THE MAKING OF THE MODERN UNIVERSITY

INTELLECTUAL TRANSFORMATION AND

THE MAKING OF THE MODERN UNIVERSITY

THE MARGINALIZATION OF MORALITY

JULIE A. REUBEN

THE UNIVERSITY OF CHICAGO PRESS · CHICAGO AND LONDON

Julie A. Reuben is associate professor in the School of Administration, Planning, and Social Policy at Harvard Graduate School of Education.

The University of Chicago Press, Chicago 60637
The University of Chicago Press, Ltd., London
© 1996 by the University of Chicago
All rights reserved. Published 1996
Printed in the United States of America
05 04 03 02 01 00 99 98 97 96   5 4 3 2 1

ISBN (cloth): 0-226-71018-1
ISBN (paper): 0-226-71020-3

Library of Congress Cataloging-in-Publication Data

Reuben, Julie A.
    The making of the modern university : intellectual transformation and the marginalization of morality / Julie A. Reuben.
        p.   cm.
    Includes bibliographical references and index.
    ISBN 0-226-71018-1.—ISBN 0-226-71020-3 (pbk.)
    1. Universities and colleges—United States—History—19th century.   2. Universities and colleges—United States—History—20th century.   3. Education, Higher—United States—Philosophy.   4. Educational change—United States—History.   5. Moral education—United States—History.   I. Title.
LA227.1.R48   1996
378.73—dc20   96-12267
                                                          CIP

∞ The paper used in this publication meets the minimum requirements of the American National Standard for Information Sciences—Permanence of Paper for Printed Library Materials, ANSI Z39.48-1984.

Dedicated to the memory of my grandmother,
Fahima Reuben

CONTENTS

ACKNOWLEDGMENTS

I have been fortunate to receive an extraordinary amount of help during the many years that I have worked on this book, and I am pleased (and relieved) to finally be able to express my gratitude in print. The first half of this book was originally my doctoral dissertation. My first debt, then, is to the faculty of the Stanford University history department. I was particularly fortunate to have as my adviser Carl N. Degler. I have benefited greatly from his breadth of knowledge, help, and encouragement. This study originated in a seminar paper written under the direction of George M. Fredrickson. My discussions with him about American cultural and intellectual history helped shape this project. I am grateful for David M. Kennedy's interest in this book and his insightful comments on my work. I would also like to thank Paul Robinson for his suggestions on my dissertation, Timothy Lenoir for his comments on an earlier version of chapter 2, and Estelle Freedman and Hal Kahn for their encouragement and advice.

My experience at Stanford was enriched enormously by the supportive community of graduate students. Becky Lowen, Linda Przybyszewski, Dale Prentiss, Michael Salman, Phil Ethington, Peggy Pascoe, Penny Russell, and Jeane Delaney all provided important help and support. Doug Klusmeyer read my dissertation and offered stimulating conversation on the question of secularization. I am especially lucky to have met Bruce Schulman the first time I walked onto the Stanford campus. He has helped me through all the challenges I have faced since then. I consider my friendship with him one of the best things about my decision to become a historian.

I also received important help from scholars outside of Stanford. James T. Kloppenberg, Dorothy Ross, James Turner, David Hollinger, George Marsden, and James Burtchaell read my dissertation. I appreciate their interest in my work and their suggestions for revisions. I would also like to thank James Turner and the second, anonymous reviewer for the

University of Chicago Press for their helpful comments on this manuscript. My editor, Doug Mitchell, has made the last stages of this project a pleasure.

Archivists at Harvard University Archives, Yale University Archives, Columbia University Rare Book and Manuscript Library, the Manuscript Division of the Eisenhower Library at Johns Hopkins University, the University of Chicago Department of Special Collections, Bentley Historical Library at the University of Michigan, Bancroft Library at the University of California—Berkeley, and the Stanford University Archives were all extremely helpful. Barbara Celone and the staff of Stanford University's Cubberley Library went out of their way to make their large collection of university materials available to me, and Sonia Moss of the interlibrary loan department at Stanford University's Green Library always quickly and cheerfully tried to get the books I needed. The interlibrary loan staff of McDermott Library at the University of Texas at Dallas helped enormously with the second stage of research.

I received generous financial assistance from a Whiting Fellowship and from a Weter Grant from the Stanford history department. The Spencer Foundation helped in many ways, first with a Dissertation Year Fellowship and then with a National Academy of Education Postdoctoral Fellowship. In addition to its financial assistance, I have had the pleasure of working with the Spencer Foundation staff as a member of the program advisory committee. Their commitment to research and education has been an inspiration to me.

I would also like to thank the editors of *Mid-America* for permission to reprint portions of my article "False Expectations: The Scientific Study of Religion in the Modern American University, 1890–1920" (*Mid-America* 7 [spring–summer 1995]).

Friends and family also helped me in many direct and indirect ways. I would like to thank Michelle Bowdler and Mary Gorman, Lise Brody, Rachel MacLachlan and Joan Goldman, Judy Calhoun, Alice Killian, Dia Michels and Tony Gualtierri, the Lovett family, Barbara Reuben, Cedar Reuben, and Neil Reuben. I was especially fortunate that my dear friend Julia Fasick was my neighbor when I was writing my dissertation. She has a unique talent for finding ways to be helpful. My parents Eliahoo and Paula Reuben have given me a lifetime of love and support.

I owe my greatest debt to Lisa Lovett, who contributed enormously to this book, and who has sustained me over the many years of research and writing.

INTRODUCTION

As part of the preparation for Harvard University's 250th anniversary, the board of overseers in 1884 adopted a new heraldic seal. The new seal placed the Latin word *Veritas,* "Truth," at its center. The new motto was closely associated with a series of reforms—including the introduction of electives, the abolition of mandatory chapel attendance, and the growth of scientific laboratories—instituted in the late nineteenth century. Charles W. Eliot, the president of Harvard who launched these reforms, summed up his view of education in these words: "a liberal education is a state of mind—nothing else . . . a certain *spirit,* or temper, toward inquiry, toward truth." The new seal, then, endorsed changes that were currently transforming Harvard from a traditional classical college into a modern research university.[1]

Although the Harvard overseers, by ratifying the 1884 crest, indicated their support for reform, they did not intend to repudiate tradition. The *Veritas* seal had ties to the past as well as associations with the future. In the 1830s, President Josiah Quincy pointed out that the first shield of the college, created in 1643, had used the motto *Veritas* inscribed across three open books. Shortly after its adoption, however, the original shield was replaced by a new one, proclaiming the college's commitment to glorifying Christ. The second seal, with its motto *In Christi gloriam,* survived until the late eighteenth century, when it was replaced by a third shield, using the epigraph *Christo et Ecclesiae,* "for Christ and Church."[2]

During his administration, Quincy unsuccessfully attempted to resurrect the *Veritas* seal. Opponents of the change charged that it would deemphasize Harvard's religious mission. Quincy tried to address this concern by emphasizing the spiritual meaning of the original seal: "The books [on the seal] were probably intended to represent the Bible; and the motto to intimate, that in the Scripture alone important truth was to be sought and found, and not in words of man's devising." In 1884 the board of overseers wanted to make clear that by instituting reforms and adopting the new

symbol *Veritas* they were not abandoning the school's traditional commitment to religion. To reinforce this message, the 1884 seal retained the epigraph *Christo et Ecclesiae.* The older motto comfortably encircled *Veritas,*
which was inscribed on three books in the center of the seal.[3]

In 1884 Harvard officials assumed that the two phrases on their new
seal were compatible. They had inherited a world view that strongly associated truth and religion. The term *truth* encompassed all "correct" knowledge; religious doctrines, common-sense beliefs, and scientific theories
were all judged by the same cognitive standards. Religious truth was the
most important and valuable form of knowledge because it gave meaning
to mundane knowledge. Religion transformed abstract knowledge into
"moral" truths—truths that guided individuals' daily actions and explained their ultimate destiny. Although the contemporary debates about
the conflict between science and religion and the veracity of traditional
Christian beliefs threatened to upset this conception of truth, Harvard
officials demonstrated with the 1884 seal that they saw no need to repudiate the close connection between religion and truth.

The Harvard officials' views about truth represented the beliefs of
most educated Americans at that time. In the late nineteenth century intellectuals assumed that truth had spiritual, moral, and cognitive dimensions. By 1930, however, intellectuals had abandoned this broad conception of truth. They embraced, instead, a view of knowledge that drew a
sharp distinction between "facts" and "values." They associated cognitive
truth with empirically verified knowledge and maintained that by this
standard moral values could not be validated as "true." In the nomencla-
ture of the twentieth century, only "science" constituted true knowledge.
Moral and spiritual values could be "true" in an emotional or nonliteral
sense, but not in terms of cognitively verifiable knowledge. The term *truth*
no longer comfortably encompassed factual knowledge and moral values.

This book examines the transition from the nineteenth-century broad
conception of truth to the twentieth-century division between facts and
values. The origins of the separation of facts and values are complex and
multi-determined, which permits them to be studied from several perspectives. The most common approach relies on intellectual biography. For
example, Robert Proctor, in *Value-Free Science?: Purity and Power in Modern Knowledge,* studies the history of Western intellectuals' views about
science and attributes the full development of the notion of value-free
science to Max Weber's work in the early twentieth century.[4]

Although I do not reject all forms of intellectual biography, my book
takes an institutional approach to the study of the origins of the separation

of facts and values. I maintain that the rejection of the broad conception of truth, encompassing both knowledge and morality, was closely tied to changes in educational and scholarly practices. In the first half of the nineteenth century the broad conception of truth, referred to then as the "unity of truth," was institutionalized into the structure of higher education. Colleges maintained a set curriculum that culminated in a senior-year course in moral philosophy, designed to draw together all higher learning. This course was frankly normative: it informed students of their duties to their family, their community, their country, and God. Moral philosophy and natural theology provided a forum in which scholars could reconcile religious doctrines with the findings of secular studies. These educational and scholarly practices made the abstract idea of the unity of truth tangible, thereby reinforcing its validity.

In the late nineteenth century, however, educational and scholarly practices that helped sustain the broad conception of truth came under attack. Many educated Americans felt that the standardized curriculum excluded instruction in important modern and practical subjects. They also noted that the college curriculum precluded advanced instruction in almost all subjects of study. They feared that the limited course of study was impeding the nation's intellectual and material progress. The debates over evolution also undermined support for natural theology, the primary means of reconciling religion and science. Natural theology seemed to limit freedom of scientific study while raising doubts about Christian beliefs. In order to advance knowledge and lay the basis for better relations between science and religion, a group of scholars and educators restructured higher education and scholarly practices in the United States.

Late nineteenth-century university reformers did not reject the ideal of the unity of truth. They did not intend to abolish morality or religion from higher education, nor did they subscribe to a model of scientific knowledge that emphasized value-neutrality. On the contrary, they hoped to create new institutional forms that would embody their belief that truth incorporated all knowledge and was morally relevant, and also provide the basis for scholarly progress.

These proved to be incompatible goals. For decades reformers unsuccessfully struggled to create universities that would serve the moral aims of the classical college while contributing to the advancement of knowledge. The educational and scholarly practices that emerged from their efforts encouraged specialization rather than intellectual synthesis. New conceptions of knowledge that associated agreement with intellectual progress discouraged professors from engaging in controversial moral issues. By the early twentieth century, the ideal of the unity of truth did not seem plausible to younger intellectuals trained in the new universities. Twentieth-century academics embraced the separation of facts and values because it fit the scholarly and educational practices that had developed over the previous fifty years. The separation of knowledge and morality was an unintended result of the university reforms of the late nineteenth century.

University leaders tried to create several different forms of modern moral education. I will discuss these efforts as three stages: the religious stage, falling roughly between 1880 and 1910; the scientific, from about 1900 to 1920; and the humanistic and extracurricular, roughly 1915–30. The notion of successive stages is, of course, an oversimplification; in reality, these various efforts overlapped and competed with one another. Nonetheless, the notion of stages is still useful because advocates of particular forms of moral education did dominate the discourse within higher education in succession and as a result of the perceived failure of the previously most promising form of moral training.

The first and most important attempt to create a modern form of moral education in the new university was tied to the reconstruction of Christianity. University reformers in the late nineteenth century, like most of their contemporaries, assumed that morality was inextricably tied to religion. The relationship of university reform to religion, however, was complicated. On the one hand, university reformers opposed the older forms of denominational control as antithetical to the progress of higher education. They thought that denominational governance led to the dispersal of scarce educational resources. They also believed that church sponsorship inhibited the development of scholarly excellence: because denominational colleges preferred to hire professors from their own denomination, they did not necessarily reward the best scholars with university posts. Finally, the reformers maintained that church sponsorship stymied intellectual progress because church leaders distrusted ideas that they perceived as contradicting church dogma.

This last charge was the most serious. It raised the possibility that religion by its very nature was antithetical to intellectual advancement and, therefore, incompatible with educational institutions devoted to intellectual progress. This possibility was the heart of the late nineteenth-century conflict between religion and science. Prominent university reformers, such as Charles Eliot of Harvard, Daniel Coit Gilman of Johns Hopkins, and James B. Angell of the University of Michigan, however, rejected this possibility. They believed that they could alter the position of religion in higher education to make it consistent with modern scientific standards of intellectual inquiry.

In the wide-ranging debates over evolutionary theory and the conflict between science and religion, American scientists and theologians tried to define the essential characteristics of science and to decide why some forms of religion conflicted with science and others did not. From these discussions emerged a rough consensus regarding science. Within higher education, supporters of university reforms came to view science as a particularly successful form of inquiry because it rejected common-sense beliefs. They thought that science was progressive because scientists were willing to test currently accepted views, refining or rejecting them when necessary. The superiority of science depended on openness: scientists had to be free to question received knowledge. The advocates of reform associated science with "objectivity," but they did not define *objective* as "value-free." Rather, they used *objective* to mean "tested through empirical application."

Educational reformers believed that universities could offer their students a modern form of religious education by promoting the scientific study of religion and modern religious practices. The scientific study of religion, its advocates projected, would help integrate religion into modern intellectual life. By the early twentieth century, however, this effort was clearly failing. Scientific studies of religion, instead of integrating religion into modern intellectual life, concluded that the "truth" of religion differed essentially from the factual truth of science. The value of religion was emotional and moral, not intellectual. In addition, students showed little interest in the new science of religion or in modern religious practices, and in many major universities these programs languished. Contrary to the expectations of its promoters, the scientific study of religion only affirmed religion's intellectual marginality.

The failure to create and maintain a modern "scientific" religious education was a blow to the new universities, but it did not completely destroy their commitment to moral education. During the early twentieth century, university educators gradually backed away from the position that there was no morality without religion and began instead to emphasize secular sources for moral development. In the late nineteenth and early twentieth centuries, science itself seemed to be a powerful source of moral guidance. University reformers thought that scientific inquiry encouraged good personal habits, identical to those advanced by liberal Christianity. They conceived of the progress of scientific knowledge in utopian terms. Scientists confidently expected to produce broad unifying theories that would explain everything from the most basic physical events to the intricacies of advanced human societies. They thought that scientific research fueled social progress and proved that traditional moral values, such as temperance and monogamy, served the survival of the human race. They also believed that science would help solve difficult new ethical problems created by modern industry. Advocates of scientific inquiry believed in the union of the good and the true, and expected that by producing better knowledge, they would become better people. The next endeavor to create modern moral education, then, naturally looked to science.

In the 1910s and 1920s university educators tried to increase the influence of science by developing "general" science courses. Universities increasingly required or strongly encouraged students to take these new introductory courses in the biological and social sciences. These courses reflected the belief that the university could best fulfill its duty to society and students through research and instruction in the biological and social sciences.

The moral aims of university scientists are often ignored because their twentieth-century successors disavowed ethical interests. The model of science as morally neutral, however, did not gain wide acceptance in the United States until the second decade of the twentieth century. At that time, biological and social scientists became uncomfortable with the claim that their disciplines were the best form of modern moral education. They rejected utopian visions of science and efforts to unify all knowledge. They maintained that their research would yield useful, "practical" information, of material and vocational utility but not of moral value.

Natural and social scientists espoused specialization, arguing that stricter standards of research would produce more reliable knowledge than their predecessors had achieved with a broader conception of scientific inquiry. They were also motivated by professional concerns, such as the desire for academic independence and positions as expert advisers. Viewed as a source of moral instruction, the biological and social sciences attracted the attention and interference of university administrators. Scientists, who wanted greater autonomy, believed that their fields could prosper by providing technical rather than moral guidance.

As academic scientists increasingly embraced the model of value-free science and tried to establish their role in the university as conducting research and providing specialized education, some scholars in the humanities and arts were eager to take over the role of moral education. Scholars in literature and the arts became vocal critics of universities' failure to provide adequate moral guidance. They presented the humanities as the means to convey traditional values and art as the expression of spiritual truths. They maintained that the humanities and arts, rather than the sciences, could provide unity and moral guidance that had been lost in the university reforms of the late nineteenth century.

Scholars in the humanities and arts recognized that there were professional advantages to taking up the mantle of moral education. Many faculty in the humanities felt that the model of specialized research was not well suited to their disciplines. Also, they had difficulty gaining support for their research because, unlike scientists, they could not claim that their research would eventually translate into practical knowledge that would aid society. They had to base their claims to service on their direct moral influence on students. As the guardians of values, humanists adopted a central, but increasingly problematic, function of higher education. By the 1930s the humanities had replaced the social sciences as the model freshman introductory course. Just as religion had been dissociated from "cognitive" truth, morality became divorced from "factual" knowledge and aligned instead with "fictive" and "aesthetic" truth. The good, then, became associated with the beautiful, not the true.

Although university administrators welcomed efforts to define the humanities as a source of moral education, they also began to deemphasize curricular forms of moral guidance in the 1910s and 1920s. They expected administrative changes and extracurricular activities to solve the problem of undergraduate character development. They hired special administrators to handle "student life," instituted programs for student advising, hired special faculty for undergraduate teaching, and created new activities such as "freshman orientation." The most important "moral reform" in those decades was the establishment of the dormitory. University administrators encouraged the building of dormitories as a way to create a moral community for students. The establishment of dormitories and the development of other extracurricular and administrative forms of moral guidance lessened the expectation that faculty should provide moral guidance and created an institutional separation between morality and knowledge.

The institutional separation between morality and knowledge mirrored the development in the curriculum. In the late nineteenth and early twentieth centuries, educators tried various ways to keep moral and intellectual training united. But these efforts failed. Developments in philosophy in the 1920s and 1930s gave intellectual credence to the changes in higher education. Logical positivism drew a sharp distinction between statements of knowledge and value judgments. At the same time philosophers began to adopt emotivist theories of ethics that associated morality with noncognitive sentiments and aesthetics.

This book, following insights from the sociology of knowledge, seeks to reconstruct the historical interaction between institutions and ideas. It responds to intellectual historians' growing interest in contextualization. Historians such as David Hollinger and Thomas Bender have argued that intellectuals work in specific institutional settings and in a particular cultural and social milieu. They have ably demonstrated that an understanding of these contexts helps clarify the development and meaning of ideas. I have pushed this concept further in order to eliminate the distinction between text and context. Neither the institutional nor the intellectual history serves merely as a context for the other: they are both equally the text of this study. I do not believe that either institutional or intellectual needs primarily determined the changes charted in this book. The two constantly interacted, and only at particular junctures did one or the other dominate.[5]

Although this book examines the changing relationship between knowledge and morality, it does not focus on the formal philosophic exposition of this problem. Instead, it explores the larger intellectual and institutional context in which philosophers considered problems of knowledge and morality. It relates developments in philosophy to the search for modern forms of moral education, but does not replicate the works of historians of philosophy, such as Morton White, Bruce Kuklick, Daniel Wilson, Guy Stroh, Elizabeth Flower, and Murray Murphey. In this book, I do not use formal definitions of the terms *knowledge* and *morality*. Instead, I try to follow the general usage of faculty and administrators involved in the development of the research university. In the late nineteenth century knowledge was increasingly equated with the findings of formal scientific inquiry. But scientific inquiry was not restricted to the academic disciplines now referred to as the natural sciences. Morality was defined broadly as precepts that help people live properly.[6]

As a history of ideas, this book would have to be classified as "middling" intellectual history. It does not focus on elite intellectuals, yet universities, as elite institutions, cannot be considered part of popular culture. It is concerned with the thought of educated Americans who participated in discussions about the nature of higher education and scholarship in the sixty years surrounding the turn of the twentieth century. Most, but not all, of the participants in these discussions were themselves connected to academic institutions as faculty and administrators.

Many of these participants, however, were "average" academics, whose work did not win them places in intellectual or educational histories. To gain a fresh and broad perspective on the changes associated with the development of the research university, I decided not to rely primarily on the "classic" texts of the university reform movement and the new academic disciplines. Instead, the bulk of the primary-source research for this book involved reading relevant articles in journals such as *Popular Science Monthly, Science, American Journal of Sociology, Educational Review, Annual Conference of the Association of American Universities, English Journal, Proceedings of the Modern Language Association, Political Science Quarterly, Religious Education,* and *Atlantic.* In the pages that follow, then, the voices of well-known intellectuals, such as William James, and of famous educators, such as Daniel Coit Gilman, are heard along with those of their long-forgotten colleagues.[7]

I have reconstructed these discussions in order to explain the origins of the separation of morality and knowledge and the changing position of morality in the modern research university. Of course, such reconstructions involve simplifications and selectivity. I quote extensively from primary sources both for illustrative purposes and as a way to give readers a sense of the language used at the time. Although historians like to focus on conflict and to delineate the range of positions held on any subject, my reading of the primary sources indicates that many participants in these discussions tried to build consensus (or the appearance thereof) by masking differences of opinion. Rather than trying to articulate and clarify their ideas, they were often purposefully vague. Their lack of clarity was often more important to historical developments than the conflicts that were not fully stated. I try to follow the primary sources, emphasizing consensus when it was maintained and explicating conflicting points of view when they dominated a particular subject.

The institutional research is based on eight universities: Harvard, Yale, Columbia, Johns Hopkins, University of Chicago, Stanford, University of Michigan, and University of California, Berkeley. I selected these institutions because of their leadership in the development of the research university during the late nineteenth and early twentieth centuries, and because of the contributions of the intellectuals who were associated with these institutions. They also provide a contrast between schools that developed from denominational colleges into major research universities and new institutions, founded during the educational reform of the late nineteenth century, and represent a combination of state and private institutions.

I examined archival sources, annual reports, and course catalogues for each of the eight universities. This book, however, does not narrate a complete history of any one of these universities. I wanted a firm institutional base on which to develop my conclusions, and I built this by emphasizing the common elements of their development. I use examples from individual institutions to illustrate particular changes. Although there may not be a counterpart for each selected example at all eight of the institutions, the examples represent experiences common to the majority of the universities included in this study.

With the exception of Douglas Sloan's path-breaking article "The Teaching of Ethics in the American Undergraduate Curriculum, 1876–1976," historians have largely ignored the history of morality in American universities. The main contribution of this book to historical scholarship is to provide the first in-depth study of moral education in the American research university. It examines the shifting position of morality during the sixty years in which the research university developed as the premier form of higher education in the United States. By exploring this neglected subject, the book helps illuminate some of the tensions that plague modern higher education and scholarly practices. In particular, it helps us understand why the ideal of value-free scholarship is such a persistent and problematic aspect of modern intellectual life.[8]

The traditional account of the history of higher education emphasizes a revolution in the late nineteenth century. According to this historical model, true higher education did not exist in the United States until the development of the modern university. This narrative highlights the role of critics, who traveled to Europe, studied at or visited universities abroad, particularly German universities, and upon returning to the United States tried to make their compatriots aware of the inadequacies of the American college. By the 1870s these enlightened critics had grown numerous and influential enough to take control of a few key institutions.

These university reformers then proceded to dismantle the old-style college. They severed the ties to religious denominations. They introduced electives and established new courses in the natural sciences, history, social sciences, and modern languages and literatures. Gradually they scaled back the number of required courses and replaced recitations with lectures, laboratories, and seminars. They also strengthened and added professional and graduate programs, expanding higher education beyond the baccalaureate degree. The new institutions apparently provided the education that people wanted and needed. They grew rapidly, while colleges that had resisted the changes struggled to survive. Eventually, institutions that had initially fought the reforms adopted the new educational practices. The old college soon disappeared, and the university became the model for higher education in the United States. Most of the educational developments in the twentieth century, according to this view, were merely elaborations on the late nineteenth-century revolution.[9]

For some time now, historians have been questioning the adequacy of this revolution model. Most of the revisionist work, however, has focused on the pre–Civil War period. Historians have taken issue with the overly negative assessments of the classical college and have presented a more sympathetic view of its educational goals and methods. They have also emphasized the relative diversity of forms of higher education in the first half of the nineteenth century and the origins of many "university" reforms in antebellum institutions. Revisionist work on the late nineteenth century has focused on institutions that were outside the university reform movement. Louise Stevenson and J. David Hoeveler, Jr., for example, demonstrate how Yale under the leadership of Theodore Dwight Woolsey and Noah Porter, and Princeton under the leadership of James McCosh, accommodated new standards of scholarship and modified traditional educational practices. These institutions defy the simplistic dichotomy of the classical college and the modern university and remind historians that the transformation of higher education was more complex than the notion of a revolution admits.[10]

Less has been done to revise the second half of the traditional historical account: the academic revolution of the late nineteenth century. This absence is in part because of the undeniably radical changes introduced in the late nineteenth century by university reformers. This book extends the revisionist scholarship to institutions that were at the forefront of university reform. It demonstrates that reformers at institutions such as Harvard, Johns Hopkins, University of Michigan, and the University of Chicago sought to preserve one of the key values of the classical college: the unity of moral and intellectual purpose. Like other revisionist scholarship on higher education, it highlights some elements of continuity over the nineteenth and early twentieth centuries to provide a more complex understanding of the development of the modern university.[11]

By focusing on reformers' commitment to the ideal of the unity of truth, this book offers an alternative to the interpretation of the ideology that shaped American universities presented in Laurence Veysey's influential book *The Emergence of the American University.* In the first part of his book, Veysey examined what he perceived to be four competing visions of higher education in the postbellum era. The first, "piety and discipline," he associated with the classical college, while the other three—"utility," "research," and "culture"—he identified as different strands of university reform.[12]

My research challenges Veysey's analysis in two ways. First, it questions the value of his tripartite division of university reform. Although Veysey acknowledged that no single educator or institution could be identified exclusively with "utility," "culture," or "research," he treated these as distinct and even conflicting visions of higher education. This book implies that these categories are anachronistic. It argues that university reformers believed in the unity of truth, which assumed that the good, the true, and the beautiful were interconnected, and that successful education promoted all three together. The reformers, therefore, believed that service, which they associated with morality, and culture, which they associated with beauty, and research, which they associated with true knowledge, were complementary, natural aims of education. In the late nineteenth century no university reformer thought of seeking one rather than another. Only from the perspective of the twentieth-century rejection of the ideal of unity do these seem to be three separate goals of education.

This book also challenges Veysey's assumption that university reformers sought to secularize higher education. By contrasting "piety and discipline" with the three reform philosophies, and by treating university reformers' religious and moral commitments as anomalies or insincere efforts to appease public criticism, Veysey implicitly argued that university reformers rejected religious and moral concerns. My research indicates that university reformers continued to view piety and moral discipline as one of the aims of higher education, but wanted to replace older, authoritarian methods with new ones.

I am not alone in questioning the assumption that university reformers intended to remove religion from higher education. In recent years there has been a renewed interest in the secularization of higher education. The leading figure in this new scholarship is George M. Marsden, who wrote the introductory overview to an important collection of essays, *The Secularization of the Academy,* and published his own study of the changing position of religion in American universities, *The Soul of the American*

University: From Protestant Establishment to Established Nonbelief. Marsden and his associates confirm that university reform was not intentionally antireligious and that the process of secularization was more problematic than standard accounts of the history of higher education suggest. Marsden views the late nineteenth and early twentieth centuries as a period of "methodological secularization," in which university leaders advocated scientific techniques, professional independence, specialization, and other changes with the goal of improving scholarship and meeting the needs of an increasingly technological society rather than of discrediting religion. These changes marginalized religion and prepared the way for "ideological secularization," the explicit rejection of religion based on intellectual skepticism and/or interpretations of the ideal of cultural pluralism. Marsden maintains that liberal Protestantism, which dominated universities from the Civil War to World War II, eased the transition from methodological to ideological secularization.[13]

This book considers secularization in the context of the changing position of morality in the university. It does not attempt to fully explain secularization; important issues, particularly the impact of the social and economic changes of the late nineteenth century, are outside its scope. It does, however, examine, in greater depth than previous scholarship, university reformers' efforts to create new forms of religious training and practice. This material complicates Marsden's account of secularization. The notion of methodological secularization implies that new emphasis on scientific technique and the changes associated with it, such as specialization and professionalization, transformed the priorities of higher education and, as a consequence, incidentally marginalized religion. Marsden maintains that methodological secularization could have been compatible with continued religious vitality. My research suggests a more direct connection between educators' commitment to scientific technique and secularization. University reformers tried to modernize religion to make it compatible with their conception of science. Religion disappeared from the university because these efforts failed, not because university educators neglected religion.

The question of the secularization of higher education is closely related to those of the secularization of intellectual life in general and of the relationship of science and religion. Marsden relates secularization to the dominance of liberal Protestantism. This aligns his work with revisionist scholarship that sees secularization as an outgrowth of religious thought rather than as the result of science triumphing over religion. James Turner's *Without God, Without Creed* is one of the best examples of this scholarship. I also show how liberal Protestantism contributed to its own demise. Particularly damaging, in my view, was liberal Protestants' tendency to equate religion with morality, and the vagueness and inclusiveness of their rhetoric. Nonetheless, I do not think historians can show that liberal Christianity, rather than science, was responsible for secularization. The development of liberal Christianity was simply too intertwined with science. To understand the secularization of intellectual life, scholars will have to examine why liberal Christians could not successfully incorporate science into a Christian framework. My research suggests that this had as much to do with changing conceptions of science as with the shortcomings of liberal Christian thought.[14]

This book also contributes to scholarship about the relationship between science and religion at the turn of the century. Responding to the fundamentalist attack on evolution, historians in the 1920s and 1930s argued that Darwin's writings had initiated a war between religion and science. Recent revisionist scholarship, on the other hand, has challenged the notion that science and religion were at war in the late nineteenth century. It has demonstrated that Christian intellectuals found ways to reconcile evolution with their religious beliefs. Although my research does not completely reject the concept of conflict, it confirms that late nineteenth-century intellectuals wanted to reconcile religion and science. Instead of focusing on Christian interpretations of evolutionary theory, I examine how intellectuals tried to reconceive the conflict between religion and science by distinguishing between theology and religion. This distinction allowed intellectuals to maintain that true science and religion were compatible, while arguing that theology had restricted the development of science. It also helped university reformers chart a new role for religion in higher education.[15]

This new understanding of the relationship of science and religion also relied on changing conceptions of science. Unlike the antebellum period, when Baconianism had dominated as the ideal, if not the practice, of science, the late nineteenth century produced a wide-ranging and complex discussion about the nature of scientific inquiry. This book contributes to the on-going explication of that discussion by highlighting the development of a "progressivist" model of scientific inquiry. This view of science emphasized open inquiry and the dynamic improvement of scientific theories, and was associated with anti-essentialism and instrumentalism. This progressivist model of science helped define the purpose and direction of university reform.[16]

A better understanding of late nineteenth-century ideas about science is also important for the historiography of the social sciences. Although most recent scholarship has traced the ideal of "value free" social science to the second decade of the twentieth century, the idea that the early history of the social sciences should be understood as a conflict between "advocacy" and "objectivity" still persists. I argue that this conception is anachronistic. Late nineteenth-century ideas about science did not associate "objectivity" with value-neutrality. Conflicts among social scientists in the late nineteenth century are better understood as developing from two different conceptions about the relationship between science and morality and the implications of scholarship for social improvement than as arising from activist and objectivist camps.[17]

The changing position of moral education intersects with many important topics in the history of American intellectual life. As Douglas Sloan has noted, "the teaching of ethics has been uniquely and inseparably connected with the most important issues of modern higher education, issues involving the curriculum, institutionalization, professionalization, epistemology, the 'two cultures' split, the community—indeed the very purposes of higher education." Because of the richness of the subject, I have had to limit discussions of issues that in other contexts would merit more extensive treatment. I have sometimes sacrificed detail in order to keep the text focused on the main narrative: the separation of knowledge and morality in American universities.[18]

In 1936, for Harvard's 300th anniversary, the university once again modified its heraldic seal. This time it dropped the words *Christo et Ecclesiae* and left the term *Veritas* to stand alone on the three open books. In some ways this change signaled the triumph of Charles W. Eliot's reforms. But it also marked the death of the old ideal of the unity of truth. The word *truth* no longer encompassed the same values it had when Eliot optimistically proposed it as the highest ideal of the university.[19]

ONE

The Unity of Truth

In an article, "The Nobility of Knowledge," published in 1874, Harvard chemistry professor Josiah Cooke pronounced that "all truth is one and inseparable." Cooke did not need to explain or defend this statement; he was simply repeating a truism of his age. In the nineteenth century educated Americans believed in the ideal of the "unity of truth." The unity of truth entailed two important propositions. First, it supposed that all truths agreed and ultimately could be related to one another in a single system. Second, it assumed that knowledge had a moral dimension. To know the "true," according to this ideal, was to know the "good."[1]

The notion of the unity of truth seemed natural to Josiah Cooke and his contemporaries because it was deeply rooted in American intellectual and educational traditions. In 1636 colonists had established Harvard, the first American college, modeled after the English colleges at Cambridge and Oxford. New Englanders carried with them an educational philosophy and practice that embraced the two major propositions of the ideal of unity. They believed that all knowledge ultimately illuminated the Divine and also that they had a religious obligation to increase their knowledge. As Calvinists, they thought that humans' capacity for accurate knowledge was destroyed by Adam's fall. Although they recognized the limits of their learning, they still studied the traditional "two books of God" to try to discern the divine will. The primary source of guidance was God's revelation communicated in the Scriptures; the secondary one was his creation. New Englanders believed that they could never fully know God, but that they could approach knowledge of the divine through careful study of all branches of learning.[2]

The colonists' model of a proper education was based on medieval scholasticism as modified by Christian humanism, particularly the ideas of the sixteenth-century French philosopher, Peter Ramus. Ramus's educational system, known as *technologia,* which meant "knowledge of the arts," or as *encyclopedia,* which meant "circle of arts," taught all the legi-

17

timate "arts," or fields of learning. It began with the dialectic, or the art of rational thought, then taught the arts of speech and communication, followed by mathematics, and then by physics, which was understood to include the whole created realm, animate and inanimate. The course ended with the study of the uncreated being, or theology. Although the arts were arranged as a hierarchy, Ramus envisioned them as a circle: the encyclopedia was the circle of arts, at the center of which stood God.[3]

Since the colonists believed that all knowledge was knowledge about God, they assumed that ultimately all truths agreed and could be unified. They thought that every educated person should know all the arts: the information yielded by one area of study was valuable only in the context of the whole. Their educational philosophy also supported the unity of knowledge and morality. The influence of Christian humanism highlighted the practical moral aims of learning and education. New Englanders rejected the Aristotelian distinction between science, or demonstration, and art, or production, and emphasized that all knowledge must result in action. They maintained that the object of learning was *eupraxia,* "well acting." Truth and goodness were one.[4]

This educational philosophy, with its dependence on medieval scholasticism, broke down over the course of the seventeenth century. The main tenets of the ideal of the unity of truth, however, survived the transition to modern philosophies. For example, the American colonist Samuel Johnson, who became the first president of Kings College (later Columbia) in 1754, broke with the educational philosophy he was taught as a student at Yale, but continued to believe that all branches of knowledge agreed and that truth and morality were united. While a student at Yale in the early eighteenth century, Johnson read the works of proponents of the new science, such as John Locke and Isaac Newton. Johnson drew on these new ideas to create an updated "encyclopedia."

Johnson rejected the Ramist classification of the arts and replaced it with his own "general View of the whole System of Learning." His system incorporated all the branches of knowledge into three large divisions: rational, natural, and moral philosophy. Like his predecessors, he expected that the college curriculum would cover all areas of learning, and he held that each area must be understood in the context of the whole. He also associated the purpose of learning with morality. The end of learning was true happiness, which Johnson defined as "*Acting* according to *Right*" and "*Thinking* according to *Truth.*" Although Johnson rejected the scholasticism of his Yale education, he incorporated the ideal of the unity of truth into his new philosophy.[5]

Two of the most important changes associated with the eighteenth-century colleges were the development of moral philosophy and the growing importance of natural theology. In the seventeenth-century classification of knowledge, ethics was subsumed in theology. By the early eighteenth century American philosophers generally identified moral philosophy as an independent branch of learning. Moral philosophy was theistic and assumed that divine laws operated in ethics as well as nature. It maintained that those laws could be discovered through the empirical and introspective study of human beings. Its scope was defined very broadly to include all aspects of human social, political, and economic relations. Its purpose was normative: the ultimate aim of moral philosophy was to serve as a guide for right living.[6]

From the mid-eighteenth century to the late nineteenth century, the most important influences on American moral philosophy were Scottish Enlightenment thinkers and the development of common-sense realism. The Scottish influence became a tangible presence with the election of John Witherspoon to the presidency of Princeton in 1766. Witherspoon, like other Scottish Enlightenment thinkers, maintained that the human mind worked through related processes or faculties: the understanding, the will, and the affections. These faculties included the capacity to perceive moral qualities. Just as people could sense the hardness of an object, they could sense the goodness of an act or idea. Witherspoon believed that human reason included a moral dimension: recognition of virtue entailed an obligation to act in a way consistent with that knowledge. He argued that empirical study of human moral capacities would yield insight into the nature and basis of duty. He was confident that this naturalistic study of ethics would support the ethics of revealed religion. The study of God's creation could, in his opinion, only enhance the truth of God's word revealed in the Bible.[7]

In the early nineteenth century, the ideas of the Scottish common-sense philosophers—Thomas Reid, Dugald Stewart, Thomas Brown, and William Hamilton—became well known in the United States. The details of common-sense epistemology are not relevant here, but it is important to note how they reinforced the belief in the unity of truth. First, common-sense philosophers maintained that knowledge was practical: truth had normative implications for action. This sustained the connection between knowing what was true and doing what was right. Second, common-sense philosophy validated the possibility of deriving knowledge from empirical study. Hence, it supported the development of a moral philosophy based on the observation of human nature. Third, it maintained that all human knowledge was based on experience of the objective world. To the extent that the world was a unified whole, knowledge would also be unified. The unity of truth was based on cosmology. Believing that the universe was created by God, the common-sense philosophers assumed that it, and knowledge of it, was rational, coherent, and congruous.

Another important development in the eighteenth and nineteenth centuries—the growth of natural theology—also rested on the assumption that the universe was created by God. Natural theology presumed that God's nature and will could be inferred from his creation. By studying nature, scholars could show that God was, for example, benevolent or wise. Natural theology provided the means for reconciling the findings of science with the Scriptures. Theologians used knowledge about nature to get a more complete vision of God. Because natural theology imbued the study of nature with supreme significance, it gained considerable support for the natural sciences.[8]

Natural theology gave a moral value to the study of nature. Calvinists believed that humans' impaired cognitive abilities (as a result of the Fall) prohibited them from accurately understanding most of the moral lessons of nature. They maintained that people must rely primarily on the Scriptures for knowledge of their duties. Over the eighteenth century, however, Americans expressed greater faith in their ability to learn from nature, and natural theology became a more important part of their intellectual lives. Natural theology assumed that knowledge derived from the study of nature helped people live more moral lives. "Every moral attribute of God which we discover imposes upon us an additional motive why we should love and serve him. Hence we see that the knowledge of God, derived from the study of nature, is adapted to add greatly to the impulsive power of conscience." According to natural theology, studying "the tiniest of insects" or "the most insignificant atom of dust" could ultimately lead to great spiritual and moral truths.[9]

By the nineteenth century, moral philosophy and natural theology had become the main pillars supporting the ideal of the unity of truth. In the early nineteenth century, Americans began to write their own moral philosophy texts, although still relying heavily on Scottish examples. Moral philosophers treated their subject as integrative. It encompassed all aspects of human nature and society; it was, in the words of Harvard moral philosopher Francis Bowen, "a general science of Human Nature, of which the special sciences of Ethics, Psychology, Aesthetics, Politics, and Political Economy are so many departments." Moral philosophers were also careful to relate their study of humanity to other natural sciences and to theology. Moral philosophy was normative as well as analytic; its practitioners translated abstract theory into specific moral prescriptions. It gave substance to the ideal of the unity of truth.[10]

The compatibility of religion and science was an important component of the ideal of the unity of truth. Natural theology took on the task of reconciling the two major sources of knowledge about the divine plan: God's creation, which included the physical world, the animal realm, and humans themselves, and divine revelation as recorded in the Scriptures. Nineteenth-century Americans were confident that natural science supported Christianity. "If God is," wrote Harvard philosopher Andrew P. Peabody, "he must have put his signature on his whole creation no less than his impress on his manifested or written word. The hieroglyphs of nature must needs correspond to the alphabetic writing of revelation." Whenever nature and the Scriptures "give instruction on the same subjects," concurred Francis Wayland, the author of America's most popular moral philosophy text, "they must both teach the same lesson." God's creation and his word must agree.[11]

For scholars in the first half of the nineteenth century, the study of nature demonstrated the truth of the Scriptures, and the Scriptures dictated the interpretation of nature. "The truths of revealed religion *harmonize* perfectly with those of natural religion," wrote Wayland. "So complete is this coincidence as to afford irrefragable proof that the Bible contains the moral laws of the universe; and hence, that the Author of the universe—that is, of natural religion—is also the author of the Scriptures." According to the ideal of the unity of truth, agreement between ideas derived from different sources constituted strong evidence of the validity of those views.[12]

Nineteenth-century scholars also believed that all truths were consistent with the highest ethical and aesthetic standards. The true was also good and beautiful. These relations were an inherent part of nature, the creation of a benevolent Deity. Thus, the world was created so that "benevolent affections" were those "which we recognize as beautiful . . . while those which indicate the malevolent affections are displeasing." God, as Wayland taught, "has arranged all things for the purpose of teaching us these [moral] lessons, and he has created our intellectual and moral natures expressly for the purpose of learning them. If, then, we do not use the powers which he has given us for the purpose for which has given them, he holds us responsible for the result."[13]

Educators in antebellum America modeled colleges according to their ideal of the unity of truth. They saw the primary purpose of college as "educating young men to the highest efficiency of their intellectual faculties, and the noblest culture of their moral and religious nature." Religious concerns determined the structure of higher education. Most colleges had official ties to a religious denomination, and many were controlled by boards of trustees dominated by ministers. College presidents (and many of the faculty) were typically ministers. Ministerial control guaranteed that knowledge of God's creation was properly interpreted in light of divine revelation.[14]

Instructors were expected to be Christians and to teach their subjects from a Christian perspective. Describing his courses in natural philosophy and astronomy, Frederick A. P. Barnard wrote, "I shall attend . . . only to the beautiful truths, which are to be read in the works of God." In addition, faculty considered the moral supervision of students to be one of their duties. By tradition, Americans presumed that college life imitated family life. College authorities saw themselves as surrogate parents, responsible for students' moral and spiritual welfare. Frequently, colleges combined marks for conduct, such as proper observance of the "Lord's day," with those for classroom performance to determine the overall academic standing of students.[15]

In this way, colleges aimed to develop the student's whole nature. Educators believed that the mind was divided into various "faculties." "By *faculty*," explained Wayland, "is meant any particular part of our constitution by which we become affected by the various qualities and relations of beings around us. Thus, by taste, we are conscious of the existence of beauty, and deformity; by perception, we acquire a knowledge of the existence and qualities of the material world." College education aimed to train each faculty evenly and in relation to the others. "When all the faculties are developed or educated together, then we have beauty and symmetry and strength and perfection of character in the result." The course of study was calibrated to train each student's powers of observation, memory, and logical reason, as well as his aesthetic taste and moral sense.[16]

Educators also expected the college curriculum to cover all branches of knowledge. In their view, a "well proportioned and superior education" was comprehensive; it included "the various branches of the mathematics," "history and antiquities," "rhetoric and oratory," "natural philosophy," "astronomy," "chemistry," "mineralogy," "geology," "political economy" and "mental and moral philosophy." Nineteenth-century educators expanded the curriculum to fulfill the traditional ideal of an encyclopedic education.[17]

The senior-year course in moral and mental philosophy, often taught by the college president, was the capstone of the college education. It drew together the knowledge learned in the previous three years and placed it in a Christian framework. Instructors taught the psychological and episte-mological theory upon which they based their educational practices. They frequently included sections on natural theology and evidences of Chris-tianity and commonly assigned as textbooks the writings of William Paley, the popular English natural theologian. They also examined social and political relations and drew out the moral lessons implicit in these. The instruction was frankly normative: professors laid out students' proper duties to themselves, their fellow humans, and God. Students were then ready to be sent out into the community, versed in the elements of the various branches of knowledge, with their "whole intellectual, sensitive, moral and religious nature" well developed.[18]

Despite a strong commitment to the ideal of the unity of truth, thinkers did not always agree with the ways in which it was translated into educa-tional and scholarly practices. Beginning in the first decades of the nine-teenth century, some educators argued that the contemporary college cur-riculum did not encompass all subjects worth studying. The growth of learning in "modern subjects," such as the natural sciences, philology, the beaux-arts, and history, and "practical subjects," such as engineering and agriculture, put pressure on the college curriculum. In the 1820s critics of contemporary higher education suggested that colleges abandon the standardized curriculum to make room for these new subjects of study. College officials responded to this criticism by sacrificing universality to maintain a common course of study. They encouraged the establishment of separate schools designed to supplement the college by offering instruc-tion in subjects not offered by the college. This strategy did not quell all criticism. By the 1870s a growing contingent of educators and scholars charged that colleges' efforts to combine spiritual, moral, and intellectual training slighted the last component. Colleges, these critics asserted, sup-pressed intellectual inquiry.

From their origins in colonial America, colleges had aimed to teach all subjects appropriate for classroom study. Over the eighteenth century educators had enlarged the original classical course to include more math-ematics, greater specialization in the natural sciences, the study of litera-ture and history, and a more prominent role for moral philosophy. As a result, nineteenth-century educators inherited a course of study without much room for growth. Commentators observed that, although the length of the college course remained the same four years prescribed in the colonial colleges, "the amount which the college is required to teach, is doubled, if not trebled." The adoption of classroom studies for professional and technical training in the early nineteenth century exacerbated this problem. Educators were forced to decide between an inclusive curriculum, covering all contemporary areas of learning, in which students could elect subjects relevant to their interests, and the uniform course of study, where all students studied a broad range of traditional subjects but did not have the opportunity to study modern or practical subjects or to pursue any field in depth.[19]

In the 1820s a small circle of educators began presenting plans for widespread reform of colleges. Led by George Ticknor of Harvard, these critics hoped to improve the quality and expand the scope of instruction in the larger colleges of the country. Ticknor argued that Harvard College should serve a wider variety of educational needs. "Harvard College," he wrote, "has abundant resources to render unnecessary the establishment of many public and private institutions, like agricultural schools, the law schools, and the other establishments for the special purposes, which . . . are already beginning or begun among us also." He criticized Harvard for confining "its instructions to a strictly marked course." He argued that by opening its course of study the college could become an important intellectual center for the country.[20]

Ticknor's call to expand the curriculum in order to cater to society's needs was not radical; Harvard had always claimed to be both universal and useful to the community. But Ticknor proposed that the college enlarge its instruction at the expense of its traditional practices. He suggested that it add electives to the curriculum, organize courses by student ability rather than class year, admit nondegree students, and arrange faculty and classes by subject departments. Ticknor was not impressed with the quality of teaching in American colleges; he thought the instruction was superficial and did not encourage deep scholarship on the part of either the student or the teacher. The proposed changes, he hoped, would improve the quality of instruction and scholarship, as well as widen the appeal of a college education, by allowing students to study modern and practical subjects.[21]

Ticknor's critique inspired only temporary changes in the Harvard curriculum. Although these reforms were short-lived, Ticknor's analysis of the problems of higher education garnered some support throughout the country. For example, a small group of instructors at Yale suggested eliminating Greek and Latin to make room for other subjects. In 1825 the Connecticut legislature joined the renegade instructors by issuing a report criticizing Yale's curriculum as impractical and regressive. Two years later the Yale Corporation appointed a committee to consider these charges. In 1828 the committee published its report, which was divided into two sections, of which the first, written by President Jeremiah Day, explicated Yale's educational philosophy and the second, written by Professor Kingsley, defended the classics. The report addressed the questions "whether it will be sufficient to make *gradual* changes [to the curriculum], as heretofore; and whether the whole system is not rather to be broken up, and a better one substituted in its stead." The force of Day's arguments supported the former position: the Yale report was an innovative and influential defense of the traditional college course.[22]

Day recast the college's loyalty to the ideal of the unity of truth by deemphasizing the value of a universal curriculum covering all branches of knowledge. He emphasized instead the importance of a unified course of study that would develop every student's full mental capabilities. Common-sense philosophy, with its analysis of the mind as consisting of several faculties, helped prepare Americans for this shift. Day distinguished the purpose of a college education "from several *other* objects and plans, with which it has been too often confounded." The proper object of the college, he wrote, "is far from embracing *every thing* which the student will ever have occasion to learn." Day fully admitted that everything worth learning could not be taught in the four-year course of study. The college, he argued, did not propose "to *finish* [a student's] education; but to lay the foundation, and to advance as far in rearing the superstructure, as the short period of his residence will admit." Day asserted that the purpose of a college education was to train all the faculties of the human mind, rather than to teach all branches of knowledge.[23]

Day shifted the emphasis of the curriculum away from its content to its value as mental training or, in his words, from the "furniture" of the mind to the "discipline" of the mind. The standardized curriculum, he argued, was essential for thorough and effective mental training. Complete and accurate understanding depended on the development of all the mind's capacities. "In laying the foundation of a thorough education, it is necessary that *all* the important mental faculties be brought into exercise," he wrote. College officials presented the curriculum as an instrument carefully designed, and uniquely suited, to train each of the student's mental powers equally and in association with the others.[24]

By invoking the concept of mental discipline, Day defended the traditional curriculum, which required all students to study a broad range of subjects and did not concede that professional and technical subjects also deserved a place in the curriculum. The study of these subjects, he argued, properly followed the completion of the college course. The student would be better equipped to prepare for a profession once he had finished the broadly based collegiate education. But why, posed Day "should a student waste his time upon studies which have no immediate connection with his future profession?" To answer this, he relied on the ideal of unity: "there is no science which does not contribute its aid to professional skill. 'Every thing throws light upon every thing.'" Without a college education, Day argued, the professional lacks "that expansion and balance of the mental powers, those liberal and comprehensive views, and those fine proportions of character" that are the aim of a college education.[25]

Although Day rejected reformers' proposal that the college teach technical and professional subjects, he was not opposed to these subjects as areas of formal instruction. He applauded the development of independent technical and professional schools and, unlike Ticknor, did not think that these schools should necessarily be usurped by large comprehensive institutions. He suggested that the country's various educational needs might best be served by a variety of institutions. He even conceded that it might be appropriate for a college like Yale, if it had ample resources, to develop other courses of study, along professional and technical lines. But he opposed such developments at the cost of the traditional college education.[26]

The Yale report of 1828 was the most influential educational statement of the antebellum period. Day successfully defended the traditional college course against radical reforms. His plan for the development of higher education was largely followed for the next forty years. The four-year classical course continued to be the standard form of higher education. Areas of study that could not be incorporated into this course were developed outside of it. Educators established new schools for scientific, technical, and professional education. A few colleges, such as Union under the leadership of Eliphalet Nott, instituted separate "scientific" courses substituting more instruction in science, modern languages, and history for some of the study of classical languages. Larger institutions, such as Yale and Harvard, developed separate schools to augment the collegiate department. In this way, antebellum educators provided for new subjects of study without displacing the unified and comprehensive bachelor of arts degree.[27]

For many years after the dissemination of the Yale report, the direction for the growth of American higher education seemed well marked. Beginning in the 1840s, however, a few educators, led by Francis Wayland of Brown and Henry Tappan of the University of Michigan, began to question whether Day's strategy suited the needs of the country. They charged that the United States had too many small classical colleges and that alternative institutions offering instruction in modern and practical subjects remained weak. They opposed the proliferation of educational institutions and argued that fewer, better equipped institutions would promote American scholarship. "The interests of society demand," wrote President Josiah Quincy of Harvard, "that the number of the greater seminaries of science should be few; that they should be highly endowed, and so constituted as to become . . . great seminaries of learning . . . whence intellectual light and heat should radiate for the use and comfort of the whole land." Instead of many institutions serving a variety of populations and needs, these educators wanted to see a few larger, more comprehensive institutions.[28]

Francis Wayland thought that separate institutions were not successfully supplementing the traditional college course. He noted that special scientific courses had not attracted the necessary number of students. He reviewed the alternative institutions of higher education created to provide technical training and deemed them all inadequate to meet the needs of modern society. "These various modifications in the form of institutions for education in the higher branches of education," Wayland argued, have "failed to answer the expectations of the public." "Nothing remained," he concluded, "but to attempt to improve the colleges themselves." He thought that the existing classical colleges should be enlarged to provide scientific and technical education.[29]

Henry Tappan also criticized the strategy of separate schools to teach professional subjects. He pointed out that professional schools of law and medicine, even when associated with colleges, seldom required "preparatory classical discipline." The college had not become, as Day had proposed, a preparatory course. Instead, the different schools remained independent and, in Tappan's opinion, incomplete. He argued that "the establishment of Universities in our country will reform, and alone can reform our educational system." "By the Universities," he explained, "we mean . . . *Cyclopaedias* of education: where, in libraries, cabinets, apparatus, and professors, provision is made for studying every branch of knowledge in full." Rather than encouraging separate institutions, Tappan wanted to create schools that encompassed all branches of study.[30]

Advocates of college reform did not reject the notion of mental disci-

pline, but they thought that the current course of study was too extensive
to be effective. "It has been assumed," wrote Wayland, "that every man
who goes to College, must take a degree; that he who takes a degree, must
be acquainted with all branches of knowledge not strictly professional,
and that he must acquire all this knowledge in . . . four years." Wayland
argued that it was impossible for students to learn all the assigned material
in the time allotted.[31]

Tappan agreed that the college course was overcrowded. "The popular
conception of education is not the orderly and gradual growth of mind
according to its own innate laws fixed by God himself, but an immense
and voracious deglutition of knowledge where the mental digestion is estimated according to the rapidity with which the subjects are disposed of."
Since the beginning of the colleges, the subjects taught "have increased
three-fold." This growth subverted the original goals of the curriculum.
"The knowledge must be more superficial, the discipline less exact. Habits
of study deteriorate." By enlarging the set course of study, critics charged,
colleges diminished their disciplinary value without providing adequate
instruction in the new areas of knowledge.[32]

These critics attributed grave consequences to the saturated curriculum. If the trend were not checked, they feared, the poor quality of higher
education would lead to widespread anti-intellectualism. "A superficial
system of study in the college will necessarily beget in the community a
habit of superficial preparation," Tappan declared. "The highest institutions will set the tone of education." Furthermore, the low grade of instruction led to dissatisfied college teachers. Because their teaching was
narrowly restricted, professors were discouraged from developing a deep
understanding of their subjects.[33]

Following the model of the German gymnasium and university, Tappan proposed limiting the collegiate course to those subjects, such as classical languages and mathematics, that were of clear disciplinary value. The
college would make no pretensions of being comprehensive and would
become the required preparation for a university education. The university
would provide thorough instruction in all branches of knowledge, and
students would be able to select their classes based on their interests and
professional aims. Wayland, on the other hand, suggested that the college design various courses of study. Students would select their areas of
specialization and their classes. They would earn a degree after they had
passed an examination in their chosen area.[34]

Wayland's and Tappan's appraisal of the shortcomings of American
higher education attracted growing interest in the 1860s. Concern about

the national economy raised support for technological and scientific education. The passage of the Morrill Act in 1862 reflected this growing interest in practical education. The Civil War, which both disrupted the research activities of scientists and drew attention to the importance of scientific expertise, also raised interest in scientific education. Scientists linked the growth of science to the reform of higher education. For example, in 1872 Joseph Henry, one of the nation's leading scientists, asserted that the growth of American science depended on "an improvement in our higher institutions of learning." In this context, educational reform took on a new urgency.[35]

In the decade following the Civil War, commentators depicted the state of American science in dark tones. "America, when compared with other first class nations," wrote chemist Frank W. Clarke, "occupies a low position in science. For every research published in our country, at least fifty appear elsewhere." Clarke blamed the difficulties of science on the shortcomings of college education. The problems identified by antebellum critics—the multiplication of colleges, the inadequacies of special courses and schools, and the restrictions of the set curriculum—were especially damaging to the natural sciences.[36]

Scientific instruction and investigation, its supporters pointed out, required expensive equipment and supplies. Many of the small, poor colleges in the country could not provide adequate materials. Faculty needed to specialize to keep up with the developments in the rapidly advancing sciences. Instead, they were required to teach a variety of subjects. The standardized curriculum did not provide enough time to teach the sciences. "Glance over the curriculum laid down in almost any college catalogue," Clarke wrote, "and see how the scientific instruction is arranged. In nearly every instance there will be found an enormous disproportion between linguistic studies and science." Special scientific courses did not offset this imbalance. Consequently, "an enthusiasm for science is dampened rather than encouraged." This, in turn, inhibited the general public's regard for the sciences.[37]

Clarke attributed the neglect of science to an improper balance between the various aims of education. He believed that the religious concerns overshadowed the needs of intellectual inquiry. Religious control of the colleges hurt science education. He blamed the proliferation of underfunded schools on sectarian rivalry. "If there were such things as Presbyterian mathematics, Baptist chemistry, Episcopalian classics, and Methodist geology, such a scattering of educational forces would be pardonable; but, as matters really stand, it is a nuisance for which no valid excuse can be found." In their hiring practices, college officials mistakenly confounded scholarship and religion. "Every year professors are chosen, not on account of scientific ability, but for reasons of a theological or sectarian character." As a result, even the well-equipped colleges did not provide the best scientific instruction.[38]

Clarke thought that the religious orientation of the colleges was also responsible for the emphasis on classical languages and rhetoric. In church-sponsored schools, "the studies which are of especial value to theological students will be given undue prominence." Scientific studies were subordinated to the needs of religious training. In contemporary colleges, Clarke wrote, "there seems to be a real conflict, not between religion and science, but between the injudiciousness of religious people and the requirements of scientific research." This conflict, Clarke and others believed, could be solved by educational reform. To encourage intellectual progress, colleges and universities had to repair the imbalance between the aims of religion and the needs of science.[39]

In addition to criticizing colleges, American scientists blamed natural theology for limiting the growth of science. For most of the nineteenth century, natural theology provided the means for demonstrating "a general accordance between the teachings of Scripture and the teachings of Nature." This entailed adapting each new scientific theory to Christian doctrine. After some contentious struggles over scientific discoveries, late nineteenth-century promoters of science rejected this process because they thought that it hampered scientific progress. Instead, they called for a new way to harmonize science and religion that would guarantee the independence of scientific inquiry.[40]

In the first half of the nineteenth century, repeated conflicts between new scientific theories and accepted religious beliefs threatened the assumption that God's works and words were always in harmony. Educated Americans argued over the atheistic tendencies of some scientific ideas, including geological theories about the age of the earth, the nebular hypothesis, and theories of polygenesis. But religious and scientific leaders explained that these disagreements simply resulted from imperfect knowledge. In these cases, scientists and theologians worked to reinterpret scientific ideas or relevant biblical passages to achieve agreement. Troublesome as these controversies were, they were generally regarded as anomalies, temporary disputes that ultimately could be reconciled.[41]

By the 1870s theologians and scientists were engaged in heated debates over the religious implications of the period's most important new scientific theory, evolution. The conflict over Charles Darwin's theory of evolution was particularly intense because the theory potentially contradicted two religious doctrines. First, it offered a nonscriptural account of the creation of species, and, second, it called into question the argument from design.[42]

The argument from design—or proof of the existence of God based on evidence of intelligence or purposefulness in nature—was considered one of the "most convincing illustrations of Supreme Intelligence." The order of nature seemed to be compelling evidence that it was created by an omniscient deity. "The force of this argument" wrote geologist Joseph LeConte, "is felt at once intuitively by all minds, and its effect is irresistible and overwhelming to every plain, honest mind." Because of the presumed strength of this demonstration of divine existence, the threat to the notion of design proved to be the most controversial aspect of Darwin's theory.[43]

Charles Hodge, a professor at Princeton Theological Seminary, was the most prominent American thinker who insisted that Darwinism opposed religion. He answered the question, "What is Darwinism?" with a blunt rejection: "It is Atheism." Hodge believed that the theory of natural selection denied "all design in nature." For Hodge and others steeped in natural theology, "the denial of design in nature is virtually the denial of God." Darwinian theory obscured God's hand in nature and, therefore, could not be true.[44]

Other scientists and theologians disagreed and sought to demonstrate that evolutionary theory did not contradict the notion of a divine plan. To show design in evolution, they minimized the role of natural selection. Natural selection seemed too harsh and random to be divinely sanctioned. Therefore, thinkers such as Joseph LeConte and James McCosh drew on the neo-Lamarckian theory of inherited traits to depict evolution as a progressive and orderly process. Development, they suggested, was God's chosen means of creation.[45]

A few writers reconciled evolution and religion without expunging natural selection. They drew on the Calvinist image of an infinite, all-powerful God, whose ways could not be easily understood by humans. George Frederick Wright argued that human beings, because of their limited vision, misperceived "the seeming waste and apparent failures and imperfections of nature." To recognize "the contrivance and foresight of a higher power," evidenced by Darwinism, one must look at the whole of creation rather than a part. Humans looked at the world as if it were made

solely for their purposes. They therefore missed God's higher plans in natural selection.[46]

Promoters of science welcomed these efforts to show that "the doctrine of Evolution is not an anti-religious doctrine" and that it is not "inconsistent with the idea of Divine design in nature." They assumed that
the successful reconciliation of evolutionary doctrine and Christian beliefs
would help the cause of science. Nonetheless, they became increasingly
dissatisfied with this process. Because reconciliation entailed adjusting scientific theories to theological doctrines, they thought that natural theology
restricted the independence of scientific investigation.[47]

In addition, the process of reconciliation seemed to become more
difficult. "The efforts at harmonization," E. L. Youmans wrote, "have generally come from partisans of opposing views, who aimed at agreement by
demanding great concessions from the opposite side. The scientists often
ask theologians to renounce the main pretensions of theology for the sake
of peace, and theologians request the scientists to eschew three-fourths of
what they believe as mere pseudo-science, that concord of opinion may be
reached." The various parties seemed to be constantly fighting over the
terms of the peace.[48]

The success of natural theology in the first half of the nineteenth century rested on a consensus about the fundamentals of religion and science.
The disintegration of this consensus in the last half of the nineteenth century undermined efforts at reconciliation. The response to a series of lectures on "The Relations between Religion and Science" given in 1884 by
Frederick Temple, later the archbishop of Canterbury, illustrates the disagreement over the essential elements of Christianity and natural science.
Temple's lectures tried to reconcile Christianity and evolution. Instead of
creating consensus, however, they spawned a debate about how science
and religion conceived of the relationship between God and nature.

Temple, a liberal theologian opposed to biblical literalism, drew on
the argument from design to show the harmony between evolution and
Christianity. But he also sought to establish the possibility of divine intervention, arguing that miracles were not inconsistent with the scientific
view of the world. He equated the problem of divine intervention with the
question of freedom of the human will. Within the uniformity of nature,
he explained, individuals could still act independently. "This breach of
uniformity is within very narrow limits," but it is essential for the existence
of moral law. Similarly, Temple argued that God produced miracles for
moral lessons. "The evidence for uniformity has never succeeded, and can
never succeed in showing that the God who made and rules the universe

never sets aside a physical law for a moral purpose, either by working through the human will or by direct action on external nature." He rejected a clockwork universe in which God could not intervene. Temple believed that scientific theories about the creation of the world and the evolution of life broke down at certain important points. They could not explain the transformation from inorganic to organic existence or the transformation from mere animal life to moral and spiritual life. These gaps in scientific explanation, for Temple, indicated the probability of divine intervention. Temple did not think that the existence of miracles threatened science. "The belief that God can work miracles and has worked them has never yet obstructed the path of a single student of science." He allowed that science might progress to a point where certain "gaps" would be filled and incidents currently considered miraculous would be explained by physical laws. "A higher physical law as yet unknown" may explain things like "our Lord's Resurrection" or "our Lord's miracles of healing." Temple maintained that science and religion could be reconciled, but he insisted that science must conform to his conception of God. He would relinquish the uniformity of natural law for the existence of miracles.[49]

Although contemporaries generally applauded Temple's reconciliation of evolution and Christianity, some recognized how tenuous such compromises were. In articles published in *Popular Science Monthly,* John Burroughs agreed that science and religion should be reconciled, but denied that Temple's lectures provided the solution. Burroughs thought that Temple had violated an essential principle of science. He argued that science holds that "the sequence of cause and effect is inviolable . . . and there is no failure and no disorder in Nature." Science, therefore, could not recognize the existence of miracles. Because Burroughs and Temple disagreed about the essential doctrines of science and religion, they could not agree about reconciling them.[50]

While agreeing, at least in theory, on the ultimate harmony of science and religion, late nineteenth-century scholars tended to break into rival camps when evaluating specific ideas. One group of thinkers emphasized the primacy of Christian beliefs. Noah Porter, professor of moral philosophy and president of Yale College, told students that "neither faith nor theology are the historical or natural foes of science and culture." His tolerance, however, extended only to scientific theories that affirmed the truths of religion. "Without God there is no well-grounded hope for science." On the other hand, promoters of science wanted religion to concede the supremacy of the scientific world view. "I cordially invite the clergy to become scientists," wrote one author in *Popular Science Monthly.* "If existing religious organizations are to be preserved, the scientific method must be unqualifiedly adopted and prosecuted in the study and teaching of religion." The gulf between people who were primarily committed to the preservation of Christianity and those who championed an independent science destroyed the consensus on which natural theology rested.[51]

Some scientists and liberal theologians came to view the reconciliation of particular scientific theories and religious beliefs as an inadequate solution to the conflict of religion and science. In addition to the growing disagreement over the priority of scientific or religious views, writers simply grew tired of the continual disputes. "As the battle subsides in one field," Youmans noted, "it breaks out in another. In the field of Astronomy, where once the conflict raged with the greatest fury, all is now serene." But, he pointed out, the conflict simply passed from astronomy to geology, and from geology to biology.[52]

The continual need to reconcile new scientific findings diminished the credibility of natural theology. Because natural theology did not preclude contradictions between religion and science, it could not refute the implications of a book like John William Draper's *History of the Conflict between Religion and Science,* published in 1874. Draper suggested that there was a permanent battle between science and religion. "The history of science," he wrote, "is not a mere record of isolated discoveries; it is a narrative of the conflict of two contending powers, the expansive force of the human intellect on one side, and the compression arising from traditionary faith and human interests on the other." The underlying harmony of which everyone spoke, Draper implied, was an illusion.[53]

The book began with the origins of science in Greek culture and then chronicled the development of Christian doctrine and its subsequent repression of science, focusing on the excesses of the Catholic Church. Although Draper cloaked his book in anti-Catholic rhetoric, he aimed its message at his fellow Protestants. Draper reminded Protestant denominations that they were not exempt from exciting "theological odium." Although Protestants lacked the civil power of the Catholic Church, they shared the repressive belief in the absolute truth of the Bible. "The two rival divisions of the Christian church—Protestant and Catholic," he wrote, "were thus in accord on one point: to tolerate no science except such as they considered agreeable to the Scriptures." Because of this, Draper implied that both acted to thwart science.[54]

Draper's *Conflict between Religion and Science* was tremendously successful. It was translated into ten languages and went through fifty printings in the United States. Draper raised questions that Americans seemed ready to contemplate: Was there an inherent conflict between religion and science? Did religion oppose scientific advance? Although intellectuals continued to believe in the ultimate compatibility of religion and science, they had to admit that it had not been realized in their time. Natural theology only achieved temporary harmony through laborious compromises that slowed the progress of intellectual inquiry.[55]

Even those who believed in the basic tenets of natural theology admitted that it worked better in theory than in practice. "I frankly confess it," wrote Joseph LeConte, "according to traditional interpretation of Scripture, there are many particular passages which seem to be in discordance with the teachings of Nature." LeConte believed that as long as science progressed, there would be continual clashes between it and religion. "We can never expect the conflict to cease, so long as science continues to advance," he wrote. "The conflict must be perpetual, and the distress and doubt occasioned thereby to the religious mind must also be perpetual, unless we rise to a higher and more philosophical point of view." LeConte came to believe that the process of reconciling new scientific theories with religious doctrines hurt religion by constantly raising new doubts about the truth of religion. For the sake of religion and science, LeConte wanted to find a new basis for peaceful relations.[56]

Because disputes over new scientific ideas would continually arise, LeConte became critical of efforts to reconcile these new theories with religion. "These schemes of reconciliation become daily more distasteful to me. I have used them in times past," he admitted, "but, now, the deliberate construction of such schemes seems to me almost like trifling with the words of Scripture and the teachings of Nature." The solution for LeConte, and other late nineteenth-century intellectuals, was to stop focusing on particular scientific and theological doctrines and instead look for a way "to adjust . . . the *general relations of science and theology*."[57]

Diminished faith in natural theology led intellectuals to search for new ways to conceive of the relationship of science and religion. Although they continued to believe in the unity of truth and the ultimate harmony of science and religion, promoters of science rejected contemporary educational and scholarly practices that integrated natural science into a Christian world view. The search for a new basis for religious and scientific collaboration, however, could not be separated from debates about the true nature of science. These debates would determine the direction of educational reform and the place of religion in the new university.

TWO

Science and Religion Reconceived

The publication of Darwin's *On the Origin of Species* in 1859 spawned a wide-ranging exchange, one that went beyond the specific question of whether evolution or special creation best explained the origin of species. Questions regarding the nature of science were incorporated in this debate because many of Darwin's critics charged that *Origin of Species* did not conform to the precepts of Baconianism, then the most widely accepted model of the scientific method. These charges forced scientists to articulate their views on scientific method, which heightened awareness of competing philosophical systems. In defending evolution, American scientists rejected Baconianism and the association of science with common-sense empiricism. They affirmed that hypotheses and theories were essential to science and that progress in science involved discrediting old ideas and formulating new theories. Some intellectuals used evolutionary theory to develop new "progressivist" philosophies of science. They rejected the notion of natural law and the idea that things could be defined by essential characteristics, and conceived of science as a particularly successful form of functional adaptation to the environment.[1]

Americans were introduced to Baconianism through the works of Scottish realist philosopher Thomas Reid and his disciples. Reid bequeathed to his American followers a simplified conception of scientific methodology, derived largely from Isaac Newton's *Regulae philosophandi* and other writings. Reid, like most of his nineteenth-century followers, equated Newtonian and Baconian theories of induction and in the name of Bacon praised the derivation of natural laws from the careful observation of facts as the path to reliable knowledge. American scholars adopted the Scottish admiration for Bacon. "The name of Lord Bacon," Edward Everett wrote in 1823, "with the single exception of Sir Isaac Newton, is the first in the modern philosophical world." In public discussions of science, Baconianism served as an emblem for sound inquiry; it provided a set of strictures that, if followed correctly, would uncover the laws of nature.[2]

According to Baconianism, the ultimate aim of science was the discovery of natural laws. These laws were conceived of as invariable series of events that regulated nature. If scientists could accurately identify all the laws of nature, scientific knowledge would be absolute and certain. Since the seventeenth century, however, philosophers had recognized that scientific knowledge was fallible and probable. The question for philosophers, then, was how to ensure that scientific knowledge was as reliable as possible. What method, they asked, would produce knowledge that approached certainty? Although philosophers debated this question, Thomas Reid and those who adopted his Baconianism emphasized induction from observable facts and the prohibition of hypotheses. According to this view, if science was built upon individual facts, and if these facts were clear and unquestioned, then the generalizations based on them would be authoritative. Baconianism prohibited the use of theory, hypotheses, imagination, and explanations that relied on imperceptible causes. These all threatened the status of science as reliable knowledge and were considered outside the realm of proper scientific procedure.[3]

Baconianism had serious conceptual and practical limitations as a description of the scientific method. Baconians praised inductive reasoning without explaining how to build reliable generalizations from the observation of individual events. Baconian philosophy did not clearly address the relationship between inductive and deductive reasoning, the respective roles of both in scientific inquiry, and the nature of scientific explanations. During the first half of the nineteenth century, several British thinkers tried to modify Baconianism and develop a more sophisticated philosophy of science. For example, in 1830 the respected scientist, John W. F. Herschel, published his *Preliminary Discourse on the Study of Natural Philosophy*. Although an admirer of Bacon, Herschel rejected strictures against deductive reasoning, hypothesis, and imagination in the formulation of scientific generalizations. He argued that scientists made important discoveries through a variety of means, some of them completely fortuitous. "In the study of nature, we must not, therefore, be scrupulous as to *how* we reach a knowledge of such general facts: provided only that we verify them carefully when once detected, we must be content to seize them wherever they are to be found." For Herschel and most other nineteenth-century philosophers of science, the method of discovery was not as important as careful testing of all theories.[4]

Positivist philosophies of science also rejected the Baconian prohibitions against hypotheses. Americans were introduced to positivist philosophies of science through the work of Auguste Comte and John Stuart Mill. Mill's *System of Logic* (1843) was the most complete explication of a positivist philosophy of science. Mill offered a more sophisticated version of inductivism than the Baconian ideal. Like Baconians, Mill maintained that all scientific knowledge was based on empirical induction and that the ultimate aim of science was the discovery of natural laws. But Mill rejected the simplistic notion of passive observation in favor of a more complex model of the process of scientific discovery and justification. Mill's conception of the scientific method allowed a role for the use of hypotheses and deductive logic, but he maintained strict standards for the verification of hypotheses, requiring that predictions deduced from the hypotheses agree with empirical observations and that no other hypotheses explain the same facts.[5]

William Whewell, a contemporary of Herschel and Mill, offered a more radical reconstruction of the philosophy of science, emphasizing the importance of both facts and ideas and allowing for a more active role for the investigator's mind in scientific discovery. For Whewell, scientific knowledge comprised both conceptual and factual elements; the best science joined "clear and consistent" ideas with "real and certain" facts. He viewed the process of discovery as creative and encouraged scientists to speculate freely. Whewell expected that scientists' speculations would be confirmed or refuted through a process he referred to as the "colligation of facts." The ability of a hypothesis to predict new facts, Whewell believed, was particularly strong proof of its truth.[6]

Despite these developments in the philosophy of science, a fairly simple Baconian model dominated public discussions of science in the United States until the late nineteenth century. Although scientists recognized that scientific practice sometimes deviated from this ideal, they used Baconianism to explain the process of scientific research. Science, as they presented it, was based on careful, unbiased observation of nature. After observation, their next activity was the classification of data. Scientific method, therefore, was identified largely with taxonomy. The purpose of the collection and classification of data was the discovery of natural laws. Once a true law was identified, it would become part of an unchanging body of knowledge. Progress, according to this view of science, entailed either discovering new laws or broadening the application of laws already known. Scientists assumed that a finite number of natural laws would eventually account for all natural phenomena.[7]

This Baconian view of science was suited to American intellectual life in the first half of the nineteenth century. During this period American science was dominated by projects that easily fit its mold. Scientists concentrated on surveying the vast geological, botanical, and zoological resources of the nation. Baconianism also matched the educational philosophy of the antebellum colleges. In the classical college, science was taught with textbooks and recitations. This pedagogical method reflected the Baconian conception of science as a limited amount of specific information about natural processes. In addition, Baconian science easily fit into a standardized curriculum that aimed to unite all learning. Baconians believed that natural laws revealed attributes of the Creator. Instructors, therefore, could relate science to moral philosophy and theology.[8]

In addition, Baconianism corresponded well to the natural theology tradition. The existence of immutable natural laws implied a lawgiver. Indeed, Baconians grounded the philosophy of science in the same religious assumptions that underlay Scottish common-sense realism: God created an orderly universe and created human beings with the capability to perceive the world about them. Science was knowledge about God's creation. Baconianism was, therefore, an important element in the ideal of intellectual unity that dominated in the first half of the nineteenth century.

Later in the century, however, public criticism of Bacon became commonplace. Beginning in the 1870s, Bacon's name became the object of disdain rather than praise. In an article in *Popular Science Monthly* in 1877, Charles Peirce wrote that "a modern reader who is not in awe of [Lord Bacon's] grandiloquence is chiefly struck by the inadequacy of his view of scientific procedure." By 1890 few American scientists claimed to be Baconians. This change took place in the context of debates over evolution. One of the most common criticisms of Darwin's work was that it violated the precepts of Baconianism. True science, these critics pointed out, was based on the careful study of observable phenomena. Natural selection could not be directly observed, and fossil evidence unquestionably demonstrating evolution had not yet been found. The critics rejected Darwin's proof from the contemporary geographical distribution of plants and animals as deductive rather than inductive reasoning. This criticism was taken very seriously and slowed the acceptance of evolutionary theory in several countries. Ultimately, however, it hurt the Baconian conception of science. By the end of the century, most scientists accepted some form of evolutionary theory. Baconianism was then associated with the reactionary forces of anti-evolution.[9]

Scientists responded to charges that evolution was not a proper scientific doctrine either by defending the empirical evidence in favor of evolution and/or by criticizing the inductive model of science. For example, one celebrated confrontation over the status of evolution took place between two prominent German biologists, Rudolph Virchow and Ernst Haeckel. Virchow, in a speech presented to the German Association of Naturalists and Physicians in 1877, criticized scientists who spoke of evolution as an established scientific doctrine; Haeckel then rebutted Virchow in his *Freedom of Science and Teaching.* The exchange created an international furor. The two positions were quickly translated into English and published, with Thomas H. Huxley supplying an introduction for Haeckel's defense.[10]

In his speech Virchow argued that scientists endangered their freedom by presenting their "pet theories and personal views" as if they were established knowledge. He argued that there was a distinction between "real science in the strictest sense of the term—for which alone . . . we can justly demand that full measure of liberty which may be called the liberty of science, or more correctly still, perhaps, *liberty of scientific teaching*—and, on the other hand, that wider domain which belongs rather to speculation." He believed that only absolutely certain science should be taught in schools and universities; evolution, in his opinion, did not pass as ascertained knowledge. He was particularly critical of the theory of human descent and argued that there was no concrete evidence in its favor. "On the whole," he said, "we really must acknowledge that no fossil type of lower human development exists." He therefore concluded that "*we cannot teach, we cannot designate as a revelation of science the doctrine that man descends from ape or any other animal.*" Virchow, like a good Baconian, demanded that scientific knowledge rest on observable phenomena.[11]

Haeckel responded to Virchow by defending the evidence in favor of evolution and implying that Virchow's weak training in morphology made him insensitive to the value of this evidence. Then Haeckel criticized Virchow's vision of science as "absolutely ascertained knowledge." Haeckel examined the various sciences. He began with mathematics and conceded that, although it rests on unprovable first principles, "mathematics practically constitute an absolutely certain and objective science." He then moved to physics, the science considered the most "exact." Most of physics, he argued, "is incapable of any exact mathematical proof. For what do we know for certain of the essential nature of matter, or the essential nature of force? What do we know for certain of gravitation, of the attraction of mass, of its effects at great distances, and so on?" As he continued through the sciences—chemistry, geology, biology, psychology, and the social sciences—he argued that each was less certain than the one before.

He concluded that there was "no such boundary line" between subjective and objective knowledge. "On the contrary," he wrote, "all human knowledge is subjective. An objective science which consists merely of facts without any subjective theories is inconceivable." If only objective facts could be taught, then nothing could be taught, for all science was, to some degree, uncertain.[12]

Scientists could respond to criticism such as Virchow's by asserting that evolution rested on observable phenomenon and/or by attacking the notion of science as completely ascertained knowledge. Their choice often reflected their philosophy of science: those who stressed the empirical evidence favored positivism, while those who emphasized the inadequacies of inductivism tended to prefer progressivist conceptions of science.[13]

According to Mill's positivism, Darwin's work did not violate proper scientific method. But this did not mean that natural selection should be considered part of scientific knowledge. The question for positivists was whether the empirical evidence confirmed the hypothesized process of natural selection and invalidated all other possible explanations. Mill thought that Darwin lacked the empirical evidence to establish natural selection as anything more than a hypothesis. Although he did not rule out the possibility that natural selection might be confirmed as scientific truth, Mill was skeptical. He was unsympathetic to natural selection as an explanation of the origin of species because it did not conform to his notion of the invariable laws of nature. Despite Mill's reservations, positivists accepted in principle that natural selection might be empirically verified as one of the absolute laws of nature. When they defended natural selection, they stressed the empirical evidence in its favor.[14]

Some American positivists, such as Chauncey Wright, defended Darwin's theory of evolution on empirical grounds. But American scientists also used the debates over evolution as an opportunity to reconsider existing theories of science. In the late nineteenth century American intellectuals participated in a wide-ranging discussion about the nature of scientific inquiry. Although no philosophical consensus was reached, a new public image of science emerged that emphasized the uncertainty of science, the importance of hypotheses and causal explanations, and the progressive development of science. Some American intellectuals elaborated on this conception and drew on evolutionary theory to develop a progressivist theory of science that rejected the notion of natural laws and emphasized the instrumental character of scientific hypotheses.[15]

In a typical American exchange, supporters of evolution responded to charges that evolution could not be considered true science by attacking the Baconian belief that scientific knowledge is certain. For example, in 1872, at a banquet honoring the British scientist John Tyndall, New York *Evening Post* editor Parke Godwin warned against dignifying evolution with the title "science." Evolution, he maintained, was not verified by the observation of facts and therefore could not be considered scientific knowledge. "Certainty is the criterion of true science," Godwin insisted. "If we give that criterion up, science loses its authority, its prestige, its assurance of march, and its sovereign position as an arbiter in the varying struggles of doctrine." Darwin's work, according to critics, relied too much on mere "suppositions" to be entitled to "the authority of scientific truth."[16]

Edward Youmans, editor of *Popular Science Monthly,* took up Godwin's criticism. He responded that Godwin's standards of science would stifle scientific investigation, for theory is essential to the progress of science. Youmans noted that "the proof of" all theories is "unquestionably incomplete," but argued that scientists did not expect "absolute verities and eternal principles." Instead, they sought "to supersede existing truth by larger truth." Youmans defended the use of hypotheses and ridiculed the Baconian standard of empirical certitude. Youmans and other supporters of evolution responded to their critics by questioning some of the central assumptions of Baconianism.[17]

In their critique of Baconianism, Americans echoed the ideas of the influential English philosopher of science, William Stanley Jevons. In his *Principles of Science,* Jevons maintained that scientific knowledge is never absolute:

> In order that we may gain a true understanding of the kind, degree, and value of the knowledge which we acquire by experimental investigation, it is requisite that we should be fully conscious of its approximate character. . . . Many persons may be misled by the expression *exact science* and may think that the knowledge acquired by scientific methods admits of our reaching absolutely true laws, exact to the last degree.

But in Jevons's view no inductive conclusions were more than probable.[18]

Late nineteenth-century American intellectuals, for the most part, embraced the view that scientific knowledge was imperfect. They frequently praised Jevons's works on logic and the philosophy of science, and his books were commonly assigned at universities in the United States. Philosophers and promoters of science alike rejected the possibility of absolute scientific knowledge. Simon Newcomb, one of America's most prominent scientists, was among those who maintained that scientific knowledge was not absolute. David Starr Jordan, ichthyologist and president of Stanford University, also insisted that science was uncertain. "It is . . . no reproach to human science," he said, "that it deals with human relations, not with absolute truths. . . . Science has no 'Ultimate Truths.' There are none known to man." It may seem strange that in a period when scientists were fighting for independence, they would deny what had previously been seen as science's greatest attribute—its certainty. But this new position was consistent with the belief that science had a privileged cognitive status and deserved to be protected from outside meddling.[19]

The new image of science also emphasized the importance of hypotheses that offered causal explanations rather than simple descriptions of nature. Chemist Josiah Cooke wrote:

> The scientific investigator is not content with a knowledge of the outward relations of phenomena. He seeks to discover the proximate causes of the order observed, and although he may not be able to reach certainty, he is not satisfied until he has framed some explanation by which he can classify his facts, and which at the same time will give form and body to his thoughts so indispensable for successful study. Hence arise of necessity the hypotheses, theories, and systems of science.

The goal of science, in this view, was to frame theories that explained observed phenomena.[20]

Jevons also confirmed the importance of hypotheses and causal explanations. In *Principles of Science* he described the scientific method as a "marriage of hypothesis and experiment." "When facts are in our possession," he wrote, "we frame an hypothesis to explain their relations, and by the success of the explanation is the value of the hypothesis to be judged." Hypotheses might have been inspired by observing nature, and they were evaluated in reference to what had been observed, but they were not part of nature. They were human inventions used to understand nature.[21]

The focus on hypotheses supported a new emphasis on the importance of human creativity in science. Chemist T. W. Richards maintained that "really original research in chemistry" required "an active and far-reaching imagination." He explained, "In any but the simplest scientific tasks, the mind of the investigator must conceive of many underlying conditions and possible modifying circumstances which are not apparent at first sight, and which demand imagination for their detection and proper adjustment." To frame hypotheses, scientists frequently relied on their imagination or chanced upon ideas. Although these hypotheses were later tested by experiments and observation, scientific theories were never completely objective. They always retained the subjective human element and, therefore, could always be revised. The old view that a scientific law, once discovered, became a permanent part of human knowledge was replaced by a new dynamic concept of science.[22]

Discredited theories became a sign of the vitality of science. What had earlier been seen as an embarrassment to its authority could now be viewed as a source of its superiority. Science was distinguished from other forms of knowledge by its progressive nature. Theories were tested and either improved or rejected. "Every science is continually learning that its supposed solutions are only apparent," wrote John Dewey. "Wrestling with the problem, there is an evolution of new techniques to control inquiry, there is a search for new facts, institution of new types of experimentation. . . . And all this is progress." Therefore, concluded Dewey, "only the worn out cynic, the devitalized sensualist, and the fanatical dogmatist . . . interpret the continuous change of science as proving that, since each successive statement is wrong, the whole record is error and folly." In rejecting the idea that science was a body of certain knowledge, intellectuals developed a view of science as a progressive process of discovery.[23]

Some thinkers used evolutionary theory to further develop this new conception of science. Although many scientists affirmed the importance of explanatory hypotheses, they did not necessarily reject the older goal of describing natural laws. Some, however, rejected the notion of immutable natural laws. They pointed out that evolutionary theory challenged one of the most basic assumptions about the universe, the existence of essential natural kinds. The various classificatory schemes of natural history assumed that every species had essential qualities that defined it. British naturalist W. B. Carpenter wrote:

> Now it seems to be a received article of faith, both amongst scientific naturalists and with the general public, that all these reputed species have (or have had) a real existence in nature; that each originated in a distinct act of creation; and that, once established, each type has continued to transmit its distinctive characters, without any essential change from one generation to another, so long as the race has been permitted to exist.

Darwinism, of course, denied that species had essential, permanent qualities. In so doing, it undermined a primary example of natural kinds and, by extension, the idea that nature is fixed and immutable.[24]

Proponents of progressivist views of science argued that the rejection of natural kinds also discredited traditional notions of natural law. John Dewey, in his essay "The Influence of Darwinism on Philosophy," wrote that "the combination of the very words origin and species embodied an intellectual revolt." To make his point, Dewey constructed a simplified history of Western thought. He maintained that ideas about nature and knowledge that had dominated for the previous two thousand years "rested on the assumption of the superiority of the fixed and final." Constants were considered real or true, and variation was dismissed as insignificant. The concept of natural law illustrated this bias by focusing only on uniform sequences of events. But Darwin had drawn attention to the significance of change. "In treating the forms that had been regarded as types of fixity and perfection as originating and passing away," Dewey wrote, "the *Origin of Species* introduced a mode of thinking that in the end was bound to transform the logic of knowledge." According to this view, science could not be considered simply the discovery of regularity in nature because nature was not necessarily regular.[25]

In addition, some philosophers maintained that the rejection of natural kinds implied an anti-essentialism. William James, in his *Principles of Psychology,* argued that things could not be defined by an essential nature. "*There is no property,*" he wrote in his chapter "Reasoning," "ABSOLUTELY *essential to one thing.*" Our perception of what is important about an object depends on why we are interested in that object. If I am writing, James said, "it is essential that I conceive my paper as a surface for inscription. But," he continued, "if I wished to light a fire, and no other materials were by, the essential way of conceiving the paper would be as combustible material; and I need then have no thought of any of its other destinations." Any given thing has infinite qualities, but we do not perceive of it in its totality; instead, we select particular aspects of it that interest us. What we consider the "essence of a thing," James believed, is determined by its dominant function. We define things by our interest in them and their use for us, ignoring unrelated qualities. Anti-essentialism, then, implied that simple, unbiased observation of facts was impossible. Rejecting essentialism, James concluded that the notion of unbiased, common-sense observation was untenable.[26]

Some intellectuals began to argue that science was distinguished by its rejection of ordinary empirical evidence. For example, George Beard, in an article in *Popular Science Monthly,* asserted that "distrust of the senses" was the first test "of scientific expertness." The attitude that motivated scientific inquiry was not faith in the certainty of observed facts;

instead, it was sustained doubt and distrust of appearances. Dewey maintained that scientific inquiry "is always more or less troublesome because it involves overcoming the inertia that inclines one to accept suggestions at their face value." What distinguishes scientific thinking from regular "empirical" thinking, Dewey argued, is the endurance of doubt and the willingness to question even the most basic assumptions about reality. Instead of viewing science as a passive process of observation, some intellectuals began to conceive of it as an active process of problem solving.[27]

Evolutionary theory encouraged intellectuals to question both the assumption that nature itself was immutable and the belief that scientists could understand nature through common-sense perception. Proponents of progressivist conceptions of science concluded that the old idea that scientific discoveries replicated nature was no longer adequate. William James noted that "up to about 1850 almost everyone believed that sciences expressed truths that were exact copies of a definite code of non-human realities." But he pointed out that this position had been almost completely discredited in the decades following the publication of the *Origin of Species.* "It is to be doubted," James continued, "whether any theorizer to-day, either in mathematics, logic, physics, or biology, conceives himself to be literally re-editing processes of nature or thoughts of God." While many scientists accepted the distinction between their theories and nature, some still held that the goal of science was to describe nature. James and other progressivists, however, argued that scientific theories were instrumental rather than descriptive.[28]

Just as Darwinism helped debunk the view of inquiry as passive observation, it also provided intellectuals with concepts to defend an alternative, instrumental view of scientific inquiry. Darwinism suggested that "human thought itself is . . . a variation (or mutation) which has been able to persist and to survive." Some American intellectuals, including William James, John Dewey, James Mark Baldwin, and Charles S. Peirce, began to look at knowledge in evolutionary terms. They viewed knowledge "as a weapon in the struggle for life" that had developed and evolved through human history. They considered ideas to be instruments, or "mental modes of *adaptation* to reality." Although these men did not agree with all aspects of each other's philosophies, their work popularized the idea that intellectual inquiry was functional and should be judged by practical results.[29]

These writers began with the belief that human intellectual capacities "are the results of natural selection." Peirce wrote that "it seems incontestable that the mind of man is strongly adapted to the comprehension of the world. . . . Certain conceptions, highly important for such a comprehension, naturally arise in his mind, and without such a tendency, the mind could never have any development at all." Basic categories of thought, such as the notions of time, space, and force, were simply ideas that had been preserved and generalized because of their utility. Baldwin held that "the most absolute and universal seeming principles of knowledge, viewed racially, are 'practical postulates' which have been woven into human thought as presuppositions of consistent and trustworthy experience. They were 'original ideas' at some time, found to be useful for the organization of knowledge and for the conduct of life." These ideas were preserved because they helped human beings adapt to the demands of their environment.[30]

Progressivist theories of science maintained that new concepts were invented and preserved in a similar fashion. People live in a world that was not fully explained and could not be fully explained because experience was ever changing. A person, confronted with a new circumstance, often did not immediately know what to do. A problem existed; the process of solving this problem was inquiry, which involved inferring new solutions from past knowledge or experience. Reflective thinking, Dewey wrote, was "that operation in which present facts suggest other facts (or truths) in such a way as to induce belief in the latter upon the ground or warrant of the former." The new inference was tested in action; if it "worked" it was preserved as true.[31]

Inquiry, viewed as the solution to concrete problems, did not yield permanent knowledge. "*Theories,*" James explained, "*become instruments, not answers to enigmas, in which we can rest.* We don't lie back on them, we move forward, and on occasion, make nature over again with their aid." Ideas were judged to be true provisionally when they resulted in successful action. But this action, in turn, led to new experiences and new problems, the solution of which might require revising previous beliefs. Inquiry was an active and continuous process.[32]

The success of all inquiry was judged by its practical results. This emphasis on the practical outcome of inquiry supported the view that science was progressive: the practical benefits of science revealed the superiority of its methods. Science was portrayed as an improvement on ordinary thinking. "Knowledge from the first, whether in the form of ordinary observation or scientific thinking," Dewey wrote, "is logical; in ordinary observation, however, the logical process is unconscious, dormant, and hence goes easily and inevitably astray." On the other hand, "in scientific thinking, the mind knows what it is about." As a result, "the logical functions are consciously used as guides and standards." Science, therefore, was a superior tool for adaptation and survival.[33]

Scientists attributed the success of science to its method. What was important about science was not any particular doctrine, which might be discredited and replaced, but rather its approach to solving problems. Science, Charles Peirce wrote, "is a living and growing body of truth. We might even say that knowledge is not necessary to science. . . . That which constitutes science is not so much correct conclusions, as it is correct method." This special method was distinguished by a variety of features, including quantification, specialization, cooperation among researchers, the development of "instruments of precision," and sheer patience and persistence. But among the various characteristics of the scientific method, two seemed particularly important: the careful verification of hypotheses and an attitude of open inquiry.[34]

According to post-Baconian views of science, scientists spent most of their time designing, conducting, and carefully observing the results of experiments. All scientific theories required verification. As Peirce explained, "the hypothesis should be distinctly put as a question, before making observations which are to test its truth." In other words, "we must try to see what the result of the predictions from the hypothesis will be." Experiments were designed to isolate natural processes that might confirm or refute a given hypothesis. To avoid error, experimentation must be "controlled by the most scrupulous care, guided by the closest discrimination, attended by the keenest analysis, and interpreted by the most vigilant circumspection," as Thomas Chamberlin, professor of geology at the University of Chicago, explained. This process of active, but carefully controlled, experimentation ensured that science still referred to external reality.[35]

The emphasis on verification provided a bridge between progressivists and others who maintained that science actually described nature: both groups agreed that observation of the external world was the backbone of scientific investigation. Although late nineteenth-century progressivists rejected the view that scientists simply observed and copied nature, they believed that scientific explanations must refer to natural processes. James explained that "although [scientific theories] are no more . . . *reproductions* of outer order than ethical and aesthetic relations are . . . they do not conflict with that order. . . . [They are] *congruent* with the time-and-space-relations." To be accepted, scientific theories must not contradict observed natural phenomenon.[36]

Although scientists constantly checked their theories by observed phenomena, they were not motivated by faith in the certainty of observed facts. Instead, this extensive verification process was fueled by sustained doubt and distrust of appearances. The key quality that distinguished scientific inquiry from ordinary inquiry, progressivists maintained, was its questioning attitude. Individuals normally tended to resist the radical questioning required by science. They generally tried to avoid doubt and uncertainty and, therefore, held on to conclusions based on everyday experience. While this empirical knowledge was sufficient for survival, progressivists argued that it would not stimulate intellectual progress. Individuals' general conservatism was compounded by social pressure to accept certain conclusions as valid. "When the community uses its resources to fix certain ideas in the mind," Dewey explained, "ideas . . . assume a rigid and independent form." Because of people's natural tendency to defend the accepted and the apparent, intellectuals had to consciously protect their right to free inquiry.[37]

In the late nineteenth century, intellectuals came to view free inquiry as the prerequisite for science. Intellectual progress, they maintained, required constant questioning. Their understanding of intellectual progress varied according to their philosophy of science. For progressivists, progress implied better functional adaptation; for others, it implied more accurate description of nature. In discussions of science, the distinction between these was often blurred and the means for measuring them left unclear. Philosophers and scientists did not fully justify how their method of hypothesis testing would lead to better knowledge. Instead, they assumed that intellectual progress could be identified by agreement. They believed that scientists studying the same problem would eventually come to the same solution. William James explained that the "only safeguard" for the fallibility of observation lay "in the final *consensus* of our farther knowledge about the thing in question, later views correcting earlier ones until at last the harmony of a consistent system is reached." Although scientific knowledge was imperfect, and scientific progress required the toleration and consideration of different theories, scientific success was marked by stasis and unanimity.[38]

The emphasis on consensus as the *sign* of scientific progress contradicted intellectuals' simultaneous commitment to conflict as a *source* of scientific progress. But this contradiction, as well as differences in opinion about issues such as the existence of natural laws and the relationship of scientific knowledge to nature, did not inhibit a new public rhetoric about science from emerging. According to this rhetoric, open-minded questioning, coupled with careful verification, accounted for the success of the

scientific method. Science, though never certain, was still a privileged form
of knowledge. It was humans' best tool in their struggle to adapt to their
environment. Scientists had to have the freedom to develop theories, no
matter how absurd they might seem, because intellectual progress depended on transcending common-sense knowledge.

Thorstein Veblen in 1908 described a "new organon" that replaced
Bacon's *Novum organum.* Modern science rejected the Baconian emphasis
on classification and natural law.

> In so far as science is of a modern complexion, in so far as it is
> not of the nature of taxonomy simply, the inquiry converges upon
> a matter of process; and it comes to rest provisionally, when it has
> disposed of its facts in terms of process. But modern scientific
> inquiry comes to rest only provisionally; because its prime postu-
> late is that of consecutive change, and consecutive change cannot,
> of course, come to rest except provisionally.[39]

Veblen identified this revolution in the philosophy of science as "the
substantial outcome of that nineteenth century movement in science with
which the name of Darwin is associated as a catch-word." Darwin, Veblen
clarified, was not solely responsible for the new view of science. Indeed,
Darwin did not write extensively about the nature of science; his philosophy of science was implicit in his scientific writings and could not necessarily be identified with the views of science that were formulated in the
fifty years following the publication of the *Origin of Species.* Nonetheless,
Darwinian evolution did precipitate the rejection of Baconianism. Darwin's critics said his work violated the Baconian method. In response, defenders of Darwin questioned the adequacy of Baconianism and drew on
the theory of natural selection to articulate an alternative, progressivist
conception of science.[40]

Progressivist conceptions of science influenced late nineteenth-century
discussions about the relationship between science and religion. Committed to the ideal of the unity of truth, intellectuals believed that religious
and scientific doctrines should complement one another, but they recognized that new scientific ideas had contradicted established religious views.
Although in most cases the disagreement was resolved by adjusting the
scientific and/or religious notions, intellectuals were disturbed by the conflicts and wanted to understand their cause. They explained these conflicts

by contrasting the ideal of progressive scientific inquiry with the authoritative methods of theology. The conflict, they concluded, was not between scientific truth and religious truth, but between the openness of scientific inquiry and the dogmatism of theology. They suggested that if religion would rid itself of dogmatic theology, science and religion would be harmonious. The distinction between religion and theology, then, provided an alternative to other methods of reconciling religion and science.[41]

Late nineteenth-century thinkers inherited the view of science as a means for understanding God through his works. Natural theology used knowledge about nature to illuminate the divine. Historians such as James R. Moore have shown how Protestant intellectuals incorporated evolution into the natural theology tradition. They argued that evolution was best understood as purposeful, rather than accidental, and that it represented God's method of creation. By giving evolution religious meaning, these intellectuals affirmed the long tradition of reconciling scientific theories and religious doctrines.[42]

Despite the successful accommodation of evolutionary theories and Protestant theologies, natural theology lost favor in the late nineteenth century. Since natural theology relied on the idea of natural law, the new progressivist views of science indirectly damaged natural theology by undermining the Baconian ideal of science. In addition, the constant need to reconcile scientific theories and Christian doctrines discredited natural theology as a means of uniting religion and science. Natural theology required that specific scientific and religious doctrines agree. This invited challenges to religious doctrines and threatened the independence of science. To avoid these problems, intellectuals wanted to find an alternative way to demonstrate the harmony of religion and science.[43]

Some approached this problem by distinguishing between knowledge about the natural world and knowledge about the supernatural realm. They simply assigned each to different categories: theology explored the supernatural, while science examined the natural. Since the two did not coincide, they could not disagree. This approach offered several advantages. It promised science and religion independence in their own spheres and thus could appeal to both scientists and theologians. It also had important precedents in philosophy and in Protestant theology, with its long history of tension between rationalism and pietism.[44]

The approach also made sense to people steeped in the natural theology tradition. Natural theology distinguished between the first cause (God) and secondary causes (natural processes). This same division lay at the heart of the idea of separate spheres. Proponents of separate spheres, however, drew different inferences from the distinction between first and secondary causes than natural theologians had done. Natural theologians believed they could elucidate the first cause by studying secondary causes. Those who wanted to segregate science and religion denied that secondary causes yielded information about anything beyond nature.[45]

Some American scientists of the period paid homage to the notion of separate spheres. For example, Joseph Henry, secretary of the Smithsonian Institution, argued that disputes between religion and science resulted from ignoring the boundaries between the two. Although he maintained that "abstract science is entitled to high appreciation and liberal support," he did not "claim for it the power of solving questions belonging to other realms of thought." He criticized scientists who pronounced "dogmatically as to the possibility of modes of existence on which physical research has not, and we think never can throw positive light." Science, he believed, should leave questions about the supernatural to theologians. At the same time, he chastised theologians who fostered "feelings antagonistic to researches into the phenomena of Nature, for fear they should disprove the interpretations of Holy Writ." Henry maintained that scientists should clearly admit the limits of their knowledge, and, in exchange, theologians should not meddle in science. This clear separation would, he believed, ensure harmonious relations between religion and science forever.[46]

Religious leaders also used the rhetoric of separate spheres. These thinkers accepted a division between the material world of nature and the immaterial realm of the spirit. For example, Reverend Charles F. Deems, in his address at the opening of Vanderbilt University, made the following distinction: "Science has the finite for its domain, religion the infinite; science deals with things seen and religion deals with things not seen." If each remained in its own sphere, Deems maintained, there would be no dissension between them.[47]

Some theologians articulated another version of separate spheres by differentiating between the definitive nature of scientific knowledge and the symbolic nature of religious truth. This view drew on the distinction between literal and figurative language, popularized by Horace Bushnell in theological works such as *God and Christ*. Bushnell, believing that there was a gulf between the natural and the spiritual, argued that literal language, which referred to objects in the world, was incapable of expressing the intangible and the infinite. Religion used figurative language and, like poetry, expressed its truths in metaphor and myth. Although Bushnell maintained that scientific and religious beliefs still had to be brought into agreement, others used his ideas about language to argue that religion and science represented different kinds of knowledge and, therefore, could not conflict with each other.[48]

As it turned out, the designation of separate spheres, instead of ending the conflict between religion and science, created its own conflicts. It was not widely accepted among educated Americans in the late nineteenth century. Those who did advance it interpreted the boundaries of each realm differently. Some writers maintained that science could not examine the origins of life or the creation of the universe. They argued that God, the first cause, created the universe and all living creatures; since science was limited to secondary causes, creation was outside its realm. "The creation of the universe and its end," asserted Charles Deems, "are not questions of science, and can be known only as revealed to faith." Parke Godwin, in his controversial comments at John Tyndall's farewell banquet, took the same position as Deems. Godwin believed that "there are some problems accessible to scientific methods and some not." The origin and purpose of the universe were, in some interpretations of separate spheres, outside the limits of science.[49]

Others had a different understanding of the limits of science and religion. For decades scientists had claimed the right to study the origins of the universe. Evolutionists clearly thought that the development of species was in the realm of science. Some scientists, such as Thomas Huxley, maintained that scientific study also extended to the source of life. Scientists generally argued that any subject that could be studied scientifically, should be studied scientifically. Instead of offering peaceful coexistence, separate spheres became another battle ground.[50]

Many religious leaders were wary of sharp distinctions between religious and scientific knowledge. Leading Protestant intellectuals did not enthusiastically adopt Bushnell's use of the distinction between literal and figurative language. Although many accepted the insight that religious truths had emotional and aesthetic dimensions, few wanted to abandon cognitivist claims for religion. Historian D. G. Hart has shown that both liberal and conservative Protestant intellectuals responded to Bushnell's ideas by asserting that theology had the same intellectual status as other sciences. Although Bushnell did not maintain that religious truths were *only* symbolic, other theologians saw this as the logical consequence of his ideas about the nature of language. Mythopoetic interpretations of the Bible, such as those advanced by David Friedrich Strauss, confirmed this danger. Few American theologians of the day were willing to emphasize the mythic quality of religious beliefs.[51]

Theologians' distrust of separate spheres was reinforced by the development of agnosticism in the 1860s. Agnostics accepted a sharp division between nature and the supernatural. They maintained, however, that human knowledge could not transcend the breach between the physical and the spiritual. Herbert Spencer, the agnostic whose ideas were best known in the United States, did not deny the existence of God. He affirmed that some power existed beyond natural phenomena, but this power was essentially mysterious: it was "The Unknowable." Agnostics argued that it was more honest and reverent to admit the limits of human knowledge than to pretend to know the divine. In Spencer's words, "the character of religious is claimed by those who figure to themselves a Creator moved by motives like their own; conceive themselves as discovering his designs; and even speak of him as though he laid plans to outwit and deceive." Spencer criticized traditional religion as ignoble and presumptuous.[52]

Agnostics asserted that "The Unknowable" provided the key to peaceful relations between religion and science. Religion, defined as feelings of awe and wonder in the face of mysterious power, could not be challenged by the advance of science. As Edward L. Youmans commented, Spencer placed the reconciliation of science and religion on a plane "that no extension of knowledge can disturb." But this was a very one-sided peace, with all the benefits accruing to science. Scientists could freely propose naturalistic explanations of the universe without reference to possible theological implications. Religion, on the other hand, could exist only negatively, as vague feelings about things unexplained by science. Consequently, Christian thinkers found the concept of "The Unknowable" an inadequate substitute for belief in a personal God.[53]

Scientists, as well as theologians, resisted the idea that humans could not know anything beyond nature. The distinction between the "seen" and the "unseen" seemed anachronistic as scientists rejected the Baconian emphasis on concrete empirical evidence and acknowledged the importance of unobservable processes in scientific explanations. More important, the division between the natural and the supernatural called into question the continuity of human experience and mocked the ideal of the unity of truth. John Dewey, for example, maintained that few scientists would accept agnosticism as a permanent solution to the conflict between religion and science. He saw agnosticism as an unstable "compromise": "it is a treaty of partition which would divide the kingdom of reality into halves, and proclaim one supernatural and unknowable, the other natural and the realm of knowledge." But, he noted, reality does not divide easily into halves. He pointed out that human beings could not be placed on either side of the division. He asserted that "a 'fact encompassing, closing in upon, absorbing every other fact conceivable,' cannot be treated as something distinct from all facts." Dewey rejected agnosticism because he believed that the universe was of a single piece and that all knowledge must ultimately be unified. Instead of agnosticism, Dewey called for a science that could incorporate spiritual and natural truths.[54]

The strong conviction that "all truth is one and inseparable" made most educated Americans averse to divorcing scientific and religious knowledge. One commentator concluded that "since neither science nor religion can claim an exclusive sovereignty over the field of knowledge; since that domain cannot well be partitioned off between them, the true way is to unite them in a perpetual alliance." Separate spheres, then, could not provide a permanent solution to conflict between religion and science.[55]

Influenced by progressivist ideas about science, intellectuals offered an alternative analysis of the conflict between religion and science. They maintained that the root problem of the religious domination of intellectual life was that it discouraged open inquiry and the discovery of new truths. If religion would adopt a scientific attitude toward inquiry, the conflict between religion and science would die out. For example, Charles S. Peirce in his series of articles, "Illustrations of the Logic of Science," identified four basic methods of "fixing belief": tenacity, authority, a priori reasoning, and science. He associated the first three with religion and opposed them to the preferred method, science.[56]

Peirce considered tenacity a purely individual form of thought. A person chose to believe something and held onto that belief even if he or she had to ignore evidence refuting it. The individuality of tenacity undermined its effectiveness. "The social impulse," Peirce explained, "is against it. . . . The man who adopts it will find that other men think differently from him, and it will occur to him, in some saner moment, that their opinions are quite as good as his own, and this will shake his confidence in his own belief." But this flaw was overcome when tenacious beliefs were provided social sanction. Peirce identified authority as a social means of eliminating individual differences of opinion. Indoctrination ensured agreement. Peirce admitted that historically this method had been extremely successful.[57]

Related to authority was Peirce's third method, a priori reasoning, or deduction from self-evident first principles. Theologians and metaphysicians relied on this method. Peirce thought that a priori thinking led to unsolvable disputes. If all parties did not accept the first principles, then they would not accept the conclusions derived from them. This, in Peirce's mind, made "inquiry something similar to the development of taste; but taste, unfortunately, is always more or less a matter of fashion, and accordingly, metaphysicians have never come to any fixed agreement." For Peirce, a priori reasoning was merely a more intellectually rigorous version of tenacity.[58]

In describing the types of thinking associated with religion, Peirce drew on popular notions about the difference between religion and science. Promoters of science depicted theologians as dogmatic and obstructionist. In their view, religious thinkers approached all questions with preconceived answers. Religious inquiry was, therefore, biased and partisan. Advocates of science also depicted theologians as stifling inquiry by accusing people who disagreed with their beliefs of endangering the welfare and morality of humanity. According to this view, theologians adopted an air of absolute authority and were intolerant of all other views. They also refused to modify their beliefs. Consequently, their thought stagnated rather than progressed. Promoters of science maintained that theologians frequently fought among themselves over small differences of opinion because they resisted foreign ideas. Among late nineteenth-century intellectuals, the term *dogma* no longer simply referred to systematic religious doctrine. Instead, *dogmatic* became a term of reproach.[59]

At the same time, intellectuals increasingly portrayed science as open, tolerant, and progressive. These differences led to opposing attitudes about truth. A theologian's "idea of truth," wrote Simon Newcomb, "is symbolized in the pure marble statue, which must be protected from contact with profane hands and whose value arises from its beauty of form and the excellence of the ideas which it embodies." The scientist had another idea of truth, "symbolized by the iron-clad turret, which cannot be accepted until it has proved its invulnerability. Instead, therefore, of being protected from violence, as if it were a product of the fine arts, violence is invited. Its weak points are sought out . . . and are exposed to the fire of every logical weapon which can be brought to bear on them." In the late nineteenth century, American intellectuals increasingly maintained that these different attitudes toward truth lay at the heart of the conflict between science and religion.[60]

By comparing religion and science, intellectuals identified what they disliked about the religiously dominated intellectual life of the day. The comparison did little to relieve fears about the incompatibility of religion and science; it only confirmed the belief that religion was inherently opposed to the advance of science. Advocates of science wanted to find a way to avoid this conclusion, while still preserving the critique of the religious attitude toward truth and inquiry. Their solution was to distinguish theology, defined as a mode of inquiry and set of doctrines, from religion, which was left largely undefined as sentiment, experiences, ritual, and ethical values. Scientific inquiry, they reasoned, was hostile to theology, but in perfect accord with religion.

The distinction between religion and theology antedates the late nineteenth century. For example, Enlightenment thinkers, such as Thomas Jefferson, used this distinction in their effort to rationalize religion. But the distinction was tainted with a negative anticlericalism until the late nineteenth century, when mainstream Protestants adopted modernist-liberal ideas. Modernist-liberals asserted that religion was broader and more important than particular theological doctrines. Henry Ward Beecher, a prominent liberal minister, wrote that "the Church, the Bible, the Creed, have been confounded with Religion. Religion is the state of man's soul, it is disposition and conduct." Modernist-liberals deemphasized theology in order to establish what they hoped would be a firmer base for Christian faith and to minimize the challenge of their own theological revisionism. Although liberals rejected many orthodox Protestant doctrines, they wanted to avoid an antagonistic posture. They did not want to be seen as attacking religion. They presented theological change as part of the natural development of religion and associated it with the progressive revelation of the divine through the evolution of human culture.[61]

Modernist-liberals viewed themselves as protectors of true Christianity rather than its enemies. They portrayed conservatives, who maintained that "there is no religion possible except on the basis of their theories," as the real threat to religion. These conservatives taught that religious faith depended on the truth of certain doctrines; if the doctrines turned out to be wrong, then people's faith was crushed. Liberals thought this was the cause of the contemporary crisis of faith. They believed that this crisis was unwarranted, because "religion is not dependent on orthodoxy, and . . . a grander religion remains when orthodoxy has passed away." The distinction between religion and theology allowed modernist-liberals to attack accepted church doctrines, while maintaining a constructive pose. Rather than allow science to undermine Christianity, modernists promised to use science to bring religious truths in line with the "new and broader knowledge" of the age.[62]

Promoters of science borrowed the distinction between religion and theology, and applied it to discussions about the relationship between religion and science. Peirce, after criticizing theologians' method of inquiry, argued that acceptance of their conclusions did not determine whether someone was religious or not. "No man need be excluded from participation in the common [religious] feelings, nor from so much of the public expression of them as is open to all laity, by the philosophical narrowness of those who guard the mysteries of worship. Am I to be prevented from joining in that common joy at the revelation of enlightened principles of religion, which we celebrate at Easter and Christmas, because I think that certain scientific, logical, and metaphysical ideas which have been mixed up with these principle are untenable?" He condemned the practice of branding someone as irreligious because they rejected certain theological doctrines.[63]

The separation of piety from the acceptance of particular creeds provided a means of reconciling religion and science while maintaining the independence of scientific investigation. The development of Andrew Dickson White's writings illustrates how advocates of science gradually recognized the utility of the distinction between religion and theology. White published his works on the relationship between religion and science over a twenty-year period. White, the founding president of Cornell University and an outspoken supporter of scientific education, first addressed the subject in 1874 in a speech, "The Battle-fields of Science," given at the Cooper Institute in New York. He published an expanded version of this lecture first as a series of articles in *Popular Science Monthly* and then, in 1876, as a successful book, *The Warfare of Science*. Twenty years later, White published his magnum opus, the two-volume *History of the Warfare of Science with Theology in Christendom.*[64]

White's message in *The Warfare of Science* resembled John William Draper's *History of the Conflict between Religion and Science:* throughout history, religion has opposed the advance of science. White elaborated on Draper by explicitly stating that Protestants were as intolerant as Catholics. He also held that despite religious opposition, scientific ideas always triumphed in the end and argued that religious intolerance hurt religion as much as or more than it hurt science. "In all modern history," he wrote, "interference with science in the supposed interest of religion, no matter how conscientious such interference may have been, has resulted in the direct evils both to religion and to science. . . . On the other hand, all untrammeled scientific investigation, no matter how dangerous to religion some of its stages may have seemed, for the time, to be, has resulted in the highest good of religion and of science." Hence, religious leaders should concede the freedom of scientific investigation.[65]

In writing *The Warfare of Science,* White endeavored to tie the interests of religion to the promotion of science. But his underlying motive was clear: to ensure the independence of science. "Science must be studied by its own means and unbiased by the motives of investigators in other fields, and uncontrolled by the consciences unenlightened by itself." White's negative appraisal of religion discredited his avowed concern for it. He blamed religion for all its disputes with science, he portrayed religious thinkers as narrow and intolerant, and he attacked out of hand all interpretations of nature derived from the Bible. In tone and analysis, White's book was similar to Draper's.[66]

When White published his two-volume *History,* however, he tried to distance himself from Draper by drawing on the distinction between religion and theology. In the preface, White referenced his earlier sympathy with Draper: he noted that he had stopped writing about the relationship of religion and science when Draper published *The Conflict between Science and Religion.* He considered it "a work of great ability, which as I then thought, ended the matter, so far as my giving it further attention." But White returned to the subject, deciding that Draper's analysis was wrong. Draper, White wrote, "regarded the struggle as one between Science and Religion. I believed then, and am convinced now, that it was a struggle between Science and Dogmatic Theology. More and more, I saw that it was a conflict between two epochs in the evolution of human thought—the theological and the scientific." White maintained that in the intervening years he had sharpened his analysis by distinguishing between religion and theology.[67]

White first introduced the distinction between theology and religion in 1896 in his *History.* Aside from this distinction, the thesis of White's later work was essentially the same as that of his earlier *Warfare.* Science eventually triumphed over its enemies, narrow-minded religious thinkers. Despite the essential continuity in his analysis, White in 1896 appeared more credible in his assumed role as defender of religion. He could freely admit that theology lost when science won without, as he had in 1876, lamely adding that the loser really benefited from defeat. "My conviction is that Science, though it evidently conquered Dogmatic Theology based on Biblical Texts and ancient modes of thought, will go hand in hand with Religion, and that . . . Religion, as seen in the recognition of 'a Power in the universe, not ourselves, which makes for righteousness,' and in the love of God and our neighbors will steadily grow stronger and stronger." Theology was vanquished, but religion remained.[68]

The distinction between theology and religion effectively calmed fears about permanent discord between religion and science. Because liberal theologians independently fostered the distinction, it provided the basis for consensus that had eluded other attempts to reconcile religion and science. Promoters of science could criticize the dogmatism that they felt inhibited intellectual progress without relegating religion to the "unknowable" and destroying the unity of truth.[69]

Intellectuals proposed a new alliance, in which scientific methods could be applied to religious questions. "It is coming to be recognized more and more clearly," wrote Ira Remsen, professor of chemistry at Johns Hopkins University, "that science can do true religion no harm, but can only strengthen it. It may modify, and has modified, dogmatic theology, but dogmatic theology is one thing and religion is another, and true religion must find a broader and broader foundation in knowledge." By discarding the practices of dogmatic theology and adopting those of science, people could progress both in their understanding of religion and in their knowledge of nature. Wedded to science, intellectuals believed that religion would experience a veritable renaissance.[70]

THREE

The Open University

Ideas about science as a form of open inquiry changed the justification for university reform. Educators did not discuss university reform in a narrow professional context. Arguments about the best form of education were intertwined with considerations of the nature of scientific inquiry and the relationship between science and religion. In the 1860s most university reformers wanted to add new subjects of instruction and viewed electives as the most expedient way to meet this goal. During the 1870s and 1880s university leaders adopted the view that science was not primarily a body of knowledge, but a tool for the production of new knowledge. Drawing on this conception of science, they redefined the aims and meaning of educational reform; instead of expanding the breadth of instruction, they sought to make all aspects of university education "scientific."

After decades of frustrated proposals to transform higher education, university reform finally achieved the needed momentum in the decade following the end of the Civil War. Social dislocation and the popular belief in the practical benefits of science built support for educational change. Because of the economic, social, and political turmoil of the previous decades, by 1870 many Americans felt that they were living in a changed world. Educational reformers maintained that colleges were ill equipped to meet the needs of these new conditions. "Our higher institutions of learning, until a comparatively recent period, have been equal to the wants of the country," wrote Frederick A. P. Barnard, president of Columbia, in 1866. "But with the advancement of human knowledge and the growing diversity of the arts of civilized life new fields are opening and new wants springing up which imperatively demand the creation of new agencies." He believed that "the educational problem of the day" was to discover how to shape colleges and universities that would meet the demands of a modern, industrial society.[1]

Barnard argued that university reform was unavoidable; if colleges did not change to meet social needs, they would simply die. To substantiate his position, he showed that college enrollments were declining relative to the population. He concluded that the classical colleges' indifference to science was the cause of the decline. He argued that popular interest in science had begun to grow around 1830 and that dissatisfaction with classical education had accompanied the new enthusiasm for science. The 1830s, he wrote, "was the era in which first arose in our country that clamor against the value of classical studies of which we have since heard so much." Barnard was not surprised that, by 1838, interest in classical colleges had begun to decline.[2]

Although the connection between popular interest in science and the declining proportion of the population attending college seems tenuous today, the explanation appealed to educators of that day. Barnard wrote in the context of a heated debate over the future of higher education. Calls for the reform of higher education proliferated. Prominent reformers, such as Charles W. Eliot of Harvard, Daniel C. Gilman of Johns Hopkins, Andrew D. White of Cornell, and James B. Angell of the University of Michigan, all pressed for the growth of modern and practical subjects, particularly the natural sciences, and the expansion of advanced instruction. "The only conceivable aim of a college government in our day," Eliot declared, "is to broaden, deepen, and invigorate American teaching in all branches of learning." The motto adopted for Cornell University at its founding in 1868, "I would found an institution where any person can find instruction in any study," reflected this renewed emphasis on an encyclopedic curriculum, rather than the mental discipline advocated by the Yale report of 1828.[3]

The expansion of the curriculum, educational reformers believed, was essential to transform American colleges into universities. The distinction between a college and a university, wrote Barnard, "is to be understood to be one not of powers but comprehensiveness. It is understood that while the teaching of the college is confined within a pretty sharply defined limit, the teaching of the university has no definite limit at all. . . . An educational institution approaches the ideal of an university in proportion as it transcends the narrow limit which is supposed to define the proper province of the college." A university, therefore, was distinguished by its size and the variety of instruction.[4]

In the 1870s Barnard and many other university leaders promoted electives as the first step toward building an "encyclopedic" university. For Barnard, this was a reversal of an earlier position. Educational reformers who disliked electives proposed to diversify the college curriculum by offering a variety of alternative degree programs at the baccalaureate level, maintaining a classical bachelor of arts, but also offering more modern subjects in bachelor of science and bachelor of literature programs. These alternative degree programs would consist of different but largely set courses of study, with only limited electives. The development of separate graduate schools would then encourage advanced study. Barnard, however, turned to electives because he believed that it was the most expedient way to expand the curriculum.[5]

Barnard's defense of electives was largely practical: given the proliferation of areas of study, it was impossible to increase the amount of instruction in modern and practical subjects, maintain a commitment to the classics, and have a single course of study required by all students. Instead of the institution deciding which was better, science or the classics, Barnard thought that the university should offer both and let students choose based on their own talents and inclinations. Other supporters of electives, such as Eliot, thought that electives would encourage more advanced study and would propel American scholarship forward. Electives, then, provided a quick way to diversify the curriculum and encourage advanced study.[6]

Although university reformers never rejected comprehensive instruction as a positive goal, they began to emphasize instead the importance of training students to think scientifically. This was reminiscent of the argument for the disciplinary value of the classics—but the desired discipline was new. Reformers sought to turn students into investigators. They extolled the search for truth as the highest purpose of the university. Since "the future of our civilization depends upon the widening spread and deepening hold of the scientific habit of mind," Dewey wrote, "the problem of problems in our education is therefore to discover how to mature and make effective this scientific habit." The inclusion of science came to mean a particular kind of mental training, rather than a particular body of knowledge.[7]

As educators emphasized scientific mental training, they minimized the importance of imparting a particular body of knowledge. Henry Burns Hutchins, Angell's successor at the University of Michigan, told a group of students:

> Your ability to accomplish results depends upon your ability *to think,* not in a dreamy, inconsequential, haphazard way, but logically, effectively and with a view to the future as well as present conditions. . . . If during your residence at the university, you have simply accumulated facts and data and principles, as stated

by others, and have not at the same time, learned to think independently and logically, then you go into the work of the world
seriously handicapped.

After all, "facts, data, principles even, are constantly changing." Instead
of being taught established truths, reformers maintained, the students of
the new university should be taught to question, test, and judge.[8]

By 1890 university reformers argued that the distinguishing feature of
universities was that they offered the mental training necessary for independent inquiry. "The primary aim of the university," according to David
Starr Jordan, president of Stanford University, "should not be to give information or opinions or trade skill, but to place the student in contact
with sources of knowledge and opinion." The emphasis on scientific mental training blurred the distinction between undergraduate and graduate
instruction. As undergraduates, students learned to think scientifically; as
graduate students, they became researchers in a particular field. Basic and
advanced instruction both taught scientific methods; the advanced students, however, used the scientific method to pursue a research program
in a particular area of study.[9]

Educational reformers argued that simply offering science courses
was not enough to teach students to think scientifically. Science had long
been included in the curriculum of the classical college. But those science
courses had been taught as recitations, in which students were expected
to memorize a body of information considered to be the basic principles
and truths of that branch of science. This was inconsistent with the view
that scientific truths were always evolving. By the 1880s scientists had begun to complain that this sort of instruction was inadequate. Science was
not simply a set of doctrines and should not be taught as such. "An impression widely prevails," Josiah Cooke, professor of chemistry at Harvard, wrote, "that however important a knowledge of the general results
of science may be, it is not necessary that the literary man or the general
scholar should acquaint himself with scientific methods. But it is obvious
. . . that no accurate knowledge of the facts of nature is possible without
a knowledge by which the facts have been established." To understand
science, Cooke believed, students had to master scientific methods.[10]

Scientists asserted that the only adequate way to teach science was
through laboratory work. As botanist John Coulter explained,

> The laboratory method means that the old recitation, which was
> the retailing of second-hand information as to facts, and second-
> hand opinions concerning them, has given place to the direct ob-

servation of facts and the expression of individual opinion concerning their significance. As a result, students are sought to be made thinking rather than memorizing machines, with the initiative power developed rather than the imitative.

In advocating laboratory teaching, scientists defined a new ideal of mental training, sharply opposed to the traditional mental discipline of the classical college. "To teach the student to think for himself, to develop in him the power of independent inquiry, whether it be original investigation, or the more common inquiries of life," geologist Thomas Chamberlin wrote, "is the ideal of the modern science teacher." Educators maintained that by practicing the scientific method, students would develop desirable habits of thinking—habits associated with the progressivist conception of science. These included openness to new ideas, reluctance to accept opinions on authority, and interest in empirical verification.[11]

Relying on these arguments, scientists convinced universities of the importance of providing adequate laboratory facilities. Before the Civil War, laboratory equipment had been uncommon. A few instructors used "experiments" to illustrate a lesson, but colleges did not provide laboratories as part of regular instruction or to encourage faculty research. In the decades following the war, scientists argued that they could not fulfill the aim of university education without laboratory equipment, and the leading universities all adopted laboratory methods. In the early twentieth century, the institutions formalized their view that laboratories were essential to the university mission, when the Association of American Universities delineated minimum requirements for scientific laboratories. Surveying changes in higher education, Angell noted in 1899 that "the method of scientific instruction has been entirely revolutionized. In the last half century, no more important step in education has been taken than in the universal introduction of the laboratory methods in the sciences." Instructors in the natural sciences adopted the view of science as a method of inquiry and successfully translated it into teaching practices.[12]

This ideal of mental training was easily generalized beyond the natural sciences. Faculty at the new universities argued that scientific methods of inquiry and teaching should be applied to all areas of study. "Science is not a function of subjects, but rather the distinctive product of a special and laborious method." The method of the natural sciences, noted William T. Sedgwick, a professor at the Massachusetts Institute of Technology,

is no longer the exclusive property of science, but has become the true method of inquiry in history, in politics, in philology, and in

nearly every modern branch of learning. . . . One of the greatest
services that science has ever done is to discover and popularize
the model method of research which all branches of learning have
hastened to adopt, and whose adoption has brought about the
scientific spirit of this age.

Intellectuals sought to apply the methods of the physical sciences to questions heretofore considered the province of philosophy and theology. In so
doing, they developed a new group of studies, referred to as the historical
sciences or social sciences.[13]

In the new social sciences, instructors used the seminar as the counterpart to laboratory studies in the natural sciences. The laboratory had become a symbol of discovery. University reformers argued that scholars
in the social sciences could teach the process of intellectual discovery by
guiding students through a research project in small seminar classes. Daniel C. Gilman, president of Johns Hopkins, explained,

In the seminary, the professor engages with a small company of
advanced students, in some line of investigation. . . . The younger
men have an opportunity of seeing the methods by which older
men work. The sources of knowledge, the so-called authorities,
are constantly examined. The drift of modern discussions is followed. Investigations, sometimes of a very special character, are
carefully prosecuted.

Thus, university professors in nearly all areas of study now agreed that
the highest aim of education was teaching methods of investigation.[14]

This new emphasis on scientific thinking transformed the meaning of
electives: no longer a means to an expanded curriculum, they became
an integral part of students' education. Reformers in the early 1870s had
viewed electives as a necessary means to expanding the curriculum. Fifteen years later, they portrayed the elective system as an intrinsically valuable embodiment of the ideals of scientific inquiry. George H. Palmer, a
philosophy professor at Harvard, noted this change when he wrote, "The
new education has accordingly passed through two stages of development.
First, in order to avoid superficiality when knowledge was coming in like
a flood, it was found necessary to admit choice; secondly, in the very
admission was disclosed a more spiritual ideal of the relation of the mind
of man to knowledge." Although Harvard had instituted electives to
increase instruction in modern subjects, Palmer insisted that the real im-

portance of electives was to encourage the proper attitude of intellectual inquiry.[15]

Palmer explained to the readers of the *Andover Review* that when he left Andover Theological Seminary in 1870 to go to Harvard, he was opposed to the elective system. But after teaching at Harvard, he became convinced of its power as mental and moral training. Harvard, in allowing students more freedom in selecting their courses than any other college, had "thrown away that established principle of American education, that every head should contain a given kind of knowledge." There was no longer any particular body of information that distinguished the educated from the uneducated. "In assessing the worth of studies," Palmer wrote, "attention was thus withdrawn from their subject-matter and transferred to the response they called forth in the apprehender. Hence arose a new ideal of education, in which temper of mind had preeminence over *quaesita,* the guidance of the powers of knowing over the store of the matters known." Like laboratory teaching, electives reflected the contemporary emphasis on methods of inquiry over bodies of knowledge.[16]

Educators aimed to teach students the value of open inquiry. Instructors expected students to question established views, learn how to gather and evaluate evidence in favor of theories, and judge for themselves the adequacy of various positions. Electives accorded well with the ideals of open inquiry because they required students to make free choices. "Choice, like other human powers, needs practice for strength," Palmer wrote. "To learn how to choose, we must choose. . . . To permit choice is dangerous; but not to permit it is more dangerous, for it renders dependency habitual." Electives, then, encouraged the same habits required by scientific inquiry, and university policies were thus seen to reflect the ideals of scientific inquiry.[17]

University reformers used this new commitment to scientific mental training to justify additional changes, such as faculty research and academic freedom. Angell noted that the old college had assumed that the student's main aim was to learn a body of knowledge, but that "in these days the ultimate end which the student is exhorted to seek over and beyond those acquisitions is the power and passion for discovering new truth." As a result, he continued, the student "is now exhorted and stimulated to test his gifts for investigation and research." Angell asserted that faculty research would encourage students in this direction: "No ambitious young teacher in our colleges now fails to make strenuous efforts to enlarge the boundaries of knowledge in the domain of learning which he is called to cultivate. The enthusiasm of the teacher is easily communicated to their aspiring pupils." In this way, faculty research became an important corollary to scientific mental training.[18]

Faculty took the lead in promoting university-sponsored research. They argued that an instructor must engage in research in order to teach students how to investigate. "The true teacher of science," said R. H. Chittenden, director of the Sheffield Scientific School at Yale, "must ever be a student, not only familiar with the past, but ever alert to interpret such signs as nature may make, quick to seize the opportunity to add to man's knowledge, to broaden and extend the limits of his chosen science." Ira Remsen of Johns Hopkins concurred: "Teachers in the university should not only teach but be engaged in extending the domain of knowledge, and trying to make investigators out of students." Research was an important extension of the new teaching objectives. Both research and training in scientific inquiry were essential aspects of the universities' new mission: encouraging the growth of science, conceived of broadly as progressive inquiry in all areas of knowledge.[19]

The idea that students should be taught scientific methods buttressed the notion that research was a primary function of the university. Researchers made better instructors because they were better able to teach scientific methods and because their knowledge was more accurate. "As a general rule," J. P. McMurrich of the University of Michigan wrote, "the investigator will prove a more capable teacher than the non-investigator for the simple reason that he will be more apt to keep abreast with the progress of his studies and inclined to rely on original sources for the information he imparts rather than seek it in the more accessible text-books." Imparting knowledge depended first on the creation of knowledge. "The primary function of a university," maintained Chittenden, "is the diffusion of knowledge. . . . Before there can be diffusion of knowledge, however, there must be acquisition of knowledge." The progressivist view of science, because it emphasized the value of new knowledge, naturally supported the growing interest in original investigation.[20]

By supporting faculty research, universities could claim that they served society in two ways: they graduated students capable of the highest form of mental reasoning, and they produced knowledge that contributed to social progress. Educational reformers argued that research and the training of investigators was one of the university's essential services to society. "It requires but a very slight acquaintance with the times in which we live," Gilman said, "to see that the progress of modern civilization is due to the uses of scientific methods, and that innumerable problems pertinent to the highest welfare of the human race remain unsolved because they have never been studied in this painstaking way." Arguments about the social value of research and its role in teaching students to think scientifically quickly became important elements in the rhetoric of university reformers. "The spirit of investigation and the pursuit of new truth should pervade every university department from top to bottom," wrote President Nicholas Murray Butler of Columbia University. Research became one of the defining marks of the new university.[21]

To promote research, educators argued, the university must encourage the freedom of thought necessary to scientific inquiry. "The essential character of the university," David Starr Jordan asserted, "is *Lernfreiheit,* freedom of learning, the freedom of the student to pursue his studies to the furthest limit of the known, the freedom of encouragement to invade the infinite realm of the unknown." Freedom implied tolerance. "It is only in the struggle of opinions," wrote University of Chicago president William Rainey Harper, "that the truth is at last ascertained. With good personal feelings, differences of opinion, are to be welcomed. . . . A frank and open expression of opinions and influences, and sincere methods of work will lead to the best results." The university, like the scientist, had to be open and undogmatic.[22]

Advocates of university reform argued that the promotion of inquiry was the overarching purpose of the university. "Among the brightest signs of a vigorous university," Gilman said, "is the zeal for the advancement of learning." Academic freedom, research, the training of future investigators and instructors, and the instilling of scientific mental habits were all aspects of this effort to further inquiry. In adopting this aim, reformers depicted the university itself as a scientific institution, its policies and values paralleling the qualities of scientific inquiry.[23]

The changing focus of educational reform left some institutions behind. Yale's declining reputation in the decades following the Civil War illustrates the changing philosophy of university reform. In 1870 Yale, more than any other college, approached the ideal of comprehensiveness. In addition to the traditional undergraduate, or "academical," department, Yale maintained separate law, theological, and medical schools; the Sheffield Scientific School; the School of Fine Arts; and a graduate division. Yale employed sixty-one instructional officers, including thirty-seven professors. It also excelled in the sciences. More than one-third of its instructors taught mathematics or science. The Sheffield Scientific School was considered one of the best centers of scientific education in the United States. Charles W. Eliot, in articles on "The New Education" published in 1869, extolled Sheffield's curriculum as "a prophecy" of the future of scientific education in the United States. In short, in 1870 Yale appeared in every sense a progressive college with potential to become a first-rate university.[24]

By the 1890s, however, few educators believed that Yale had realized its earlier promise. Many Yale faculty members dissented from its policies. Although scientific education at Sheffield flourished, the number of faculty had more than tripled, and a sizable share of the new instructors taught "modern subjects," some university reformers viewed Yale as a conservative holdout, resisting the essential spirit of university reform. In 1899, when President Timothy Dwight announced his retirement, one professor predicted that if Dwight's successor did not represent a clear break with the past, many of the young faculty would leave Yale rather than continue under its "medieval" practices.[25]

The decline in Yale's standing is generally traced back to the leadership of Noah Porter, president of Yale from 1871 to 1886. His vehement defense of the classical college earned him a reputation as the leading opponent of university reform in that period. Yet Porter's conservatism was not evident at the beginning of his career; at one point, it seemed that he might even become a reformer. He opposed narrow sectarianism in religion and education and was an internationally respected philosopher and psychologist. He had studied in Germany, respected German standards of scholarship, and, like many university reformers, hoped that American education would emulate certain features of the German university.[26]

Porter never opposed the development of universities, nor did he depreciate the natural sciences. He argued that science instruction was an essential part of the college curriculum. But he disapproved of the reform measures of Barnard, Eliot, and others. In particular, Porter resisted the introduction of the elective system because it undermined the position of classical languages and mathematics as the basis of all collegiate education. These studies, Porter believed, were the most effective means of mental training and, as such, essential to any higher study.[27]

Porter contended that universities had to be built on top of the traditional college. To defend this view, he pointed to the German educational system. There, students went through rigorous training in the gymnasium before being admitted to the university, where they could pursue their studies in freedom. The college, he argued, was the American counterpart to the German gymnasium. Advocates of electives were mistakenly trying to turn the college into the university. Reformers proposed

> to attach to the college some features which properly belong to the university, viz.: freedom of election, the gratification of special preferences and tastes. But they fail to provide or require the feature which gives the university its dignity and invests its name with special honor, and that is a *thorough discipline previously undergone and a liberal culture already attained.*

Porter argued that without maintaining strong classical colleges, Americans could not create proper universities.[28]

When Porter retired, Timothy Dwight was elected president of Yale. Like his predecessor, Dwight saw a university as several schools organized around the classical college. He also believed that the best means to meet the demand for increased instruction in scientific subjects was the separate scientific school. "The evils of the elective system are thus avoided, while its most important advantages are secured." Dwight agreed with reformers such as Barnard and Eliot that a university should include comprehensive instruction, but he rejected their reliance on electives as the means to universality. Instead, he advocated the development of separate, but closely associated, schools.[29]

Dwight developed his educational philosophy years before he became president. In 1870 and 1871 he had written a series of articles explaining his views on how to transform Yale into a true university. He advocated strengthening the various schools "outside" the college—that is, Sheffield Scientific and the professional schools—and making them equal partners in a university system. "The spirit of the University, must be the spirit of unity and fraternity. If one member suffers, the sentiment must be that all the members, of necessity, suffer with it." Thus, Dwight believed that the Yale Corporation and the president should take more responsibility for the financial security and intellectual prestige of the associated schools. He believed that the president should not teach in a particular school or associate himself primarily with any one school, as Porter did with the college.[30]

As president, Dwight had an opportunity to put his ideas into practice. In his inaugural address, he declared "Yale College is to be a University," and he soon had the name of the institution officially changed to Yale University. He refused to teach in the college or handle any of the college discipline. He saw himself as representing the whole university and appointed deans to oversee the individual schools. He worked to increase

the size of the endowment, the number of faculty, and the number of buildings. Despite these achievements, however, Dwight was unable to quell the
dissatisfaction of the faculty and alumni who wanted Yale to become a
modern university. Yale still seemed unacceptably backward.[31]

Dwight failed to convince people that Yale was a true university because he clung to outmoded ideas about university reform. While Porter
had defended the classical college and attacked university reformers, other
university leaders had been developing ideas that made his and Dwight's
notion of a university obsolete. It was no longer sufficient that a university
be comprehensive, it also must embody the ideals of scientific inquiry.
William Graham Sumner, one of Porter's severest critics at Yale, developed this argument in his article, "Our Colleges before the Country," published in 1884. Sumner affirmed the importance of a full and varied curriculum. But he also promoted innovations, such as the elective system and
the replacement of recitations with lectures, laboratories, and seminars.[32]

Sumner appropriated Porter's defense of the traditional college curriculum as mental training and turned it against him. He conceded that
the traditional curriculum provided a distinctive mental discipline, but he
questioned its value. Classical education, Sumner wrote, "has distinct and
mischievous limitations." It teaches students how to "recite" and memorize, but "when they try to acquire something, to make it their own, to
turn it into a concise and correct statement and utter it again, they cannot
do it." They "accept authority too submissively" and argue with "dialectical ingenuity" rather than with a firm grasp of the problem. On the other
hand, when subjects like history are taught according to scientific methods, students receive an exercise in "analysis and investigation of relations
and sequences," rather than simply memorization. Free course selection
and scientific teaching methods, Sumner maintained, were intrinsically
valuable intellectual exercises.[33]

Despite Porter and Dwight's efforts to transform Yale into a comprehensive university, Yale was still viewed as the paragon of conservatism.
Only after Arthur T. Hadley took over the presidency in 1899 was Yale
finally recognized as a modern university. He adopted the new view of
science and its place in the university, stating that "it is not the subject
that makes the course scientific; it is the method." He wrote that "science
is not a department of life which can be partitioned off from other parts;
it is not the knowledge of certain kinds of facts." Instead, "it is a way of
looking at life and dealing with life; a way of finding out facts of every
kind and dealing with interests as varied as the world itself." Yale finally

embraced scientific inquiry in all areas of learning and life as the primary aim of the university.[34]

When educational reformers elevated the pursuit of new truth as the highest ideal of the university, they did not intend to renounce all the traditional aims of the American college. Leaders of the new universities continued to believe in the unity of truth and expected that intellectuals' reliance on common methods of inquiry would tie the different areas of study together. They also planned to institute new practices that would draw together the research ideal and a morally relevant education, emphasizing both service to the community and the development of individual character. Universities, reformers believed, should encompass students' intellectual, moral, and spiritual education.

Reformers wanted to build universities that incorporated all areas of culture. "It cannot be said too loudly or too often," wrote Eliot, "that no subject of human inquiry can be out of place in the programme of a real university." Educators believed that comprehensive institutions should include religion as well as science. At Columbia Butler identified "the scientific, the literary, the aesthetic, the institutional, and the religious" as the five primary "aspects of life and civilization," and expected all five to be incorporated in the organization of the university. Butler intended that moral education would be an integral part of the new expanded college curriculum.[35]

University reformers still believed that all knowledge taught in the university would ultimately agree. Jordan wrote, "All real knowledge is a help to all other." The university promoted the unity of truth by bringing the fields of study together. Butler viewed the "historic faculty of philosophy," or the nonprofessional departments, as "the essence of a university and its true glory." It represents, he wrote, "the unity of knowledge and the true catholicity of scholarly investigation. Through it each department of study is kept in sympathy with its fellows, and each strengthens and supports the rest." The university provided an institutional cincture for the different areas of inquiry.[36]

Because of their commitment to free inquiry, university officials could not ensure that the contents of all instruction agreed. Although they accepted a certain amount of disagreement as the cost of intellectual progress, they believed that ultimately scientific study would produce consensus. "Individuals will err; generations will labor under false ideas; domineering intellects will dazzle for a time the ordinary mind; error like disease must be clearly understood before the mode of correction can be formulated," Gilman acknowledged. "But," he reasoned, "there is no better way known to man for securing intellectual and moral integrity than to encourage those habits, those methods, and those pursuits which tend to establish truth." Educators believed that scientific investigation would gradually solve disputes and replace errors with truth. Patient, open, scientific study, explained one University of Michigan professor, would eventually discover "the underlying unity and harmony of things." Through scientific study scholars would reach consensus on disputed issues and ultimately come to understand the larger order of the universe.[37]

Amid these temporary conflicts of opinion, educators expected the university to be bonded by a common "spirit of inquiry." Harper told faculty at the University of Chicago that he "did not demand unity of opinion" but did ask "for unity of spirit." Harper, and other university leaders, wanted a common commitment to the "spirit" of open inquiry. Intellectuals believed that commitment to scientific ideals could link different fields of study. Robert Wenley of the University of Michigan argued that "no conflict can exist" between the natural sciences and philosophy because they "possess this in common—they search for the truth free from all trammels of dogmatic presupposition . . . their object must be the same, even if they view it from different sides for different purposes." They "both are 'science' in the broad sense of the untranslatable term, *Wissenschaft*." Reformers expected that shared methods of inquiry could provide a "new unity" for higher education.[38]

This new unity included traditional moral concerns of the college. Like college authorities before them, university officials conceived of knowledge as a guide to living. Intellectuals, influenced by Darwinian evolution, viewed knowledge as a tool, its value to be tested through application. John Dewey frequently reminded his readers that the "value [of knowledge] rests in solving the problem which has arisen, viz., that of securing a method of action." "The final purpose of knowledge is action," echoed Jordan. "Knowledge," agreed Clyde Votow of the University of Chicago, "is not an end in itself, but an instrument for the use toward the common good." Ultimately, universities encouraged the growth and spread of knowledge for moral reasons: they believed that knowledge helped people live better lives.[39]

This view of knowledge corresponded to an expansive vision of the mission of education. "I believe," John Dewey wrote, "that education is the fundamental method of social progress and reform . . . the community's duty to education is, therefore, its paramount moral duty." Advocates of university reform shared this conception of education as an important force for community betterment. "In these modern days," declared Butler, "the university is not apart from the activities of the world, but in them and of them. It deals with real problems and relates itself to life as it is. The university is for both scholarship and service; herein, lies that ethical quality which makes the university a real person, bound by its very nature to the service of others." The modern university, like the traditional college, was a servant of society, dedicated to its material and moral improvement.[40]

University officials continued to view character development as one of the most important functions of education. Butler wrote that despite the wide and varied interests at Columbia, "there is one aim which all faculties and schools, all teachers and scholars, have in common—the building of character." Eliot agreed that "a sense of duty to students in respect to the formation of character" was "characteristic of all the American faculties." University reformers did not distance themselves from the college's traditional concern with individual virtue.[41]

Many educational leaders placed particular emphasis on the ethical side of education. When considering the presidency of the University of California, Benjamin Wheeler wrote to Eliot that he was "interested in nothing so much as education in its application to individual character." He said that he might accept the position, despite his doubts about his administrative abilities, because it "offers to the right man undoubtedly great opportunity for shaping and uplifting." Wheeler went to California because he believed he could exert greater moral influence as a president of a large university than as a professor of Greek.[42]

Hadley also wrote privately that he cared most "about the ethical side" of his teaching. At his inaugural as president of Yale, Hadley identified the "central problem" of his administration as meeting "the world's demands for progress on the intellectual side, without endangering the growth of that which has proved most valuable on the moral side." Educators believed that they "must hold up true ideals of life." "The university," wrote Harper, "should take definite steps to protect its constituency against . . . vice and demoralization."[43]

University officials rejected the restrictions of the classical college, but they still embraced its commitment to character formation. Instead of maintaining the elaborate rules regulating student behavior that were common to the antebellum college, university officials believed that they would influence students by adhering to the ideals of open inquiry. They emphasized the moral benefits of the freedom of the university. George Palmer argued that the elective system, because it required students to exercise their will, "uplifts character as no other training can." The leaders also associated scientific inquiry with personal virtue. "The scientific habit of mind," wrote Francis Peabody of Harvard, calls "for perfect fidelity, transparent sincerity, and instinct for truth, an unflagging self-control; and these are quite as much moral qualities as intellectual gifts." The new mental training also promoted beneficial personal habits.[44]

Although university reformers frequently emphasized the ethical value of scientific inquiry, they still believed that religion was the most important basis for morality. "The fundamental characteristic of the scientific method is honesty," wrote Ira Remsen. "I believe that the constant use of the scientific method, must in the end leave its impress upon him who uses it. . . . A life spent in accordance with scientific teachings would be of a high order." But Remsen and his colleagues did not propose that scientific methods alone could provide adequate ethical training. Although he thought that scientific habits "practically conform to the teachings of the highest types of religion," Remsen asserted that "science cannot now, and I do not believe ever can take the place of religion in some form." University reformers were not willing to advocate a completely secular ethical training, while university officials still associated morality and religion.[45]

In the late nineteenth century most American academics maintained that Christianity was responsible for the development of the highest ethical standards. They expected that religion would continue to define moral ideals and conduct. In the same vein, leaders of university reform connected ethical training with religious education. Eliot opposed the secularization of public schools because he thought that it was impossible to teach "morality apart from religion." To provide an effective moral education, the university must also be religious. "Religion must form the axis of personal character," wrote Jordan, "and its prime importance the university cannot ignore." Officials at Columbia affirmed that "an ethical training to be lasting and effective must be religious." Educators agreed that, in practice, it was impossible to draw a sharp line between the ethical and the spiritual.[46]

Educators believed that the university had an "obligation to cultivate the religious spirit." Neglect of the "religious side" of human nature would degrade "education as a whole." Despite this belief, they felt that religion had been responsible for repression in American colleges, and they feared that it might conflict with their new commitment to scientific education. Educational reformers eased the tension between the desire for moral training and their anxiety about religious oppression by adopting the distinction between theology and religion. They identified denominations as the institutional counterpart to theology and as the true cause of repression in the colleges, and asserted that universities, independent of church control, could be truly free religious institutions.[47]

Eliot's changing attitude about the role of religion in the university illustrates the value of the distinction between religion and theology for educators who disliked the religious restrictions of the antebellum college but who did not want a completely secular university. When Eliot was elected president of Harvard in 1869, he was already a leading advocate of increased scientific training and university reform. Like many reformers, Eliot saw religion as a major obstacle to the improvement of higher education. He criticized the common practice of selecting ministers to head universities and colleges. "It is gradually becoming apparent that even the colleges are suffering from this too exclusively clerical administration." Eliot looked forward to a time when colleges would be run by professional educators. He also wanted to decrease the importance of natural theology and moral philosophy in the college curriculum. At his inaugural address, Eliot praised the sciences but was critical of philosophy, the subject that had traditionally been associated with the defense of religion in colleges. "Philosophical subjects," he said, "should never be taught with authority. They are not established sciences; they are full of disputed matters, and open questions, and bottomless speculation." He asserted that these subjects could be taught as the history of opinions but not as certain knowledge.[48]

Eliot began his administration with plans to promote science and decrease the presence of religion at Harvard. He thought that the dominating influence of religion was inimical to the proper spirit of the university. "The very word education is a standing protest against dogmatic teaching," he proclaimed at his inauguration. "The notion that education consists in the authoritative inculcation of what a teacher deems true may be logical and appropriate in a convent or a seminary for priests, but it is intolerable in universities and public schools, from primary to professional." Given these sentiments, it was natural that Eliot would want to reduce the influence of religion at Harvard.[49]

Eliot soon realized that the question of the appropriate position of religion in the university was more complicated than he had recognized. He was prepared to oppose the efforts of narrow-minded people to restrict, in the name of religion, what was taught at the university, but he had not considered how to include religion in the university in a manner consistent with its ideals. He had to face the question of incorporating religion in the new university when dealing with the divinity school. When Eliot became president, the Harvard Divinity School was in poor shape. It continued to decline, despite the addition of two professorships, during the first years of his administration. Eliot recognized the problems in his *Annual Report* for 1874–75 and expressed his regret over the divinity school's condition. He did not, however, express much optimism for its recovery. "To remedy the feebleness of the School," he wrote, "seems to be beyond the power of its learned and devoted Faculty, of the Governing Boards, and of the Administration of the University. The causes of its depression lie beyond their control." Eliot thought that uncertainty about the place of religion in modern intellectual life outweighed efforts to improve the divinity school.[50]

Eliot's own doubts about religion and the ministry fueled his pessimism about the future of theological education. He thought that seminaries were losing students because of the constraints placed on ministers. "The ministry," he later wrote, "seems to be a profession which is not as untrammeled as the other learned professions, and which subjects a man, as he grows older and wiser, to grave temptation to insincerity." The problem with the ministry was that it demanded loyalty to outmoded theological dogma. Teaching such doctrine violated Eliot's intellectual ideals.[51]

Before Eliot could devote his energies to saving the divinity school, he had to convince himself that its curriculum could be consistent with the ideals of a university education. By drawing on the distinction between religion and theology and new ideas about science, Eliot decided that a minister's education need not be dogmatic. Shortly after despairing of its future, Eliot embarked on a vigorous campaign to reform the divinity school. The campaign consisted of two changes: deemphasizing the role of theology in the curriculum and hiring a multi-denominational faculty. First, he proposed that "in a rightly constructed course of university study in divinity, dogmatic theology would occupy an exceedingly small place." Other "proper university subjects," such as ethics, ecclesiastical history, and Hebrew literature, would make up the bulk of a minister's training. "These subjects," he wrote, "are by common consent as liberal and as unsectarian as chemistry, philosophy, or history. . . . [They] possess an exalted and enduring intellectual interest which makes them a necessary part of a comprehensive scheme of university instruction." Religion, which was much broader than theology, could be taught in the same manner as other university courses.[52]

Eliot also thought that the dogmatic aspect of theology could be negated by hiring faculty from various denominations. He proposed that theological education could become "scientific" by presenting a variety of views. Religious denominations made theology offensive by demanding that their ministers believe in its tenets as absolute truth. If a divinity school were not controlled by a single denomination, Eliot reasoned, then students would be free to judge theology with an open mind. In such a school, "young men may study theology and the kindred subjects with the same freedom of spirit with which they study law in a law school, or medicine in a medical school." Drawing on the association of science with freedom, Eliot proposed that a divinity school, if free from denominational control, could offer as "scientific" an education as other professional schools.[53]

Eliot believed that he had found a formula for an acceptable university divinity school. If it were genuinely nondenominational and emphasized religion rather than theology, he believed, such a school could be conducted on a scientific basis. In 1879 he enthusiastically led a campaign to raise funds to endow five professorships in the divinity school. He then took an active interest in finding scholars from a variety of denominations, who had been trained in historical and critical methods, to fill the new chairs.[54]

At the end of his career Eliot remained so pleased with the reorganization of the divinity school that he included it in a list of his nine most important achievements during his forty-year term as president. He promoted its curriculum as the solution to ministerial education in the modern age of science. He maintained that ministers trained in nontheological "unsectarian" religion could serve the spiritual needs of their community without violating their own intellectual integrity. The reorganization of the divinity school seemed to make Eliot more comfortable with the topic of religion generally. In the 1880s he began to write more about religion, arguing that religiosity was an essential human characteristic. He also began to defend the unsectarian university as a positive religious institution.[55]

Eliot likened the distinction between religion and theology to the distinction between an unsectarian and a denominational college—a view that was essential to public acceptance of university reform. He did not, however, invent the notion of a nondenominational Christian school. Throughout the nineteenth century, state universities and some private colleges designated themselves as such. But they generally took on the nondenominational status as a necessity and had to fight the perception that they were irreligious institutions, dangerous for impressionable youth. Eliot, on the other hand, successfully argued that unsectarianism was not simply a practical necessity, but a positive good. He, and other university reformers, convinced a good part of the educated public that the best form of religious education was open and free.

Eliot's view of the unsectarian university as a positive religious institution was best developed in his 1886 debate with James McCosh, president of Princeton. The two men were asked to debate "the Place which Religion should have in the College," before the Nineteenth Century Club. In his address Eliot distinguished among three types of colleges: the denominational, the partially denominational, and the undenominational. This typology was opposed to McCosh's, which admitted only two categories, the religious and the irreligious. Eliot wanted to emphasize that all of these institutions were religious, though in different ways.[56]

Eliot tried to present each of the three types of institution in a complimentary light. "The frank and positive attitude of a thorough-going denominational college commands a perfect respect," he said. "There is doubtless a place and function for such colleges in a nation which is divided, as ours is, into many religious communions, discriminated not only by differences of dogma and ritual, but also by differences of race, social level, and habitual political proclivity." Given that parents wanted to educate their children according to their own beliefs, Eliot admitted that denominational schools were necessary and useful.[57]

Despite his recognition of the legitimacy of the denominational school, Eliot questioned the value of institutions that served single segments of the population. In another context, he described "the education of young members of single denomination apart from the youth of other denominations" as an "enfeebling" practice. It "keeps them in ignorance of the conditions of the real world into which they must go out." In addition to the ill effects on students, he thought education should destroy rather than perpetuate such distinctions among Americans. "The philosopher will complain," he told the Nineteenth Century Club, that the denominational school "does not yield the best fruits of real culture— namely, openness of mind, liberality of sentiment, and breadth of sympathy." To offset such narrowness, he suggested that the proper use of a denominational school was to educate rural youth for a couple of years before sending them to a larger college.[58]

Eliot next described the partially denominational school. Religious practices at these schools varied considerably. Some still retained mandatory prayer, some did not; some required religious tests for faculty, while others let the practice die; some still hired only ministers as presidents, while others selected laymen. These practices varied so much because the partially denominational college was really a denominational school in the process of evolving into a fully unsectarian institution. The extent to which a college dropped its denominational practices depended on the liberality of the community it served. Eliot worried that inconsistent practices might mislead parents about the extent of religious supervision that their children received, but he praised the partially denominational schools for responding to "the general movement of society towards toleration" of religious differences.[59]

Eliot then turned to his preferred type, the unsectarian institution. "The best test of genuine unsectarian quality in a college is diversity of religious opinion among its teachers." Unsectarian colleges also selected laymen as their heads and chose men from a variety of denominations to serve on their governing boards. They did not maintain a church with a single preacher, "because that church would be justly regarded as a church of the denomination to which the preacher belongs." They could, however, offer Sunday-evening services led by visiting ministers representing a variety of denominations, encourage students to join local churches of their own choice, and conduct short daily prayers "without any homily, or other opportunity for dogmatic teaching."[60]

The public frequently misperceived the unsectarian institution's impartiality toward various forms of religion as indifference to all religion. "Hasty or bigoted people may easily say—this college does not know truth from error, pays no allegiance to our one truth in religion, teaches, by act if not by word, that all religions are equally true or equally false, and that no particular religion is necessary; in short, this college is Godless." Eliot thought that this opinion mistook religious tolerance for religious indifference. Viewing the unsectarian university as godless, Eliot maintained, "grievously . . . mis-represents the true theory of religious toleration." Instead of hurting religion, he argued, tolerance was the best policy for the preservation and growth of religion.[61]

The unsectarian college included religion in "the same serious, candid, and truth-loving spirit" as all other subjects. This practice, Eliot asserted, undermined the widespread misconception "that there is an opposition between the fundamentals of religion and modern science." Instead of promoting conflict, the unsectarian college illustrated "the unity in aim and spirit of all genuine study and teaching, no matter what the subject." Hence, universities, by jettisoning theology and denominational creeds, treated religion like all other intellectual subjects. Eliot was confident that this intellectual equality would promote the interests of true religion. He believed that through scientific study people would come to agree about basic religious truths.[62]

Throughout his career Eliot maintained that there was a place for the denominational school. But he grew increasingly certain that such institutions could not be considered universities. "The great universities," he declared in 1891, "cannot be conducted as strict denominational organizations." Pledges to denominational creeds conflicted with the university's commitment to free inquiry. The scholar "pursues truth eagerly . . . without due regard to its possible effects on venerable associations, precious feelings, or traditional sanctities." Universities welcomed religion, but refused to protect any doctrines from open investigation. Religion, if true, would survive and flourish in a university dedicated to openness and freedom.[63]

More conservative educational and religious leaders disagreed with Eliot; they wanted either strict or moderate denominational control. At the other end of the spectrum from Eliot's unsectarianism was strict denominationalism, and church officials argued that denominational control was essential. "To be without a creed," declared Justin A. Smith, editor of the Baptist *Standard,* "is to be without a belief. . . . No denominationalism means in practice the utter neglect of religious influence of any kind, and a spirit of indifferentism, or more often of positive infidelity." These leaders rejected the distinction between theology and religion and continued to associate piety with the acceptance of particular beliefs.[64]

More moderate educators, such as Eliot's debating partner James McCosh, downplayed the importance of denominational creeds but insisted that religion was too important to be left without any positive support. McCosh pointed out that "unsectarian" was "a negative phrase; excluding much, but including nothing fitted to attract the mind." In an unsectarian school, religion would be "merely tolerated . . . as if the college was afraid or ashamed of it, and wished to confine it as much as possible." Religion, "a truth from its very nature above all other truths," McCosh insisted, could not be left to the whim of individual students. Students must be instructed in basic Christian beliefs.[65]

Moderates, like McCosh at Princeton and Porter at Yale, did not accept Eliot's call for complete freedom of inquiry. They thought that Christianity provided the "essential condition" for all knowledge and culture. "We hold," wrote Porter, "that religion controls and tempers culture, in order to stimulate, refine and elevate it; and culture, in its turn, enlightens and liberalizes religion." Consequently, they rejected the view that "our investigations should be unbiased and untrammelled by any traditional creeds." Instead, they insisted that true intellectual and moral progress was possible only within the limits of Christian theism. According to this view, the institution must protect Christianity. "No voice against Christ should ever be raised within its recitation rooms, in its chapel, or in its society, or exhibition or commencement platforms," wrote one educator. "Freedom of thought or speech cannot be stretched to warrant such license." These educators continued to interpret Eliot's call for complete freedom as a guise for Godlessness.[66]

Despite these strong sentiments, Eliot's notion of the unsectarian university triumphed. Over the 1870s and 1880s freedom from church control became accepted as a principle of university reform. Andrew Dickson White named "unsectarianism" as the first "guiding idea" leading the movement for improved scientific education. "There is no other possible basis for the development of great institutions for scientific and industrial education . . . to put them under control of any [religious] synod, conference, association, council or convention is to strangle them." This idea quickly spread to all forms of modern education. "The notion that the Christian Church is to monopolize and manipulate education," one observer declared in 1881, "is antique for our time and for all time." University leaders agreed that denominational control unnecessarily thwarted the goals of educational reform.[67]

The creation of new universities in the late nineteenth century reflected the contemporary aversion to church control. When planning the Johns Hopkins University in 1874 and 1875, its board solicited the advice of presidents of other universities. White immediately suggested that the institution "not be allowed to lapse into the hands of any single religious sect or body. Nothing can be more unfortunate." For the new university's first president, the trustees selected Daniel C. Gilman, who agreed with White about the dangers of sectarianism.

The institution we are about to organize would not be worthy of the name of an University if it were to be devoted to any other purpose than the discovery and promulgation of the truth; and it would be ignoble in the extreme if the resources . . . should be limited to the maintenance of ecclesiastical differences or perverted to the promotion of political strife.

The Johns Hopkins trustees agreed and established the university on a nondenominational basis. At its inaugural in 1876 Eliot praised "the absence of sectarian control" over the new university.[68]

Officials at Johns Hopkins endured numerous attacks by religious leaders and papers, claiming that the young university was irreligious. Nonetheless, Gilman defended its position on religion and anticipated future public acceptance of nondenominational schools. "It is my belief," he reported in 1888, "that the apprehensions which were once felt that a university, bearing no ecclesiastical name and requiring no religious tests, would be necessarily adverse to Christian influences, have nearly if not quite disappeared from the minds of all well-informed persons." Gilman expected that people would soon recognize that a university could be both religious and unsectarian.[69]

Other new universities followed Johns Hopkins and rejected associations with churches. In the late 1880s, when Leland Stanford was planning the organization of Stanford University, he resisted the offers of the Methodists to conduct the university under their auspices. Instead, founders Leland and Jane Stanford instructed the trustees "to prohibit sectarian instruction, but to have taught in the University the immortality of the soul, the existence of an all-wise and benevolent Creator, and that obedience to His laws is the highest duty of man." David Starr Jordan, the first president of Stanford University, praised the institution's religious independence. "It is the free investigation and promulgation of truth which is the function of the university. But the denominational school must also stand for the defense of certain doctrines as the ultimate truth," he wrote. "The school cannot serve two masters; and the school maintained for special work of the part cannot meet the needs of the whole." Colleagues elsewhere agreed with Jordan that denominational affiliation obstructed the true purpose of the university.[70]

Nonsectarianism became a point of orthodoxy among educational reformers. In 1891, when the Baptist Education Society led a fund-raising drive for the new University of Chicago, the *Educational Review* published an editorial blasting efforts to establish denominational schools: "The wickedness of this movement for sectarian universities is only exceeded by its folly. Everyone who contributes a dollar toward the establishment of a sectarian university is paying to exalt the narrow, the petty, the uncharitable, and to substitute for the pursuit of truth the perpetuation of sectarian belief as the aim of our higher education." Disapproval of sectarian control hurt efforts to raise money. "Sectarian!! Sectarian!! Baptist!! Baptist!! that is the eternal cry in nearly every office," complained the chief fund raiser, "and our utmost endeavors on the street and in the papers are powerless to arrest the note of alarm." Clearly, by this time distrust of church-dominated universities had overwhelmed fears of irreligion in unsectarian institutions.[71]

The changed attitude toward church-sponsored universities transformed the identity of the new University of Chicago. William Rainey Harper, its first president, wanted the school to become a great university, and by 1890 such aspirations precluded denominational identity. "Individuals, or the state, or the church may found schools for propagating certain special kinds of instruction, but such schools are not universities, and may not be so denominated." Despite the role of the Baptist Education Society and its original charter requiring that the president and two-thirds of the board of trustees be "members of regular Baptist Churches," the University of Chicago never operated as a Baptist institution.[72]

The one area of the University of Chicago that retained an active denominational identity was the divinity school. As a condition of John D. Rockefeller's gift to the university, the Baptist Union Theological Seminary became its divinity school. Harper had misgivings about this association. He agreed with Eliot's critique of the ministry. Students whose "educational training has taught them to think" were refusing to become ministers because "those who have undertaken it are forbidden to think except within the narrowest limits." Theological training epitomized the dogmatic education reformers opposed.[73]

The University of Chicago could not conduct a divinity school along traditional lines. "The interest of the University," explained Harper, "is distinctively in a School of Theology which shall partake exclusively of a scientific character." Such a school could "not be limited by the influence of a single denomination, nor indeed any group of denominations." Harper proposed that the university dissociate itself from the Baptist Union Theological Seminary and "establish a separate Divinity School, non-denominational, co-ordinate with the other Graduate Schools of the University." Although he did not succeed in severing the divinity school's ties to the Baptist denomination, negotiations with church leaders produced a statement agreeing that the school "must be carried on in accordance with university ideals of freedom of investigation and teaching; that all its classes be open . . . to students of all forms of religious faith;

and that its faculty be recruited from the ablest scholars, irrespective of religious denomination." The trustees of the seminary promised to reject didactic practices in favor of the new standards promoted by educational reformers.[74]

In addition, Harper invited other denominations to move their theological schools to the area and to affiliate with the university. If a fully independent divinity school was impossible, he hoped at least to create a multi-denominational community. "The intercourse between students of these different schools tends to impress upon them the unity of Christian work and the students generally in the University are led to acknowledge the uniformity of purpose of the theological halls." Officials at other universities, including Columbia, the University of California, and the University of Michigan, also encouraged religious groups to establish schools associated with their universities. Reformers viewed such institutional arrangements as a way to encourage interdenominational cooperation, to broaden the educational opportunities of divinity students, and to provide university students with free access to instruction in religious subjects.[75]

Older reform-minded institutions also cut traditional ties to religious denominations. At Columbia, Seth Low recognized the importance of religious independence. After becoming president, he distanced himself from church-related activities, going so far as to resign from the vestry of his own church. He downplayed Columbia's relationship with the Episcopalians, emphasizing instead the religious diversity of the university's board of trustees and its freedom from "sectarian control." Low's successor, Nicholas Murray Butler, also stressed Columbia's "catholicity of temper and tolerance of mind" in regard to religion. The only appropriate religious designation for Columbia, he maintained, was "Christian." "Unless a university entirely abandons its own peculiar aim and becomes merely an instrument of propaganda for some specific doctrine, it cannot in its institutional capacity go beyond this."[76]

When Arthur T. Hadley became president of Yale in 1899, he, too, wanted to distance the university from its long association with the Congregational Church. Like other educational reformers, Hadley thought that religion should be subject to the same standards of inquiry as all other subjects of study. "In old times most people took their standards of morals and religion ready made. They accepted the creed of their church because it was the creed of their church." But not in this "age of individual freedom," explained Hadley. "The men of to-day claim a right to do their thinking for themselves." Religious education must reflect this change. University educators insisted that their students have religious freedom.[77]

Hadley thought that theological training particularly needed reform. Under the current educational practices, he did not think "our divinity student at the end of his course able to take a position of leadership, to give counsel in questions of morals and faith, such as the physician can give in questions of health or the engineers in questions of buildings." He pushed the faculty of the divinity school to revamp its curriculum. In 1914 the school's name was changed to the Yale University School of Religion to symbolize the resulting changes. "We are contrasting a University School of Religion," explained the secretary of Yale, "with a local, denominational seminary of theology. Now between the words religion and theology there is a great gap. . . . The word religion is broader and more vital." The once conservative Yale had denounced the dogmatism associated with theology and embraced the freedom of scientific inquiry.[78]

By the end of the nineteenth century, educational leaders presented nonsectarianism as an essential feature of university government. Their views received financial sanction in 1906, when the Carnegie Foundation decided to exclude denominational institutions from its new program of retirement pensions for faculty. The foundation gave several reasons for excluding denominational schools, ranging from the practical concern that denominational sponsorship encouraged the proliferation of smaller, weaker institutions to the intellectual concern that denominational sponsorship interfered with scholarly freedom. In justifying the decision, Henry Pritchett, president of the foundation, relied heavily on Eliot's vision of the "unsectarian" university. Pritchett insisted that the decision was not a result of hostility to denominations or to Christian education. "Least of all does [Carnegie] desire to hamper in any way the cause of religion," Pritchett said. "His purpose was to serve primarily the cause of education, and as a matter of educational administration, it has seemed unwise to place a college under the control of another organization of whatever the cause."[79]

Eliot hoped that the Carnegie Foundation's policy would "induce institutions of learning to rid themselves completely of [denominational] control." Not all schools, of course, abandoned their denominational affiliation, but many did. Carnegie's policy accurately reflected the success of the educational reforms begun thirty years earlier. The idea of educational independence was now clearly established. Nondenominationalism had been freed from the taint of irreligion and elevated to an important principle of religious and intellectual freedom. Freed from church control and dogmatic denominational creeds, reformers believed that universities could develop a new kind of religious education and scholarship.[80]

FOUR

The Reconstruction of Religion

Between 1870 and 1890 university reformers refashioned course work related to religion. In 1870 religious instruction in colleges consisted of required courses in moral philosophy, often supplemented by lectures on natural theology or the evidences of Christianity. By 1890 these courses had disappeared from the university curriculum. In their stead, faculty advanced a variety of electives related to religion. These classes, they hoped, would provide the core for an emerging academic discipline, the "science of religion." Intellectuals conceived of this new science as the answer to their search for a religiously significant and scientifically respectable education.

In the early 1870s educators began to consider natural theology an inadequate form of religious education. At Columbia, Frederick A. P. Barnard proposed in 1871 that the board of trustees form a committee to decide the future of the course on "the evidences of natural and revealed religion." A temporary instructor was teaching the course, but there was general agreement that the course was unsuccessful. While Barnard admitted that "it is desirable that every student should be instructed in the important subject of the foundations of religion," he suggested that the course be changed from a requirement to an elective. The outgoing instructor suggested that the course be moved from the senior year to an earlier year and that it be combined with another subject, such as the fine arts. Barnard agreed that such a course would be "much more attractive" than the current course, but he did not think such a change was feasible because it would require drastic revision of the course of study. In the end, Barnard could not find anyone appropriate to teach the class. The dearth of adequate instructors was understandable, he thought, given the intellectual climate of the time. In 1877 he abandoned his search and hired a philosophy assistant to teach psychology instead.[1]

Over the next decade, other reform-oriented schools discontinued lectures on natural theology and evidences of Christianity. The University

88

of California offered its last class in natural theology in 1871. At Harvard, Professor Andrew P. Peabody in 1872 stopped assigning a text on the "evidences of Christianity" in his moral philosophy course. By the end of the 1870s, the University of Michigan also omitted the "Evidences of Christianity" from its description of philosophy courses. Johns Hopkins University, University of Chicago, and Stanford University, all newly founded institutions, never established courses on the evidences of Christianity or natural theology. Only Yale, under the conservative leadership of Noah Porter, still required its students in the 1880s to take its class, "Natural Theology and Evidences of Christianity."[2]

Also in the 1870s moral philosophy began to be discredited as intellectuals criticized college philosophy courses as too "theological." In a letter to the editor of the *Nation* in 1876, the psychologist G. Stanley Hall suggested that the magazine examine the poor condition of philosophy in American colleges. Even at "our best institutions," Hall explained, there "are few if any branches which are so inadequately taught as those generally roughly classed as philosophy." Hall blamed the shortcomings of American philosophical instruction on "the persistent use of [works of Scottish philosopher Sir William] Hamilton, [Joseph] Butler's 'Analogy [of Religion],' and a score of treatises on 'moral science' which deduce all ground of obligation from theological considerations." Philosophy courses suffered because they were taught by "one of the older and 'safer' members of the faculty, under the erroneous belief that it should be the aim of the professors in this department to indoctrinate rather than to instruct— to tell *what* to think, than to teach *how* to think."[3]

In the same issue of the *Nation,* William James echoed Hall's concerns in his anonymous article, "The Teaching of Philosophy in Our Colleges." "The philosophical teaching, as a rule, in our higher seminaries," he wrote, "is in the hands of the president, who is usually a minister of the Gospel, and as he more often owes his position to general excellence of character and administrative faculty than to any speculative gifts or propensities . . . his classes are edified rather than awakened." Students "leave college with the generous youthful impulse to reflect . . . dampened and discouraged . . . by the lifeless discussions and flabby formulas they have had to commit to memory." James argued that moral philosophers stifled all true inquiry by requiring students to memorize philosophical doctrines.[4]

By presenting students with a set of established "truths," critics charged, moral philosophy undermined the real purpose of philosophy. "As for philosophy," James wrote, "its educational essence lies in the quickening of the spirit to its *problems.* What doctrines students take from their teachers are of little consequence provided they catch from them the living, philosophic attitude of mind, the independent, personal look at all the data of life, and the eagerness to harmonize them." Philosophy, according to James, should encourage questions about "man in his relation with the universe," not provide authoritative answers. James's and Hall's views were consistent with the developing ideals of science; they emphasized the importance of open inquiry and minimized the significance of particular doctrines. Educational reformers increasingly applied these new standards to philosophy instruction.[5]

Required courses in moral philosophy, like the natural theology course before them, vanished from university curricula. Harvard changed its ethics course from a requirement to an elective in 1875. The University of California until 1879 continued to require students in the colleges of letters and literature to take moral philosophy. After 1879 most of its instruction in philosophy was temporarily suspended. When the subject was resumed five years later, the required course in moral philosophy was replaced by an elective, entitled "Elementary Ethics, Historically Treated." By the end of the 1870s Michigan also had discontinued courses in moral philosophy. Other reform-oriented institutions followed the advice of Hall and James and replaced required courses in mental and moral philosophy with a variety of electives taught from a historical and critical perspective.[6]

Despite the elimination of the traditional moral philosophy requirement, educators continued to associate philosophy with moral and religious education. University presidents felt that it was important to hire philosophers who were independent thinkers and whose views seemed credible in an institution devoted to scientific inquiry. But they also wanted philosophers who were sympathetic to Christian beliefs and values. "Few colleges want or are likely to want teachers of philosophy, if their philosophy is at war with the fundamentals of Christianity," explained James B. Angell of the University of Michigan. In short, reformers sought philosophers who could steer safely between iconoclasm and dogmatism. But the path to a nondoctrinal theistic philosophy was not always evident. Consequently, university officials could not rely on philosophy as the basis for modern religious training.[7]

Changing expectations about the nature of philosophy and its role in the reconciliation of religion and science also made it difficult for university administrators to hire philosophers in this period. For example, Daniel C. Gilman, president of Johns Hopkins, found it nearly impossible to select a philosophy professor. Gilman was committed to science, open inquiry, and ethical and religious education, and believed that these were compatible. In answering a letter from a minister who was concerned about the religious beliefs of the university's future philosophy instructor, Gilman wrote, "I should be sorry to see fetters put upon a professor in any department of science—as to what [he] should or should not hold. Our plans look toward the freedom of 'the University,' and not to the restrictions of 'the College.' We shall welcome discoverers and investigators, if we can induce them to come among us, and shall give them abundant opportunities to exercise their gifts." But, he continued, "we are also fully alive to the importance of sound philosophy especially in relations to the questions of . . . a faith which exercise[s] the minds of thoughtful men everywhere."[8]

Gilman hoped to find a philosopher who could bring religion and ethics in line with modern thought. Although he was unwilling to impose a particular creed, he wanted a "strong and right minded philosopher— one who can awaken and lead forward students." In another letter, he affirmed his views on "the importance of ethical instruction." But, he confessed, "I cannot *find the man;* if you can find him for me, I will give you a premium." He wanted a philosopher who could "meet modern philosophical discussions and tendencies," someone who had "not only high intellectual and moral qualities but vigor, tact, enthusiasm, sagacity and that sort of courage which neither dreads nor provokes controversy." Gilman thought that the ideal philosopher would avoid both destructive criticism and unquestioning adherence to tradition.[9]

Gilman sought a philosopher who would harmonize religion and science, but he was unsure about what sort of philosopher could best accomplish that goal. He considered several appointments. After unsuccessful negotiations with Robert Flint of Edinburgh and William James, Gilman decided to postpone his search. "We are not yet agreed," he explained, "as to whether it is more important to have a professor of the History of Philosophy, or a Professor of Psychology,—or of ethics." Instead of picking a permanent professor in a particular field, Gilman hired three part-time instructors: Charles S. Peirce, G. Stanley Hall, and George S. Morris. All three men professed the desire to accommodate religion and scientific inquiry. For several years Gilman staffed the philosophy department with the three of them and avoided deciding which man offered the most promising line of reconciliation.[10]

Gilman realized that he could not hold onto the three part-timers forever and would have to come to some conclusion about the future of philosophy in the university. In 1883 Morris wrote Gilman to tell him about a possible full-time opening at the University of Michigan. Although Gilman liked Morris "very much" and considered him "a very safe man—intelligent, catholic, well read, accessible, [and] cooperative," he also thought that Morris was "not quite forcible enough," so he did not try to keep him at Johns Hopkins. The possibility of losing him induced Gilman to settle matters in philosophy. The following year, he announced that the university had designated Hall as the permanent head of the philosophy department, thus ending the part-time arrangements with Peirce and Morris. Gilman appreciated Hall's vigorous personality, his outspoken defense of psychology as "Christian to its roots and centre," and his efforts to align psychology with Hopkins's growing biology department. In selecting Hall, Gilman seemed to have secured a professor who incorporated religion into the realm of scientific inquiry.[11]

Gilman's long-delayed decision turned out to be ill fated. In April 1888 Hall accepted the presidency of Clark University and left Johns Hopkins without a philosophy department. Gilman did not repeat his search for a leading philosopher. Instead, he hired Edward H. Griffen as professor of the history of philosophy and dean of the undergraduate students. Griffen had been a professor of mental and moral philosophy at Williams College. He was known as "a man of high character" with safe religious beliefs. Gilman expected him to be "accessible to parents, students, and colleagues"; conduct daily prayers; teach the undergraduate course on logic, ethics, and psychology; and be a "moral and intellectual force among the undergraduates." "The duties," Gilman explained to Griffen, "are not those of a University professor, as they are commonly understood, but those of a College President." Gilman had finally decided that it was too difficult to find a philosopher who combined both scientific and religious respectability. He had come to believe that the ethical and spiritual education of the undergraduates was more important than developing a distinguished philosophy department.[12]

Gilman's difficulties in selecting a professor of philosophy, though extreme, were not unique. For example, at the University of California, banker and regent D. O. Mills endowed a "Professorship of Intellectual and Moral Philosophy and Civil Policy" in 1881. The university searched for three years before finding an appropriate person to fill the chair, finally selecting George H. Howison in 1884. Howison was typical of the first generation of professional philosophers: an idealist whose views were consistent with Christian theism, he also believed that philosophy should be independent of church doctrine. He believed that a professor of philosophy "should have no church affiliations. He needs to stand free, I think, in a degree that hardly any other sort of teacher does, from any pledges about doctrine." Accordingly, Howison did not try to resurrect the old required course work in mental and moral philosophy. Instead, he offered philosophy electives, emphasizing the history of modern philosophy.[13]

Philosophers like Howison at the University of California, Morris at the University of Michigan, and Josiah Royce at Harvard were interested in questions addressed by theologians, such as the existence of God or the nature of human immortality, but they were not committed to orthodox doctrines. However, their courses on ethics and the philosophy of religion still reflected their theistic philosophy. Howison, for example, in 1884 began teaching a course, "Elementary Ethics, Historically Considered," which included "a critique of Perfectionism and Hedonism, of Necessity and Freedom, of Optimism and Pessimism." This course became a staple in the Berkeley department. In 1887 he introduced two courses on the philosophy of religion: "The Philosophy of Religion, Historically Considered—God, duty and immortality, as treated by the leaders of philosophy from Anaxagoras to Lange" and "Philosophy of Religion: The Rational Foundations of Theism—A Critique of Mill's *Three Essays* and Kant's *Dialectic of Pure Reason*." Similar courses were taught by other philosophers during this period. For a time, then, these idealist philosophers seemed to combine religion and a commitment to university reform.[14]

Despite the prominence of idealists such as Howison, Morris, and Royce in the first generation of professional philosophers, traditional religious concerns became more marginal within philosophy. Younger philosophers, who did not find neo-Hegelian idealism adequate, often chose simply to avoid the intellectual problems associated with theism. Instead, they turned to more technical problems in epistemology, logic, and the history of philosophy. As a result, university presidents found it more difficult to find professors interested in theistic philosophies. When John Dewey left Michigan for Chicago in 1894, President James B. Angell could not find a replacement. He wanted a believing Christian interested in the philosophy of religion or ethics. He tried unsuccessfully to convince George H. Palmer of Harvard, Howison of Berkeley, and Henry C. King of Oberlin to accept the post. "After two years search to secure a suitable American," Angell gave up and decided to "risk . . . taking a foreigner." He hired Robert M. Wenley of Glasgow.[15]

The declining interest in questions relating to theism created conflicts between younger philosophers and their older colleagues. When Arthur T. Hadley became president of Yale in 1899, he inherited a philosophy department rent by in-fighting. George T. Ladd would not cooperate with the other members of the department who did not propound his idealist philosophy. Edward W. Scripture felt his colleagues were ruining his work and discriminating against his graduate students because of his "lack of sympathy with metaphysical speculation." The department reflected conflicts within the newly professionalizing discipline of philosophy. More professionally oriented philosophers pushed for technical, specialized, "scientific" studies, while their more traditional colleagues, although also claiming the mantle of science, preferred broad consideration of questions about the nature of life and the universe. In this struggle, Scripture represented the wave of the future, while Ladd's position, though never obsolete, became a minority within the discipline.[16]

The marginalization of religious concerns was reflected in the changing philosophy curriculum at universities. In 1870 two of the four required philosophy classes—moral philosophy, mental philosophy, logic, and natural theology—at the University of California dealt directly with religious and moral concerns. Fifteen years later, even the idealist Howison offered eight courses in philosophy, only one of which, an elective on ethics, was devoted specifically to those issues. By 1900 the philosophy department offered thirteen courses. Howison's "Elementary Ethics, including Civil Polity" (a combination of two previously separate courses) was still the only class explicitly devoted to religion or morality. In 1915 only three out of thirty-one classes were devoted to ethics or the philosophy of religion. The bulk of the department's courses were related to the history of philosophy or psychology. By that point, intellectual problems associated with theism no longer dominated the attention of academic philosophers.[17]

While the association of philosophy and religion waned over the last decades of the nineteenth century, scholars outside of philosophy began studying religion. In 1885 Howison's "Elementary Ethics, Historically Considered" was the only course at California related to religion or morality. Fifteen years later thirteen such classes were offered, including classes on biblical literature, the history of the Christian Church, and the philosophies and religions of China. The philosophy department sponsored none of them. By 1915 Berkeley's catalogue included nineteen classes related to religion or morality, offered in seven separate departments.

The pattern at Berkeley was typical of other universities, which also developed new courses related to religion. For example, in 1885 conservative Yale offered three courses related to religion, the traditional requirement of "Ethics, Natural Theology, and the Evidences of Christianity," a graduate philosophy course in ethics, and an elective in Hebrew. By 1900 Yale had become one of the leading institutions for the study of Semitic languages and literature and offered more than fifty courses related to religion. During the same period, Johns Hopkins expanded its Semitic department and its course offerings in Indian religions and church history.[18]

These new courses were not devoted to the traditional metaphysical questions, but instead explored "the human side of religion." Herbert B. Adams described his course in Jewish and church history as "ancient sociology." "It involves an historical study of Chaldea as background for Jewish history, and of Egypt and Phonecia, as well as of Jewish history proper. Special attention is directed to the study of Hebrew institutions." Most courses on the Bible were taught from a historical or literary perspective. Frank K. Sanders of Yale organized his course "Biblical Literature in English" "on the principle of chronological and historical connection." In addition to introductory courses on biblical literature and history, universities offered advanced courses involving philological analysis of the Bible and other ancient religious texts.[19]

By the early twentieth century the new fields of comparative religion and the psychology of religion had made their way into university curricula. At Berkeley, Professor John Fryer taught two classes on Asian religions in 1900. In 1903 George Stratton offered an advanced course on the psychology of religion. The next year Professor Pliny E. Goddard taught an anthropology course entitled "The Religious Practices and Beliefs of Non-literary Peoples." These new courses represented the growing interest in the origin, development, and psychological and social significance of religion. They were part of the development of the scientific study of religion, which educators hoped would provide the basis of a spiritual education perfectly suited for the modern university.

University reformers expected that the new courses on religion would provide the basis for effective, modern religious training. This expectation was based on a series of assumptions about the problems of traditional religious education. They thought religion suffered from its association with outmoded theological doctrines. They hoped that scientific study would modernize religious beliefs. Reformers wanted a "modern reconstruction of religion," which would develop "a new conception, a new expression, a new administration of religion, fitted to the modern-world and the current need." They also assumed that students were uninterested in religion because they associated it with dogmatism. It followed, then, that once students realized that the new courses were taught scientifically, they would take them. Educators admitted that the spiritual benefits of such courses were indirect, but they thought that students would be impressed with the value of religion and struck by the basic truth of Christianity.[20]

The development of the scientific study of religion in the 1890s complemented liberal Protestant leaders' desire for "religious reconstruction." Liberals believed that they were living in a period of tremendous intellectual change, which would inevitably influence religion. Reverend Henry Ward Beecher wrote in 1882, "That a great change, progressive and prophetic, is passing over the public mind in matters of religious truth, there can be no doubt." Instead of fighting these changes, Beecher proposed to examine their causes and nature and provide articulate leadership for the new religious movements.[21]

In examining the causes of religious change, Beecher discussed the significance of science. New scientific theories, particularly evolution, forced people to reconsider their religious beliefs. "To admit the truth of evolution is to yield up the reigning theology. It is to change the whole notion of man's origin, his nature, the problem of human life, the philosophy of morality, the theory of sin, the structure of moral government as taught in the dominant theologies of the Christian world." Although evolutionary theory discredited many time-honored religious beliefs, Beecher refused to view it as the enemy. "Science is truth; Truth loves the truth." The project for Beecher and other religious liberals was to use scientific theories as instruments of religious reconstruction.[22]

Liberals applied evolutionary ideas to their views of religion. As a result, they rejected the assumption that religion was static and perfect. They believed that Christianity should progress as culture evolved. "Progress in doctrine and life is a necessary experience of a living church," affirmed Charles Briggs of Union Theological Seminary. University reformers were sympathetic to the liberal religious movement and thought that universities could be instruments of religious progress. "Religion is not a fixed thing, but a fluent thing," Charles W. Eliot observed. "It is, therefore, wholly natural and to be expected that the conceptions of religion prevalent among educated people should change from century to century." Because universities facilitated "the increase of knowledge, and the spread of the spirit of scientific inquiry," they also had a part to play in the "changes in religious beliefs and practices."[23]

University reformers admitted that university instruction sometimes led students to question the religion in which they had been reared. "The scientific attitude of mind cultivated in most colleges as well as universities," noted William Rainey Harper, "distinctly opposes the acceptance of truth on the basis of another person's authority. The college student passes through an evolution both intellectual and moral. He is taught to question everything. . . . This same questioning attitude must inevitably include matters of religion." The open-minded inquiry of the university extended to religious as well as all other ideas.[24]

Believing in the progress of ideas, university leaders presented the discrediting of some religious beliefs as an inevitable part of progress. They maintained that destructive criticism cleared the way for a new and more vigorous form of religion. The "loss of religious faith," Eliot argued, is not necessarily bad. It depends on "what kind of a faith is lost. . . . There have been, and there are, a great many religious faiths which it is a great happiness to lose. Among these I count many of the ordinary beliefs among so-called Christians. To lose a religious belief may, in my view, be cause of the profoundest thankfulness." Leaders of university reform who were sympathetic to the modernist impulse in religion affirmed that many old doctrines should be superseded by modern beliefs.[25]

Advocates of modern religion rejected the concept of orthodoxy and believed that religious doctrines should be treated like scientific theories, constantly challenged and tested, revised and enlarged. "Orthodoxy is, in the Church, very much what prejudice is in a single mind. It is the premature conceit of certainty," observed Phillips Brooks, a leading liberal minister. Religious doctrine, like prejudice, must "be kept open for revision and enlargement, if it can be always aware of its partialness and imperfection, then it becomes simply a point of departure for newer worlds of thought and action, or we may say, a *working hypothesis,* which is one stage of the progress toward truth." Change in religion, like change in science, was supposed to represent improvement and growth.[26]

University reformers believed that freedom implied tolerance for different views. Consequently, they thought that this new, modern religion would be more tolerant than older, dogmatic forms of Christianity. Harper thought that the university must have "a religion of toleration. One's neighbor must be allowed to differ." Educators considered "tolerance" an important "characteristic of the scientific spirit and of the scientific method." Although researchers disagreed with one another in every important area of study, they continued to share a "common spirit of search." The same spirit should be cultivated in religion. "An important by-product will be an increase of tolerance, which is a real charity of mind and not to be identified with indifference or mere vagueness of thought." Tolerance would promote a "catholicity of Christian feeling" and encourage students to be broadminded. Tolerance, however, was not an end in itself. Many advocates of religious progress ultimately hoped that this broadmindedness would lead to new religious unity.[27]

University reformers wanted their institutions to play a constructive role in the development of this religious unity and to help create a modern religion. "Religion cannot contain anything that reason rejects," wrote John Coulter of the University of Chicago. "This means that . . . all the triumphs of reason must ever be consistent with religion; and that loyal affection and a trained mind are helpmeets of religion." Universities, reformers argued, should devote their intellectual resources to the reconstruction of religion.[28]

Harper, who was a celebrated biblical scholar as well as a university reformer, wanted the University of Chicago to become a center for the new scholarly study of religion. To be scientific, he thought, such study must be free from theological control. He was eager, therefore, to ensure that these subjects were protected from interference by the Baptists and by John D. Rockefeller, who had founded and financed the school.

Harper, who had accepted the position of president of the new university, set himself up as a test case to establish the independence of religious thought at the university. In 1891 he decided to write Rockefeller about his unconventional religious views. A few years earlier, Augustus H. Strong, a prominent Baptist, had raised questions about the orthodoxy of some of Harper's biblical teaching. At that time, Harper had informed several of the theologians affiliated with the Baptist Union Theological Seminary in Chicago of his opinions. Although they did not agree with him, they thought he was sound in the "essentials" of the Christian faith. Harper reminded Rockefeller of the incident and told him that he was not completely satisfied with the outcome of those talks. He wanted to reopen the question of whether "my positions were such as to make it inappropriate to take the office of president." He wanted, in short, to test Rockefeller's tolerance of openminded questioning of religious doctrines.[29]

Harper told Rockefeller that some of his opinions "would bring down upon my head and upon the University the indignation of some of the Baptist denominational papers." He wanted to know whether such opposition would prevent him from presenting his views. Harper explained that he was about to deliver a series of lectures on the Books of Genesis and Exodus, "in which I shall undoubtedly say many things that the ordinary public will not accept." Harper suggested that Rockefeller convene a group of Baptist leaders to decide if the lectures were acceptable to the denomination. Then, Harper concluded, "I may know whether I shall have the privilege of teaching my views in the University of Chicago; and I may decide in case this privilege is not granted me whether, under the circumstances, it is wise for the university and for myself to accept the position." Since Harper had earlier indicated that he could not "consent to accept a position in which that privilege will be denied," his letter was a thinly veiled threat that he would quit if his freedom of speech were not guaranteed.[30]

Rockefeller communicated through Henry L. Morehouse of the American Baptist Home Mission Society. Morehouse sent a letter to Harper that was intended to deliver "a heavy blow." He angrily reminded Harper that he had already accepted the presidency and that he should not be raising objections at this point. In addition, Morehouse wrote, "Mr. Rockefeller has neither the time nor inclination to decide mooted theological questions and to assume the responsibility of saying what you teach." Although annoyed by his letter, Rockefeller granted Harper's independence.[31]

Harper was pleased with Morehouse's response and formally accepted the presidency soon after receiving his letter. "My conscience," he wrote, "is free. I have told 'the whole truth and nothing but the truth.' I am ready to go to Chicago. . . . I do so, however, with the understanding that the platform is broad and free; that everybody has known beforehand my position and situation, and that I am free to do in the way of teaching what, under all circumstances, seems to me wise." He secured freedom for his own teaching and the principle of independence from denominational control for all professors studying religion.[32]

As president, he transferred the departments of Semitic language and literature, biblical and patristic Greek, and comparative religion from the divinity school to the faculties of arts, literature, and science in the university. "The theological seminaries of the country," Harper explained, "have not been intended to serve as laboratories for the working out of problems, but as training schools for the instruction of skillful propagandists." On the other hand, "there exists in the university the spirit of research," which was crucial "for the investigation of the many phases of the religious life and of the many questions which form a part of the religious education." Harper began to pave the way for the university to honor free inquiry and to encourage the scientific study of religion.[33]

University reformers believed that religious courses could be taught according to the same scientific methods used in other classes. In the words of Clyde Votow of the University of Chicago,

It is not desired that the colleges should set themselves to promote particular denominational organizations, creeds, rituals, or politics. Let them teach religion in the same historical and scientific way that all other subjects are taught. Let the empirical method be employed, with a calm, clear, appreciative, constructive and practical mind, ready to see the facts as they emerge from study, ready to interpret the facts in light of all we know.

"Religion," concurred Raymond Knox of Columbia, "can and should be studied in the same spirit of inquiry, candor, and freedom from bias which alone makes study profitable in any field of inquiry." Religion did not have to be taught in the dogmatic fashion of theological schools; it could be incorporated into the university on the same basis as all other modern subjects.[34]

Although educators emphasized the scientific and cultural nature of the new courses on religion, they still thought the classes had a spiritual value. Harper argued,

If the university promotes the study of religion, a larger respect and appreciation will be accorded these subjects by students as well as by people at large, because the problems are problems on which learned and scientific men are at work. An influence will be set at work to counteract the marked tendency of that which religion represents, on the ground that religious feeling is something peculiar to women and weak men.

Harper thought that the cultural status of religion would improve if it was associated with the masculine sphere of science, rather than the increasingly feminized church. University reformers believed that scientific studies of religion offered a potent antidote for the contemporary perception that religion opposed intellectual progress.[35]

Harper thought that religion was losing its power among educated Americans because of its association with dogmatic and illogical thinking. Professors attributed students' lack of interest in religion to a similar cause: students were repelled by the didacticism of traditional religious instruction. "The trouble with your average student is not that he is narrowly sectarian and intolerant," wrote Benjamin Bacon of Yale, "rather that he will hold Bible study in more or less contempt, as a mere pretext for 'preaching.'" Educators predicted that when students discovered that university classes were "scientific" rather than "devotional," they would be more interested in religion. "The average university student is interested in Bible study, but he wants a fair, scientific, modern discussion of the problems offered," explained one instructor. University leaders thought that students respected science and that they would respect religion more when they realized that it, too, could be "scientific."[36]

Educators believed that more students would take classes in religion if the classes were taught scientifically. Students would thus experience spiritual as well as intellectual growth. Frank K. Sanders said that although the student's spiritual development was not the purpose of the courses in Yale's department of biblical history and literature, "it is believed that a fair and square study of the biblical material cannot help promoting that effect." The scientific study of religion encouraged, rather than excluded, personal involvement in religion. Bacon argued that

> it is just by making the courses purely—but not for that reason coldly, or unsympathetically—scientific, objective, critical and historical that they will become most surely effective in the interest of genuine religious culture. The religious culture will necessarily be incidental and not direct; it will be such as each student's own heart prompts him to draw from it in the privacy of his own reflection, not the moralizing or preaching of some representative of this sect or that.

Studying religion scientifically would indirectly stimulate students to be religious. The university, by offering courses in religion, would serve the cause of religious awakening.[37]

Between 1890 and 1920 the scientific study of religion flourished. Most scholars in the new field were sympathetic to religion and wanted to show that it had an important role in modern scientific culture. To demonstrate its value, intellectuals focused on its psychological and social functions. This approach, however, did not produce modern religious beliefs, as predicted. Instead, the scientific study of religion only affirmed religion's intellectual marginality.

"Religion as a subject of speculation is as old as human thought," commented a professor of comparative religion in 1893. But, he observed, "religion as an object of investigation is one of the most recent of sciences." This new field included diverse areas of study, as indicated by the variety of university courses on religion. It incorporated subjects that had once been part of theological training, as well as studies in the new social sciences. Intellectuals hoped to meld these diverse subjects into a comprehensive science that would guarantee religion a prominent place in modern intellectual life.[38]

Toward the end of the century scholars in biblical studies began to declare their allegiance to scientific methods of inquiry and their independence from theological studies. Advances in critical biblical studies also created new areas of specialization, such as archaeological studies of Mediterranean history and philological studies of ancient religious texts. Scholars in these fields examined the development of particular religious traditions, most commonly Christianity, but also Judaism, other ancient religions, and the great religions of Asia.

In addition to these studies of individual religions, proponents of the new science envisioned investigations of religion as general phenomena. Social-scientific studies of religion exemplified the aspirations of the new science. British anthropologists James George Frazer and Edward Burnett Tylor examined the origin and development of religion in their classic works, *The Golden Bough* and *Religion in Primitive Culture.* Pioneer sociologists, including Emile Durkheim and Max Weber, turned their attention to the role of religion in society.[39]

In the United States the psychology of religion captured the attention of intellectuals and became the most fashionable area in the new science of religion. In 1882 G. Stanley Hall published an early essay on adolescent conversion experiences. The field took off in the 1890s with the work of Edwin Starbuck and James Leuba. William James's *Varieties of Religious Experience,* published in 1902, was an immediate success. It lent prestige to the subject and increased Americans' interest in it. James's work was followed by numerous other books, including texts by George A. Coe, Edward Scribner Ames, and James B. Pratt. Introductory volumes, such as Ames's *Psychology of Religious Experience,* included chapters on "primitive religion" and the history of religion. The psychology of religion subsumed other areas of study.[40]

The growth of the science of religion depended on the intellectual developments discussed in chapter 2: the idea of science as a method and the distinction between theology and religion. Intellectuals viewed the scientific study of religion as an extension of the proposition that scientific methods could be applied to social and intellectual life. "Science has conquered one field after another, until now it is entering the most complex, the most inaccessible, and, of all, the most sacred domain—that of religion," began Starbuck's *Psychology of Religion.* "The Psychology of Religion," he wrote, "has for its work to carry the well-established methods of science into the analysis and organisation of the facts of the religious consciousness." Psychologists studying religion planned to apply methods of scientific inquiry to examine the facts of religion.[41]

In his intellectual autobiography, George Coe described the first of several steps that brought him to the psychology of religion. In college, he had had a biology teacher who encouraged him to read Darwin. "For me an issue was squarely joined. It concerned chiefly the validity of a method. How is truth to be found in matters of this kind? I settled the question," he recalled, ". . . by solemnly espousing the scientific method, including it within my religion, and resolving to follow it wherever it should lead." The desire to create a science of religion rested on the assumption that scientific inquiry was the most reliable source of knowledge in all fields.[42]

Coe took his second step toward the science of religion when he decided that theology contradicted the principles of scientific inquiry.

> Theology, as it came to me, depended for its validity upon its primary discipline, apologetics; but apologetics took its conclusion for granted from the outset. . . . There was involved an assumption that there is a kind of authority that can settle details of fact, or of value, or of duty before we have inspected them, whereas the method of the sciences and of historical criticism proceeded in the opposite direction.

Other devotees of the psychology of religion similarly rejected the restrictions of theology. Ames wrote in his autobiography *Beyond Theology,* "The minister's world has always seemed to me more or less prescribed. The truths he should know were largely *given,* given in revelation and weighted with divine and unquestionable authority." The new science appealed to thinkers who opposed the methods of theology but did not want to abandon religion altogether.[43]

Proponents of the science of religion communicated their hostility toward theology in their scholarship. William James, in *The Varieties of Religious Experience,* defined religion as "*the feelings, acts, and experiences of individual men in their solitude, so far as they apprehend themselves to stand in relation to whatever they may consider the divine.*" He admitted that this definition omitted "theologies, philosophies, and ecclesiastical organizations," which he considered of secondary importance. Theology, in his opinion, grew out of and depended on personal experiences. "The truth is that in the metaphysical and religious sphere, articulate reasons are cogent for us only when our inarticulate feelings of reality have already been impressed in favor of the same conclusion." James based his study on the presumption that religion was not best understood as a set of theological doctrines.[44]

Other practitioners of the new science shared James's view of the relationship of religion and theology. In 1904 Starbuck noted that "intellectualism in religion has been almost entirely discredited in recent years. Among the empiricists in the study of religion, there is not one, so far as I know, who is able to find that the intellectual, ideational, rational, cognitive processes perform more than a mere by-play in the drama of the personal life." Five years later Jean Ellen Harrison, in an essay evaluating the progress of the study of religion since Darwin, reiterated this position. "The ultimate and unchallenged presupposition of the old view was that religion was a *doctrine,* a body of supposed truth. It was in fact what we should now call Theology." The new science of religion rejected this view as "a profound error or rather a most misleading half-truth. Creeds, doctrines, theology, and the like are only a part, and at first the least important part, of religion." The science of religion dismissed theology as a relatively unimportant part of religious life.[45]

Scholars promoting the scientific study of religion hoped to show that religion could persist in a culture dedicated to scientific inquiry. Starbuck confided privately that he hoped his studies of religion would "work toward making religion as large as life again." James, in his preface to Starbuck's *Psychology of Religion,* wrote that "rightly interpreted, the whole tendency of Dr Starbuck's patient labour is to bring compromise and conciliation into the long standing feud of Science and Religion." About his own work on religion, James confessed that he hoped "to make the hearer or reader believe, what I myself invincibly do believe, that, although the special manifestations of religion may have been absurd (I mean its creeds and theories), yet the life of it as a whole is mankind's most important function." Most of the American practitioners of the new science of religion hoped that they could save religion from discredited theologies.[46]

Researchers emphasized the constructive aspect of the new science. Morris Jastrow, Jr., of the University of Pennsylvania, wrote:

> If the progress that the science of religion has made during the past two or three decades brings out one fact clearer than any other, it is that any fears as to the possible detrimental influences of the study of religion as it exists to-day, are idle and without any reasonable foundation. The historical study of religion serves

as a powerful illustration, nay, may truly be said to furnish *the* most powerful illustration for the permanency of religion as a factor in human life, both of the individual and the species.

Instead of undermining religious faith, he expected the science of religion to demonstrate the enduring value of religion.[47]

Ames made similar claims for the psychology of religion. "The final realm of scientific study has been the inquiry into the psychology of religion, a searching quest into human nature itself to discover, if possible, the inner sources of religious attitudes and behavior. . . . It turns out that science, on its own method and in its own terms, discovers the reality of religion as a vital and universal aspect of human life." The science of religion established that religion should survive even after scientific ideas had displaced basic theological tenets.[48]

Academics studying religion began with the presumption that theological doctrine was of secondary importance, so they sought to determine the primary character of religion. In approaching this problem, they began with the post-Darwinian premise that all mental life was adaptive and purposeful. "In the sphere of religion," James Leuba explained, "this doctrine means not only that every pulse of religious life includes ideas and feelings but also that it finds its objective expression in action." These actions served to further the survival of the individual and the species. Intellectuals sought to determine the true nature of religion by uncovering its particular evolutionary role. Scientific studies defined religion in terms of its social and psychological function.[49]

William James's *Varieties of Religious Experience,* the most influential work in the psychology of religion, illustrates this functional approach. James began by criticizing traditional definitions of religion. He thought that religion was too diverse and too vague to be defined by "any single principle or essence." "Let us not fall immediately into a one-sided view of the subject," he wrote, "but let us rather admit freely at the outset that we may very likely find no one essence, but many characters which may alternately be equally important in religion." Instead of defining religion, James proposed to examine what religion does. He sought to uncover the underlying significance of being religious.[50]

James found that religious people had a certain kind of attitude about their lives and the world. They faced life and its demands with a seriousness and enthusiasm absent in others. This attitude, James believed, made "a tremendous emotional and practical difference." "For when all is said and done, we are in the end absolutely dependent on the universe," so that to survive we must make "sacrifices and surrenders of some sort." For the nonreligious, "the surrender is submitted to as an imposition of necessity, and the sacrifice is undergone at the very best without complaint." But for the religious, James observed, "surrender and sacrifice are positively espoused: even unnecessary givings-up are added in order that the happiness may increase." Religious belief apparently made it easier for people to adjust to their environment. *"Religion thus makes easy and felicitous what in any case is necessary;* and if it be the only agency that can accomplish this result, its vital importance as a human faculty stands vindicated beyond dispute." From an evolutionary standpoint, religion helped people psychologically adjust to the world's objective demands.[51]

Although James emphasized the psychological value of religion, he thought it served a social purpose as well. He examined the social benefits of religion in his chapters on "the value of saintliness." He applied evolutionary standards to determine the social value of saints, in an attempt to "test saintliness by common sense, to use human standards to help us decide how far the religious life commends itself as an ideal kind of human activity." This method, he explained, "is but the elimination of the humanly unfit, and the survival of the humanly fittest, applied to religious beliefs." He concluded that "economically, the saintly group of qualities is indispensable to the world's welfare. The great saints are immediate successes; the smaller ones are at least heralds and harbingers, and they may be leavens also, of a better mundane order." Religion, James concluded, is essential both for the individual's survival and for the improvement and development of society.[52]

Other intellectuals studying religion agreed with James on the evolutionary value of religion, although they sometimes offered different appraisals of religion's most important function. Coe, for example, stressed the social role of religion rather than its psychological returns. He identified religion with "sociality" and argued that religion is the prime force in the development of a more ethical society. Religion, he wrote, "refuses to take human nature as static datum eternally resistant to social ideas, but insists upon the possibility of fundamental changes, and sets us the task of building a new race, a regenerate race!" Despite differences of emphasis, the two men agreed that religion served vital functions, both in personal growth and in moral inspiration.[53]

The new science of religion fulfilled most of the promises of its advocates in regard to the reconciliation of religion and science. Their positive depictions of the social and psychological values of religion were consistent with the reigning liberal Protestantism. They quelled doubts about the obsolescence of religion in modern society by demonstrating that it filled essential human needs. They showed that scientific methods could be used to study religion. But these studies still did not succeed in reintegrating religion into modern intellectual life. Scholars could not build a bridge from the functional importance of religion to the truth of even the most basic religious belief: the existence of a supernatural being. In the end, the antitheological stance of these studies widened the gulf between the intellectual and the devotional.

James made the most sophisticated attempt to join the functional analysis of religion with a scientific evaluation of religious beliefs. Despite his antitheological bias, James recognized that he could not completely discount religious doctrines. "We are thinking beings, and we cannot exclude the intellect from participating in any of our functions. . . . Conceptions and constructions are thus a necessary part of our religion." Furthermore, he realized that not all of his readers would be satisfied with a functional explanation of religion. "How, you say, can religion, which believes in two worlds and an invisible order, be estimated by the adaption of its fruits to this world's order alone? It is its *truth,* not its utility, you insist, upon which our verdict ought to depend." Hence, James proposed to test the extent to which the science of religion could corroborate the content of religious beliefs.[54]

To explore whether "the sense of divine presence [is] a sense of anything objectively true," James examined mystical experiences. During these experiences, people feel directly connected to the supernatural realm. James thought that mysticism might provide adequate proof of a supernatural realm. But after scrutinizing mystical experiences and efforts to erect a theistic philosophy from these episodes, he sadly concluded that "the attempt to demonstrate by purely intellectual processes the truth of the deliverance of direct religious experience is absolutely hopeless." Mystical states were too personal and too idiosyncratic to be "authoritative" for anyone but "the individuals to whom they come."[55]

The only general conclusion that James could draw was that "rationalistic consciousness, based upon the understanding and the senses alone" is not the only "kind of consciousness." Mystical experiences "open out the possibility of other orders of truth, in which, so far as anything in us vitally responds to them, we may freely continue to have faith." The "subconscious" identified by modern psychologists could explain these nonrational mental states. Or, James proposed, perhaps people actually communicate with supernatural beings through their subconscious. This last hypothesis, he emphasized, is an "overbelief," that is, a personal conjecture that is not scientifically provable.[56]

Despite his own desires, James concluded that the science of religion could not demonstrate the existence of a superhuman order. Still, he thought that the scientific study of religion—of which he wrote figuratively in the feminine gender—might help with the modern reconstruction of religious doctrine. "An impartial science of religions might sift out from the midst of their discrepancies a common body of doctrine which she might also formulate in terms to which physical science need not object. This," he wrote, "she might adopt as her own reconciling hypothesis, and recommend it for general belief." James recognized that this was a modest proposition—a far cry from the definite scientific proof of a personal God for which some of his contemporaries might have hoped. Nonetheless, he offered it as a means of integrating religious beliefs into modern thought.[57]

The influential part of James's work was his bold analysis of the psychological value of religion; his tentative conclusions about the supernatural had little impact on the scientific study of religion. Other intellectuals studying religion did not bother to try to evaluate the validity of religious beliefs. After a religion's evolutionary importance had been affirmed, the content of religious doctrines seemed insignificant. Most psychologists simply excluded questions about the existence of God. "To describe the workings of the human mind so far as these are influenced by its attitude toward the Determiner of Destiny," James Pratt explained, "is the task of the psychology of religion. As its name implies, it means to be psychology—that is, it means to be a science. Human experience is the subject of its investigation. It aims at nothing metaphysical or transcendental." Questions about the existence and nature of God remained outside the realm of the psychology of religion.[58]

Faculty studying other branches of the science of religion agreed that the supernatural was outside the realm of scientific investigation. Morris Jastrow, Jr., wrote that comparative religion must omit "all such factors as special dispensation and miraculous intervention. Not that the historical attitude involves disbelief in a supernatural order, but it protests against the encroachment of this order into a foreign domain. Unless human history is to be explained by a thorough study of causes and results, and by an exclusive regard to human conditions, no explanation in the real sense of the word is possible." Ephraim Emerton, a professor of church history at Harvard, agreed; scientific methods of history could not determine divine providence and, therefore, must eliminate supernatural elements from historical accounts. "The superhuman," he wrote, "is not a subject for the historical record. The *belief* in the superhuman . . . because a fact of human experience, has its historical record that can be studied historically." Ironically, the scientific study of religion, which was originally conceived as a positive alternative to agnostism, concluded that questions about the supernatural were outside the realm of human knowledge.[59]

Biblical criticism developed in parallel fashion during the same period; its emphasis changed from validating the Bible through factual study to elucidating the text's "poetic" character and psychological value. Biblical criticism had its roots in theological apologetics. American scholars, influenced by Germans, undertook critical studies of the Bible in the beginning of the nineteenth century. These early studies emerged in the context of theological disputes between New England Congregationalists and Unitarians. Scholars such as Moses Stuart used critical studies to demonstrate that the authority of the Bible supported their church's doctrinal positions and/or discredited those of their competitors.[60]

In the late nineteenth century biblical scholarship in the United States grew rapidly, while its relationship to doctrinal issues became more complicated. Disputes about theological doctrine became intertwined with, and overshadowed by, questions about appropriate scholarly methods and attitudes about "inerrancy" of the Bible. The debate between Calvinists and liberals merged into a conflict over "conservative" biblical studies and "higher criticism" of the Bible. Calvinists, led by the Princeton theologians Charles Hodge and Francis L. Patton, promoted a "conservative" model of biblical criticism, based on the Baconian conception of inductive science. The "higher critics" borrowed heavily from German scholars and adopted progressivist views of science.[61]

The conservatives used inductive studies to try to demonstrate the authenticity and integrity of the Scriptures. At the same time, they analyzed works of higher criticism that challenged traditional beliefs about the authorship of the Bible and its historical veracity to show that the work was based on unproven assumptions and faulty methods of scholarship. Like opponents of evolutionary theory, conservatives used the Baconian model of science to discredit higher criticism as unscientific because it relied on unproven hypotheses rather than factual observation. Since they thought that Christianity was based on the belief that the Bible was the word of God, and that this belief would be undermined if the Bible were untrue, they viewed their own critical studies as an essential defense of Christianity and higher criticism as a threat to it.[62]

Liberals, on the other hand, accepted the validity of the progressivist conception of science. They argued that scientific criticism must be "broad and open." They defended the use of hypotheses and maintained that the rejection of older interpretations of the Bible in favor of new theories represented the progress of knowledge and religion. Although they regretted the skeptical tone of some of the European criticism, higher critics thought that their biblical scholarship served the cause of Christianity. Liberal biblical scholars, such as William Rainey Harper, sought to unite intellectual and devotional approaches to the Scriptures. Conservatives, Harper charged, were "narrow and dogmatic"; they sacrificed the intellectual aspects of the Bible by refusing to accept the findings of scientific scholarship.[63]

Liberal critics believed that an accurate knowledge of the Scriptures was essential to the Christian faith. They maintained that the best way to acquire an accurate understanding of the Bible was through historical research. Joseph Henry Thayer, a New Testament scholar at Harvard University, explained that historical scholarship "looks at the Biblical books in their original relations; strives to ascertain and take into account the particulars relative to time, place, person, which called them forth, and shaped them." They thought that historical and philological scholarship would uncover how and when the Scriptures were written and help identify inaccuracies and inconsistencies in the text.[64]

Liberals maintained that the existence of errors in the Bible did not invalidate it as "the word of God." They argued that the Scriptures were written by imperfect humans, who were nonetheless inspired by God. "Let us proclaim," wrote Harper, ". . . the divine origin and character of the Bible. Yet, on the other hand, let us recognize that it has also a human origin." Biblical critics studied the human origins of Scripture. In the process critics tested, and sometimes invalidated, traditional religious beliefs. Although this process might seem initially harmful to religion, liberal scholars thought that it would yield new beliefs "which will prove far more satisfactory than any tradition based upon the supposed dogmatic necessity." By identifying problems in the text, they "purified" the Bible, helping expose its divine core.[65]

In addition to providing a more accurate knowledge of the Bible, liberals thought that historical research would help efforts to reconstruct religion. They thought that if they demonstrated that some biblical views had developed in response to particular sociological conditions, they could, if those conditions were no longer relevant, dismiss those views as irrelevant to modern Christianity. Hence, aspects of the Scriptures that seemed repugnant to modern Americans could be explained away through historical scholarship. Higher critics also thought that scholarship would expose the process of religious evolution, allowing modern believers to identify with only the "highest" aspects of Christianity and helping them contribute to its progressive development.[66]

In the late nineteenth century advocates of higher criticism established themselves in the new research universities and their nondenominational divinity schools. Their acceptance of progressivist models of science and their commitment to the reconstruction of religion placed them, rather than the conservative critics, in the mainstream of university reform and scientific study. In this context, biblical scholars defined their research as separate from denominational debates about doctrine. Instead, they saw their work as a way to integrate religion into the intellectual life of modern society. Like their colleagues in other branches of the science of religion, they hoped that, ultimately, their scholarship would unite devotional and scientific concerns.[67]

By the early twentieth century, however, some biblical scholars had begun to tacitly accept the separation between the intellectual and spiritual. Frank C. Porter's presidential address of 1908 before the Society of Biblical Literature reflected this change. Porter, a Yale professor, explored the relationship between higher criticism and religious faith. He began by noting an inverse relationship between scientific knowledge of the Bible and popular appreciation. "The Bible is better understood by scholars today than ever before, but it seems to be at the same time less generally used and less enjoyed." Porter wanted to know whether "scientific study" of the Scriptures "stimulates or dulls the sense of their poetic beauty or spiritual value." Porter acknowledged that higher criticism, whatever the intent of its practitioners, might inhibit religious faith rather than encourage it.[68]

In addressing this problem, Porter first reiterated the standard position of his generation of biblical scholars: scientific scholarship is helpful to religious faith. But in analyzing how scholarship contributes to faith, Porter admitted that the spiritual value of the Bible rested in its emotional power rather than its factual content. The parts of the Bible with the most "religious use" are "meant to be enjoyed rather than give information, to inspire rather than instruct." Scholarship does not "improve" the religious value of these passages. Indeed, scholars had to overcome the bias of their "scientific training and habit of thought," which taught them that "the world of facts and ideas imposes itself upon us as a thing of greater reality than the world of imagination and feeling." Biblical critics had to recognize that "poetic truth has no less validity and much more value than historic fact" and "to admit that to enjoy a book is a greater thing than to understand it." Although Porter wanted to avoid the separation of the "scientific study" and "religious use" of the Bible, his own analysis pointed toward the opposite conclusion: scientific knowledge had little spiritual value.[69]

In 1908 Porter hesitatingly articulated a position that was becoming accepted among more American biblical scholars: the Bible was a work of literature and the "truths" contained within it were "poetical" rather "scientific" and "factual." Factual truth uncovered through scientific study did not validate the "spiritual" truths of religion or uncover a "purified" divine message. Academics increasingly referred to the Bible as literature. Richard Green Moulton, of the University of Chicago, was one of the leading advocates of the literary study of the Bible. He believed that the form of the Bible, its numbered chapters and verses, mistakenly led people to view it as a work of philosophy or history. He maintained, on the contrary, that the Bible was a work, or a series of works, of literature. He believed that literature contained "wisdom"—"the devout contemplation of life, as distinguished from analysis"—that yielded factual and rational knowledge. In Moulton's view, such "wisdom" was "truer" than factual knowledge. The Bible was "great" literature because of the force of its wisdom, but it was not qualitatively different from other pieces of literature.[70]

By the early twentieth century many liberal American biblical critics conceded that divine truths were not susceptible of scientific study. The spiritual message was contained in the Bible's poetry, not its history. Historical study, although it increased knowledge about the Scriptures, did not serve devotional purposes. They articulated a new "mythopoetic" interpretation of the Bible, attributing its value to the feelings it evoked rather than to the literal meaning of the words. When explicitly addressing the issue of the truth of religious beliefs, the new scholars of religion said that they were not making any judgment. "I conceive it to be wholly aside from my duty," stated Emerton, "to consider the truth or falsehood of any doctrine, orthodox, or heterodox." But the implicit message of the scientific study of religion was that the intellectual content of religion was unimportant; it did not matter whether doctrine was true or false. What made people religious was what they felt and did, not what they thought.[71]

Scientific studies did not repair religion's intellectual reputation. Morris Jastrow wrote,

The hands on the clock of time cannot be turned backward, and it is idle therefore to look forward to a period when religion shall again become the mainspring of intellectual and material progress. Nor is such a condition to be desired. The true sphere of religion lies elsewhere. Its province is not the investigation of scientific problems, nor the creation of new arts, but the directing of human life into proper channels, and serving as a beacon light illuminating the path of mankind towards its goal, whatever we may conceive that goal to be.

It was clear, though, that for Jastrow science determined this "goal," while religion only inspired humans to strive for it.[72]

The message that emerged from scientific studies of religion was that religion had no intellectual content. The psychology of religion and other kinds of social-scientific studies maintained that religion had an inspirational rather than an intellectual role. Biblical studies emphasized the poetic rather than the factual "truth" of Christian beliefs. Rather than unifying religion and science, these studies relegated them to different areas of life: science to the intellectual and religion to the inspirational. Although they affirmed the permanence and importance of religion, at the same time they reduced it to a psychologically and socially useful fiction. The scientific study of religion did not restore its place in the intellectual life of the nation.

Not only did studies of religion fail to serve as a basis for an effective, modern religious education, but universities that tried to build major programs in religious studies were plagued by student indifference. Yale's experience illustrates the problems universities faced in trying to build programs in religious studies. Soon after Arthur T. Hadley became president of Yale, Frank Sanders began lobbying him for more support for the biblical literature department. "It has seemed to me that we have a unique opportunity here at Yale for developing a school of Biblical research to which there will not be a superior in the country," he wrote to Hadley. Sanders thought that he could achieve "remarkable results" by unifying the work of instructors in the divinity school and the university, and by hiring a couple of new professors. Hadley approved of Sanders's plan. "There is no department which is more fundamentally important than yours, and we ought to omit no efforts to give it the advantages it deserves," he wrote, assuring Sanders of his help. University administrators like Hadley wanted their institutions to offer religious education and supported faculty who promised viable "scientific" programs of study.[73]

When Sanders left his chair in the university to become dean of the divinity school, he wanted to be replaced by "a first class, all round Biblical Literature man," rather than a narrow specialist. He strongly advocated hiring Charles Kent, then a professor of biblical literature at Brown University, because he believed Kent's personality would attract undergraduates. Kent was hired, but his courses did not draw many students. When Hadley refused to give Kent a raise because of his low student enrollment, Sanders became defensive. Sanders maintained that it was not Kent's fault that his classes were unpopular. He said that students did not take the classes because they did not understand the scientific nature of the courses and that Kent had no opportunity to distinguish his classes from the traditional, didactic Bible study. "In relation to the academical men he still has his place to fully make," Sanders explained. "This takes time and experience. Under our prevailing system the Biblical Department is very badly handicapped, because there is no opportunity of putting the *real* aims, methods and course of the Department before the students at the psychologically appropriate time."[74]

Other universities had similar problems drawing students. The University of Chicago planned an ambitious program in religious studies, based on the departments of biblical literature and comparative religion that Harper had moved from the divinity school to the university. Harper envisioned a variety of courses taught at different levels and appealing to different kinds of students. For example, the department of biblical and patristic Greek offered elementary courses for "students preparing for the ministry," who did "not have the time to fully develop original interpretations of the New Testament." In keeping with Harper's desire to foster biblical scholarship, the department also taught advanced courses. "It is earnestly hoped, moreover, and confidently expected," the university bulletin read, "that there will be those who desire to become in a larger sense independent New Testament Scholars. It is with a view to serving efficiently this latter class . . . that a large range of elective studies is provided."[75]

The courses in the departments of Semitic language and literature, biblical and patristic Greek, and comparative religion never attracted many university students. One instructor wrote Harper complaining that divinity students were not required to take the courses offered by the department of comparative religion. "The numbers outside of the theological students who will take these courses are exceedingly few," the instructor explained. The department needed divinity students to survive. Because of low student interest, these departments never effectively separated from the divinity school.[76]

Some departments originally devoted to religious studies gradually lost their religious orientation when students did not enroll in the classes. For example, at the University of Chicago, the department of biblical literature in English, which was originally designed to attract nonspecialists, particularly undergraduates, to biblical studies was converted into the department of literature in English in the academic year 1897–98. The study of other classical literature as well as some literary criticism was added to its curriculum. The department, however, still retained a special place for the study of the Bible. One of its stated purposes was to give "persons who may not be special students of languages opportunity for extending their knowledge of literature as a subject of universal interest in liberal education." The department's introductory statement went on to note that "this consideration has special application to the Sacred Literature of the Old and New Testament." The new department intended to "carry on work hitherto done by the Department of Biblical Literature." The new department was more popular than the original one but still much less popular than such departments as English, history, or sociology. In 1903 the department was reorganized again as the department of general literature; its courses combined great works, comparative literature, and literary criticism. Biblical literature was still included but made up a smaller part of the curriculum. The department's courses were open to upper-division undergraduates and graduate students. The only concession to the original purpose of encouraging biblical studies was that freshmen and sophomores could take courses on the Bible, but not the other courses offered by the department.[77]

Lack of student interest also shifted the focus of the Semitics department at the University of California away from its original interest in biblical literature. The Semitics department was founded in 1894, with a local rabbi volunteering instruction in Hebrew and biblical criticism. By 1900 the department was well established. The original "honorary instructor" and another associate professor taught courses in Hebrew, biblical archaeology, Old and New Testament criticism, Jewish literature, Aramaic, and Assyrian. The department's courses, however, were not very popular. In 1899–1900, out of twenty-eight departments, the Semitics department was twenty-seventh in terms of student registration.[78]

In 1904 the head of the Semitics department left Berkeley for another institution. The university took advantage of his departure to change the focus of the department by promoting an instructor whose specialty was Arabic. Under the new administration, the department endeavored "to give the Arabic a place of at least equal importance with Hebrew." This change was "demanded by the intrinsic value of Arabic philology and Arabic literature, by the fact that it is still the spoken language of millions of people and the literary and religious language of millions more, and by the fact that Mohammedanism is a decisive factor in many of the world's great political and economic problems of to-day." The department supplemented its original biblical courses with new nonreligious classes, such as commercial Arabic.[79]

Some professors of religion responded to lack of student interest by denying the devotional aspect of their courses. Moulton, the primary instructor of biblical Literature in English at the University of Chicago, tried to improve his credibility by distancing himself from religion. When Harper asked him to speak at a student vesper service, Moulton declined. Although he was "anxious . . . to use every opportunity of speaking before the members of the university on biblical literature," he explained, "I desire to avoid delivering in public addresses of distinctively devotional or religious character." Moulton did not want students to associate his teaching with preaching. This was a growing concern among biblical professors. A survey of the needs of biblical departments, conducted in 1915, emphasized that "the department must be placed on a basis which is absolutely independent of all specialized religious activities of the college." Educators originally promoted the scientific study of religion because it would serve both intellectual and spiritual concerns. Ironically, the faculty teaching these courses felt that they had to dissociate themselves from religious activities in order to maintain their credibility among students.[80]

The absurdity of attempting to draw students to courses on religion by denying their religious content was apparent in a poll conducted in 1911 by a professor at the University of Pennsylvania. He drew up a list of topics for a class in biblical literature. The topics, such as "Man's Place in the World—The Story of Creation" or "The Things That Shape a Nation's Character," deemphasized the Bible in favor of "social" and "scientific" themes. The instructor asked the students if they thought the title was "catchy," if it would "attract the average student" to a Bible class, and if the student would "be likely to attend the class again when he discovered the real meaning of these topics." He wanted to know if students would be more interested in studying biblical themes if they did not know that they were from the Bible.[81]

The instructor discovered that the "the most favorable topic omits any biblical reference, and the least favorable one is expressed in definite religious terms." He concluded that the results "show a most decided trend of liking away from the personally religious to the broader and more scientific interests of modern days." The professor was not discouraged by these findings; he still believed that students would be interested in biblical studies if they were taught from a modern perspective. He seemed unaware of the contradiction involved in trying to lure students to classes that were originally designed to increase students' respect for religion, by concealing their religious content.[82]

Unlike the instructor, some of the students polled recognized the futility of attracting students to Bible classes with nonbiblical discussion topics. When asked if the student would be likely to continue to attend the class "when he discovered the real meaning of these topics," one student replied simply, "No. The real meaning should be presented first." Another reportedly said the topics were "not catchy but *deceitful.*" Others said they would stay in the class if the topics "were discussed in the way their headings indicate." Clearly, these students did not want to take classes with a hidden religious purpose.[83]

Faculty's assumption that students avoided classes because of their devotional intent created a division between educators who wanted religious studies to renounce all constructive spiritual purposes and those who wanted to make them more explicitly devotional. Educators who were particularly concerned about the religious lives of students began to question the assumption that the academic study of religion would be inherently religious. One educator wrote that

> critical courses in the Bible might be anything but religious. An emphasis on facts and dates and construction may give valuable information, but it does not necessarily give the religious impulse. . . . It is possible to study the Bible as literature and get little religious value from the experience. The same results might be secured from the study of any other literature, and the scientific method might be secured from any of the sciences.[84]

These educators concluded that true religious education must be explicitly, not indirectly, devotional and began to advocate more explicitly devotional classes. Even Harper, the tireless promoter of the scientific study of religion, turned to explicitly devotional classes when his plans for the scholarly study of religion languished. In 1897 he announced a new experiment: Sunday-morning Bible classes taught by members of the divinity school. He thought that these classes should be demanding enough to deserve university credit, but that the spiritual purpose should be manifest.

> It might be possible for such work to be conducted with no more a religious spirit and with no more spiritual profit than a course in trigonometry, but such is not the purpose of the course proposed. The work is undertaken with the single thought in mind, to enable the students to know God in his dealings with man as illustrated in the history of the chosen people and in the peculiar events connected with the life and times of Jesus Christ.

If scientific methods did not lure students to classes on the Bible, Harper was willing to try to attract them by offering credit for more traditional Sunday-school classes.[85]

By offering credit for the Sunday-morning classes, Harper attempted to keep religious education at least marginally within the university curriculum. Most other university educators interested in students' religious lives turned their attentions away from the standard curriculum. Harrison Elliot, then of the International Committee of the Young Men's Christian Association, recognized that the "attempt to make a curriculum class deal with this personal [religious] message at once endangers its academic standing." But he believed that universities should not simply ignore students' spiritual development. He pointed out that regular university courses could be supplemented by extracurricular classes, which would address the question, "What does the Bible mean to me?" At many research universities, classes offered by the YMCA and other student organizations became the primary source of religious education.[86]

By the 1920s many educators accepted that courses related to religion would not become a new, more effective form of religious education. Without this motivation, scholars lost interest in the science of religion. The scientific study of religion, declined rapidly in the 1920s. Educators increasingly relied on extracurricular activities to serve students' religious needs. In so doing, they reinforced the functional differentiation of religion and science that emerged from the scientific study of religion. By depending on extracurricular activities for devotional education, university officials created an institutional arrangement that cemented the separation of the intellectual and the devotional.[87]

University reformers did not intend to create a sharp divide between courses on religion and extracurricular religious activities. They thought religious activities should be integrated into the intellectual life of the university and should reflect the institution's commitment to openness and freedom. Attempts to design modern religious activities paralleled university reformers' efforts to reconstruct religious beliefs through the scientific study of religion. Ironically, as universities came to rely more heavily on extracurricular activities as the basis of campus religious life, they also retreated from their efforts to create a modern form of religion and allowed students to pursue whatever kinds of religious activities they desired.

While university reformers were encouraging the development of new courses in the science of religion, they were also modifying their institutions' religious activities to make them consistent with the values of open inquiry. Advocates of religious reform focused much of their attention on chapel services. Over the last decades of the nineteenth century the most controversial change was the introduction of voluntary rather than compulsory chapel. State universities generally led the movement toward voluntary chapel. The University of Michigan experimented with voluntary prayers in 1871. Initially, President Angell was skeptical about the reform. He wrote his father-in-law in February 1872, "we are still continuing the experiment of voluntary attendance at prayers, and though I keep expecting it will fail, it does not yet." The experiment coincided with a religious awakening at the university and with significant improvement in students' behavior at chapel. Consequently, Angell deemed the experiment a success and made voluntary chapel a permanent policy of the university.[88]

Universities that had developed from denominational colleges, such as Harvard and Columbia, found it more difficult to abandon the tradition of obligatory chapel. Charles Eliot considered abolishing compulsory prayers soon after he became president of Harvard in 1869, but was strongly discouraged from raising the issue. In 1871–72, prayers were suspended for five months while the campus chapel was being renovated. When there was no noticeable increase in student misconduct, Eliot proposed to the board of overseers that chapel become voluntary. The board, however, rejected the suggestion. At Columbia, President Barnard made a similar suggestion in his 1874–75 annual report. He discussed the many practical problems associated with compulsory chapel, such as difficulty in enforcing attendance, student rowdiness at services, and problems accommodating the growing numbers of students. Despite Barnard's report, the board of trustees at Columbia did not institute voluntary prayers. Practical problems alone did not convince governing boards to abandon compulsory prayers.[89]

The association of voluntary prayers with the ideals of freedom and openness finally provided the needed impetus to institute optional chapel. George Palmer, who had articulated the view that electives were intellectually and morally superior to required courses because they allowed students to exercise free choice, applied similar arguments in favor of voluntary chapel. When Charles Eliot asked Palmer to lead summer chapel services in 1882, he refused. He said that he enjoyed "taking morning prayers" with the students and would like to lead them, but he would do so only if they were voluntary. "I will gladly be [the leader] so soon as our governing board will treat religion as a matter capable of interesting a man who is not forced. At present, methods discarded in the secular sphere as unserviceable because having no solid roots in character are still reckoned good enough for religion." Palmer thought that the adoption of electives, but not of voluntary prayers, indicated a greater commitment to students' intellectual development than to their spiritual growth. Compulsory chapel "is not respectful," Palmer wrote, "and would not I think be persisted in if our aim in religious training were as single as it is intellectual." Palmer maintained that free election, in both religion and course work, developed students' minds and wills.[90]

Instead of viewing required daily chapel as a sign of a school's commitment to religion, educators began to present compulsory prayers as an insult to religion and a barrier to true spiritual development. "The college," wrote David Starr Jordan, "will not make young men religious by enforced attendance at church or prayer meeting. It will not awaken the spiritual element in students' nature by any system of demerit marks." Charles Henderson of the University of Chicago agreed. "Since a free and sincere conviction is of the essence of a real religious faith, and compulsion in all its forms is essentially futile and immoral, absolute freedom of thought and expression is guaranteed [to students in the university]. This liberty cannot rightfully be construed as a sign of indifference or undervaluation of the Christian religion by the governing bodies." Advocates of religious reform thought that freedom developed "a more manly and efficient type of religious character on the part of the students, the result of self-control and deliberate choice." They maintained that efforts to compel religious observance betrayed doubt about the power of religion.[91]

Governing boards responded sympathetically to appeals for voluntary prayers that emphasized their benefit to religion and their relationship to larger university ideals. In 1886 Francis G. Peabody, who had recently been placed in charge of college chapel services at Harvard, used these arguments to secure the approval of the board of overseers for voluntary prayers. The trustees of Columbia followed suit in 1891 when the university's chaplain retired. Johns Hopkins, Stanford, and the University of Chicago all opened with optional religious services.[92]

University officials were optimistic about voluntary religious services. Seth Low of Columbia announced soon after the introduction of voluntary chapel that "the change thus effected has justified the hopes of those who favored it . . . the service was devout and hearty. The attendance, also, was more representative than before of the university as a whole." Shortly after the University of Chicago opened, Harper reported that chapel services, "though voluntary, are well attended, the room being practically filled and some days many being compelled to stand." Ernest D. Burton, professor of New Testament Greek, described them as "characterized by reverence and genuine religious feeling." Educators asserted that students were responding to religious appeals that were "vital rather than perfunctory."[93]

Voluntary chapel reflected the university's allegiance to freedom and its commitment to an anti-authoritarian religious life. The religious service itself was also altered to establish open and nondogmatic religious practices. David C. Gardner reported on Stanford's efforts "to bring a modern, vital religious method to the student body" at the Pacific Coast Conference of the Religious Education Association. He emphasized Stanford's innovative chapel service. "In our college church," he said, "we have no traditions, we say no creed, we use no liturgy. There is no social unification, and no obligation to support the cause." In addition to being voluntary, revamped chapel at universities was to be free from the constraints of orthodox creeds and rituals.[94]

University officials at some institutions experimented with their chapel services to make them genuinely nondenominational and attractive to students. One of the most common innovations was a program of visiting ministers. Instead of having the president or chaplain officiate at all services, schools invited ministers from a variety of denominations and churches. In 1881 Harvard instituted the practice of hiring five ministers from different churches. Eliot considered innovations in chapel services to be an essential part of university reform. "There is no more characteristic feature of Harvard University than the conduct of its religious services. It expresses its liberality as regards opinions, its devotion to ideals, and the preciousness in its sight of individual liberty," Eliot wrote shortly before he retired.[95]

Other universities instituted systems of rotating ministers from various denominations. David Gardner invited Unitarian, Episcopalian, Congregationalist, Baptist, and Presbyterian ministers, as well as a local rabbi, to lead services in the Stanford church. The University of California asked leading liberal Christians and ministers from a variety of local churches to speak to its students. At the University of Michigan, student guilds representing a variety of churches arranged for speakers from their denominations. Yale, Columbia, and the University of Chicago invited guest ministers and had faculty members take turns leading chapel services.[96]

University officials wanted students to hear representatives from different denominations, but they did not encourage these speakers to discuss the distinctive theological positions of their denominations. They wanted religious services to be "simple, direct, and manly." The purpose of a university chapel service was to present the "Christian religion and Christian morals in the broadest and most fundamental sense of those terms." Chapel should be "as broad and tolerant as the spirit of the University." By inviting guest ministers, university officials hoped to emphasize "fundamental truths in regard to which all Christians unite," rather than to highlight denominational differences.[97]

Universities also shortened chapel services and replaced sermons with simple prayers and songs, in order to reduce the doctrinal component of chapel services. "In music and prayer . . . the mind is at work in a region which is no longer the region of pure thought; it is much nearer the springs of feeling and action, where no expression is adequate and hence all expression takes the tynge of symbol." Universities paid particular attention to music. The University of Michigan published its own hymn book, "in an effort to make a Hymn and Tune Book suitable for undenominational schools and colleges, and accurate as regards both the words and music." Harvard improved the music at its chapel services by instituting a boys' choir. "The Choir, made up of University students and Cambridge school boys," Eliot reported, "has undoubtedly helped to maintain and increase the general interest in the Chapel services." By the time Eliot retired, Harvard was spending $4,000 a year on chapel music, more than the average faculty member's salary.[98]

In addition to voluntary chapel services, university reformers encouraged a wide range of extracurricular religious activities and organizations. The chaplain or a faculty member frequently served as adviser for these student groups. Some universities formed umbrella organizations, such as University of Chicago's Christian Union and Harvard's Phillips Brooks House Association, to stimulate and coordinate the activities of student religious groups. University officials viewed these groups as evidence of the success of religious reform. They felt that students voluntarily participating in religious activities proved that a vital religious life was possible without coercion.[99]

Harvard, Yale, Columbia, Johns Hopkins, University of Michigan, and University of Chicago all had buildings to house the student religious groups. University officials emphasized the symbolic importance of such buildings. President Dwight, at the inauguration of Yale's Dwight Hall, spoke of the significance of a building devoted to religious purposes. He predicted that the building would influence "the inmost life of hundreds of young men."

> We do not learn our lessons or grow in our minds and thoughts from books only. The silent teachings of what we see enter often more deeply into our souls by reason of their very silence. We can resist or contradict the teacher who speaks with a living voice, but the power of art or architecture is almost like the power of another's life which manifests itself in our presence; it steals in upon us so gently and with so little of self-assertion or opposition, that we yield to it almost before we are aware.

The very presence of the building, Dwight thought, would turn students' attention to religion.[100]

Educators believed that buildings communicated the university's values. The message might be explicitly written, as in the inscription above the entrance of Columbia's Earl Hall: "erected for the students that religion and learning may go hand and hand and character grow with knowledge." But buildings did not need words; their existence and style revealed much about the priorities of an institution. A building used only for religious functions "by its place among others and by its quality shall worthily symbolize the place of religion in the mental life of the university."[101]

For this reason, several universities also built impressive chapels during this period. Columbia, for example, had conducted daily chapel services for over a century in buildings used for academic as well as religious purposes. Beginning in 1895, President Low began to make appeals in his annual report for money to build a separate chapel. While Low praised the university for maintaining "chapel services without interruption, even under the unfriendly conditions described," he thought that "the testimony to the religious life will be more unequivocal when its chapel services are held in a suitable building wholly consecrated to the purpose."[102]

In 1903 Low's pleas finally resulted in an anonymous donation of $200,000 "for the erection of a University chapel." When the building was completed in 1906, President Butler praised its "dignity, appropriateness, and great beauty." The building had "already made a deep impression both within and without the University," he wrote. "Now that a splendid building is provided for religious worship," Butler predicted that chapel service would "be a far more important factor in the daily life of the University than ever before." Butler considered the new chapel a potent expression of the importance of religion at Columbia.[103]

John D. Rockefeller, in his gift for the University of Chicago, expressed this faith in the symbolic importance of buildings: "As the spirit of religion should penetrate and control the University," he wrote, "so that building which represents religion ought to be the central and dominant feature of the university group." He wanted the chapel "to embody those architectural ideals from which the other buildings, now so beautifully harmonious, have taken their spirit, so that all the other buildings on the campus will seem to have caught their inspiration from the Chapel and in turn will seem to be contributing their worthiest to the Chapel." The university buildings would then "proclaim that the University in its ideal is dominated by the spirit of religion, all its departments are inspired by the religious feeling, and all its work is directed to the highest ends." Jane Stanford insisted, for the same reasons, that the Stanford church be the university's most elaborate building, located at the center of the campus.[104]

While chapels and buildings housing student Christian associations were tangible monuments to religion, they also physically separated religion from the academic functions of the university. The physical segregation symbolized universities' failure to use extracurricular relibgous activities to integrate spiritual and intellectual concerns. Reformers' efforts to create modern religious practices were plagued by the same problems that undermined courses in the science of religion: inability to articulate modern religious beliefs and lack of student interest.

In their effort to avoid theological doctrines, university officials fixed upon ethics as the common core of religion suitable for discussion in modern chapel services. William E. Hocking explained that "in order to shear the sermon of its possibilities of mischief," universities eschewed "points of doctrine and difference." Religious discourse "thus moves into the field of general ethics." Educators thought that moral lessons, unlike theological doctrine, could receive the common assent of openminded, modern people.[105]

University officials presented ethical precepts as the original intention of primitive Christianity and the true substance of modern, scientific religion. "Religion," wrote Clyde Votow of the University of Chicago, "as interpreted by Jesus . . . means reverence, trust, obedience, faithfulness, industry, sincerity, honesty, truthfulness, righteousness, justice, purity, honor, kindness, sympathy, helpfulness, health, and happiness. Religion is an ideal of life." These original moral ideals, Eliot predicted, would survive as the "superstitious accretions" built up around the Christian religion were "stripped away by inexorable science." Science would validate the traditional moral values of Christianity, even if it repudiated all other Christian beliefs.[106]

By making ethics the focus of religion, university officials avoided questions about the intellectual status of Christianity. "Do not, for the sake of all you hold sacred, allow the existence of intellectual difficulties to interfere with the progress of your practical religious life," Harper told students at the University of Chicago. "Many men think that unless all their intellectual problems are settled it is impossible to live a truly religious life. A more mistaken notion never entered a man's head." Educators told students not to "think you have lost your religion," if "you find yourself stopped by the creeds or the traditions of the body of religious men with whom you are associated." They encouraged students to view religion as something that was "lived" rather than examined intellectually.[107]

The emphasis on conduct over creed submerged religion into daily activity. "Christianity exists to-day, not in creeds, but in the lives of men, and not in individual men, but in men as parts of the social organism," an instructor at the University of Michigan explained. "It is embodied in their institutions, in their tools, in all their instruments of progress, in all their means of communication, in their laws, their prisons, their asylums, their schools, their places of business." The association of religion with ethical living made explicit religious sentiments unnecessary. The "religion of the twentieth century," wrote Jordan, will be a "working theory of life. It will be expressed in simple terms or it may not be expressed at all, but it will be deep graven in the heart. In a wise and helpful life it will find ample justification." Christianity, as presented in university chapels, became little more than appeals to clean living and good citizenship.[108]

Talks to students and university chapel services reflected this attenuation of religion. In describing Harvard's Noble lectures to a prospective speaker, Eliot wrote, "These lectures are intended to lead young men to an imitation of Jesus, but they need not be technically religious in subject or treatment. Subjects taken from literature, philosophy, or sociology are entirely permissible." Sermons in campus chapels often focused on the general problems of student life rather than on explicitly religious questions. In 1904 chapel services for juniors and seniors at the University of Chicago opened with a series of faculty talks on "the choice of a profession." In addition to Charles Henderson's talk "The Outlook in Christian Service," students listened to faculty speak on "The Outlook for the Teacher," "The Outlook in Medicine," ". . . in Music," ". . . in Law," and "The Chances in Chemistry." University officials also spoke about the school of education, the university library, the university museums, and the University of Chicago Press. In an effort to be relevant to students' lives, sermons lost their distinctly religious character.[109]

At the University of Chicago, students criticized the school's chapel services for not being "completely religious in character." An editorial in a student publication complained that "the exercises, as held at present, consist of a short prayer, a chant by the choir, the dean's announcements for the week, and an entertaining address by some professor, upon a topic with little bearing upon religion." The professor's address, students complained, made the average student forget "he is attending a religious service. He is in a lecture room again, and listening to a lecture." Religion became so identified with daily concerns that it was unrecognizable as religion.[110]

Shortly after the University of Chicago opened, Rockefeller's secretary asked several of the faculty to comment on the school's religious atmosphere. Ernest D. Burton responded by praising the university's active religious life and its tolerant attitude "toward varying religious opinions." He expressed one reservation, however: "If I forecast any danger, it is that too loose an interpretation shall be given to the term Christian, and that from the desire to recognize the fullest liberty of all, it shall come to be considered out of place to express any but the most general Christian sentiments." Burton accurately predicted the outcome of universities' efforts to create modern religious practices. To avoid religious beliefs that might be considered dogmatic and nonscientific, university officials relied heavily on ethical precepts. Instead of creating a vital modern religion integrated with the university's intellectual life, chapel services and university addresses offered a diluted, almost secular version of traditional religion.[111]

University leaders also found that vountary chapel services failed to draw large numbers of students. Presidents at schools with voluntary prayers admitted that student attendance was poor. Lack of student interest killed daily chapel at the University of Michigan. In the 1890s daily services were quietly dropped in favor of twice-weekly afternoon vesper services. Stanford offered religious services only on Thursday afternoon and Sunday morning. Officials at other institutions complained of low student attendance. Only fourteen students on average attended morning prayers at Johns Hopkins during the 1896–97 academic year. Around the same time at Columbia, the average daily attendance at chapel was reported as thirty. President Butler's prediction that the new chapel would increase attendance at religious services proved false. Student participation remained a problem at Columbia, and efforts to build up attendance even one day a week by inviting prominent speakers and engaging the cooperation of fraternities met with little lasting success. In 1914 the secretary of the Columbia YMCA concluded that "the chapel is of very small force in the college life, and to build it up requires an infinite amount of patience and personal work." "Vital," modern religious services did not draw students to chapel.[112]

The University of Chicago had similar problems attracting students to chapel services. President Harper thought that poor attendance at chapel was hurting the university's reputation and injuring the spiritual and moral life of the school. After five years the officials at Chicago decided that voluntary chapel did not work. "We have tried every legitimate means of making the service attractive," wrote Charles Henderson. "So far as I can learn there is not an institution in the country which enjoys a large attendance of students without requiring it." Despite his original belief that "compulsory attendance would produce hypocrisy and create a prejudice against religion," Henderson recommended that Harper institute compulsory chapel services for undergraduates. In 1897 the University of Chicago devised a system of rotating chapel services that required all undergraduates to attend one service a week.[113]

Yale witnessed other universities' problems with student participation before it considered voluntary chapel. Religious reform began later at Yale than at the other schools. Arthur T. Hadley, Yale's first nonclerical president, took office in 1899. Hadley wanted to reform Yale without destroying all its traditions. Under his administration, Yale retained its "time-honored institution" of compulsory chapel. Hadley defended compulsory chapel on practical rather than religious grounds. "Daily chapel exercises seem to me to be valuable," he wrote in a letter. "I would not go so far to say that they were a necessity. The lack of such services interferes with the coherence of the student body." But, he continued, "I doubt very much whether the religious spirit is greatly affected by the presence or absence of such exercises." Others apparently shared Hadley's attitude. "Public sentiment at Yale supports the requirement, but for reasons which are largely secular, or show little appreciation of the exercise as a devotional one," observed one faculty member. "Students and alumni in large numbers express their approval of required prayers because of the inspiration which comes from seeing so many students together, and feeling one's self a member of a great institution." In Hadley's mind the benefits of required chapel were similar to those of a football game: they increased community spirit and loyalty to the institution.[114]

Compulsory chapel solved the problem of student attendance, but, as Hadley realized, it did not guarantee student interest in religion. Although all Yale college students had to attend chapel, only a small proportion joined the church "on confession of faith." In 1901 Yale officials recognized that there was not enough student interest to support a voluntary daily religious service. When Yale dropped compulsory attendance twenty-five years later, it abandoned daily chapel services as well.[115]

Educators had similar problems attracting students to other university-sponsored religious activities. Students were uninterested in lectures by well-known religious figures. When Charles Cuthbert Hall, the liberal president of Union Theological Seminary, gave the Noble lectures at Harvard, President Eliot's secretary reported to the donor that "the audiences have been large and good, but you would be disappointed in the relatively small number of the younger under-graduates. It is not that they have been crowded out, but simply that the form of successful appeal to the religious instinct of boys that age seems yet to be discovered." Several years later, Hall's colleague, Harry Emerson Fosdick, delivered a series of popular lectures at Columbia. "The audience, averaging between 300 and 400 each night," reported the Columbia alumni paper, "was obviously made up of men who wished to gain the largest outlook on life and who were deeply interested in the problem of working out a positive, constructive, religious faith." Privately, the organizer of the talks admitted that he "was not fully rewarded in the number of under-graduates that I hoped would attend."[116]

Although a minority of students were actively involved in campus religious life, many of them did not sympathize with the modernist leanings of university officials. Students who were religious and participated in activities were frequently satisfied with the religion of their youth, and they were not always sympathetic to efforts to create a modern religion. Advocates of religious reform expected student organizations to be an integral part of the modern university's religious life. Students did create religious societies during these years, but they did not conform to the ideas of reformers.

University reformers assumed that students, because of their contact with the university's intellectual life, would be dissatisfied with traditional forms of religion. They discovered that this was not the case. Officials at Yale were unhappy when Catholic, Methodist, and Episcopal students formed separate groups for students belonging to these churches. "These organizations," one professor wrote, "represented a tendency distinctly un-Yale in character, toward separation rather than unification." Officials were afraid that the groups would divide "the religious life of college into sects." They persuaded the students in these denominational organizations to combine their activities with those of the Student Christian Association. "Thus that unity in religious work has been secured which has come to be more and more the spirit of the age." Yale succeeded in temporarily suppressing denominational religious activities.[117]

At several institutions officials were disappointed to discover that students preferred the Young Men's and Women's Christian Associations to more liberal campus-based Christian societies. The YMCA, under the leadership of Dwight Moody, was more conservative than many leaders of the new universities. Although it was not affiliated with any particular church, the YMCA adopted "the Portland test," which limited full membership to men who had joined "evangelical" churches. University reformers did not approve of the evangelical bias of the YMCA and encouraged students to form more inclusive religious groups.[118]

When it opened in 1891, Stanford University organized the liberal Students' Christian Association. Soon after, the YMCA organized its own groups. The university organization, explained John Mott, a prominent leader of the American YMCA,

> included both men and women, and had no evangelical test. I suppose fully 9/10's of the members were evangelical church members. They conducted a meeting at regular intervals which was most interesting, profitable, reposeful, and spiritual. And yet after a few weeks experience they found that certain fundamentally important things were not being done and could not be done with

freedom by their organization without offending certain highly respected members who did not believe in Christ as Lord. They, therefore, formed a Y.M.C.A. and Y.W.C.A.

Mott believed that a nonevangelical religious group could not succeed because it was "impossible to unite all its members in any form of practical Christian work or spiritual study and worship." Although Mott's explanation was self-serving, YMCAs and YWCAs survived at universities when more liberal organizations failed.[119]

Like leaders at Stanford, Harper was wary of the YMCA and wanted the University of Chicago Christian Union to be the most prominent and active religious group on campus. The YMCA, however, "looked upon the new University of Chicago as a strategic center and was very anxious that a college association should be formed under the most favorable auspices." Harper resented the activities of the YMCA because he thought its representative was trying to discredit the campus-sponsored Christian Union. Because of his pledge of free and voluntary religious practices, Harper did not stop the organization of a YMCA and YWCA. "Under a rule of perfect freedom from constraint," Charles Henderson reported in 1892, "three Christian Societies have already been formed and have begun work; The Christian Union, for all who 'profess and call themselves Christians'; the Y.M.C.A. and the Y.W.C.A. for the more evangelical persons who feel the need of the means of more direct Christian work." Although Harper did not want the YMCA to compete with the university Christian Union, he did not feel free to stop it from forming a campus chapter.[120]

The experience at the University of Chicago was similar to that at Stanford. Campus YMCAs commonly provided various services, including publishing a handbook for incoming students. Despite Harper's objection, the YMCA rather than the Christian Union took over these duties. Within a few years, it was clear that the YMCA and the YWCA were more successful than the liberal Christian Union. Harper expressed his disappointment with this situation to Chaplain Henderson. Henderson responded by pointing out that the YMCA and YWCA "are the hope of real devotional life in the University. . . . Instead of discouraging them I believe we should do all in our power to cheer them." Given students' general indifference to religious activities, the "patient and zealous" activity of any religious organization was a promising sign.[121]

The commitment of universities to religious freedom made it difficult for officials to proscribe students' religious expression, even when it was opposed to liberal sentiments of the university. At Johns Hopkins, students petitioned the board of trustees to allow the evangelist Billy Sunday to speak on campus. Arthur O. Lovejoy, professor of philosophy, protested the board's affirmative answer. Billy Sunday, Lovejoy wrote "is a man who, whatever his possible usefulness in dealing with certain classes of people, represents, both in his intellectual temper and his taste, an attitude which should be antipodal to that of any body of university men." President Frank Goodnow told Lovejoy that the board felt that "it was practically impossible for them to refuse a petition . . . to use the University premises for the purpose."[122]

Advocates of religious reform originally viewed voluntary, unsectarian religious practices as a step in the development of a modern scientific religion. Educators' inability to integrate religion into the intellectual life of the university, combined with general student indifference to university-sponsored religious activities, pushed university officials away from the original intentions of religious reform. Instead of providing a new religion based on a modern scientific model, educators began to interpret the ideals of free and open inquiry as involving the toleration of a variety of religious beliefs and practices rather than the creation of a new modern religion.

Increasingly, university officials found themselves encouraging whatever religious activities interested students. Even the strongest campus religious organizations struggled to get students to participate in their programs. The surviving papers of the Columbia University Christian Association reveal a constant battle against student indifference in the first decades of the twentieth century. Leaders of the group frequently remodeled their programs to attract more students to Bible classes and other activities. In the early 1910s the association began to concentrate on getting students involved in local churches. This was the beginning of a focus on denominational rather than unsectarian religious activities. "The final aim of all religious work at the University is to bring all of its members into closer relations with the churches to which they belong, of whatever faith and denomination," concluded a report of 1916 examining the university's religious activities.[123]

At this time religious denominations also became more interested in universities outside their control. They began to send representatives to work at state and other nondenominational universities. In the 1910s "the denominational university pastorate" won acceptance. Despite initial misgivings, university officials began to welcome representatives of various religious denominations to their institutions. After World War I the campus ministry became the backbone of university religious programs.[124]

By the 1910s many educators had retreated from their efforts to create modern, unsectarian religious practices. They hired chaplains to oversee and promote these activities. They welcomed student groups and representatives from religious organizations, offering them the use of beautiful campus buildings devoted to religious purposes. But educators no longer tried to shape students' religious character. In the modern research university, religion would simply coexist along with many other university-sanctioned activities.

The adoption of this laissez-faire attitude toward religious activities coincided with efforts to distance curricular studies of religion from devotional aims. Together, these changes represented reformers' failure to integrate religion into the intellectual life of the university. University reformers were unable to maintain the unity of spiritual, moral, and intellectual education. In practice, the university's adherence to scientific standards of inquiry precluded a strong religious presence in higher education.

FIVE

Scientific Substitutes for Religion

The failure to create and maintain a modern "scientific" religion was a blow to the new universities, but it did not completely destroy their commitment to moral education. The leaders of university reform in the late nineteenth century steadfastly maintained that moral development was one of the primary missions of higher education. During the early twentieth century, university educators gradually backed away from the position that there was no morality without religion and instead emphasized secular sources for moral development.

American intellectuals who led the battle for university reform in the late nineteenth century held onto the ideal of the unity of truth. They hoped to update the antebellum Christian synthesis with a new scientific synthesis. University reformers discussed the moral value of science in two distinct ways. First, they believed that "scientific inquiry," viewed as a general approach to the discovery of knowledge, encouraged certain moral traits and therefore served as an "indirect" form of moral education. Second, they thought that particular scientific disciplines produced knowledge that was morally relevant because it could provide standards for individual behavior and social norms. Educators considered the biological and the social scientific disciplines to be the most fruitful source of this kind of "direct" moral education.

The possibility of scientific morality was controversial. Since the Enlightenment, intellectuals had advanced scientific morality both to undermine and to advance religion. Intellectuals opposed to the authority of the church extolled the superiority of science and predicted, either directly or by implication, its eventual triumph over religion. The most prominent example of this tradition in the nineteenth century was Auguste Comte's positivism. In his *Cours de philosophie positive* (1842), Comte had presented three stages of human knowledge: the theological or fictitious, the metaphysical or abstract, and the scientific or positive. Comte had celebrated the superiority of the scientific over the theological, and its inevitable defeat of earlier modes of thought. He had designed a religion of humanity to replace Christianity and other theistic religions that had developed during the theological and metaphysical stages.[1]

The United States did not have a strong tradition of antireligious advocacy of science. The tenor of the American Enlightenment was "moderate," advancing a "rational" Christianity rather than a materialistic scientific philosophy. In the early nineteenth century, evangelical Protestantism, common-sense realism, and Baconianism had dominated intellectual life and left little room for presumptuous claims for science. Only late in the century did a small group of vocal agnostics and non-Christian theists raise the threat of science deposing Christianity. In this context, advancing scientific ethics could be seen as antireligious.[2]

In general, intellectuals who advocated scientific ethics at the expense of Christianity were excluded from the reform-oriented universities. For example, in 1870 Charles Eliot planned to hire John Fiske to teach history at Harvard. The year before Fiske had given a series of public lectures at Harvard on positivism, extolling the ideas of Comte and Herbert Spencer. The lectures were reprinted in the New York *World,* identifying Fiske as a professor at Harvard. The lectures and the misrepresentation of Fiske's position caused controversy. Some of the Harvard overseers objected to the apparent university endorsement of Fiske's views. James Freeman Clarke wrote Eliot that he opposed Fiske "being again presented to the public as a teacher in the University" because "Positivism is understood to imply, among other things, a relegation of all opinions concerning God and the Infinite to the region of the unknown—which is equivalent to Atheism." Fiske had openly challenged Christian theism, and this made him too controversial to be appointed to a university position. Eliot withdrew his support of Fiske and appointed Henry Adams instead. Adams's views were no more orthodox than Fiske's, but his public support for science did not extend to open hostility to Christianity. Many university presidents followed this pattern of willingness to hire faculty who supported scientific morality, but not those who were openly antagonistic toward religion.[3]

Many scholars who believed in the moral relevance of science entered university faculties and administration in the late nineteenth century. Some, such as scientists John Coulter of the University of Chicago and Nathan Shaler of Harvard, were eager to help reconcile religion and science by demonstrating the scientific basis for Christian morality. Just as university reformers had relied on their association with liberal Protestantism to gain acceptance for the distinction between religion and theology, they depended on a similar alliance to promote scientific morality. Liberal Protestants adopted an expansive vision of scientific knowledge and wanted to incorporate science into a Christian framework. They welcomed scientific support for Christian morality as proof of the underlying truth of Christian beliefs.[4]

Some scientists believed that the mental discipline acquired through the study of nature would produce intellectual clarity on moral questions. For example, C. Riborg Mann, a physics professor at the University of Chicago, thought that the human mind developed from the concrete to the abstract. Individuals' ability or inability to organize, understand, and manipulate their physical experiences determined their abilities in the more abstract realms of morality. "Since the content of the words and phrases that we use in language is thus determined by the mental pictures that we have formed from our concrete experiences with physical nature it is of the greatest importance that those pictures be clear and definite," he stated. Developing competence in the physical sciences provided the necessary base for all other areas of intellectual life. "The concrete pictures of system, order, and organization, which result from the scientific study of natural phenomena, are necessary to system, order, and organization in the worlds of intellect and the soul. Were the natural world a physical chaos, the mind would be a mental chaos, and the soul an ethical chaos." Moral reasoning required the intellectual skills secured through scientific study.[5]

In addition to portraying the scientific method as a form of mental discipline, university educators presented it as a form of moral discipline. The argument held that students, by learning to think scientifically, also developed good moral habits: the view of science as an "indirect" source of moral education. Students learned moral values as a natural by-product of any scientific education, no matter what the subject of study. Some educators even maintained that this "indirect" education was the best possible form of moral training. The "highest type of character," university reformers asserted, developed only under "conditions of freedom."[6]

The notion of scientific training as a form of moral education rested on the image of science as a virtuous occupation. As historian David Hollinger has shown, scientists in the late nineteenth and early twentieth centuries appropriated religious virtues for their own legitimation. They created an "ethic of science," which emphasized moral values, such as veracity, universality, and self-abnegation, and presented scientists as the true representatives of these values. University educators helped popularize this image of the scientist. They associated "the man of science" with characteristics such as "a passion for knowledge, the love of truth, honesty, patience, singlemindedness of mind, simplicity of character, humility, reverence, [and] imagination." Although they acknowledged that not all scientists possessed such "great attributes," they thought that science "tends to develop them in all her followers."[7]

University leaders associated the "ethic of science" with the values of Christianity. "The righteous man," wrote political scientist Jesse Macy, "is one who keeps an open mind to all truth; the lost soul is one who rejects the spirit of truth. The modern scientific spirit is simply the Christian spirit realized in a limited field of experience." Through scientific training, university educators promised to instill this "spirit of science" in students. Scientists such as Ira Remsen of Johns Hopkins presented laboratories as a source of moral uplift as well as a tool for the advancement of knowledge. Faculty insisted that science courses include laboratory instruction because "that special mental and moral discipline which is appropriate to the science can be secured only by wrestling with its problems as they actually present themselves to the investigator." By imitating the professional scientist, students imbibed the values of scientists.[8]

Educators thought that students, even those who did not plan to become professional scientists, benefited morally as well as intellectually from scientific study. They envisioned universities graduating students with ideal "scientific" characters. This character training, like the older moral philosophy, was supposed to prepare students for their social and political responsibilities as community leaders. Intellectuals commonly associated science and democracy. Macy wrote that "science and democracy have come into the modern world at the same time. They are mutually related as cause and effect." Educators as diverse as Charles Eliot, Arthur Hadley, and John Dewey maintained that scientific virtues were essential attributes of citizens in a democracy. Echoing this rhetoric, Randolph Bourne, then a student at Columbia, described the ideal college graduate as possessing "scientific" qualities. "We want citizens who are enthusiastic thinkers, not docile and uncritical followers of tradition; we want leaders of public opinion with the scientific point of view: unclassed men, not men like the leaders of the passing generation, saturated with class prejudices and class ideals." Subjected to the powerful but indirect moral discipline of scientific training, students were expected to mature into strong, honest, useful men.[9]

In addition to the morals inculcated through scientific study, university leaders expected that knowledge produced through scientific research would be morally relevant and that scientific knowledge would become part of students' direct moral education. They believed that all scientific knowledge had moral value, because it contributed to the progress of civilization. Certain sciences, particularly biology and the social sciences, were seen as potential substitutes for the older moral philosophy. These sciences would provide practical guidance on vexing moral questions involving both individual behavior and social practices.

The proponents of science believed that civilization was steadily progressing and that the United States was at the vanguard of such progress. They thought that America was an advanced society because it was scientific, Christian, industrial, and democratic—characteristics that were both the cause and consequence of progress. Although some of their contemporaries feared that material and technological advance might threaten moral progress, university leaders maintained that all progress was interconnected and mutually dependent. "In whatever light we look at it," wrote sociologist Franklin Giddings, "the assumption that we can have material betterment without the mental and moral elements of progress is absurd."[10]

Although they maintained that all development was interconnected, supporters of university reform generally thought that science drove progress. The progressivist model of science that became popular among late nineteenth-century academics viewed science as a tool in the development of human civilization. Science, itself the product of the evolution of human reason, provided people with conscious control over their environment and themselves. Thus, it opened the possibility for human beings to direct and quicken the path of evolution. All science, according to this view, was "applied" and "practical" because it contributed to the future well-being of the human race. This broad conception of the practicality of science reflected the desire of philosophers of science and liberal Christians to collapse dualisms, such as "material" and "moral," and "secular" and "sacred."[11]

Science, as the engine of progress, was automatically considered a human good. "Science," wrote Daniel C. Gilman, "is rapidly lifting the mist which has rested upon the conditions in which the human race is placed; every new and fundamental discovery is fraught with world-wide benefits, sooner or later to be developed." Utopian literature helped popularize this "perfectionist" vision of science. The popularity of Edward Bellamy's *Looking Backward* (1888) illustrates the promise of applied science. Bellamy's vision of the future, however we may view it today, reflected a widespread belief that technologies derived from advances in knowledge could eventually solve all serious moral and social problems.[12]

Educators portrayed all scientific training as ultimately improving the lives of individuals and the quality of civilization. David Starr Jordan wrote,

> In science we find the bases for the development of the finest of fine arts, that of human conduct. As we better understand the universe around us, our relations to others and to ourselves, the behavior of our race becomes rationalized. It becomes possible to keep ourselves clean, and to make ourselves open-minded, friendly and God-fearing. In the achievements of science, therefore, we may properly find the only permanent wealth of nations.

Even the most utilitarian science, such as agricultural research, took on moral value. "The amount of wheat, rye, meat, cotton, and wool, *per capita,* increases from decade to decade," stated Giddings, "and it cannot be denied that to lessen the awful sufferings from starvation and cold, from which, until recent years, the world was never even comparatively free, is an advance in human well-being." Agricultural research, educators proclaimed, would increase not only the wealth of farmers, but also the health and well-being of others, the prosperity of the nation, and intercourse between nations; it might even promote world peace.[13]

While they believed that all scientific knowledge would, at some time and in some way, further the well-being of people, educators acknowledged that some types of scientific knowledge contributed more directly to moral progress than others. The sciences were commonly perceived as proceeding along a continuum, from the physical sciences to the biological and then to the social sciences, such as economics and sociology. As the sciences advanced on this spectrum, their applicability to morality increased. Thus, physics produced knowledge about the cosmos, served the state, and supported technological innovation: all of indirect, but relatively remote, moral value. Sociology, on the other hand, addressed issues such as the ideal family structure, which had direct and immediate moral implications.[14]

University leaders looked primarily to the biological and social sciences to give substance to the ideal of the unity of truth. Many faculty hoped that these sciences would produce a modern "synthesis" that would supersede the Christian synthesis of antebellum moral philosophy. They thought that evolutionary science, like moral philosophy, could fulfill both tenets of the ideal of unity: it could draw together various branches of knowledge and provide normative guidance on personal and social issues.

Evolutionary theory in the late nineteenth century seemed to promise the desired scientific synthesis. Progressive evolutionism dominated American biology and shaped much of the social thought of the day. It seemed to link "the natural sciences with those subjects that deal with human progress in physical, social, political and economic respects" and to provide "an orderly conception of the world and human experience." Because a wide range of disciplines, from geology to sociology, adopted evolutionary approaches, many intellectuals believed that these disciplines could be synthesized into an overarching evolutionary philosophy that would offer a comprehensive view of life.[15]

Scholars in many different fields believed that their disciplines exemplified the unifying potential of evolutionary theory. Geologists, ecologists, and geographers all claimed for their disciplines a special unifying function. For example, Thomas Chamberlin of the University of Chicago wrote that "geology is to be studied comprehensively as the evolution of the earth and its inhabitants." He believed that geology encompassed everything from the physical development of the planet to the psychic and cultural development of humans. Geology, therefore, related a wide range of subject matter to create "a really broad view of the world of which we are a part." Representatives of other "central" sciences, such as Chamberlin's colleague in ecology, Warder Clyde Allee, envisioned a similarly comprehensive mission for their disciplines.[16]

Social scientists also promised to provide a new scientific synthesis of knowledge. They interpreted the spectrum of sciences as a "hierarchy of knowledge." Because their disciplines were at the apex of this hierarchy, they maintained that they served as the "science of sciences." In the United States sociologists most often claimed this role. Albion Small, for example, described sociology as "an attempt to organize a *Novum Organum* of all the sciences that contribute to our understanding of life." It aims "to take the last word of every science that gathers knowledge about man and combine it with the last word of every other human science, to form the completest view of human conditions possible up to date." Sociologists, following the example of Comte, were particularly interested in organizing the various branches of scholarship.[17]

Some anthropologists also perceived their discipline as a synthetic rather than a specialized science. "While each separate department of science is busy adding new data," wrote John Flagg, a lecturer on anthropology at the College of Physicians and Surgeons in Boston, "anthropology fits each new fact, so far as it bears on the problem of man, into its proper place in the whole. . . . The real value of anthropology . . . is to take the place that philosophy occupied in the old scholastic system." Anthropologists also saw themselves as uniting the biological and social sciences. Harvard professor Roland B. Dixon explained that anthropology has two aspects, the biological and the cultural. "On the physical side anthropology touches and interlocks with the biological sciences, so on the cultural side it is closely related to the historical and humanistic sciences. The scope of anthropology is thus very wide, since it includes virtually everything that is pertinent to the history of the human race." This synthetic view of anthropology dominated in Great Britain. In the United States, the influence of the anti-evolutionary leader, Franz Boas, and the imperative to study the disappearing Native American cultures fostered a more specialized conception of anthropology, focusing on the study of "primitive" cultures. The ideal of the social sciences forming a modern substitute for moral philosophy was, therefore, not as prominent among American anthropologists as among other social scientists.[18]

The old moral philosophy had offered normative guidance as well as intellectual synthesis. Evolution, in order to replicate its role, would also have to address specific moral questions. Many promoters of science thought that an evolutionary ethics was possible. Historian Robert J. Richards has shown how several prominent British and American intellectuals explained the evolutionary origins of morality. Rather than assuming that science excluded human values, these intellectuals looked to evolution for moral guidance because they perceived it as "objective science." Arthur T. Hadley, for example, in his article "The Influence of Charles Darwin upon Historical and Political Thought," explained that evolution provided a definite standard by which people could judge competing ethical claims: behaviors that enhanced personal and group survival and growth were good and those that did not were bad. Hadley and many of his contemporaries thought that evolutionary theory proved that survival was the ultimate aim of existence and, therefore, the final arbiter of moral values.[19]

Proponents of evolutionary ethics assumed that the individual scientific disciplines would determine what behavior and values promoted survival and growth. According to Clyde Votow of the University of Chicago, scientific knowledge would help answer "the supreme human problem": how to live. "The sciences of biology, psychology, anthropology, history and sociology," he wrote, "are furnishing to us the new knowledge, interpretation and correlation of the facts of human experience which enable ethics to become the best promoter of the common good." Research and education in the biological and social sciences were expected to yield direct benefits for both personal and social ethics.[20]

Like their predecessors, the new generation of academic scientists made broad claims for the social and moral value of biological knowledge. Ernest Gale Martin of Stanford wrote,

> There is an increasing appreciation on the part of progressive thinkers of the importance of applying biological principles and the biological viewpoint to the interpretation of history if a sound and just interpretation is to be had. Hand in hand with the acceptance of this principle, and directly correlated with it is the recognition of the fact that the future course of civilization will be determined largely by the extent to which its leaders are informed in and able to make use of biological conceptions as aids to the interpretation of current events and as guides to plans for events that are to come.

Biology, according to this view, was the key to human behavior and, therefore, also the key to human improvement.[21]

Ethically minded scientists thought that biology contained lessons for personal behavior. "It is a very significant fact that the rules of conduct for the best development of men, discovered first by the experience of the human race, and afterward formulated as religious precepts, have now been established as laws of biology," wrote John Coulter of the University of Chicago. Educators embraced the notion that biology encouraged clean living and good habits, and they looked to it as a form of moral training. They pointed out that many moral issues traditionally addressed by religion, such as sexual relations, could be studied by biologists. They argued that "many of the worst sins . . . responsible for the undoing of many individuals are physical in nature, such as intemperance and sexual perversion. Any effort to reform men who are habituated to such indulgences will be greatly helped by methods based upon physiology and hygiene." According to this view, biology rather than the Bible would provide the authority for the Ten Commandments.[22]

Scientists maintained that biological research assisted social ethics as well as personal morality. It would help address contemporary social problems, such as inadequate housing and unsafe work conditions. "Many of the great moral and religious problems to-day are biological. Community work is largely founded on biological laws." By sponsoring biological research and instruction, universities served the larger community. "Social morality has no better servant and helper to-day than biology, and the study of this subject in our colleges has a splendid moral influence." Academic scientists presented temperance, sexual hygiene, public health reforms, and eugenics as some of the potential moral benefits from biological research. These convictions drew many academic scientists into these reform movements.[23]

The movements most closely associated with the biological sciences were health reforms. Health had long been associated with morality, and the increasing prominence of scientists in these movements in the late nineteenth and early twentieth century did not sever this connection. Indeed, academic scientists discussed health in moral terms and used the example of health benefits to explain the value of their research. Some health movements, such as temperance and sexual hygiene, tried to influence individuals' behavior. Scientists like David Starr Jordan—who opposed the consumption of all "unnatural stimulants," such as coffee and alcohol—looked to biology to show the evolutionary advantages of such restrictions and thus to provide scientific sanction for traditional Christian morality.[24]

The union of science and Protestant moralism was evident in the efforts to regulate sexual behavior. The social hygiene movement aimed to fight venereal disease and restrict prostitution. These goals were similar to those advanced by the nineteenth-century social purity movement, which had been led largely by devout Protestant women. The social hygiene movement united the leadership of medical professionals, such as Prince A. Morrow, with the support of committed social reformers, such as Jane Addams, and university leaders, such as E. R. A. Seligman and Charles Eliot. The movement also diverged from its predecessor by supporting public discussion of sexuality and emphasizing sexual satisfaction within monogamous marriage rather than fighting the sexual double standard. Despite these differences, the social hygiene movement, like the social purity movement, was committed to the values of sexual self-control and the primacy of the family. To contemporaries, it seemed to represent a prime example of the application of scientific knowledge to the cause of moral progress.[25]

Similar coalitions of academic leaders and scientists, physicians and social reformers united over other public health reforms, such as the quality of water and milk supplies and the control of contagious diseases. These movements were also viewed as moral reforms, although they did not focus on individual behavior. They were part of the shift of attention from personal morality to social ethics in the late nineteenth and early twentieth centuries. Public health reforms were cast in terms of Christian values, such as "brotherly love and responsibility" and "protection of the innocent." University administrators saw the development of bacteriology as an important opportunity for their institutions to serve the public, and they encouraged their faculty to work with regional health boards. They also took responsibility for educating the public regarding problems of public health, as well as other social concerns, and convincing the public that the solution of these problems required "substituting scientific cooperation for partisan government."[26]

One of the most prominent "biological" social reforms was eugenics. Scientists presented eugenics as the application of scientific knowledge to enhance the "survival and growth" of society. Following the common assumptions of the era, intellectuals translated evolutionary advantage into moral advance. Eliot, for example, considered knowledge of heredity second only to "open-mindedness" as the most important contribution of natural science. He believed that knowledge of heredity would change many social customs. "It will promote, on the one hand, the occasional production of illustrious men, and, on the other, the gradual improvement of the masses of mankind. The moral benefits will surely flow from our generation's study of heredity." University leaders presented their support for eugenics research as one of their prime contributions to the moral progress of the nation.[27]

Eliot and many of his contemporaries assumed that genetics could improve the moral as well as physical character of individuals and society. Jacques Loeb, for example, speaking on the "physiological basis of altruism" to an undergraduate sociology class at the University of California, maintained that ethics was the expression of instincts, such as motherhood, and that these instincts were "chemically and hereditarily fixed in us in the same fashion as the shapes of our bodies." Loeb's views were shared by many outside physiology, including psychologists and social scientists.[28]

Social scientists made even stronger claims for the moral relevance of their disciplines. The ties of the social sciences to morality were clearly evident in intellectual and institutional roots. The older moral philosophy had had two branches, mental philosophy and political economy, which had gradually become independent areas of study. By the late nineteenth century mental philosophy had developed into psychology, and political economy had spawned economics, political science, and sociology. Although leaders of these new sciences rejected moral philosophy's "dogmatic" approach, they preserved its interest in ethical questions.[29]

The social sciences had strong institutional ties to the political and social reform movements of the period. The American Social Science Association, founded in 1865, was the first organization devoted to promoting the social sciences. Its membership included government officials, leaders of charity organizations and reform associations, journalists, and educators (including prominent university reformers, such as Eliot, Gilman, and Andrew Dickson White). The ASSA linked the investigation of social problems with efforts to eradicate the evils associated with modern industrial life.[30]

As the social sciences developed within the university, they retained their ties to social reform and ethics. Many early academic social scientists, such as Charles F. Dunbar, William Graham Sumner, Francis Amasa Walker, Albion Small, George T. Ladd, and John Bascom, entered the field through journalism, the ministry, public service, or moral philosophy. Some of their colleagues were academically trained social scientists who had originally intended to pursue other professions. For example, Henry Carter Adams was an aspiring journalist before he attended Johns Hopkins for graduate training, and Richard T. Ely had intended to enter the ministry before he went to Germany to pursue his doctorate.[31]

After the doctorate in philosophy, or Ph.D., became the standard requirement for university posts, many social scientists continued to combine, either sequentially or simultaneously, "practical" efforts to improve the quality of human life with their academic careers. Woodrow Wilson's career as a professor, university president, and politician was exceptional only because of his success and prominence. Many social scientists were involved in contemporary social or political movements either as activists, advisers, or publicists. For example, Herbert Baxter Adams of Johns Hopkins helped form the Workingmen's Institute and the Baltimore settlement house, Lawrence House. He also became involved in Baltimore politics, supporting municipal reform. E. R. A. Seligman of Columbia was active in the Society for Ethical Culture and the University Settlement and Greenwich House, and served as an adviser on city, state, and federal commissions. Charles Merriam of the University of Chicago served as a Chicago alderman and ran unsuccessfully for the post of mayor. He and many of his colleagues in the social sciences were active in political and social movements in Chicago. Like biologists active in eugenics and hygiene reforms, social scientists involved in campaigns to address problems in municipal government, labor conditions, urban housing, rural schooling, immigration policies, race relations, and myriad other issues, saw their activities as a natural component of their role as scientists.[32]

The new social science disciplines of the late nineteenth and early twentieth centuries had much in common with the older moral philosophy and the reformist ASSA. Social scientists continued to maintain ties to nonacademic individuals and groups. For example, in 1912 "professors and teachers" made up only 20 percent of the membership of the American Political Science Association. Social scientists viewed their disciplines as concerned broadly with improving the quality of human life and determining how individuals and society could best approach an ideal life. They expected to produce knowledge that would provide guidance on contemporary social problems. Because they looked upon social woes as moral problems, they thought of their efforts to improve society as a moral service.

Intellectuals' belief in the moral relevance of scientific knowledge has been obscured by the later twentieth-century conception of value-free science. Historians, looking back at disputes among early social scientists, often explain them as a battle between one group trying to create an objective, value-free science and another group that wanted to combine scholarship, ethics, and activism. This dichotomy is anachronistic; before the 1910s American intellectuals did not generally equate scientific objectivity with moral neutrality. The first generation of professional social scientists disagreed about many things, but they shared a commitment to producing reliable knowledge about the social realm that was of moral value.[33]

Social scientists' concordance on the moral value of scientific knowledge was confused by their dissension over issues of social policy and by their different understanding of the relationship of "objective science" to morality. All the social science disciplines were troubled by serious disagreements during the early period of their professional development. Economics, as the first field to professionalize, was also the first to experience these disputes. In the 1880s, just as political economy was being accepted as an essential discipline in a well-equipped university, a bitter and public battle developed between members of the "new school" of historical economics and advocates of the classical tradition of political economy. The division between these two groups was broad, encompassing their views about the nature of scientific inquiry, assumptions about human nature, and understanding of acceptable public policy. Between 1890 and 1910 the lines between these two camps blurred, as economists adopted marginalist theories and put aside some of their fundamental disputes.[34]

I will examine in some depth the debates between the classical and historical economists to demonstrate that, despite other disagreements, both groups believed that science had moral value. William Graham Sumner, Simon Newcomb, Charles Dunbar, and J. Lawrence Laughlin led the classical side. This group was distinguished by an outspoken defense of laissez-faire as the best possible economic policy. Sumner, for example, considered state intervention in the economy a form of robbery, inevitably hurting the middle classes. "The state, it cannot too often be repeated, has nothing, and can give nothing which it does not take from somebody. Its victims must be those who have earned and saved, and they must be the broad, strong, middle classes, from whom alone any important contributions can be drawn." The economists of the classical school opposed proposals for economic reform, particularly those associated with the labor movement and populism, as inconsistent with sound economic science.[35]

In the 1870s and 1880s economists' defense of laissez-faire was closely tied to their ideas about science. On the whole, the classical economists followed John Stuart Mill's views about the scientific method and its application to the study of human society. Mill had revised the Baconian conception of science by rejecting the opposition between inductive and deductive reasoning. He viewed deduction as a series of interpretations of generalized inductions and, therefore, as based ultimately on observation. He followed the Baconian tradition, however, in affirming the existence of natural laws, uniformities in the universe that can be considered universal and immutable.

According to Mill, natural laws also governed individuals and society. Through the application of proper scientific methods, scholars could discover these laws. Mill doubted that the social sciences would ever achieve the predictive power of the physical sciences, but believed that, if properly developed, the social sciences would "be most valuable for guidance." He thought that eventually the social sciences might be able to explain, "in any given condition of social affairs," the causes, the direction of development, the future effects, "and by what means any of those effects might be prevented, modified, or accelerated, or a different class of effects might be superinduced." The social sciences would help shape social policy.[36]

Although Mill clearly saw practical applications for the social sciences, he did not want to emphasize them. He believed that the underdeveloped state of the social sciences was due to people's premature desire for "therapeutics of the social body." He also distinguished between the "science" and "art" of politics. Social science, he maintained, would eventually help leaders understand how they could accomplish their ends, but it would not decide what those ends should be. The "imperative mood," or what ought to be, was outside the realm of science; these moral questions were a matter of the social "arts."[37]

The American classical economists reflected Mill's influence. They defended the use of deductive logic as consistent with empirical science. They held onto the idea that immutable laws governed human society. Sumner wrote that "the natural laws of the social order are in their entire character like the laws of physics." The classical economists designated the discovery of these laws as the prime goal of the social sciences, and they believed that any sound economic policy must work in harmony with the actions of these laws. Laissez-faire fit well with this conception of harmonious adjustment and with the distinction between the science and art of political economy.[38]

The new school, led by Richard T. Ely, Simon Patten, Richard Mayo-Smith, and Henry Carter Adams, supported state and private intervention in the economy to achieve social goals. Their views on policy, like those of the classicists, were tied to their ideas about science. The historical economists, instead of following the Baconian ideal or Mill's revision of it, adopted the newer progressivist model of science. They believed that societies evolved over time and that economic "laws" were not immutable but relative to particular social organizations. Ely explained that economic life, "as it is understood by representatives of the new school, is not something stationary: it is a growth. What is, is not what has been, nor what it will be." He applied the same principle of growth to science: it evolved and was related to the society in which it was produced. Classical economics, Ely argued, did not discover immutable laws but rather "described the economic life of commercial England in the nineteenth century."[39]

The new school rejected the notion of static, immutable laws and the idea that the purpose of science is the unearthing of these laws. "The new method," wrote Mayo-Smith, "does not give us principles which . . . are unchangeable, perpetual, and cosmopolitan. Neither does it lay down laws which can be applied by rule of thumb to every new economic and social problem, wherever occurring, or under whatever circumstances. Such a science is, on the face of it absurd." Economists of the new school rejected the idea that economic principles, or any scientific notions, were absolutely true. Science changed as human knowledge advanced and as the conditions under study evolved.[40]

Instead of uncovering immutable laws, the historical economists wanted to undertake empirical studies that would help guide social policy. "All we seek now," explained Mayo-Smith, "are certain empirical generalizations which will guide our judgment in approaching practical problems." The historical economists rejected Mill's distinction between art and science. "There is," wrote Adams, "no such sharp line of distinction between the science and art of economics as has been commonly exposed." They viewed science as an instrument that could be used to further the progress of civilization.[41]

According to the historical economists, human beings had acquired the intellectual ability, through science, to manipulate the environment in order to facilitate individual and social growth. "The law of evolution, with its 'survival of the fittest' and its 'adaptation to environment,'" explained Adams, "comes to be the basis of a scientific theory of revolution or of reformation; for the fittest type to survive may first exist in the conscious purpose of society, and be realized by means of an environment arbitrarily determined." The historical economists, like most of their contemporaries, associated evolution with progress and believed that through scientific study they could help direct social growth.[42]

The historical economists thought that industrial development had created serious social problems and economic injustices that should be corrected. Intellectuals, they maintained, should study the economy "to guide and direct the forces which control the production and distribution of economic goods, that they may in the highest degree subserve the ends of humanity." Ely believed that the ultimate aim of economics was to help structure a society that encouraged "the most perfect development of all human faculties in each individual which can be attained." He associated this goal with the realization of "the ethical ideal of Christianity." Although not all of Ely's collaborators shared his religious vision, many did, and those who did not still viewed economics as a tool of moral and social reform.[43]

Both schools of economists believed that they practiced objective science and addressed moral issues in an appropriate scientific manner, but members of each school believed that their opponents violated proper scientific methods and misunderstood the ethical role of the scientist.

The classicists maintained that economic science was objective because it was grounded in the observation of empirical reality and that the laws it discovered were permanent and real. They saw economics as morally relevant because they believed that economic laws were essentially normative and that a proper economic structure sustained the virtue of a nation. The classicists also believed that the study of political economy would improve citizens' civic participation and guide public policy. Simon Newcomb, for example, could agree with the new school that the "ultimate objective" of the study of political economy was "the improvement of society." The results of scientific study should be used to achieve social goals. "The school of non-interference," wrote Newcomb, "claims, as a general rule, these ends are best attained by giving the adult individual the widest liberty within the limits prescribed by considerations of public health and morality." Conservative economists recognized that their research contained lessons for contemporary society, but they presented these lessons in terms of restraint and inaction rather than intervention and reform.[44]

The classicists accused the new school economists of violating the strictures of objective science because they adopted an activist approach to both scholarship and public policy. Although they believed that scientific laws implied normative rules, conservative economists criticized the new school for using ethical ideals to guide scientific research. By focusing on what "ought to be," scholars blinded themselves to what "actually is." "Times without number," lamented Newcomb, "I have seen educated men refuse to accept a statement of fact, not on the ground that it was not a fact, but that it was not *necessarily so,* or *might* be different, or *ought* to be different." The classicists believed that the distinction between art and science must be maintained, or else wishful thinking would color scientists' observations and cloud their reasoning. They felt that by collapsing this distinction, the new school economists violated the scientific method.[45]

The historical school turned this charge back onto their conservative opponents. They argued that classical economics was essentially deductive, based on a few a priori principles rather than on inductive research. "The old method," wrote Richard Mayo-Smith, "is essentially deductive. It finds certain premises which are true, and reasons from these premises to the solution of specific problems." This approach, he contended, was undermined by empirical research demonstrating that the "first principles" of classical economics were not universally valid. "Experience showed that at different epochs in civilization, and among differently situated nations at the present time, the premises would require very great modifications." The classical school, their opponents countered, violated scientific principles by ignoring the results of empirical research.[46]

The new school economists believed that the classicists disregarded the most important principle of science: openmindedness. According to their progressivist model, the worst crime against science was dogmatism. Proponents of progressivist science opposed theology because it employed apologetics to justify beliefs handed down by tradition or authority. In the social, political, and economic realm, "partisanship" was the equivalent of theological dogmatism. The historical economists denied that there were any "partisan" principles that should be accepted absolutely.

The new school economists thought that the classical school dog-matically accepted laissez-faire without testing it historically. This, they charged, violated proper scientific methods. "Political Economy is neither a religious creed to be used to excommunicate all heretics, nor a legal code by which to condemn malefactors, but a body of experience to guide us in the conduct of social economic life," wrote Mayo-Smith. "The inductive method forbids its being used for the private purposes of the priesthood or the judges, for new experience may teach us new solutions and new expedients." Innovation was the essence of scientific and social progress; there were no normative economic laws that must be accepted at all times and in all conditions.[47]

Historical economists argued that activism, as long as it was not dog-matic, was not inconsistent with their position as "objective" scientists. Science, according to their view, did not preclude ethical stands. Historical economist Edward Bemis wrote to his conservative colleague, J. Lawrence Laughlin, "I, of course, agree fully with your idea of the importance of a judicial scientific truth-loving spirit. I do not understand, however, that such is inconsistent with the holding and expressing of personal opinions on economic questions." Scientists, however, had to accept their positions provisionally, test them, and be willing to change them, if further empirical inquiry suggested that another view was more adequate. They had to con-sider all other positions with an open mind and be willing to accept the hypothesis that best fit the existing evidence. Since knowledge could only be tested through application, the new school economists believed that they should carefully study the historical consequences of particular eco-nomic policies. Knowledge of the past would provide some information about the likely results of future policies and provide the basis for intel-ligent social "experimentation." Future progress depended on testing new policies that would help American civilization solve its pressing problems.[48]

The debate between classical and historical economists peaked in the late 1880s. Economists interested in the professional development of their discipline sought to find some common ground in the 1890s. This search was facilitated by two important intellectual developments. First, ad-vocates of laissez-faire and proponents of activism adopted similar views about the nature of scientific inquiry. Economists who supported a range of policy positions concurred that scientists did not uncover regularities in nature, but rather invented concepts that helped human beings "navigate" through experience. In addition, the development of marginalist econom-ics provided a bridge between the classical school and the new historical school. Marginalist economics, which in the early twentieth century became the dominant theoretical orientation among American economists, supported reformism. Up until the 1920s economists agreed that their discipline had significant ethical applications.

The influence of John Stuart Mill's ideas about science diminished in the 1890s as the ideas of another English philosopher of science, Karl Pearson, took hold among American economists. Pearson's *Grammar of Science,* published in 1892, rejected the older idea of scientific law, which conceived of laws as rules that existed in nature (or society), regulating natural (or social) phenomena. This older idea posited that these immutable laws existed independently of human beings, who discovered them through scientific study. Pearson thought of scientific laws as human constructions that provided a brief, formulaic representation of a large amount of human experience. "We are thus to understand by a law in science, *i.e.* by a 'law of nature,' a *résumé* in mental shorthand, which replaces for us a lengthy description of the sequences among our sense-impressions. Law in the scientific sense is thus essentially a product of the human mind and has no meaning apart from man. It owes its existence to the creative power of his intellect." Natural laws, according to Pearson, did not point to the existence of a superhuman "law-giver," nor should they be considered normative.[49]

Pearson's notion of science as a human creation overlapped with the progressivist view of science. Pearson emphasized the method of scientific inquiry rather than its content. "The field of science is unlimited; its material is endless, every group of natural phenomena, every phase of social life, every stage of past or present development is material for science. *The unity of all science consists alone in its method, not its material.*" He saw science as a form of mental and moral discipline. He believed that "inculcating scientific habits of mind will lead to more efficient citizenship and so to increased social stability." He thought that scientific knowledge had "practical" value. Pearson also emphasized the role of imagination in scientific inquiry. Conservative economists, such as Charles Dunbar and Arthur T. Hadley, drew on the newer conceptions of science to champion laissez-faire.[50]

There were important differences between Pearson's and progressivist views of science, but these could be mediated more easily than earlier conflicts. The progressivist model pictured scientists as active and engaged, advocating competing hypotheses until consensus formed around the one that best survived the verification process. It emphasized change and presented science as progressing through the displacement of once accepted doctrines. Pearson regarded the ideal scientist as impartial and thought that scientific laws were universal in the sense that all people with "normal" minds recognized their validity. He saw the progress of science as consisting of one true formula being replaced by another that encompassed a larger range of human experience. These differences would become important in the 1920s, but for twenty years after the publication of the *Grammar of Science,* social scientists could mask these differences in the rhetoric of their common "search for truth."[51]

Those same years saw the development of marginalist economics. Marginalist theorists, led in the United States by John Bates Clark, reinterpreted the classical notion of value and based it on utility. *Utility* was defined broadly to encompass basic material needs as well as more refined desires. Marginalism quickly gained favor because it explained troubling aspects of the contemporary economy, such as inequality in competition and the effect of monopolies, and provided an optimistic analysis of the compatibility of industrial capitalism and social justice. Marginalism also allowed for universal economic principles as well as some variation over time. It was abstract and compatible with the idea that scientific knowledge is conceptual rather than representational. Moreover, it was mathematical, giving economics the form (and prestige) of an exact science. Economists who held any of a variety of positions on social reform could accept marginalist analysis.[52]

The declining influence of Mill and the development of marginalism did not eliminate all conflict among American economists. Disagreements about substantive economic policies and different theoretical positions persisted after the rapprochement of the 1890s. But for a couple of decades, at least, economists were no longer divided over their conception of science and its proper relation to morality. Historical economists and marginalists, reformers and conservatives could agree that economics had practical moral application. "Economics to me," explained historical economist Edward Bemis, "is something more than a cold blooded analysis and criticism of industrial society and theories of reform. It is itself a means for reforming and uplifting said society." Irving Fisher, a leading marginalist, agreed that "not only can society be reformed, but to do so is the principal service of economic and social sciences." Even the conservative Hadley used his presidential address to the American Economic Association in 1898 to urge economists to take an active role in solving social problems and use their science to address the central problem of morality: the best way for humans to live, individually and together.[53]

Other social science disciplines experienced similar discord over substantive and methodological questions, but they agreed that the ultimate aim of their disciplines was to improve human life and perceived this goal as a moral mission. Frank Goodnow, the first president of the American Political Science Association (APSA), maintained that political scientists should study "what is and what should be." He believed that political science would not simply describe political reality but also help shape that reality. Goodnow's colleagues agreed that political science had practical application. Henry Jones Ford, a later president of the same organization, asserted that "political science is not merely historical, but is a genuine science in that it can supply plain interpretation, clear foresight, and practical guidance to those who consult it. The state of political science may be fairly compared with that of medical science. The one has much the same relation to the body-politic that the other has to the physical body." Political scientists perceived their task as the study of political institutions with the goal of improving them.[54]

Political scientists conceived of the practical applications of their scholarship in moral terms. They viewed political relationships as ethical. Westel Woodbury Willoughby, for example, treated the relationship between the individual and the state as a question of "ethical obligation." Others also employed moral rhetoric. Jesse Macy, in his presidential address before the APSA, associated "truth" with "righteousness and justice." "Truth," he told his audience,

> expresses the correspondence between righteousness and justice; it is realized by harmonizing external conduct with a subjective state of mind. . . . Righteousness remains an aspiration or a mere dream until it is realized in just human relations. The men of science become traitors to the spirit which gave birth to their order if they stop short of carrying their devotion to truth into every field of human relation.

Political science, by nature of its subject matter, was inevitably related to ethics. "The ultimate object of political science," remarked A. Lawrence Lowell, summing up the views of his colleagues, "is moral, that is the improvement of government among men."[55]

Although Lowell's fellow political scientists could easily assent to his statement, they had greater difficulty deciding how they, as scientists, would accomplish this moral end. Lowell's immediate predecessor as president of the APSA was James Bryce, the British ambassador to the United States and the author of the respected book, *American Commonwealth*, published in 1888. Bryce argued that political science was primarily a historical rather than an abstract science. The data of political science were the histories of particular communities. Political scientists organized this data to better comprehend the principles or laws that governed political communities. Bryce believed that the knowledge produced by political scientists had practical value, but he denied that it could "provide authoritative solutions for current problems and controversies." Bryce recognized that other political scientists had such aspirations. He, however, maintained that political scientists served society through the education of leaders and citizens. "Cherish no vain hopes of introducing the certitude or the authority of science into politics," he told the members of the APSA in 1908. "If you help to create among the most enlightened part of a nation the right temper and attitude, if you strengthen their sense of civic duty, if you enforce the need there is for accurate knowledge of facts and intelligent reasoning from the facts, you will have done as much as can be expected and more than has ever yet been accomplished."[56]

Other political scientists, however, claimed a more active role in politics. Although few made any claim to absolute certitude for their discipline, most American political scientists believed that they should formulate public policy as well as educate the populace. Charles Beard believed that political scientists could "form connections with state and national officials" and "find abundant opportunities to help in drafting bills, devising ways to meet specific legislative and administrative problems and in a hundred other matters." Lowell suggested that they should serve as advisers to political reformers. These reformers, Lowell noted, "need advice from people who are really familiar with the actual working of many political institutions. In short, they need men with a scientific knowledge of the physiology of politics." Political scientists saw themselves as an important resource in public affairs.[57]

In addition to their differences regarding direct versus indirect influence on politics, political scientists did not agree on exactly how to combine "scientific objectivity" and political activism. Some political scientists maintained that they could "take stands" on unsettled political questions as long as they kept the proper scientific attitude of open inquiry. Advocates for opposing positions, explained Macy, "must maintain the open mind and be ready to accept the other's conclusions if a preponderance of evidence is found in its support. One who argues against socialism should be in a state of mind to become a socialist if his arguments are effectively answered. It was this quality in scientific debate, which was so impressive to those who first experienced it." Others, such as Lowell, questioned whether scientists could be openminded while advocating a position, and suggested that scientists should not take a position before investigating an issue. The scientist, explained Lowell, "must not set out with a prejudice for or against particular institutions, or, indeed, regard politics for an immediate moral standpoint; for if he does he will almost inevitably be subject to a bias likely to vitiate his observation." Still others, while accepting activism, emphasized scientists' moderation in political controversies. "There is a general conviction," wrote Albert Shaw, then president of APSA and editor of *Review of Reviews,* that political scientists

> have a large common stock of sincerity and of intelligence, and a habit of mind which checks controversial attitudes and faddish enthusiasms, where questions of clear fact and of scientific bearing are essentially involved. For that reason, our students of political science are obtaining an ever-increasing influence as a moderating and mediating element in the processes of our political life.

These differences, though significant, did not undermine the general consensus among political scientists that their discipline had practical moral relevance.[58]

Sociologists also merged science and ethics. Divisions in the 1890s between Albion Small and Franklin Giddings did not upset the general reformism and moralism of the discipline. Some of the nation's pioneer sociologists, including Small, came to the discipline from the ministry. Consequently, sociologists had strong ties to the social gospel movement as well as to more secular progressive reforms. Indeed, sociology developed in large part as a response to agitation for social and political change.

Small explained that sociologists examined problems first raised by popular leaders. "The doctrines of professional sociologists are attempts to substitute revised second thought for the hasty first thoughts composing the popular sociologies in which busy men outside the schools utter their impression." They did this to help make reform movements a more effective means of social amelioration. "Science makes common cause with every other human interest when it insists that there must be adequate investigation and formulation of the conditions of human welfare before there can be any credible programmes for the wholesale promotion of welfare." Giddings shared this conception of sociology as a guide for social reform movements. "Private philanthropy vies with legislation in attempts to improve the general life-conditions of the masses. Much of this is mischievous. Gradually, however, the intelligence of the community is enlisted, and philanthropic passion is in a measure brought under direction of reason, and so is made more efficient for good." Giddings, Small, and their associates considered themselves the "intelligence of the community."[59]

Like other social scientists, sociologists viewed their ties to social reform in moral terms. Giddings regarded the union of scientific intelligence and enthusiastic benevolence as a "profound moral experience." Through this marriage, "the social mind" would "develop an ethical character" essential for the progress of society. Small believed that sociology would settle the contemporary confusion over moral standards. He rejected the notion of conflict between the scientific study of "what is" and the examination of "what ought to be." He maintained that "sociology would have no sufficient reason for existence if it did not contribute at last to knowledge of what is worth doing."[60]

In the early twentieth century, sociologists used the concept of "social control" to combine science and practical moralism. Led by Edward A. Ross, they posited that society, to survive and evolve, must shape individuals' feelings and behavior to serve group needs rather than individual interest. They then focused their attention on the processes that facilitated social attachment. By understanding these processes, sociologists could manipulate them to create social harmony. Sociologists also turned to social psychology and the formation of personality. This knowledge would help shape a new social education, "through which all members of the coming order shall get a wider outlook, a higher and clearer idealism, and so be prepared to create that free, righteous and joyful system of life to which they aspire." The consensus regarding reform survived among sociologists into the 1910s.[61]

Psychologists in the late nineteenth and early twentieth centuries also shared this reformist orientation. Like other social scientists, psychologists retained the ethical concerns of moral philosophy, even while they distanced themselves from this heritage. Historian of psychology John M. O'Donnell notes that "the discipline developed and flourished not primarily as a community of pure scientists but as a scientistic response to this search for social and philosophical order." Psychologists adopted the scientific method not to reject the goals of moral philosophy but to find more reliable solutions to problems than they thought would be possible with the older, "dogmatic" approach. Some psychologists portrayed their discipline in utopian terms, promising knowledge about human nature that would ultimately lead to human perfection.[62]

Until the 1910s social scientists generally agreed that the aim of their research was the production of morally relevant knowledge. Only in the late 1910s and 1920s did advocates of value-free science gain a significant voice in American intellectual life. The association of "objectivity" with moral neutrality significantly changed the debates among social scientists. Before that time, however, social scientists eagerly portrayed their work as an instrument of moral progress.

University reformers wanted their institutions to serve the public and to train moral leaders. They viewed public service as the modern incarnation of higher education's traditional moral mission. In the late nineteenth and early twentieth centuries, university presidents typically hired all faculty themselves. They contacted friends and associates at other institutions to find out about the intellectual interests and personal qualities of potential faculty. Just as they preferred faculty who were sympathetic to religion, presidents sought out faculty who defined their work in moral terms. In building their faculties, therefore, they were sensitive to the moral value of the various disciplines. University administrators hired faculty who had research interests in areas with important "practical" applications and with ties to contemporary social causes. They approved of courses that educated students about ethical issues and encouraged student involvement in social reform.

University presidents promoted and publicized research and teaching that helped fulfill their institutions' dedication to public service. This reflected educators' sincere commitment to an ideal of educated social leadership. Educators believed that universities were public trusts created to advance the needs of humanity. Emphasis on service also suited university leaders' need for funding to sustain institutional growth. To appeal to philanthropists and legislators, university reformers underscored the practical value of the knowledge produced through faculty research and the future service of their students. In this case, idealistic and materialistic needs converged to reinforce the ethical orientation of the university.[63]

Under these conditions, educators favored the disciplines they associated with human progress. The biological and social sciences both benefited from this policy. For example, Daniel Coit Gilman frequently spoke of the important relationship between biology and medical advances. He praised biological research because of "the promises it holds for improving the health of people," and built at Johns Hopkins one of the most advanced and influential biological science programs of the day. Other university administrators devoted resources to biology because they identified biological research with medical advances and service to humanity.[64]

Faculty understood administrators' interest in public service and accordingly highlighted the contributions of their disciplines. One biology instructor maintained that biology courses served as "the most normal possible introduction to the very practical art of living." Faculty often presented their courses as contributing to students' moral development. This view of biology instruction was consistent with the progressivist conception of science as an instrument in the adaptation and evolution of humanity, and was a natural extension of biologists' optimistic predictions regarding the practical application of their research.[65]

One of the ways in which faculty underscored the practical benefits of biology was by championing hygiene instruction. "During the last two or three decades," wrote Alan W. C. Menzies of the University of Chicago,

> scientific method has been increasingly applied to the solution of problems bearing upon the health of the individual and of the community. Out of the region of controversy, in the study of problems of the maintenance and preservation of health, there has thus come to maturity during comparatively recent years a body of organized knowledge, of which the cardinal facts and broader methods may, perhaps, be grouped together under the title "general hygiene."

Emphasizing the value of this research for individuals and students, Menzies urged that universities institute courses in general hygiene.[66]

University leaders embraced this suggestion and presented hygiene instruction as a form of moral education. "Health," G. Stanley Hall asserted, "means wholeness and holiness and is the best natural basis of the new practical Christianity." Universities instituted elective and in some cases required courses in hygiene. For example, at Harvard in 1919 Henry K. Oliver donated money to establish a professorship in hygiene. The professor of hygiene was expected to give a required course of fifteen lectures on practical hygiene for freshmen, as well as elective courses in hygiene. In the same year Harvard received an appropriation from the U.S. Interdepartmental Social Hygiene Board to organize a department of hygiene. The curriculum of the department included "courses and conferences in informational hygiene, and courses, conferences and training in the applications of hygiene, emphasizing with appropriate and due proportion and with proper tact and persistency the serious importance of venereal diseases, their causes, carriers, and prevention, and emphasizing at the same time the other important facts and applications of general hygiene, individual hygiene, group hygiene, and intergroup hygiene." Other universities established similar hygiene instruction.[67]

Faculty also advocated social causes associated with their disciplines. Academic biologists, for example, advanced eugenics and introduced it into university curricula. Geneticists, such as Raymond Pearl and Herbert S. Jennings of Johns Hopkins and Edward M. East and William E. Castle of Harvard, gave the movement scientific leadership. Castle's book *Genetics and Eugenics,* published in 1916, was widely used in college courses and went through four editions in fifteen years. Most American colleges and universities offered courses specifically in eugenics or general genetics course that included eugenics material.[68]

The social sciences, even more than the biological sciences, prospered on the promise of their moral value. University reformers championed instruction in the social sciences as a form of community service. Andrew D. White, for example, urged the Johns Hopkins trustees to establish "very thorough courses" in the neglected areas of "political and social economy." "The want of knowledge among our best educated men on these subjects is something most disheartening; and I feel that some of the worst mistakes that have been made in our country are directly traceable to the lack of this kind of knowledge among the men to whom we entrust our legislation." If universities were to fulfill their traditional aim of training community leaders, they had to encourage the development of the social sciences.[69]

Johns Hopkins did develop a prominent program in the social sciences, led by Herbert Baxter Adams. Adams believed that he had established "a great department of history and politics," which was both "a place of instruction and a centre of scientific publication" and "a school of practical affairs, having history and politics for its liberal basis and affording useful training in administration and social science." He encouraged students to take a scholarly and an active interest in political and social causes. The Johns Hopkins Studies in Historical and Political Science published numerous studies of local government aimed at supporting reform efforts. Many of the young men who studied with Adams at Johns Hopkins entered politics or public service. Gilman supported Adams's program and praised the study of politics at Hopkins for graduating students who were "wise interpreters of politics . . . strong promoters of democratic institutions," and "firm believers in the merit system of appointments, and in local self-government." By offering social science instruction, Gilman believed that Johns Hopkins ministered to the welfare of the nation.[70]

When Gilman expanded social science instruction at Johns Hopkins to include economics and sociology, he hired faculty with a strong commitment to reform. Ely, the leader of the historical school of economics, was the university's first permanent appointment in economics. Although Gilman had misgivings about Ely, he appreciated his commitment to Christian ideals and reform. Gilman also praised sociology because of its "practical" applications. In an address before the alumni, he commended the introduction of sociology into university curricula, noting that "the demand for educated men to take leading positions in charitable and philanthropic associations is one of the most encouraging signs of the times." Throughout his tenure, Gilman thought of the social sciences as distinguished by "their service to the individual and their service to the state."[71]

Johns Hopkins University's moral orientation in the social sciences was not unique. John Burgess, the founder of the School of Political Science at Columbia University, envisioned a training ground for public service. Columbia's president, Frederick A. P. Barnard, explained that the school was "designed to train men for domestic or diplomatic civil service, or to prepare them to discharge intelligently such duties of public life as may devolve upon them as members of our state or national legislature." The school, which became a major center for graduate training in the social sciences, only accidentally shifted its focus from the education of "men of affairs" to the training of scholars. The unexpected demand for men with Ph.D.s to fill the new faculty positions in the social sciences, and the corresponding failure of efforts to create a "German-style" civil service in the United States, changed the career goals of the students of the school. In the late nineteenth century, however, when academics and activism still blended, this change did not seem to be such a great deviation from Burgess's original intent.[72]

Social science programs were designed to train public officials. This aim was a professionalized version of the goal of the older moral philosophy: preparing all students to be upstanding citizens and leaders of their communities. Given their similar aims, it is not surprising that courses in the social sciences retained moral philosophy's normative cast. The University of Michigan, for example, planned a series of courses in political science in 1881. The first course was "Political Ethics," structured to provide students with a proper basis for judging individuals' relationship to the state and the relations between different governments. Following this, students could select from "The Idea of the State," "Nature of Individual, Social and Political Rights," "History of Political Ideas," "Government of

Cities," "Theories and Methods of Taxation," "Comparative Administrative Law," and other specialized classes in law and diplomacy.[73]

Social science courses were heavily oriented to issues of contemporary social concern. All the universities included in this study sponsored classes examining social problems and/or strategies for reform. At the University of California at the turn of the century, for example, Professor Jessica Peixotto taught "Contemporary Theories of Social Reform," which examined "the programmes and principles of the leading reform movements of the day"; "History of Social Reform," "an historical review of those social movements usually roughly grouped as socialistic"; and "Contemporary Social Problems," "a series of lectures on problems of immediate social interest by members of the faculty and others." These courses suited President Benjamin I. Wheeler's view that "the ultimate task of the state university . . . is the finding out of the way of truth in matters which concern the well-being of the community and of man in society." Social science instruction helped universities discharge their commitment to social improvement.[74]

At the University of Michigan, Henry Carter Adams taught "Problems in Political Economy," which discussed "The Immigration Problem; Industrial Crisis; Free Trade and Protection; The Railway Problem; The Municipal or Trust Problem; Taxation," while his colleague Charles Horton Cooley taught "Problems in Sociology," "a study of the laws of population, degeneracy, the liquor problem, poor relief (public and private), vagrancy, crime and penology, the divorce problem, the assimilation of the foreign element in American population, the development of cities, the tenement question, slums, social settlement, and other sociological questions of present interest." These sorts of courses ensured that interested students were familiar with controversial public issues and offered ethical solutions to these problems. Although individual instructors had different views on what constituted an ethical solution to a given problem, the social sciences in this period favored moderate reforms that seemed to balance the ideals of individual liberty, compassion for others, and social harmony.[75]

Even at schools like Harvard, where conservative, antireformist social scientists such as Charles Dunbar held senior positions, the social sciences addressed the problems of contemporary social reform. Charles Eliot offset the influence of Dunbar by hiring social science faculty who were active in local charities and reform organizations. He hired Edward Cummings in 1891 to teach sociology in the political economy department.

Cummings had been influenced by British trade unionism and urban social settlements; he served on the Board of Boston Associated Charities
and was active in penal reform. He offered courses such as "Principles of
Sociology," "The Social and Economic Condition of Workingmen," and
"Socialism and Communism—Utopias, Ancient and Modern." When
Cummings left Harvard in 1900, Eliot hired Thomas Nixon Carver to
replace him. Like Cummings, Carver was active in Christian social reform,
serving as chairman of the Social Service Committee for "The Men and
Religion Forward Movement." Among other courses, Carver taught
"Methods of Social Reform." In these contexts, Eliot encouraged critics
of the status quo to speak to students. For example, he asked Thorstein
Veblen to give four lectures on "Socialistic Speculation after Marx" as
part of Carver's course on social reform.[76]

University officials invited instruction about controversial political issues because they believed universities should provide leadership on social
problems. In 1902 Columbia accepted a gift to hire Felix Adler, head of
the Society for Ethical Culture, as professor of social and political ethics.
President Nicholas Murray Butler recognized that Adler's reform interests
would make his instruction "more vital and practical and less purely academic than would otherwise be the case." He praised this interest in contemporary problems, stating that "it is natural and appropriate that the
universities, and Columbia University in particular, should be looked to
to formulate and enunciate such principles and to hold them steadily before the students and the public." Although they did not want to hire radi-
cals, university administrators encouraged teachers engaged in issues of
current import.[77]

Other presidents sought out and hired faculty with experience in reform organizations. At Stanford, the first economist David Starr Jordan
hired was Amos G. Warner, who had earned his Ph.D. in Adams's program at Johns Hopkins and had then served as superintendent of charities
in Baltimore. His courses involved students in practical social services.
Warner died in 1900, but faculty-community activism survived him. Professor Walter G. Beach, author of *Sociology and Social Problems,* and
Margaret M. Lothrop, a lecturer in economics who served on the board of
directors of the California State Conference on Social Work, were active
in social reform. Social scientists at many universities coordinated classroom work with practical work at settlement houses and other community
organizations.[78]

Like many social reformers outside the universities, faculty viewed
their reform activities as a religious mission. At University of Chicago,

Charles Henderson, who served as the campus chaplain, taught classes on social reform. At Harvard, Eliot saw the social sciences as related to the social gospel movement. "The new sociology, based on the Gospel doctrine of love to God and love to man," he wrote, "seeks to improve environment, the rectification of vice-breeding evils and wrongs, and the actual realization of the ideal, 'Thou shalt love thy neighbor as thyself.'" He committed Harvard to this view by supporting Francis Peabody's teaching in social ethics and by encouraging donations for the permanent endowment of a social ethics department.[79]

Yale president Arthur Hadley wanted to develop a program similar to the social ethics program at Harvard. He believed that ethics should be studied scientifically and should become, like economics and politics, one of several related disciplines in the social sciences. Hadley envisioned a scientific ethics that was independent of, but cooperative with, religion. Irving Fisher, professor of economics, agreed "that ethics should ultimately be classified among the social sciences." Together they discussed the possibility of including courses in ethics as part of the social science instruction. Their plans, however, were frustrated by the hostility between Charles Sumner in social science and members of the theology school, which precluded the desired cooperation between religion and science.[80]

In the 1910s and 1920s university educators, missing the unity provided by the course in moral philosophy, tried to develop introductory "survey" and "orientation" classes. At some institutions these courses were required, while at others they were voluntary. In almost all cases, the courses were developed first in the natural and social sciences. In 1922 a committee of the American Association of University Professors (AAUP) surveyed orientation courses at American colleges and universities. It found that most aimed "to give the student a stimulating and intelligent interest in the main human problems of the present" and to provide "an introductory survey of a considerable portion of the field of collegiate study." This reflected university reformers' view that evolutionary science furnished a basis for integrating knowledge and offered moral guidance. Another common aim of these courses was to teach students scientific methods, thereby instilling in them the values of the scientific investigator.[81]

These courses reflected late nineteenth-century views about the moral value of the biological and social sciences. Educators thought of biology in connection with character training. "The acceptance by educational institutions of the principle that civilization is a biological phenomenon," Ernest Gale Martin of the Stanford biology department asserted, "brings them face to face with the necessity of shouldering an additional burden in the course of preparing leaders for the civilization of the future, by including in their plans of instruction training in biology for citizenship." Such biology instruction would examine "human behavior as the manifestation of the reactions of the most highly organized living things to the whole world of nature, animate and inanimate." A comprehensive course would encompass the various specialties within biology and would touch on related sciences. Developing biology instruction for "citizenship" would, therefore, involve the cooperation of faculty in botany, zoology, bacteriology, physiology, genetics, ecology, and geography.[82]

Stanford University introduced new biology and social science requirements in 1920 to provide students with a synthetic view of humanity. The university encouraged them to use this knowledge to improve themselves and society. Stanford's required biology course attempted "to present to beginners by means of lectures, illustrations, demonstrations, and laboratory exercises the fundamentals of biology in its broadest sense." It began with the study of "protoplasm, the common living substance of all plants and animals," and continued through the study of cells to simple and complex organisms, the laws and mechanism of heredity, evolution and adaptation of organisms, the ecological and geographical distribution of plants and animals, and "man's place in nature." Throughout the course, "the relations of living things to their non-living environment" was considered.[83]

Stanford coupled general biology with a required general social science course, "Problems of Citizenship." This class was designed as an introduction to the social sciences; it included lectures by faculty in a variety of departments and discussion sections led by special instructors. Like the general biology requirement, Stanford's citizenship course was comprehensive. It was designed, explained its director, Edgar Eugene Robinson, "to present the salient features in the bases and background of present-day society, and to consider the place of education in modern life and the political equipment of the citizen and to examine in detail the fundamental political, social, and economic problems of the American people." It began where the biology course ended, discussing the "Bases of Civilization, including such subdivisions as Physical Environment of Modern Man, Man's Cooperation with Nature, Science and the Scientific Method, Fundamental Social Institutions, Races of Mankind." It then examined the "Historical Development of American Society . . . Political Equipment of the Citizen . . . Political Institutions and Problems . . . Economic and Social Institutions and Problems . . . [and] Education for Citizenship, including such subdivisions as Agencies for Publicity, the Development of Community Life, Opportunities of an Individual in a Democracy." Stanford's required biology and social science classes were intended to provide students with an evolutionary overview of nature and man, and to help them use this knowledge to address contemporary social problems.[84]

Other universities joined the natural and social sciences in an evolutionary framework in an effort to offer students an intellectual synthesis and moral direction. University of Chicago's first successful general education courses, "Botany 5: Organic Evolution" and "Zoology 5: Evolution, Eugenics, and Genetics," were biology courses. These courses became the basis for a broader general science course, "The Nature of the World and Man," that incorporated the physical sciences into an evolutionary framework. This course began with the nature of matter, moved on to the character of chemical processes, then to the origins of the earth and the evolution of plant and animal life, and ended with the human evolution.[85]

University of Chicago extended the evolutionary framework from the sciences to the social sciences. It developed a social science survey course, "Man in Society," to follow "The Nature of the World and Man." The social science survey course began with the evolution of man and continued "up through the record of man's achievements to the major problems with which he is faced at the present day." Together, these courses fulfilled the university's commitment "to help each student to acquire such a knowledge of the physical universe, of the history of the race, of the structure of society, and of the nature of the individual, that, taking his stand at the center of his own being, he may have a sense of where he is." These courses were optional, originally open only to the top one hundred entering freshmen.[86]

Dartmouth and the University of Minnesota introduced similar "evolutionary overviews" as part of their required freshman "orientation" curriculum. Dartmouth developed two courses, "Evolution" and "Problems of Citizenship." The course on evolution, directed by William Patten, was conceived as a "tour through the universe, or the manufacturing plant in which the young man is about to play his part as an intelligent worker." It was viewed as a foundation for future classes in philosophy, sociology, biology, and the physical sciences. "The Problems of Citizenship" provided an introduction to the social sciences to prepare students for the responsibilities of citizenship. Minnesota developed a single survey course covering the natural and social sciences. The class was intended "to orient the student in the world of nature, and of organized society, and to arouse in him a consciousness of his relationships and a realization of his responsibilities." These courses, like the ones at Stanford and Chicago, aimed to provide moral as well as intellectual guidance.[87]

Columbia University also considered a combined natural and social science survey course, but decided that it was not feasible because of the difficulty of finding qualified instructors. Instead, Columbia developed a social science orientation course, "Introduction to Contemporary Civilization." This course began by discussing human nature and the relationship of human beings to the environment; it then offered a brief overview of Western society from 1400 to 1870 and a history of the "great nations" from 1871 to the present. The longest portion of the course was an examination of the "insistent problems of today," such as imperialism and "backward people," nationalism and internationalism, conservation, industrial problems, "problems of political control," and educational problems. Columbia published its syllabus for "Introduction to Contemporary Civilization," and the course was adopted at other universities. In 1929 Columbia developed it into a two-year course jointly sponsored by the departments of economics, government, history, philosophy, psychology, and sociology. In exchange for participating in the program, these departments offered no other courses to freshmen or sophomores.[88]

Like Columbia, most of the other universities that instituted required orientation courses during the 1910s and 1920s relied heavily on the social sciences. For example, Williams College developed a course called "American National Problems," Princeton created "Historical Introduction to Politics and Economics," and Amherst introduced "Social and Economic Institutions." These courses reflected the growing belief that the university could best fulfill its duty to society and students through research and instruction in the social sciences. Historian Clayton C. Hall argued that

> those universities will best serve the public interests in the immediate future which are first and best in historical investigation and in the study of the science of law and of government in its application to the vital questions affecting the well-being of human society . . . from those halls will come forth men qualified to help in the formation of an enlightened public opinion and to take a guiding part in public affairs; men who, speaking above the strife of tongues, can say with authority which commands attention: "This is the way, walk ye in it."

The promotion of the study of the social sciences became, according to this view, a moral mission.[89]

For educators, World War I seemed to reinforce the need for instruction in the social sciences. Samuel P. Capen, director of the American Council of Education, insisted that "the core of a modern liberal education must be the social sciences. Out of the chaos of war and the still greater turmoil that has succeeded arises one categorical imperative for the college. The modern educated man must know his world." Capen maintained that ignorance of social and political developments had "led to the awful calamities of the past five years." Universities had to ensure that these would not be repeated. "However useful as specialties other subjects may be, or however interesting as avenues of self-development, they can not now without a background of social science constitute a liberal education." University leaders increasingly viewed the social sciences as the most important area of instruction.[90]

Although ethics did not become a branch of the social sciences, the two were closely intertwined in the minds of many American academics. Through the 1910s social scientists portrayed themselves as agents of moral progress. University administrators welcomed and rewarded this conception. The phenomenal growth of the social sciences, before there was any clear consensus regarding the intellectual achievements of these disciplines, is evidence of university reformers' strong desire to continue the traditional association of higher education and moral leadership.[91]

University reformers built up programs in the biological and social sciences in part to foster community welfare and to provide moral education. Initially, using science to advance moral concerns complemented universities' efforts to reconstruct religion on a scientific basis. Eventually, however, scientifically based moral education shifted from supplementing religious morality to serving as a substitute for religion. Ambiguities within liberal Protestantism and assumptions about the cognitive superiority of science facilitated this change. The development of naturalistic ethics also helped convince educators that universities could fulfill their moral obligations without a specifically religious orientation.

Ambiguities in Christian modernism blurred the distinction between religious and secular ethics. Advocates of modernism, as was discussed in chapter 4, often identified morality as the essence of religion. Some went further and equated morality with religion. From this position, educators could easily treat science as a substitute for religion, because they perceived that it advanced morality. In this way, a sort of "religion of science" entered universities through the back door, not as an agnostic attack on Christianity but as an outgrowth of Christian modernism.

David Starr Jordan's attitudes toward religious and moral education provide an example of how support for modernized religion could turn into support for a purely scientific ethics. Jordan spoke about religion within the idiom of modernist Protestantism. He believed in the existence of a divine being. "Man cannot worship himself," he wrote. "Righteousness is not the work of humanity, but of God in humanity, and only this can man worship." He also accepted the ideals of Christianity. "Whatever our creed or philosophy, we must recognize this fact, that all progress toward the ideal manhood is progress in the direction of Christly living. . . . The goal of evolution is Jesus Christ." Like many other modernists, Jordan saw Christian ethics as proof of the superiority of Western society.[92]

Jordan supported liberal religious causes; he served on the board of directors of the Liberal Congress of Religion. He also championed universities' efforts to reconstruct religion. He believed that the freedom and individualism of the new university were consistent with the needs of religion. He thought that "freedom of thought and action would promote morality and religion, that a deeper, fuller religious life would arise from the growth of the individual." He expressed confidence in the open university's ability to reconstruct religion.[93]

Although Jordan's statements about religion used the language of Protestant modernism, he had little reverence for traditional Christian practices and doctrines. Unlike many of his colleagues, who assumed that the new "scientific" religion would confirm much of traditional Christianity, Jordan thought that modern religion would evolve according to the model of the Shinto religion of Japan, which he described as a faith that "has no creed, no ceremonies necessary to its practice, no sacred legends or mysteries, and nothing of the machinery of spiritual power which characterizes great religions in other countries." Jordan also praised Shintoism because "it makes no proselytes" and it "opposes no belief and insists on none." Its sole function was ethical, he believed. "It is the animating spirit that causes a Japanese to love his children, be kind to his wife, to help the stranger, to be loyal to Japan, to devote his life to his service, and above all . . . to do no act which is unworthy of his class of Samurai, of his education or of his training." Thus, Jordan comfortably equated religion and morality.[94]

By equating religion and morality, Jordan saw no need for an explicitly religious curriculum; as long as students learned the highest ethical values, the aims of religion would be fulfilled. He believed that science, particularly evolution, would provide standards for correct behavior. Then moral training could be based on science rather than on religious education. The ethics curriculum at Stanford followed this path. In 1891–92, the first year Stanford offered classes, the only course related to religion was an ethics course in the philosophy department. It covered such topics as "development of the ideas of God, freedom, duty, soul, [and] immortality" and considered "the grounds for the acceptance of these ideas."[95]

The next year the department of ethics and ethical literature was created. The department rejected the explicitly religious intentions of the traditional moral philosophy courses. "The aim of this department is the inductive study of ethical conduct. No attempt will be made to construct an abstract metaphysical or theological theory of life." Instead, the department would try to find "by scientific investigation, the laws and tendencies actually ruling in the complex world of human life, and to study the evolution of moral ideas and conduct." The courses included "Ethical Literature of the Bible." Although it avoided "theological doctrines," this course considered "the relation of the thought of the Old and New Testaments to present life."[96]

The ethics department remained unchanged for the next few years. In 1894–95, Professor Wilbur W. Thoburn joined the department and began teaching a course with President Jordan called "Organic Evolution." This course became the basis for the department of bionomics, which was created the next year. The introduction to the department explained that the name *bionomics* had been "proposed by [English social theorist] Patrick Geddes to include the science of descent and adaption and evolution." The department covered all phases of organic life. "In the case of man, an attempt is made to base the study of higher intellectual, social, and religious life on the exact knowledge of his animal nature, and to apply the chief factors of evolution to the interpretation of human tendencies and relations." In the new department, Thoburn taught "Applied Bionomics" and "Religion and the Teachings of Christ," as well as "Organic Evolution" with Jordan. Because Jordan preferred this "scientific" approach to religion and ethics to a literary approach, the department of ethics and ethical literature was disbanded the next year.[97]

The department of bionomics thereafter became the center for ethics teaching. The department's new introductory statement reflected this fact. "It is believed that an inductive study of human life furnishes the basis for determining duty and responsibility. Students who are preparing for settlement work, the ministry, or related lives of activity will be received as majors in this department." In this context, moral concerns were placed in the framework of the findings of the natural sciences. The department had only a short life because Thoburn died before the 1898–99 academic year.[98]

Thoburn was personally religious and served as an informal minister at Stanford, counseling students who had religious doubts. He perceived his work in the bionomics department as engaging science in the service of Christianity. Jordan also portrayed the department as a service to religion. Like most of their colleagues, Jordan and Thoburn assumed that morality and religion were intertwined and that science, by providing a foundation for morality, would help modernize religion. But, as the history of ethics instruction at Stanford illustrates, scientific moral education could easily replace an explicitly religious education.[99]

The department of bionomics basically turned evolution into a new religion: it explained the cosmos, human beings' place in it, and their moral obligations. The tendency to find a replacement for religion in an all-encompassing evolutionary theory was common in the late nineteenth century. William James, for example, remarked that "the idea of universal evolution lends itself to a doctrine of general meliorism and progress which fits the religious needs of the healthy-minded so well that it seems almost as if it might have been created for their use. Accordingly, we find 'evolutionism' interpreted thus optimistically and embraced as a substitute for the religion they were born in." In universities' efforts to reconstruct religion, Protestant modernism could merge into this kind of "religion of evolution."[100]

This tendency for science to supersede, not simply support, religious morality is evident in the rhetoric of university educators. For example, John M. Coulter, a professor of botany at the University of Chicago, gave an address, "Science as a Teacher of Morality," at the Religious Education Association convention in 1905, in which he assured his audience that "the subject does not imply that science can replace religion as a teacher of morality; but that in so far as it contributes anything to morality it reinforces religion." But he went on to suggest that science, because of its superior cognitive status, provided a more reliable authority for morality than religion did.

> The world, like the individual, grows in knowledge; and the childhood of the race received as commands what maturity recognizes as statements of eternal truth, infinitely more binding than any

commands could be. There is no resenting truth, or no quibbling about it; and obedience is imperative. . . . I count this scientific attitude towards morality to be a distinct contribution towards its enforcement.

In other speeches, Coulter explicitly maintained that morality based on science would be more authoritative than morality based on religion.

A fundamental contribution of biology that has reacted favorably upon religion is the increasing body of knowledge in reference to the effect of conduct upon the welfare of the human body. So long as proper personal conduct is a religious demand only, it is observed only by those strongly dominated by the religious impulse, and even with them the pressure of personal interest is rather vague and distant. But when this religious demand is reinforced by a biological demand, proper conduct is observed by many who are not dominantly religious, and upon even those who are religious the pressure of personal interest becomes more definite and immediate.

Coulter was still within the broad program of modernist Protestantism: he wanted to use science to "prove" the truth of Christian beliefs. But as his own language reveals, science, once accepted as a superior source of knowledge, could easily become a superior foundation for morality.[101]

Science seemed to produce reliable, authoritative knowledge, while religion seemed to create endless disagreements. Thomas C. Chamberlin, a geologist at the University of Chicago, warned that the current doubts about traditional religious beliefs might hurt morality. "There is imminent danger that in this cutting loose from the forms of moral truth found serviceable in the past there may be an estrangement from the moral essence that lies back of them." This, he believed, was a danger that must be avoided. "It is preeminently important therefore that the fundamental factors of morality be inculcated on bases that are not the special subjects of questioning." The solution he proposed was a scientifically based morality. "It is therefore especially felicitous that it should now appear that intellectual success through the scientific method is conditioned on an adherence to moral law. It is peculiarly happy that this moral influence, resting thus upon a strictly intellectual basis, should have a new and large recognition in institutions like this." Chamberlin did not think that scientific morality ruled out religious morality. "Moral influence," he concluded, "thus stands on two feet, and if, for any reason, there be tremblings in the one, there is an easy resting over on the other." Science, as the stronger of the "two feet," was for Chamberlin the form of moral training that universities should cultivate.[102]

Academic scientists, such as Coulter and Jordan, believed that science could discover a set of reliable moral precepts. They assumed that this scientific morality would closely resemble traditional Christian morality. Because they also associated the "essence" of religion with morality, they came close to treating science as a modern alternative to religion. They avoided this position by maintaining that religion would still have a distinct role because it would invest this scientific morality with "sentimental force." They thus echoed the findings of the new science of religion, which tended to strip religion of its cognitive value while celebrating its emotional role.[103]

Scholars who believed that science would reinforce Christianity came to a position similar to that of the scholars who hoped to reconstruct Christianity through the scientific study of religion. Instead of creating a modern version of the partnership that had existed between natural theology and biblical theology, they posed a functional division between science and religion.

Albion Small's career in sociology illustrates the difficulties inherent in trying to use science to reinforce Christianity. Small considered himself a Christian. He described his religion as his "attempt to make Jesus Christ the Pattern and Power of [his] life." He dedicated himself to "find[ing] out what the Pattern and Power of Jesus Christ mean in terms of my own daily work."[104]

Small combined his religious and scholarly interests by teaching classes such as "The Sociology of the New Testament." This course was designed "especially for students in the Divinity School" who were interested in understanding "the ideal of society contained in the Gospels" in terms of "contemporary social conditions." Small assumed that sociology would support Christian morality. He did not, however, expect that it would demonstrate that Christian ethics were divinely sanctioned. In fact, Small rejected all absolute moral standards, believing that ethics should be determined by social utility. "The men whose function is to generalize methods of moral valuation," he argued, should "stop juggling with absolute standards that are not absolute, and frankly . . . undertake the work of organizing knowledge of relative utilities into the largest philosophy of ends which our intelligence can construct." Nonetheless, Small continually maintained that this "philosophy of ends" would be consistent with traditional Christian values.[105]

Small also believed that sociology and Christianity served different functions. Sociology, through empirical studies, defined "proper" moral standards. Religion, on the other hand, ensured the "maintenance of influences that impress the importance and authority of ultimate standards, and exert constant moral pressure towards the application of the standards." Because Small believed that religion only enforced the values that scholarship defined, he rejected the idea of a Christian sociology. "A Christian attitude," he argued, "no more makes a social, than an electrical, engineer." He believed that Christian sociology would be as absurd as a Christian chemistry or mathematics.[106]

Although Small was personally sympathetic to religion, he nonetheless, like the scholars who forged the new science of religion, only confirmed its intellectual marginality. Religion had no relationship to the production of knowledge or the establishment of truth. The church, in Small's system, was dependent on the university for the content of its ideas, not the other way around. By maintaining that science was the most reliable source of moral values, Small further undercut religion. He advanced the possibility of a nonreligious moral education and, in so doing, negated the most pressing demand for a religiously informed curriculum.

In the universities of the late nineteenth and early twentieth centuries, there was no sharp division between educators who saw science as a support for religious morality and those who advocated independent secular moral education. The first position merged into the second in the thought of such educators as Jordan, Thoburn, Coulter, and Small. These men extended the cognitive authority of science to morality. At the same time, they equated religion with morality and slighted its intellectual value. They created a rich rhetoric extolling the moral value of scientific inquiry. When efforts to create a modern religion failed, educators searching for secure avenues of moral training naturally turned to science.

Developments in moral theory supported educators' new emphasis on scientific morality. In the late nineteenth century, academic philosophy was dominated by idealism. Idealist philosophers, such as George Holmes Howison at the University of California, George Herbert Palmer at Harvard, George Trumbull Ladd at Yale, and George Sylvester Morris at Johns Hopkins and the University of Michigan, assumed an intimate connection between religion and ethics. During the early twentieth century, naturalism supplanted idealism at the dominant form of American philosophy. Philosophers, such as John Dewey, George Santayana, and Ralph Barton Perry, articulated naturalistic ethical theories that divorced moral questions from the problems of theism. These theories buttressed the view that moral education could be separated from religious education.[107]

John Dewey's ideas were particularly influential in the early twentieth century. In 1908 Dewey and his former colleague at the University of Chicago, James H. Tufts, published *Ethics.* Within months of its publication, thirty colleges adopted it as a textbook for ethics courses. The book was so popular that it went through twenty-five printings before Dewey and Tufts revised it in 1932. The two men rejected supernatural accounts of morality and instead presented it as a natural development from social life. They acknowledged that morality had been confused with religion because "the religious has often been the agency through which certain of the characteristics of the moral have been brought about." But they differentiated religion, which relates "man's life to unseen powers or to the cosmos," from morality, which "concerns itself, not with unseen beings or cosmic reality, but with human purposes and the relation of man to his fellows." They explained that "for religion, conscience may be the 'voice of God'; for morality, it must be stated in terms of thought and feeling." Dewey and Tufts rejected any necessary connection between moral and religious education.[108]

Instead of coupling morality and religion, Dewey and Tufts associated ethics with the natural and social sciences. "Moral life," they explained, "is called or stimulated by certain necessities of individual and social existence." The aim of morality was to "transform both natural and social environments" in order to build an "ideal social order." Ethics, therefore, depended on knowledge of nature and society. "These relations to nature and society are studied by biological and social sciences. Sociology, economics, politics, law, and jurisprudence deal particularly with this aspect of conduct. Ethics must employ their methods and results for this aspect of its problem, as it employs psychology for the examination of conduct on its inner side." For Dewey and Tufts, secular subjects were an important source of moral guidance.[109]

Naturalistic ethical theories, like the one expounded in Dewey and Tufts's *Ethics,* helped universities shift their attention from religious to scientific morality. This was particularly important as universities' efforts to reconstruct religion floundered. Even without a thriving religious program, university leaders could claim to provide effective moral training. "The center of gravity of the curriculum has undoubtedly shifted. Courses in Christian Ethics, Moral Philosophy, the old Metaphysics, and such works as Butler's Analogy have become more or less obsolete in modern colleges," acknowledged Samuel C. Mitchell, president of the State University of South Carolina. "While this is true," he continued, "I am not prepared to say that the present curriculum is less ethical in either its content or outcome than the old one which it displaced." The modern college, Mitchell insisted, "with its curriculum dominantly scientific and social, is, in my opinion, unquestionably more stimulating to manly endeavor in moral and civic causes than was the old system." The sciences, independent of any explicitly religious education, could provide students with adequate moral education.[110]

From the beginnings of the university reform movement, educators acknowledged the moral value of science. They maintained that scientific inquiry developed good habits among its practitioners and that scientific knowledge contributed to individual and social betterment. They conceived of science not as a threat to religion, but rather as its support. They expected that scientific knowledge would dovetail with and provide additional evidence for religious morality. But as intellectuals expounded on the virtues of scientific morality, religion was relegated to the background, and science alone took on the mantle of moral education. For a time, at least, it seemed possible that science could save the universities' commitment to the unity of truth.

SIX

Value-Free Science

University administrators' plans to use the biological and social sciences as secular substitutes for religion soon came into conflict with younger faculty's conception of their disciplines. Academic scientists coming of age in the early twentieth century rejected the utopian visions of science and the ideal of the unity of truth that had been so important to their predecessors. They embraced specialization and rejected efforts to synthesize all knowledge. They began to see the interests of their disciplines in a model of science that stressed the importance of factual description rather than constructive adaptation to the environment and that associated objectivity with the rejection of moral values. In adopting this new conception of science, faculty defined their role in the university as producing research and providing specialized training. This more limited role gave scientists more autonomy and freedom from adminstrative supervision.

Even faculty who subscribed to the ideal of unity found that the increasing specialization of research thwarted efforts to synthesize various branches of knowledge. Although they accepted, in principle, that the sciences "must be so connected as to form a unity," with a "science of science" drawing the lower branches together, they found it impossible to agree on such a classification. These difficulties surfaced, for example, during the organization of the International Congress of Arts and Science planned in conjunction with the 1904 Universal Exposition in St. Louis. Instead of having separate meetings representing different disciplines, the organizers of the congress decided to have scholars in all fields meet "with the definite purpose of working towards the unity of human knowledge, and with the one mission, in this time of scattered specializing work, of bringing to the consciousness of the world the too-much neglected idea of the unity of truth." The aim of the congress was to incorporate recent scholarly advances into a new synthetic framework.[1]

The committee in charge of the congress agreed on a program designed by Harvard psychologist Hugo Münsterberg. Münsterberg devised an elaborate classification separating all subjects of inquiry first into theoretical and practical sciences, then further dividing these into 8 major divisions, covering the normative, historical, physical, mental, utilitarian, regulative, and cultural sciences. These divisions were split into 24 departments, which in turn were subdivided into 129 sections. In each of the departments, scholars were asked to speak on the fundamental conceptions, principles, and methods of their subject. This arrangement was supposed to group all subjects of inquiry in their logical order and reveal underlying relations between the various branches of scholarship.[2]

Münsterberg's plan engendered much opposition. The sociologist Albion Small privately described it as "an effort of the scholastic imagination utterly untempered by practical judgement." He predicted that "instead of having a display of the unity of science," the congress would "be a show of the disunity of scientists." William Rainey Harper agreed with Small's judgment and tried to convince the organizing committee that the plan would irritate working scholars. "It is arranged from the point of view of the specialist in *correlating* research, not from the point of view of those who are *conducting* research. It completely ignores or subordinates what is uppermost in the interest of the latter, namely the problems that they are working on." Harper predicted that scientists would not feel qualified to discuss the unity of truth and would resent being forced to address this theme rather than their own research. The plan, he thought, would either alienate potential speakers or elicit only vague platitudes.[3]

John Dewey raised these reservations in a letter to the editor of *Science.* Dewey supported the congress's focus on "the unity of human knowledge" as "an idea that is rational and feasible, and which would probably command general if not unanimous assent." But he opposed Münsterberg's elaborate classification, describing it as a "sectarian intellectual idea representing some particular *a priori* logic." By providing "ready-made a plan or map of the interrelation" of all knowledge, Dewey thought, the committee limited "the freedom and completeness of the intellectual discussions of the congress," thereby violating the spirit of scientific inquiry. "The essential trait of the scientific life of to-day is its democracy, its give-and-take, its live-and-let-live character." Dewey argued that unity had to emerge naturally out of the process of free and open inquiry and could not be imposed from without. He pointed to the "most active sciences of the day" with "bi-fold names—astro-physics, physical chemistry, geo-physics, physiological chemistry, psycho-physics, [and] social psychology" as proof that scientists were breaking down "artificial walls separating different sciences."[4]

Münsterberg responded by denying that his program curtailed the speakers' freedom and affirming the necessity of some classification. "The principles which are sufficient for a mere directory would never allow the shaping of a programme which can be the basis for synthetic work. Even a university catalogue begins with a certain classification, and yet no one fancies that such a catalogue grouping inhibits the freedom of the university lecturer." He agreed that freedom of inquiry was essential and "has made the specialistic sciences of our day as strong as they are. But it has brought at the same time this extreme tendency to disconnected specialization with its discouraging lack of unity . . . if we want really to satisfy, at least once, the desire for unity, the longing for coordinations, then the hour has come in which we must not yield to this live-and-let-live tendency." He did not believe that unity would emerge naturally out of free inquiry, as Dewey proposed. It had to be created through a well-ordered, community effort.[5]

Neither Dewey's freedom nor Münsterberg's order successfully gave substance to the ideal of the unity of knowledge. Münsterberg admitted that the congress did not fulfill all his expectations. Many of the speakers did not treat "the topic for discussion of which they were invited." Some disagreed "with those logical principles which had led to the classification." For example, the chair of the sociology section protested the classification of sociology as a "mental science." "The classification of the sciences of this Congress," he declared, "has done more to throw the subject into confusion than any other event of recent years. I regard it as a retrograde movement so far as sociology is concerned." Important American intellectuals, such as William James, refused to participate because they disliked Münsterberg's system building. Others simply ignored the theme of the congress and spoke narrowly, as Harper had predicted, on the topic of their own research. Münsterberg could not impose his vision of the unity of truth on his fellow scholars.[6]

Like Münsterberg's attempt at unifying science, Dewey's expectation that unity would emerge out of the freedom of scientific inquiry also went unfulfilled. In 1907 Dewey helped organize a series of talks by Columbia professors. Like the Congress of Arts and Science, "the express purpose of these lectures was to counteract the strongly particularistic tendency of modern scholarship." A "representative of each of the several great departments of study" was asked to explain "in simple and non-technical language what his field of work was, what its methods, and what its main problem." The resulting publication, instead of leveling the boundaries between disciplines, bolstered them. It lacked an introduction summing up or relating the various lectures, and the speakers themselves made no consistent effort to place their discipline in a larger framework of knowledge. On the contrary, each address was printed as if it were a separate pamphlet, with its own title page, publication information, and pagination. Only the binding of the book provided unity.[7]

In 1929 Columbia University, to celebrate its 175th anniversary, again sponsored a lecture series surveying contemporary scholarship. Like those of 1907, these lectures featured individual faculty discussing their own disciplines. Dixon Ryan Fox, who edited the lectures for publication, explained that this format was chosen "not only for the practical reason that no one felt competent to undertake the whole, but because such a partnership of specialists would symbolize the modern university." This time, however, Columbia made no pretensions to offset specialization and unify knowledge, or even to cover the whole field of knowledge. Although Fox acknowledged that "inclusiveness" would have been "ideal," he said that such a broad scope would have taxed "the endurance of the university audience." So instead the organizers simply decided that seventeen lectures would fit into the academic year and selected that number of subjects "arbitrarily . . . as contributing a representative sample of the whole." The selected disciplines were not "more important" than those neglected. Since the purpose of the lectures was to illustrate "the progress of learning in America," rather than to demonstrate the unity of knowledge, any active discipline was as good as another.[8]

The difference between the aim and scope of the 1907 and the 1929 lecture series mirrored scientists' changing attitude about specialization. More and more scientists had begun to see specialization not as a necessary evil to be offset when possible, but as a positive and essential feature of science. Unity appeared, then, to be a spurious ambition. "No one any more," the economist Rexford Tugwell explained, "can hope to understand the whole of science as was very definitely hoped by the scientists a century or two ago; and so modern scientists gradually have abandoned the hope of a great, inclusive integration in favor of frankly specialized work in particular fields." Scholars in the natural and social sciences began to view specialization as a sign of the maturity of their disciplines.[9]

In the biological sciences, this new attitude toward specialization was related to the rise of "experimentalism." Historians of biology generally agree that the standards of scientific practice changed significantly between 1880 and 1920. Experimental biology replaced the naturalist tradition. The new approach emphasized function rather than form and structure, internal factors rather than external influences on the organism, and laboratory work rather than field research. It relied on carefully designed experiments and quantitative data.[10]

This emphasis on experimentation killed hopes that biology might provide a synthesis of the natural and human sciences. Younger biologists, such as Jacques Loeb and Thomas Hunt Morgan, rejected the progressive evolutionism that had seemed so promising to David Starr Jordan and his contemporaries. They criticized their predecessors for straying from careful, minute research. Raymond Pearl of Johns Hopkins University said of late nineteenth-century morphology that "all was well" when biologists stuck to their "purely descriptive purpose," but that they undermined their work when they strayed into philosophy. "The business only began to go bankrupt when it took on an essentially metaphysical purpose, and a logically bad, not to say hopeless one, at that." Modern biologists had learned not to make the same mistake. Edmund B. Wilson explained that experimentalists avoided philosophy. "The biologist as such is occupied only with the protoplasmic living system that he can see, handle, dissect and subject to experiment." Wilson admitted that this method examined "only one side of the great problem" of life, "but the difficulties there encountered," he explained, "are quite enough to tax all the resources of his science." Experimental biologists resolved to stick to concrete, carefully defined issues and leave more amorphous problems to others.[11]

Experimentalists believed that the biological sciences were firmly based in the physical sciences. They generally rejected the idea that they should search for the special "life-force" that "animated" living organisms. Instead, they viewed organisms as physico-chemical systems. "There seems to be no valid reason to believe that organisms differ essentially from non-living systems as regards the conditions under which the processes underlying vitality take place," maintained Ralph Lillie of Clark University. Experimental biologists clarified that they were not necessarily advancing a materialist philosophy. On the contrary, they simply found it "profitable to assume that the integrating and organizing activities of living systems are fundamentally analogous to the equilibration automatically accomplished in non-living systems." They were unconcerned with the "philosophical implications" of such an approach and advanced it only as a valuable research strategy.[12]

Biologists limited the scope of their science in order to make it more reliable. After decades of debating different theories of evolution, biologists wanted to replace "empty speculation" with "ascertained knowledge." They believed that such knowledge was possible only through focused studies that were designed to produce data that would answer a particular question. Other biologists had to be able to repeat and extend these studies. The results had to be tested and refined. Knowledge would be expanded slowly through this exhaustive process of confirming and building upon previous research.

This experimental approach encouraged specialization. Scientists studying a related set of problems split off into semi-autonomous disciplines. Wilson even denied that biology was a coherent science. "The word does not, in fact, denote any particular science but is a generic term applied to a large group of biological sciences." Instead of a unified biology, there were the separate sciences of embryology, cytology, zoology, physiology, and so forth, related by a common interest in "the phenomena of life." Scientists encouraged the growth of new fields with "bi-fold" names, such as biochemistry and biophysics, not as a way to forge unity but as new, fruitful areas for specialized research. Increasing resources for research from universities, foundations, and government agencies sustained the experimental orientation among biologists and thus advanced the subdivision of biology.[13]

Along with the greater specialization by subject matter, biologists and other natural scientists began to view "pure" and "applied" science as forms of functional specialization. In the late nineteenth century, the progressivist conception of science had rejected sharp distinctions between pure and applied science by presenting all scientific inquiry as a form of problem solving. In the 1910s and 1920s the relationship between pure and applied research became a common subject of discussion in scientific circles. Scientists distinguishing between pure and applied research did not claim that the two produced different kinds of knowledge; instead, they based the distinction on scientists' motives and role in the production of knowledge. Pure science was motivated by "the desire to understand," while applied science grew out of "the desire to direct our actions to achieve predetermined ends." Pure scientists pushed the boundaries of knowledge forward. Applied scientists then used this knowledge to solve practical problems. The "inventions" of applied science were the "outgrowth of investigations that were conducted without thought of practical uses, but were searching after truth alone." According to this model, pure science was the first and necessary step toward the eventual application of scientific knowledge. In some cases, a single scientist conducted all stages of the process from discovery to application. But more often, scientists specialized, based on their personalities, talents, and opportunities, in either pure or applied research.[14]

Experimental biologists generally considered themselves pure scientists. The experimental orientation did not eliminate practical and ethical issues from the discussion of biology, but biologists won the respect of their colleagues by avoiding rather than addressing these issues. Experimentalists distrusted broad assertions about the value of scientific knowledge. "The biologist is apt, perhaps too apt," wrote Wilson, "to emphasize the bearing of his work on problems of human life—psychological, social, political, ethical. No one supposes that all the intricacies of the social organism are at present within the reach of the biological searchlights; far from it." In public lectures and popular writing, biologists continued to trumpet medical advances made possible by biological research. Individual researchers continued to be motivated by their interest in social, political, and ethical problems. But such issues were excluded from the scholarly presentation of scientific research. The new disciplinary discourse favored technical language and abstruse rather than applied research.[15]

Social scientists embraced specialization and stricter standards for scientific research with even greater fervor than their colleagues in the biological sciences. In the late nineteenth century academics had split political economy into the separate disciplines of economics, sociology, and political science. At the start of the twentieth there was considerable tension between the new disciplines over turf and legitimacy. Within universities the social sciences competed with each other for resources within combined departments and lobbied administrators for departmental independence. Efforts to take on the task of unifying all knowledge only exacerbated these tensions.[16]

Few scholars were willing to recognize sociology, or any other science, as the summit of all knowledge. Albion Small, who offered sociology as a vehicle to synthesize all human knowledge, realized that only a small minority agreed with his vision. Small privately admitted that "only here and there a sociologist in the world takes the same view" of sociology's relationship to other sciences. "Practically nobody representing the sciences logically included within Sociology gives the view any toleration whatever." To avoid antagonizing their colleagues, many sociologists carefully denied that sociology had "imperialist" designs on other disciplines. No science, explained University of Missouri sociologist Charles Ellwood, "should be taught chiefly as an aid to, or illustrative of, some other science. Each science, in a sense, exists for itself,—that is, represents some relatively independent human interest, and has a right to claim that it should be studied for its own sake." In this context, no single discipline could credibly claim to coordinate the rest.[17]

Other sociologists recognized that contemporary intellectual conditions were hostile to the kind of synthetic science Small envisioned. The modern university encouraged a division of labor; sociology had to find its place within that division, not try to overcome it. "A living science," wrote Franklin Giddings, ". . . grows from a distinct nucleus. It becomes every decade more clearly individuated." To succeed sociology would have to be "something that can be presented in the class-room and worked over in the seminarium." Only "when sociology has as distinct a place in the working programme of the university as political economy or psychology," would "its scientific claims . . . be beyond cavil." Giddings's view on the role of sociology, rather than Small's, triumphed within the discipline. Sociologists realized that their discipline would advance faster as a specialized field than as a synthetic subject.[18]

Younger scholars raised theoretical objections to the notion of a synthetic science. Robert Hoxie, a political scientist at the University of Chicago, criticized Small's ideal of an *"all-inclusive, all-sufficing* science of human experience" as unscientific. "It is one thing to assert that human experience is one unified whole. It is quite another to assert that it can be scientifically apprehended as such." The purpose of science was explanation and interpretation, but it was not possible to explain a thing by itself. Therefore, a science claiming to explain all human experience had to do so in reference to "something outside this experience." "There can be no final or absolute synthesis" of the various sciences, maintained Hoxie, "except on the basis of some extra-scientific presupposition—some standard of values intuitively or authoritatively established." Hoxie argued that a synthetic understanding of human experience was possible only from a poetic or theological perspective. This represented a sharp break from the ideal of unity and the tradition of moral philosophy, which had been understood as the science of all human experience.[19]

In addition to favoring clear lines between the various social sciences, younger scholars favored specialization within individual disciplines. In 1929 Jessie Bernard noted that specialization had been a major trend in sociology in the previous decade. She saw three kinds of subfields within sociology. The first resulted "from marginal contacts with other sciences, like social psychology, social geography, social biology." The second resulted "from the application of the sociological viewpoint to specific problems and institutions, like criminology, educational sociology, the sociology of the family." The final category represented the "division of labor in research, like rural and urban sociology." These specialties had advanced to a point where each was "a separate social science in itself, with its own techniques, its own problems, its own viewpoint." Only "very exceptional men" could grasp and keep abreast of sociology as whole. Bernard saw this specialization as positive and interpreted it as evidence that sociology was maturing into a proper science.[20]

Scholars in other social sciences shared Bernard's attitude toward specialization. Wesley C. Mitchell, surveying advances in economics for the Columbia lecture series, noted that "in the last twenty-five years [i.e., since 1904] specialization has grown so rapidly that it sometimes seems to threaten the unity of economics." But, he explained, this "threat" was not serious because it reflected an outmoded understanding of economics. Specialization was only problematic if one thought that a unified economic theory was the primary contribution of economists. "The fears that economics is disintegrating are well founded from the viewpoint of one who takes conventional economic theory to be the common bond." But traditional economic theory was declining in importance, because more and more economists viewed themselves as behavioral scientists. Like other social scientists, economists increasingly understood their research as addressing one small part of "the great problem of human behavior." Mitchell noted that "if we think of economics as concerned with human behavior, all the specialists however schismatic, are enclosed within the fold." Studies of personnel administration, business cycles, public utilities, labor unions, "or any special problem in the long and shifting list," did not need to be unified into an overarching theory of economic activity. If they helped illuminate one area of human behavior, they were valuable.[21]

Like biologists, social scientists saw cross-disciplinary research as a road to increased specialization rather than synthesis. Social scientists, such as Charles Merriam, encouraged scholars in one field to borrow research methods and conclusions from other fields. Merriam wanted his colleagues to draw on statistics, psychology, biology, neurology, geography, and other sciences to study political phenomena. "In dealing with basic problems such as those of the punishment and prevention of crime, alcoholism, the vexed question of human migration, the relations of the negro, and a wide variety of industrial and agricultural problems, it becomes evident that neither the facts and the techniques of economics alone, nor of politics alone, nor of history alone, are adequate to their analysis and interpretation." He hoped that cross-disciplinary research on particular problems would rid political scientists of the habit of spreading "so broadly over so wide a field that they are likely to get aëroplane views" and instead would encourage "the high-power microscopic examination of problems that is so essential to penetrating understanding."[22]

Social scientists associated this increased specialization with improved methodological standards. Younger scholars, such as sociologists F. Stuart Chapin and William F. Ogburn, criticized the state of their disciplines. Chapin, writing in 1914, considered sociology "an extensive and ill-defined body of knowledge" rather than a science. He thought that sociologists relied on "too much deductive philosophic generalization and far too little inductive verification." Consequently, "the progress of achievement" that marked the natural sciences eluded sociology. In all the social sciences, younger scholars, concerned about the lack of prestige and progress of their disciplines, exhorted their colleagues to become "scientific."[23]

They tried to turn their disciplines into "natural sciences" by imposing strict standards for scientific research. They introduced many of the changes adopted by biologists a decade earlier, such as greater quantification, efforts at experimentation, and distrust of philosophy. Read Bain of Miami University exemplified this attitude when he declared, "Sociology is a natural science. . . . Its methods are not uniquely different from those of other sciences. The only data with which it deals are those that are observable by the senses aided by the objectifying devices of logic, mathematics and instrumentation." Although not all social scientists would have agreed with Bain, there was a distinct shift in the social sciences to more "objective" methods of research.[24]

Beginning in the 1910s some social scientists aggressively advocated statistical analysis as the key to scientific reliability. Use of statistics was supposed to make the social sciences exact and objective. "The quantitative expression of social fact is to be preferred for scientific purposes whenever it can be used," asserted Stuart Rice of the University of Pennsylvania. "It reduces individual bias to a minimum, permits verification by other investigators, reduces and at the same time makes evident the margin of error, and replaces the less exact meanings of descriptive words with the precision of mathematical notation." Within the academic discourse, numbers seemed to confer authority. Many social scientists naively felt that statistics produced an unmediated picture of reality and, therefore, seemed to be free from problems of interpretation.[25]

Statistics, they believed, would provide a corrective to the overly deductive nature of early social science. Social scientists interested in the philosophy of science pointed out that all scientific "laws" were really statements about the probability of recurrent sequences of events. The social sciences seemed less successful than the natural sciences because social phenomena were less regular than those studied by the natural sciences. The exceptions to natural "laws" were, therefore, infrequent and less disturbing than the continual deviations from social "laws." Statistics seemed to offer a method for overcoming this problem. Social scientists could measure the probability of events rather than rely on unreliable generalizations.[26]

In addition to using statistics, social scientists looked for other ways to improve their research techniques. They frequently lamented that, unlike natural scientists, they were not able to perform experiments. They sought ways to compensate for the missing laboratory by controlling and standardizing their research. They promoted case studies, field research, and large-scale social surveys. The aim of these methods was to collect a wide variety of empirical data that could be organized and analyzed. Eventually social scientists would complete enough studies to make comparisons of the findings. These comparisons would provide the basis for generalizations regarding social structure and human behavior.[27]

The aim of the methodological innovations was to make the social sciences more "empirical." Social scientists returned to the Baconian model of building generalizations from individual facts. "The present has been termed 'the inductive era,'" wrote economist Frederick C. Mills. "For the economist of today facts constitute not only the ultimate test of theory but, probably to a greater conscious extent than formerly, facts constitute the raw material from which theories are to be cast." Social scientists believed that their conclusions were only as reliable as the data on which they were based. The main thrust of the new movement among social scientists was to find suitable research data. This orientation favored concrete, visible, discrete, and recurrent phenomena. Some researchers argued that the social sciences should study only observable behavior and should ignore people's conscious intents and values. Others believed that such a limit would render human action incomprehensible; they favored instead the development of techniques to objectively study nontangibles, such as attitudes and ideas.[28]

Although they disagreed about what constituted appropriate data, social scientists agreed that theory should have only a limited role in empirical science. Like biologists, social scientists denounced broad assertions as empty speculation. They wanted their colleagues to eschew theoretical discussion and focus on the careful study of specific issues. In the 1920s the terms *philosophical* and *theoretical* were used as synonyms for *unscientific.*[29]

Social scientists who renounced theory did so in an effort to lessen disagreements within their disciplines. In the late nineteenth century intellectuals had advocated the scientific study of humans as a way to solve the perennial contests between different schools of theologians and philosophers. Because they rejected dogmatic presuppositions in favor of free and open inquiry, they expected these new sciences to break through interminable debates about a priori principles and gradually establish a factual understanding of human nature and society. But in the end social scientists found themselves embroiled in as many conflicts as their dogmatic predecessors.

Around the turn of the century social scientists were self-conscious about the number of disagreements among scholars in the same or related fields. But despite their discomfort, they denied that these conflicts reflected a lack of credibility. "The present position of any science," argued Giddings, "cannot be determined by arraying its contradictions and inconsistencies." Scientific growth, he reminded his readers, always entailed conflicts of opinion. Nonetheless, Giddings's true hope for sociology was a "steady and gratifying progress toward scientific consistency and rigor of method." Social scientists who held the progressivist conception of science maintained that conflict was a natural part of the process of scientific inquiry, but believed that consensus represented progress. For this reason they were ambivalent about conflicts within their disciplines.[30]

Economist Henry Rogers Seager shared Giddings's attitude about consensus. In the 1907 Columbia lectures on the sciences, Seager joked that once "it was understood that the social sciences would next be taken up, some one in this audience said, 'Now they will begin to talk about what they don't know.'" Seager admitted that economists still talked "about what we don't know," but he predicted improvement. "The dogmatic orthodoxy of the past has been succeeded by an exuberant heterodoxy which gives so great prominence to the disagreements among economists that the agreements are easily overlooked. This disputatious period is gradually passing in its turn and a new body of principles is emerging." As Seager's remarks reveal, social scientists were eager to show that they could settle disputed points and that their disciplines were progressing.[31]

By the the 1920s, however, younger social scientists had begun to view discord as antithetical to science. Frank Fetter of Princeton University maintained that disagreements among economists indicated that economics was not yet a science. The "diversity of opinion in the fundamentals among leading exponents of the subject argues strongly that economics is still a philosophy—a general attitude of mind and system of opinion—rather than a positive science." Social scientists increasingly emphasized consensus as a distinguishing feature of scientific research. Mitchell, for example, presented the "slackening of doctrinal controversy" among economists as proof that the discipline was becoming scientific. "I think that we debate broad issues less, because increasing concern with factual observation is breeding in us a more scientific and a less dialectical temper," he said. Younger social scientists presented increasing scientific rigor as a solution to disciplinary discord, and they viewed consensus as a sign of scientific success.[32]

Many of the younger generation of scholars thought that eliminating ethical concerns was the key to achieving scientific rigor and intellectual consensus. These scholars viewed morality as a matter of personal preference. They argued that ethics contaminated scientific research by confusing subjective values with objective facts. "Nothing," maintained A. Gordon Dewey of Columbia, "is more liable to lead astray than the injection of moral considerations into an essentially non-moral, factual investigation." According to this view, one of the main reasons why social scientists did not agree on the results of their research was that moral concerns colored their interpretation of facts; similarly, moral aims had undermined the research of their predecessors.[33]

On the basis of this criticism, some social scientists began to insist that ethical neutrality was an essential condition of scientific research. "Another implication of the natural science viewpoint in sociology," wrote George Lundberg of the University of Pittsburgh, "is the abandonment of the ethical and moralistic approaches which at present encumber social research." To be truly scientific, Lundberg believed, scholars had to avoid ethical questions about what ought to exist and concentrate only on what is. "Economics," Willford I. King of the National Bureau of Economic Research insisted, "is a mathematical science dealing with the relationship between a certain class of causes and their effects, and deals wholly with what is and not with what ought to be." Unlike the first generation of social scientists, members of the younger generation maintained that scientific disciplines should be descriptive and not evaluative.[34]

Not all social scientists agreed that objective science had to be value-free. Some thought ethical neutrality was an impossible goal and believed that instead of avoiding ethical judgments, social scientists should clearly distinguish between factual statements and moral values. Since their research was so closely related to moral concerns, Frank Knight, an economist at the University of Chicago, did not believe social scientists could ignore all questions of "what 'ought' to be." But, he wrote, "what can and must be done is to separate the ideas of truth and ethical significance in the mind of the worker who is interested and understands both. We must know when we are stating facts and when we are passing judgement, and must make it unmistakably clear in our exposition which we are doing." Still other social scientists held onto the older ideal of a morally engaged scholarship that would contribute to the development of a scientific ethics. By the 1920s, however, this last group had dwindled to a vocal minority. Most social scientists agreed that ethical "detachment is a *sine qua non* of scientific method."[35]

The new emphasis on scientific rigor and ethical neutrality did not sever the traditional bond between the social sciences and social reform. Social scientists in the 1920s, like their predecessors, viewed themselves as important resources for the solution of social and political problems. Indeed, they were eager to take part in public affairs and were frustrated that their views were not more highly respected. "The plain fact," lamented George Soule, director of the National Bureau of Economic Research, "is that whereas most people trust the word of the natural scientists as a matter of course, neither the ordinary leader of public life nor the ordinary private citizen has, until within a few months, thought of accepting economics as a body of contemporary and exact knowledge from which guidance may be derived in action." Soule and other social scientists thought that they would increase their influence in society if they improved their credibility as scientists.[36]

The desire for greater credibility was one of the most important motives pushing social scientists to raise their standards of research. They reminded their colleagues that natural scientists' expert advice was sought out much more than that of social scientists, and usually contended that social scientists deserved their ill-repute. In this vein, Harvard political scientist William Bennet Munro asserted that "the science of government has been probably the least successful of all the sciences in building up a set of principles upon which any body of men can agree. . . . As a result of this backwardness in what may be called the pure science of politics, there has been almost no applied science of government worth its name." Social scientists believed they had to improve the reliability of their research findings in order to solve the problems of society.[37]

Social scientists preserved their predecessors' interest in contemporary social and political issues, but they tried to forge a new model of the relationship between knowledge and practice. Earlier social scientists had mixed practical and intellectual concerns. Scholars coming of age in the 1910s, however, embraced the distinction between pure and applied research. "In approaching problems of economic welfare," wrote Raymond T. Bye of the University of Pennsylvania, "the surest procedure is to make a clear separation of pure from applied science. Pure science confines itself to accurate description of phenomena; it explains what is and how it works and what are its effects, but it does not concern itself with what ought to be nor tell us whether the effects are good or bad." Applied science, on the other hand, "takes the knowledge acquired from pure science and applies it" to the practical problems affecting humans. "The two go hand in hand; but the former must precede, for without it the latter is without a proper means for the accomplishment of its task." Social scientists argued that the functional distinction between pure and applied research was especially important in the social sciences because of the danger of moral bias. Because of their subject matter, social scientists were much more likely than natural scientists to corrupt their research with prejudgments. "The cool, careful analysis of the disinterested investigator, pursuing for the time being, at least, knowledge for knowledge's sake, without any intruding ideas about welfare," concluded Bye, "is the surest way toward the ultimate promotion of economic well-being." Ironically, social scientists like Bye believed that disinterested, value-free science was a prerequisite for effective social reform.[38]

In addition to distinguishing pure from applied science, some of the younger social scientists insisted that applied scientists must differentiate means from ends. They argued that science could not help determine policy goals. Scientific study, by learning more about the interaction of individuals and social institutions, could expose the consequences of certain policies. Applied scientists could use this knowledge to predict the outcome of proposed policies and to recommend which policies would best achieve given ends. In the words of George E. G. Catlin, "it is indifferent to the scientists what goods a man may happen to value. The business of the scientist is to study those methods which a man must adopt to attain this or that end *if* he happen to choose it." In its extreme form, this distinction reduced the social scientist to a technician who could help implement but not determine public policy.[39]

More often scholars presented the ideal of the "social engineer," who could impartially design policies to produce the common good. Even the "social engineer" represented a narrowing of social scientists' reform aspirations. Intellectuals had lost faith in the idea that material, intellectual, and moral progress were bound together, so that advances in one area automatically translated to advancement in all. "With the decline of the Spencerian doctrine of inevitable progress," Read Bain wrote, ". . . the view of most sociologists has been that there is no such thing as 'progress in general.'" A given society could become technologically more sophisticated without becoming more literate; its population could become healthier without becoming more moral. Younger social scientists believed that they could offer expert advice on the material problems of society without having to address ethical implications.[40]

The "scientific" warfare of World War I helped undercut the idea that intellectual and technological developments are always good. After the war, James Rowland Angell, a psychology professor at the University of Chicago and later president of Yale, commented that

> science as such has no political or ethical prejudices, no preferences, no convictions. It will serve autocracy as readily as democracy; in the hands of the Bolsheviki it will destroy as willingly as it will construct in the hands of others. The individual scientist may have what aims he will, be they good or evil, high or low; the scientific discovery which he makes, once published, may be exploited by another for ends wholly different.

In this context, rhetoric about the great beneficence of science, so common a decade earlier, was impossible. Instead, intellectuals had to specify the practical advantages of scientific progress. Like the content of scientific research itself, these benefits were increasingly defined in concrete and material terms. Science became associated with technology and "efficiency" rather than "valuation" and "human interest."[41]

The transformation of the standards of scientific research involved a change in intellectuals' conception of scientific inquiry. In the 1920s American academics largely rejected the progressivist view of science in favor of objectivism. This objectivist view of science adopted aspects of Baconianism that scholars had disavowed thirty years earlier. The progressivist conception had renounced the Baconian model of passive induction and had presented science as a form of controlled problem solving. Science involved questioning accepted notions, posing alternative explanations, and verifying hypotheses through active experimentation. Scientific inquiry, according to this view, was creative and dynamic. As in the older Baconian model, science still required careful empirical study, but this came in the final stage of verification, not in the first stage of hypothesis formation.[42]

New discussions about scientific method were motivated by the view "that the old standards of objectivity are not adequate to produce 'objective' science." While the progressivist model of science had taken an eclectic approach to the source of scientific knowledge, the "objectivist" model insisted that induction was the basis of all scientific generalizations, thereby reviving the Baconian emphasis on induction. Intellectuals once again maintained that science began with the careful observation of facts. Instead of conducting empirical research to verify hypotheses, scientists believed they should construct their theories from observations of empirical data. Theory should not direct research, but should be formulated from it. "When definite contact is made between factual investigations and economic theory," wrote Mitchell, "it is rather to test theory than to verify it. That change in wording from 'verification' to 'testing' is significant." Mitchell used *test* rather than *verify* to indicate that observation of facts should guide theory and not vice versa. "Theory that is not based upon logical inferences from sense-experience is not sound theory," wrote Bain. Objectivists reversed the progressivist view of the relationship between hypothesis and observation; empirical research became the first, not the last, step in the scientific method.[43]

Younger scientists also redefined *objectivity.* Earlier proponents of progressivist conceptions of science had adopted "anti-essentialism," which denied that objects were clearly defined by any fundamental feature. Instead, they argued that an observer's interest in an object determined the properties that defined it. On the basis of anti-essentialism, progressivists rejected the idea of passive observation. "Objective" and "unbiased" research referred to scientists' willingness to question established theories and to discard old theories if new ones better explained the empirical data. The term did not refer to the disinterested study of phenomena. It did not mean that scientists began their research free from values, aims, and theories. Indeed, the progressivist view of science had maintained that researchers' "interests" spurred inquiry and thus were essential for scientific progress.

Now scientists renewed the ideal of passive observation. Objectivists identified objectivity with detachment. The objective scientist was supposed to examine data without being influenced by "preconceived ideas." Unbiased observation, explained A. B. Wolfe of Oberlin College, "means in the main freedom from personal or class interest, from dogmatic egotism (assuming that one's ideas are more valid that the next man's simply because they are one's own), from metaphysical presuppositions, and from any desire either to condemn or to praise the facts as they are, and consequently without any desire to make them appear what they are not." According to the objective model of science, scientists were supposed to turn their minds into blank slates, recording what occurred without actively pursuing specific theories.[44]

Objectivists emphasized unbiased observation of facts in an effort to improve the reliability of scientific knowledge. "The aim," explained biologist Ralph Lillie, "is to ascertain impartially the actuality of the case, that which is *so,* quite independently of what our wishes or fears or other prepossessions may be." They equated reliability with agreement. Objectivity, explained George Lundberg, "consists fundamentally in the similarity of responses to a situation by large numbers of people." Consensus, which was viewed as a sign of scientific progress, held a privileged status in the progressivist conception of science. The progressivists had thought that scientists would agree upon the theory that provided the greatest degree of functional adaptation to the environment; this theory would be considered "true" until a better theory was formulated. Objectivists, however, lost faith in the possibility of agreement about what was the "greatest degree of functional adaptation." This standard was too abstract and too personal. Instead, they thought that people would generally agree about what they could see, hear, and feel. Hence, the first and most important step in the production of scientific knowledge was the collection of empirical data upon which scientists could agree.[45]

Although the objectivists reintroduced aspects of Baconianism, they did not reject all aspects of the progressivist view of science. Most objectivists rejected the notion of absolute natural laws. They viewed scientific conclusions as probabilistic descriptions of natural events. They thought that hypotheses and theory had a legitimate, if subordinate, role to play in science. They accepted that scientific concepts change and agreed that there were no eternal scientific truths. Despite these similarities, the new emphasis on objective observation undercut progressivists' position that science was morally relevant. The emphasis on empirical observation favored studies of behavior rather than amorphous values, and the new meaning of objectivity required that scientists excise their ethical concerns from the presentation of their research. Morality was supposed to be excluded from science.

Although scientists' motivation for adopting objectivist standards of research was to improve the reliability of scientific knowledge, they found that the concept of value-free science offered other advantages as well. University adminstrators felt obliged to scrutinize anything related to the morality of their institution. Hence, faculty who addressed subjects that were related to morality faced stricter limits on their academic freedom, and departments involved in the "general education" curriculum experienced more interference from administrators over the kinds of courses offered and the faculty hired to teach them. By promoting the new conception of science and rejecting responsibility for moral education, faculty could lobby for greater separation between research and teaching, and more autonomy within the university.

University officials' commitment to provide moral guidance to students sometimes backfired and discouraged faculty from defining their disciplines in ethical terms. For example, policies on academic freedom seemed to punish faculty whose teaching and research addressed controversial moral issues. The debates over academic freedom in the early twentieth century subtly redefined the expression of ideas as a moral rather than an intellectual act. Since university officials maintained the right to supervise faculty morality, this legitimated the regulation and prohibition of certain kinds of presentation of ideas. In theory, the content of ideas was not judged, just the expression. But in practice, it was difficult to divorce content from expression; by proscribing certain kinds of presentation, universities effectively limited the types of ideas discussed. Because the character of faculty who taught morally relevant subjects was especially important, these faculty could expect more surveillance and less independence than their peers. For them, the line between intellectual expression and moral action became dangerously blurred.

Although university presidents maintained that faculty had full freedom of intellectual inquiry and expression, they insisted that all faculty have a good moral character. They treated morality as an unquestioned requirement for the job. Daniel Coit Gilman of Johns Hopkins wrote that "in the selection of the officers of the university, the trustees have been governed by but one desire—to secure the services of those who were most competent to advance and to teach the sciences they profess." But he went on to say that the trustees "expect each teacher to set an example of upright moral conduct." Educated Americans agreed that university professors should conform to certain standards of moral conduct. In 1912 the president of Stanford explained that "so long as collegiate training of young men and university research are entrusted to the same group of teachers, these teachers cannot escape responsibility for the moral and intellectual ideals of those under their charge." College students required moral guidance; in order to provide it, educators reasoned, the teachers themselves had to be moral.[46]

Faculty were accorded intellectual but not moral freedom, freedom of ideas but not of behavior. University administrators wanted to maintain a clear line between ideas and acts. On the University of Chicago's tenth anniversary, President Harper discussed academic freedom at length. He began by strongly affirming the institution's commitment to free inquiry. He said that if "an effort is made to dislodge" a professor for religious or political sentiments, "the institution has ceased to be a university. . . . Neither an individual, nor the state, nor the church has the right to interfere with the search for truth, or with its promulgation when found." He asserted that no permanent member of the faculty had been or ever would be fired for expressing his views, no matter how odious those ideas might seem to others. The only case where a professor's "resignation will be demanded, and will be accepted, [is] when, in the opinion of those in authority, he has been guilty of immorality, or when for any reason he has proved himself to be incompetent to perform the service called for." University leaders set up a dichotomy between academic freedom and moral turpitude; the former was to be safeguarded, while the latter was rooted out.[47]

University leaders used this dichotomy to explain their personnel practices. It seemed to provide a rational map to the contentious and confusing ground of faculty qualifications. For example, a worried parent sent a letter to President Henry Pratt Judson, Harper's successor at the University of Chicago, complaining about the bad influence of two professors, one of whom was involved in a divorce, while the other held unconventional theological views. Judson responded that the first individual was no longer connected with the university and explained that "a man's social and marital relations are, of course, considered, on the question of his fitness to teach college students." The second professor, Judson maintained, was protected by the university's commitment to academic freedom. "The charter of the University provides for the utmost breadth of theological opinions among the faculty, and to dismiss him on the alleged ground would be an undoubted violation of that charter."[48]

University presidents felt obliged to dismiss teachers who crossed the bounds of acceptable conduct. David Starr Jordan explained that he had asked Thorstein Veblen, who had had extramarital affairs, to resign because the "University cannot condone these matters, much as its officials may feel compassion for the individual." The administration at Johns Hopkins was forced to dismiss its leading psychologist, James Mark Baldwin, in the wake of a sex scandal. Another famous psychologist, John B. Watson, was fired when he became involved in a messy divorce, precipitated by an affair with a medical student at the university. When university presidents fired faculty for moral turpitude, no one questioned their right to do so. The offending instructor either left quietly, maintaining his privacy when possible, or else departed amid a public scandal. But none of the offenders' colleagues publicly charged the administration with overstepping the bounds of authority. These dismissals were accepted as necessary, though unfortunate.[49]

University administrators implemented the moral turpitude policy with few problems. There probably were many transgressions that went unpunished, as well as many unknown cases of enforcement. These are largely lost because universities' right to demand moral rectitude went uncontested. For the same reason, historians have ignored moral turpitude cases. The cases have been discussed only as events in individuals' biographies. Academic freedom, on the other hand, was hotly contested and has received much scholarly attention. The two problems, however, became closely intertwined in the early twentieth century. Since moral turpitude was seen as a legitimate cause for punishment, it could be used to delineate the outer limits of academic freedom. Academic freedom cases, then, can be seen as struggles to define the line between immoral action and acceptable intellectual freedom.

In the late nineteenth century universities dismissed several faculty under suspicious circumstances. In these cases, observers felt that the president of the institution had violated the instructor's academic freedom by punishing him for the expression of ideas. For example, when Jordan fired Edward A. Ross in 1900, most people considered the action an outright violation of academic freedom. Ross had annoyed Jane Stanford by speaking out against Chinese immigration and the use of coolie labor. Stanford demanded that Jordan fire Ross. Jordan initially opposed the decision and confidentially said so to Ross. When Jordan could not save Ross's job, Ross made the "facts" of the incident public. Ross's dismissal appeared to be a clear instance of retaliation for the expression of views offensive to Jane Stanford and contrary to her business interests. Some of Ross's colleagues resigned in protest, faculty and administrators at other institutions complained, and newspapers publicly criticized Jordan.

Jordan tried to legitimate his action by reinterpreting the case as a moral violation. He wrote to the presidents of other major universities to explain himself. In these letters, he maintained that Ross was fired for improper conduct, not for the expression of his views on Chinese labor or any other issue. Jordan explained that Jane Stanford had objected not to Ross's opinions but to his "erratic" behavior that made him a "menace to the good work of the institution." Jordan acknowledged that he had initially opposed firing Ross because he respected his intellect and research. At this point, Jordan had thought that Ross's behavior was not a manifestation of bad character, viewing it as something that could be modified. But he confessed to his colleagues that Jane Stanford was a better judge of character than he. Ross's subsequent behavior, exposing and misrepresenting confidential information, Jordan wrote, "have lost Dr. Ross the respect of most of his colleagues, and have largely justified Mrs. Stanford's view of the matter." Jordan felt that Ross's behavior demonstrated that he was, as Jane Stanford had maintained, a dishonorable man.[50]

The Ross case and the other academic freedom cases in the 1890s prompted a flurry of writing about the nature of university professors' rights and responsibilities. A decade later one question dominated the discourse on academic freedom: can professors abuse their right to intellectual freedom, or is freedom of inquiry an absolute right? Consensus formed on the side of the possibility of abuse, and much of the writing about academic freedom was devoted to delineating what constituted an illegitimate use of an academic position. To preserve the sanctity of ideas, writers focused their attention not on *what* professors said, but on *how* they expressed it. They categorized the presentation of ideas as a form of behavior and maintained that it should be regulated, like all other behavior, according to accepted standards of ethical conduct.

William Rainey Harper equated the abuse of academic freedom with actions that "bring reproach and injury to [a professor] and to his institution." Such injurious actions included misrepresenting "untested" ideas or "unsettled" opinions as the "truth," propagating "partisan" views, using "sensational methods" to influence students or the public, speaking "authoritatively" on subjects outside his specialty, or failing to exercise "common sense." A professor, Harper concluded, "ought not to make an exhibition of his weaknesses so many times, that the attention of the public at large is called to the fact. In this respect he has no larger liberty than other men." Although Harper admitted that a permanent member of the faculty should not be dismissed for any of the above "weaknesses," he asserted that university officials should be careful not to give permanent positions to people who behaved in these ways. Andrew West of Princeton specified that faculty should have temperate judgment, be "wise in counsel, considerate in action, tactful in winning men, swift to help, and slow to harm." He thought that "plain common-sense, open-eyed sympathy, tolerance, modesty, [and] balance" were some of "the old undramatic virtues needed to guarantee that the free professor or the free faculty will be beneficently free."[51]

The discussions of academic freedom became a vehicle for setting norms of academic discussion. Administrators and faculty maintained that the mode of expression had an effect separate from the content of the ideas. John Dewey wrote,

The manner of conveying the truth may cause an irritation quite foreign to its own substance. This is quite likely to be the case whenever the negative rather than the positive aspect is dwelt upon; wherever the discrepancy between the new truth and established institutions is emphasized, rather than the intrinsic significance of the new conception. The outcome is disintegrating instead of constructive; and methods inevitably breed distrust and antagonism.

This kind of analysis implicitly made faculty responsible for the reaction of their audience. In the discussion of academic freedom, writers often conflated professors' actions with the effect on their audience: speaking in a proper academic manner and not provoking controversy or conflict were treated as the same thing.[52]

Some educators proposed giving the right to free expression only to professors who did not abuse it. "Before we talk of larger freedom," Andrew West wrote, "we must be sure in a given case that the individual professor . . . is fit to be free." West believed the best solution to problems of academic freedom was to employ professors who had the requisite "virtues" to exercise freedom responsibly. If this was impossible, a university would have to grant its faculty less freedom. Other university leaders, like West, also tended to define academic freedom circularly: professors whose ideas raised no questions were fit to express themselves, while those who attracted negative publicity were acting irresponsibly. "Professors of established reputation, good judgment and good sense rarely if ever find themselves under serious criticism from any source," wrote Nicholas Murray Butler of Columbia. "Such men and women may hold whatever opinions they please, since they are in the habit of expressing themselves with discretion, moderation, good taste and good sense." On the other hand, there were some faculty whose statements attracted public censure. Butler drew a distinction between the "manner" and "matter" of intellectual expression, and he assumed that faculty who attracted public scrutiny did so by the manner and not the content of their speech. "It is a misnomer," he argued, "to apply the high and splendid term 'academic freedom'" to these cases. Instead, he viewed them as "exhibitions of bad taste and bad manners." The faculty involved were irresponsible agitators, not victims of "improper attacks" on their scholarly freedom. "The serious, scholarly and responsible investigator is not a demagogue, and demagogues should not be permitted to take his name in vain." Faculty who needed the protection of academic freedom, by this reasoning, did not deserve it.[53]

This reasoning allowed university administrators to assert that their institutions were fully committed to academic freedom, while still being able to regulate faculty speech. By defining the presentation of ideas as an act independent of the ideas expressed, by establishing normative guidelines for appropriate scholarly presentation, and by judging presentation by audience reaction, they could limit freedom of speech by labeling the provocation of controversy as a moral indiscretion. After defending the right of professors to speak on public issues, President Lowell of Harvard added this qualification: "All this refers, of course, to opinions on public matters sincerely uttered. If a professor speaks in a way that reveals moral obliquity, he may be treated as he would on any other evidence of moral defect; for character in the teacher is essential to the welfare of the students." Faculty could find themselves guilty of moral turpitude because they spoke in an unscholarly, undignified, or provocative manner. How professors expressed their ideas was now classified as a form of moral behavior, not as part of the process of intellectual inquiry.[54]

Faculty leaders did not oppose the distinction between the manner and content of intellectual expression. In 1915 the American Association of University Professors issued its seminal report on academic freedom. The AAUP committee agreed that professors had to conform to the dictates of appropriate scholarly behavior. "The liberty of the scholar within the university to set forth his conclusions, be they what they may, is conditioned by their being conclusions gained by a scholar's method and held in a scholar's spirit; that is to say, they must be the fruits of competent and patient and sincere inquiry, and they should be set forth with dignity, courtesy, and temperateness of language." The committee also acknowledged that faculty might have to censor themselves when teaching undergraduates. It maintained that professors had special responsibilities in teaching immature minds and that they should "present scientific truth with discretion," introducing new ideas slowly, with respect for students' own beliefs and traditions, "and with due regard to character-building." In public as well as in the academy, the AAUP believed, professors should avoid "exaggerated statements" and "intemperate or sensational modes of expression." The committee stressed that it did not advocate "the absolute freedom of utterance of the individual scholar"; rather, its goal was for professors, rather than university administrators or trustees, to decide if and when another professor had abused the privilege of academic freedom.[55]

By associating controversy with inappropriate behavior, policies on academic freedom refused to protect any professor who addressed a topic that, in a given time and place, was inevitably provocative. For example, during World War I, expression of doubts about U.S. entry into the war or about the draft immediately aroused conflict. University administrators branded faculty who spoke against war policies as "disloyal" and accused them of encouraging people to dodge their duties as citizens. During the previous decade philosophers, such as Josiah Royce, had elevated "loyalty" to the highest moral virtue, and universities had aimed much of their moral education at graduating "good citizens." Hence, charges of disloyalty and bad citizenship were clearly understood as moral indictments. University officials interpreted opposition to the war as instances of moral turpitude rather than as legitimate cases of academic freedom, and they dismissed faculty accordingly.[56]

This was Columbia's defense after firing James McKeen Cattell and Henry Wadsworth Longfellow Dana in 1917. Both men had attracted considerable public attention because of their opposition to the draft, and both were later dismissed by the board of trustees. A university report defended the trustees' decisions, noting that "ultimate decisions as to whether the influence of a given teacher is injurious to private morals or dangerous to public order and security, is one which the Trustees may neither shirk nor share nor delegate." Columbia officials believed that Cattell and Dana had transgressed moral norms and, therefore, deserved to be fired. The AAUP Committee on Academic Freedom agreed with the principle, although it disagreed with its application to Cattell's case. The AAUP "has never declared it to be an infringement of academic freedom," wrote committee chairman Arthur Lovejoy, "to remove a teacher for grave delinquencies, or for violations of professional ethics, or for gross and habitual discourtesy." Moral concerns clearly overrode faculty's right to free speech.[57]

As a result of the early twentieth-century discourse on academic freedom, university leaders identified certain kinds of speech as unethical and unprofessional. They regarded public controversy as an indication that professors had used prohibited manners of expression. This limitation of the scope of academic freedom made scholars more reluctant to associate their disciplines with controversial moral questions. In addition, faculty who taught subjects identified with morality found themselves under particular scrutiny. For example, the trustees of Johns Hopkins University took particular interest in social science instruction. They regarded "the discussion of current political, economic, financial, and social questions before students of this University as of such importance that the lessons should be given only by the ablest and wisest persons whose services the

University can command." In 1894 the trustees formed a committee to consider the best way to ensure responsible instruction in these fields. At the University of Chicago, President Judson also maintained that "the trustees in the university have a right to know what doctrines members of the faculty are teaching in social and especially on ethical subjects and how they are presenting these doctrines." University officials believed they should supervise the teaching of ethical issues as part of their responsibility to enforce standards of moral conduct. This kind of scrutiny increased the appeal of the ideal of value-free science.[58]

Throughout the period under consideration university presidents normally had final authority over all staffing decisions. They were often actively involved in the selection of faculty and commonly inquired about a candidate's background, views, and character before approving a new appointment. As the faculty grew more specialized, university presidents accorded them—particularly department chairs—more voice in choosing their colleagues. The selection of the instructional staff had always required balancing administrative and faculty priorities. In the early twentieth century faculty had made some progress in gaining more influence over appointments. The concern about professors' character threatened to tip this balance back toward the university president.[59]

Scientists were particularly wary of administrative interference in faculty selection. They felt that nonspecialists could not appropriately evaluate the needs of their disciplines. At University of Chicago, for example, Charles Otis Whitman thought that President Harper's lack of knowledge about biology had cost the university some of its best faculty. Whitman was particularly angry that Harper had not tried to keep an instructor that Whitman had selected, Shosaburo Watase. Harper thought Watase, who had few students, was an "expensive luxury" and did not offer him a permanent appointment. Whitman considered Watase "the broadest and soundest student of cellular biology" and an "honor to the University." These sorts of incidents made faculty jealous of their authority and independence, and caused them to look askance at changes that threatened to restrict their freedom in the selection of colleagues.[60]

In addition to supervising faculty, administrators took a greater interest in those subjects they considered central to the moral mission of the university. In the 1910s university officials, troubled by the low enrollments in science courses, began to pressure faculty to change their instructional methods. Under the elective system, only a small proportion of students chose to study science. For example, at the University of California, Berkeley, in 1925–26 only 3 seniors majored in the department of bacteriology, 3 in biochemistry, 4 in botany, and 18 in zoology, while 133 majored in English and 177 in history. In the Yale College class of 1926, 2 students majored in biology, compared to 217 in English and 54 in history. In the same year 111 Harvard undergraduates (3.7 percent of the student body) majored in biology, while 673 students (22.2 percent) majored in English and 263 (8.7 percent) in history. George Herbert Mead of the University of Chicago lamented, "No one will question that science in the colleges of this and other universities has not had the importance and popularity that it should have, that this element of our modern education is by no means represented in the results of education in accordance with its importance." Although the exact distribution varied from school to school, most university officials were disappointed by students' lack of interest in the natural sciences.[61]

University administrators blamed the lack of interest on scientists and the specialized nature of their classes. They charged that faculty designed courses in the natural sciences to train future specialists rather than to integrate science into a program of general education. Nicholas Murray Butler complained in 1919:

> Despite the vast expenditure of the past fifty years for equipment and teaching the natural sciences . . . we have not made chemistry, physics and biology part of the mental furniture of persons who are called educated. . . . The teachers of all these sciences have almost uniformly proceeded as if every student who came under their influence was to become a specialist in their particular science. They have mistaken the training of scientists for the teaching of science.[62]

To rectify this situation, administrators pressured science departments to make introductory courses more relevant to the interests of students majoring in other disciplines. They tried to increase the influence of science and offset some of the criticism about overspecialization by instructing scientists to develop "general" science courses. For example, at the recommendation of its board of overseers, Harvard introduced in 1922 a general biology course, "Life and Its Environment." President Lowell encouraged the development of such courses by having the Committee on Instruction monitor courses to ensure that they were "cultural" rather than "vocational" in orientation. The Committee on Instruction lamented that students and faculty tended to view certain disciplines as "designed peculiarly for general culture, and certain others as designed for the scholastic training of specialists. . . . The Committee believes that such a distinction is unfortunate, and that, so far as possible, every department ought to provide courses for students who are not to be specialists in it."[63]

Although Lowell acknowledged that there was no sharp line between "vocational" and "cultural," he believed that there was a difference of emphasis. The proper emphasis for a college course was the mastery of a subject for the purpose of the development of a student, not for preparation for a career. "Cultural" courses contributed to a student's personal growth. Lowell thought that all college subjects should be "cultural." He also suggested that faculty reduce the number of advanced courses they offered and develop general survey courses that were primarily "cultural." These courses ideally related their subject matter to the personal and social interests of students. For example, "Physiology 1: Elementary Anatomy and Physiology" was described as treating "the subject both from a scientific point of view and from a practical point of view. Personal Hygiene and the practical guidance of a man's life are an important part of the teaching. It is intended for general culture, not for students of Medicine."[64]

Although scientists designed new introductory classes, some faculty resisted pressure to radically reorient their undergraduate instruction. Disputes emerged over the best format for science courses. Faculty found themselves in conflict with colleagues and students over the campaign for science orientation courses. At Harvard, for instance, the student council published a report in 1926 evaluating the college's educational practices. The students were generally enthusiastic about the undergraduate curriculum at Harvard. One exception to this endorsement was their attitude toward the courses offered in the natural sciences. The students maintained that the science courses in the undergraduate curriculum were inappropriate for the general student. The students proposed that the college design a general science survey, "presenting, without laboratory work, the more important principles of astronomy, geology, physics, chemistry, botany, zoology." They envisioned a class that explained "the scientific point of view," "develop[ed] the philosophical significance of scientific progress," and demonstrated how "man's increasing control over nature has changed his way of looking at life." Students wanted to learn about the cultural impact of science rather than the research techniques and problems of a scientific discipline.[65]

These Harvard students understood that their vision of science instruction challenged the priorities of their teachers. "The committee is aware that professors of science will object that laboratory work is essential to teach the scientific method. But it is the opinion of the committee, all of whom have performed the laboratory exercises now required, that they do not teach the scientific method." The students pointed out that in introductory classes students do not perform scientific research. "The work consists of stereotyped experiments, every operation is carefully prescribed in advance, and the results already known." Students saw little value in repeating these acts of mock discovery. Laboratory work, which had been one of the key elements of university reformers' program for active learning, appeared to students to be nothing more than rote performance.[66]

The Harvard student council was joining a larger debate over the nature of instruction in the natural sciences. Since the late nineteenth century educators had seen laboratory work as the defining feature of university science instruction. The laboratory epitomized training in the scientific method and the university's commitment to graduating students prepared to think independently. Critics of laboratory work, by doubting the value of all students learning how to conduct scientific research, called into question the moral and intellectual claims of the ideal of scientific "mental training." Some scientists agreed that students needed a different sort of introduction to science. Insisting upon laboratory instruction, argued T. W. Galloway of Beloit College, had served "to retard the development of biology to its rightful place as one of the most foundational and catholic of all educational fields." Galloway favored the movement to create new introductory science courses that provided an overview of humankind's place in the world and emphasized scientific knowledge that was applicable to students' lives. Scientists like Galloway also advocated the development of "cultural" science courses. They focused more on the history and philosophy of science than on the concepts and methods of individual scientific disciplines. This movement launched the history of science as "a distinct branch of teaching and research."[67]

Research scientists responded to their critics by reiterating their faith in laboratory work as the best form of mental training. "It is fair to assume that college graduates would be best prepared to meet life's problems if they were trained in research methods," wrote James M. Anders, professor of medicine at the University of Pennsylvania, in 1929. "They could accurately collect and evaluate and correlate facts appertaining to any department of the curriculum; their thinking would thereby assume a wider scope and prove more constructive. More than this, they would thereby attain a higher level of initiative, conception, and vision." These scientists maintained that students in science classes did not have enough opportunity for laboratory research. They argued that lectures and textbooks still occupied too much of college science teaching. The way to improve science instruction was to increase, not eliminate, student research.[68]

Many scientists simply refused to concede that specialized science education was inappropriate for the general student. Like their predecessors, they insisted that all students benefited from the mental discipline of the laboratory. Others did not even try to justify the value of science instruction for nonspecialists. They frankly admitted that the aim of science courses was to provide professional training for future scientists.[69]

Most scientists at the leading universities were uninterested in fulfilling the role of a generalist unifying knowledge for the benefit of undergraduates. As a result, plans for a scientifically based moral education languished at most institutions. Orientation courses on evolution, like the ones designed by the University of Chicago and Dartmouth, did not become a common feature of American undergraduate education. Although the number of colleges offering freshman orientation courses jumped from ten in 1918 to seventy-nine in 1925, only a few adopted courses that relied heavily on the biological sciences, and some of these were short-lived. Even the University of Chicago's "Nature of the World and of Man," a model for other science orientation courses, did not survive beyond the 1920s. In the early 1930s, when Robert Maynard Hutchins, the new president of the University of Chicago, lobbied for the development of general education courses, the faculty in the biological sciences were among the most resistant in the university.[70]

At Stanford University, where the head of the biology division, Ernest Gale Martin, had enthusiastically endorsed biology for "citizenship," science faculty still asserted their preference for specialized instruction. In 1929 a committee formed to examine the ideals and future development of the Stanford School of Biological Science reported that the faculty felt that the "curriculum must be arranged and conducted on a professional basis for a career in biology." The committee acknowledged that "many feel that the School owes it to other schools of the University to conduct some courses of a cultural nature as a general University service." Although there was some support for such courses within the school of biology, there was also considerable concern "that the necessary energy and money spent on such courses would be more profitably expended in professional work."[71]

Social science orientation classes lasted longer than those in the natural sciences, but even these faced faculty resistance. Some universities established general courses in social science but dropped them after a few years. Yale in its 1922–23 annual report announced "a new general course giving a broad introduction to social science." In 1925 Percy T. Walden, dean of freshmen, announced that the course "was handicapped by adverse conditions" and had to be discontinued. University of Chicago's first attempt at a social science orientation course, "Man in Society," also fell apart after a few years. These difficulties probably reflected inter- and intra-disciplinary conflict about the content and purpose of a general course in the social sciences. Since survey courses had been conceived as a way to demonstrate the unity and purpose of a field of study, increasing specialization and debates over the nature of scientific research made it particularly difficult to design these courses. Social scientists discussed introductory courses at their conferences and in their journals throughout the 1920s. These discussions often led only to the acknowledgment that a "divergence of opinion" existed regarding these introductory courses and that no single model could be recommended.[72]

As social scientists attempted to rid their research of value judgments, they became more sensitive to and critical of moral aims in their teaching. Disagreements about the purpose of the introductory courses affected even those universities that had successfully established such courses. Columbia's "Contemporary Civilization" course and Stanford's "Problems in Citizenship" course were both established after World War I to educate students about the problems of modern society and to train them to be better citizens. In the mid–1920s social scientists began to question whether citizenship training was a suitable goal. During a discussion about orientation courses at the American Political Science Association, participants pointed out that "as yet 'effective citizenship' is undefined, and that this constitutes a major problem for those interested in a course having citizenship as a major goal." Another round-table discussion at the APSA concluded that, like political science research, the subject matter of the courses "will tend more than at present to be approached as a problem in human behavior. The purpose of study will come to be . . . attempting to recognize and understand the behavior patterns working out in . . . social relations." Social science instruction at major research universities reflected scholars' new emphasis on value-neutrality. By 1930 there was a trend away from basing required orientation courses in the social sciences. In 1934 Stanford changed the title of its citizenship course to "Introduction to Social Problems" and altered the requirement to allow students to elect it or another introductory social science class. As the ideal of value-free science became widely accepted in the universities, social scientists rejected the notion that their disciplines should provide the college curriculum with unity and moral purpose.[73]

Social scientists also became more uncomfortable with elective courses that focused on social problems and reforms. Jessie Bernard noted in 1929 that the number of sociology classes devoted to practical problems and social ethics was declining. "Sociology was making headway toward overcoming . . . the 'social science' strain in its ancestry," she reported approvingly. University leaders increasingly viewed classes on social problems and their treatment as "professional courses." For example, in 1920 President Lowell tried to move the social reform courses offered by Harvard's social ethics department to the divinity school because he thought they were more appropriate for students preparing for careers in social service than for general college students. Richard Cabot, chairman of the social ethics department, resisted this change. Lowell, instead, gradually eliminated the department and replaced it with a sociology department headed by Pitirim Sorokin, who was opposed to a reformist and ethical orientation in the social sciences. Several other universities, including Columbia, University of Chicago, and University of Michigan, created professional schools of social work and moved the reform-oriented courses to those programs. This institutional change sharpened gender divisions within academia: moral concerns were related to the "feminine" profession of social work, while science was associated with "masculine" virtues of detachment and impartiality.[74]

In part as a result of their new commitment to value-free science and in part from a desire for more institutional autonomy, faculty in the natural and social sciences tried to establish their primary position in the university as researchers rather than undergraduate teachers. In selecting this professional role, science faculty were redefining the relationship between teaching and research. Late nineteenth-century university reformers had linked research and teaching. They had argued that the primary aim of the university was to train students to think "scientifically," the only way to teach scientific thinking was through practice in scientific research, and the only person who could direct research was the active scientist. Research, then, was essential preparation for effective university teaching. Teaching was also believed to help research, by forcing faculty to articulate and defend their ideas. This model of the relationship between research and teaching reigned until about 1910. For example, in 1906 the Association of American Universities sponsored a conference session addressing the question, "To what extent should the university investigator be relieved from teaching?" David Starr Jordan began the discussion, declaring that "teaching without research is not university teaching." He went on to explain why teaching and research were mutually beneficial.

He suggested that universities should not hire individuals for research-only positions but rather should arrange teaching conditions so that all faculty could comfortably teach and complete their research. None of the participants disagreed with his conclusion. Arthur T. Hadley summed up the group opinion, "We do not want the two things separated, we want them combined."[75]

University leaders' assumption that research and teaching were mutually beneficial was challenged in the second decade of the twentieth century. Critics of the new university charged that researchers neglected their teaching and were out of touch with their students. They argued that research abilities should not be the primary consideration for hiring college faculty. Some scientists responded to this criticism by arguing that research should be considered an independent mission of the university. Even if research did not enhance a professor's teaching, they maintained, universities should still support scientific research for its own sake. They emphasized the value of scientific research to society and pointed to the use of science in the recent war as evidence. These scientists encouraged university officials to think about the university's traditional role of social leadership and service as several distinct tasks. They thought that producing knowledge, training professionals, and shaping the character of citizens could be approached as separate jobs accomplished by different sectors of the university.[76]

Scientists wanted universities to dedicate more facilities and resources to research, to free a larger portion of the faculty's time for research, to specify research as the prime criterion for appointment and promotion, and to create special research professorships and institutes devoted to particular scientific problems. They used the growing number of private research laboratories and industry-sponsored laboratories to strengthen their case. They argued that there was "a real danger that investigation will be led captive by industry, that the distinctions between pure and applied science may be obliterated, and that research will get into dangerous proximity to the patent office." Scientists maintained that the university, because it employed researchers in all areas and left them free to determine the goals of their research, filled a unique role in stimulating new areas of research. The university's "breadth of interest, wide range of contact, unusual freedom of relationship, and spontaneity" offered an indispensable research environment that should be nurtured. Scientists encouraged university administrators to present their schools as research institutions and not simply educational institutions. They maintained that this was an important part of the university's service to society: since progress in pure science was viewed as a prerequisite for progress in applied research, the support of pure research would aid the technological progress of society, without subordinating scientific research to immediate pecuniary goals.[77]

In addition, private industry and independent research foundations threatened to lure faculty away from the universities. President Marion LeRoy Burton of the University of Michigan explained that the university had to improve conditions for research in order to prevent scientists from leaving to go to research institutes. He outlined a plan for special research positions, periods of leave from classroom teaching and general laboratories, and cooperation in publication. "We all owe it to one another and the University to create an environment in which scholarly work can flourish, in which it is fully expected that time must not be consumed with too many distractions, and where sound, substantial scholarship is rated above public recognition of a superficial type or even social graces of a high order, important as they are for every university community." Outside pressure encouraged universities to view research as a basic aim of the university, independent of its value for teaching.[78]

Natural scientists were more successful than social scientists at carving out an independent realm for research. The lack of student interest in the natural sciences probably helped in this regard. The social sciences were some of the most popular subjects among undergraduates. For example, the economics department had the largest group of majors in the class of 1926 at Stanford, the second largest at Harvard and Berkeley, and the third largest at Yale. Social scientists could not minimize their undergraduate teaching responsibilities. In addition, natural scientists had access to more outside research support through foundations and corporations. Nonetheless, social scientists emulated, with some success, the research practices of natural scientists. With funding from the Carnegie Foundation and the Rockefeller Foundation, social scientists established the National Bureau of Economic Research and the Social Science Research Council to help fund and coordinate research. In addition, several universities set up internal social science research facilities, such as the Local Community Research Committee at the University of Chicago and the Institute of Social Science at the University of California, Berkeley. Support for this kind of independent research increased faculty's autonomy within the university.[79]

Biological and social scientists had decided that their professional advancement depended on the quality of their research, not on their position as moral leaders. As a result they concentrated on improving the reliability of the knowledge they produced. This motivated stricter standards of research. It also encouraged the adoption of the ideal of value-free science because morally charged subjects created conflict and undermined the authority of the discipline. Academic scientists tried to increase the prestige of their research by maintaining that it was the only source of factual truth and a precondition for technical progress. They then translated this prestige into increased security within the university. By the 1920s most natural and social scientists defined their academic role in terms of specialized instruction and the advancement of scientific knowledge, effectively undermining plans to make their disciplines the basis of a new secular moral education.

SEVEN

From Truth to Beauty

The development of the modern humanities was closely related to the efforts to find a secular substitute for religiously based moral education and to the adoption of the idea that science was morally neutral. As faculty in the biological and social sciences increasingly rejected moral aims, their colleagues in literature and the arts also began questioning the use of evolutionary sciences as the basis for the ideal of the unity of truth. In the early twentieth century some faculty in departments of language, literature, rhetoric, philosophy, and history argued that scientific knowledge could not provide moral guidance or intellectual coherence. They looked instead to a revival of a "humanist tradition." They argued that the humanities provided the best basis for inculcating moral values. They associated morality with the beauty of art, rather than with the truth of science.

The contours of the modern classification of academic disciplines into the natural sciences, the social sciences, and the humanities developed slowly over the late nineteenth and early twentieth centuries. Of these groups, the humanities was the last to establish a sense of corporate identity. The late construction of the humanities as a common set of subjects seems contrary to what one might expect, given the humanities' strong ties to tradition. To establish the distinctiveness of their fields and their role in higher education, scholars in the humanities highlighted their bonds to the past and their prominent role in earlier forms of higher education. The modern notion of the "humanities," however, developed in the 1910s and 1920s in response to changes in the definition of science and the structure of higher education.[1]

The disciplines that make up the modern humanities—language, literature, art, philosophy, and history—did not yet form a coherent group in the early twentieth century. Despite history's belletristic past, academics in the late nineteenth century had aligned it with the social sciences, particularly political science, rather than with language and literature. Only as the social sciences became more ahistorical, and as historians developed new interests in intellectual and cultural history, did history develop strong ties to literary studies. Even so, history throughout the twentieth century has vacillated between the social sciences and the humanities both in its disciplinary identification and its institutional classification.[2]

Philosophy was also difficult to categorize. In discussions of the curriculum, educators sometimes grouped it with the social sciences, sometimes with literature and the arts, and sometimes, following practices of the antebellum college, with mathematics. Philosophers themselves were divided over whether they should try to become a specialized science or a broadly "humanistic" discipline. Today, philosophy is consistently classed as one of the humanities, but the intellectual interests of some philosophers ally them with cognitive science, linguistics, mathematics, and other "scientific" disciplines.[3]

Proponents of art instruction were divided between those who envisioned the university offering professional artistic training and those who believed that art instruction in the university should be modeled after the historical and critical study of literature. Efforts to expand art instruction in the nineteenth century floundered as scholars tried to articulate the purpose of such instruction. They debated questions such as whether universities should aim to prepare professional artists; whether it was worthwhile for general students, who did not plan to become artists, to study painting, sculpting, acting, composing, and other aspects of the production of art; and whether art could be taught separately from the technical aspects of art production. In addition, teachers of the visual and performing arts were divided between their ties to institutions outside the university, such as museums, theaters, and conservatories, and potential professional opportunities within the university.

Finally, approaches to the study of language and the analysis of literature often seemed in conflict and the institutional interests of the classical languages and modern languages seemed to be opposed rather than complementary. The intellectual concerns of scholars in languages and literature during the late nineteenth century had divided them internally and had united certain groups with proponents of science and religious liberalism. The most prominent fault lines were the comparative value of studying classical or modern languages and literature and the gulf between advocates of philological studies and professors who approached literature as a form of art related to other arts. The division was complex: philologists who studied classical languages shared interests with philologists who studied modern languages. Philologists also had ties to biblical critics and to scholars in other fields who advocated a greater emphasis on scientific research. Likewise, both classicists and scholars who wanted to study literature as an art form shared ideas and an interest in expanding the curriculum to include other fine arts. They were aligned with efforts to expand electives and increase the variety of the curriculum. All scholars in the modern languages had an interest in eliminating required courses and entrance examinations that favored the classical languages over modern languages. This united them with faculty in the natural and social sciences, who saw modern languages as an important tool for their students. But scholars in the modern languages were divided over the propriety of teaching recent literature and American literature. Classicists, of course, had an interest in maintaining requirements that made the study of Greek and Latin a distinguishing feature of the bachelor of arts degree. This united them with professors who taught rhetoric and had seen the role of rhetoric in the curriculum shrink with the spread of electives. Rhetoricians, though, tended to be generalists opposed to specialization and research, while many classicists favored specialized research. These divisions prevented scholars in the humanities from seeing themselves as a group united by common educational goals and distinct from other scholars in the university. In this context, then, it was not at all clear at the end of the nineteenth century that these disciplines shared common institutional or intellectual interests and would in a few decades be grouped as one of the basic divisions of American academic life.[4]

Faculty in literature and the arts used the need for moral education and the idea of value-free science to further their own notions about how scholars should study and teach literary, philosophical, and historical subjects. Some believed that literary studies, history, and philosophy had gone off track in the attempts to make their scholarship scientific. In the classical and modern languages, academics agreed that the study of literature should take an equal, and perhaps superior, place to specialized philological and historical research. In philosophy, one group asserted the importance of broad, idealistic philosophical inquiry to replace or at least supplement specialized research. A similar position emerged among a group of historians, who thought that the study of the development of human civilization was getting lost in narrower historical investigations. In the early twentieth century this diverse group of scholars began to refer to themselves as "humanists."

Humanists argued that their predecessors had mistakenly adopted the methods of scientific research and that their colleagues were killing the humanities with specialized research. They maintained that the mission of the humanities was to preserve, understand, and help others develop an appreciation for the "best" expressions of human ideals. They wanted art, poetry, and prose to be taught for their beauty and the "truth" of their spiritual ideals, and not primarily as examples of grammatical forms, artistic technique, or methods of logic. They maintained that the humanities, reoriented to this mission, could offer a secular equivalent of religion.

Almost half a century before this view triumphed in the American university, Matthew Arnold had articulated a similar conception of the humanities. In his book, *Culture and Anarchy,* published in 1869, Arnold had attributed the social and political unrest of the time to a lack of intellectual authority. Believing that social anarchy was a symptom of cultural drift, he had pressed for a revival of serious thought, literature, and art. He believed that such a revival required new dedication to the perfection of humanity through the pursuit of "sweetness," or beauty, and "light," or intelligence.

Arnold devoted much of *Culture and Anarchy* to distinguishing his ideal of culture from other, "false" notions. First, he insisted that true culture was not merely pedantic scholarship; it should not be confused with the superficial study of the university designed to mark the upper classes from the rest of society, nor with more serious scholarship pursued to satisfy personal curiosity. He also wanted to distinguish his view of culture from the "mechanistic" ideals that predominated in English society. He thought that his contemporaries so valued means or, in his term, "machinery," that they lost sight of the ends that these means were to serve. They confused natural resources, wealth, technology, and bodily health as aims in themselves, rather than as valuable means to the good life. He was also critical of the ideal of culture promoted by traditional "puritan" religion. Churches too often promoted a dogmatic moralism ("hebraism" in Arnold's terminology) without encouraging an intelligent exploration of what was "right." True culture, Arnold argued, balanced "hebraism" with "hellenism," which aimed "to find the intelligible law of things" and judged "right" by "light."[5]

Arnold's effort to distinguish "true" culture from "false" prefigured later humanists' critique of science and their substitution of art for religion. Arnold implied that promoters of science were responsible for the overvaluation of machinery, and he dismissed the new scientific education as narrowly technical. "The university of Mr. Ezra Cornell," Arnold wrote, ". . . seems to rest on a misconception of what culture truly is, and to be calculated to produce miners, or engineers, or architects, not sweetness and light." Later humanist critics saw this as an accurate assessment of all modern universities. Arnold also came close to offering "culture" as a secular substitute for religion. He argued that religion and culture shared the same goal: the perfection of humanity through the "harmonious expansion of those gifts of thought and feeling, which make the peculiar dignity, wealth, and happiness of human nature." But because hebraism had led religion to emphasize duty over intelligence, Arnold believed, "culture goes beyond religion, as religion is generally conceived by us" in "harmonious expansion of *all* the powers which make the beauty and worth of human nature." Arnold maintained that "poetry," not religion, best represented his ideal of culture.[6]

Like later humanists, Arnold could be interpreted as promoting "culture" as opposed to science and religion. But Arnold was too committed to the ideal of the unity of truth for such antagonism. Arnold, like promoters of science, celebrated the end of dogmatism: "now the iron force of adhesion to the old routine,—social, political, religious,—has wonderfully yielded." He praised free inquiry, the acceptance of new ideas, and "seeing things as they really are." He also maintained that culture was compatible with religion. "He who works for sweetness and light, works to make reason and the will of God prevail." Arnold spoke to the concerns of liberal Protestants by presenting culture as a means of reviving and reforming religion. Although Arnold believed that many religious leaders and promoters of science were misled by hebraism and "machinery," he held out the possibility that all might want the same thing—the unity of truth, goodness, and beauty—and that they might cooperate in attaining it. In his own day Arnold was generally viewed by Americans as a friend of religious liberalism, who wanted to preserve the beauty and morality of religion while rejecting theological dogmatism.[7]

University presidents of the period hired faculty—such as Charles Eliot Norton at Harvard, Hiram Corson at Cornell, and George Edward Woodberry at Columbia—who shared Arnold's view of culture. Their interest in the arts was seen as one contribution to the university's larger effort to provide modern moral and spiritual education consistent with scientific inquiry. These professors thrived in the new universities dedicated to the ideal of science as free and open inquiry. Although they were critical of aspects of the intellectual life of the academy, their criticism was not directed at university reform per se, which, after all, had opened up the curriculum to the subjects that they taught.[8]

By the early twentieth century, however, proponents of Arnold's conception of culture had become some of the most outspoken critics of the ideal of scientific inquiry and its translation into the educational practices of the university. They used the dissatisfaction with scientific education to point out what they believed were the distinctive contributions of their own disciplines. A group called the New Humanists, led by Irving Babbitt of Harvard, advanced these charges with particular force. The New Humanists argued for a reform of higher education, a reorganization of literary studies, a return to classical standards of criticism, and a rejection of naturalist philosophies of humanity and the cosmos. Their analysis of the problems of higher education and the humanities overlapped with the views of other scholars who did not share their commitment to classical philosophy. As a result, the New Humanists had more success in stimulating an interest in humanistic reform than in institutionalizing their own philosophic ideal.

Babbitt presented the first major statement of the New Humanist position in 1908 in his book *Literature and the American College.* He questioned the widespread belief in the moral value of the social sciences. The social sciences represented to Babbitt the dangerous merging of what he believed were the two major modern "dogmas," naturalism and humanitarianism. Naturalism, derived from Baconian science, viewed human beings as extensions of their environment. Humanitarianism, an outgrowth of Rousseau's romanticism, sought to adjust society to the needs of the alienated individual. Together, Babbitt argued, these led to the development of the social sciences and the idea that moral problems could be solved through social engineering.

In *Literature and the American College,* Babbitt tried to maintain a tone of moderation regarding the assumptions of the social sciences. He stated that he was opposed not to science or humanitarianism as such, but to their imperialist designs on other philosophies. "The more scientific progress and the more social pity the better. Exception can be taken to these things only when they are set up as absolute and all sufficient in themselves; when the Baconian would substitute quantitative and dynamic for human standards, or the Rousseauist would exalt social pity into the place of religious restraint as the very keystone of the arch of human nature." But despite this eclectic stance, Babbitt clearly believed that scientific humanitarianism was a dangerous source of moral decay: it left people seeking false solutions to moral problems, while at the same time masking the failure of their efforts. "Our lapse into moral impressionism is also hidden from us by the rapid advance of physical science," he wrote. "We assume that because we are advancing rapidly in one direction we are advancing in all directions; yet from what we know of man in history we should rather be justified in assuming the exact opposite." Scientific progress, Babbitt implied, was a source of moral decline.[9]

Other humanists agreed that science was not an adequate source of moral guidance. Edwin Greenlaw of the University of North Carolina maintained that the dominance of science in higher education promoted false values. "Left to themselves," he wrote, "both science and social studies minister chiefly to worldly advancement, to the amassing of wealth, to the pursuit of a happiness that is wholly material." He thought that scientific ideals had infused contemporary culture with a narrow and dangerous notion of progress. Consequently, people placed all value in the future and ignored the past. They prized the growth of industry, cities, and commerce, without considering the quality of life as a whole. Greenlaw did not advocate a "war on science," but insisted that the impact of science must be "humanized" by the influence of literature and art.[10]

The New Humanists' critique of science became more pronounced as the movement gained ground. In the 1930 collection *Humanism in America,* editor Norman Foerster maintained that humanism evolved as it addressed new conditions. The humanist of the renaissance, Foerster explained, had had to offset the excessive otherworldliness of the Church. Modern humanists had a different enemy: science. "To-day its great foe is thisworldliness, obsession with physical things and the instincts that bind us to the animal order—in a word, the many forms of naturalism that have all but destroyed humane insight, discipline, and elevation." An important part of the initial self-definition of the modern humanities was the perceived need to serve as a counterbalance to the influence of science in American intellectual life.[11]

The New Humanist critique of science reflected scientists' own redefinition of scientific inquiry. The humanists accepted the image of science as value-free, but they drew different conclusions than scientists did about the scope of science. The humanists argued that all significant human experience was subjective and value-laden, and that objective, value-free science was not suited to understand it. In his essay "The Pretensions of Science," Louis Trenchard More of the University of Cincinnati addressed the "false claims . . . being advanced" under the name of science. The most dangerous of these claims, he argued, was "that the phenomena of the subjective world also lie in the field of science." This pretension supported the "pseudo-sciences of psychology and sociology." More decried scientists who "would have us believe that all truth is scientific and that the conclusions of self-examination are but guess-work." More and other humanists rejected behavioral studies in the social sciences as absurd and dangerous. They complained that scientists set themselves up as the best authorities on human nature and experience and then proceeded to deny the existence of the most significant elements of that experience.[12]

The New Humanists wanted to limit the realm of science and establish the humanities as an appropriate means to human self-understanding. "It is the false claims of these pseudo-sciences which must be exposed and renounced," concluded More, "in order that humanism may come again into its own as the arbiter of character." But before the humanities could adequately fulfill this role, the study of literature, art, and philosophy would have to be radically reformed. The New Humanists charged that in the name of research, academics produced careful philological studies but lost sight of the meaning of literature. Literary scholars, falsely valuing progress, overlooked the superiority of classical literature and classical aesthetic and moral norms. They also fell victim to romanticism, idealizing self-release and individual expression over self-restraint and universal values.

The New Humanists wanted to reconstruct literary education so students would become linked to a tradition of "great" Western literature. They saw literature and the arts as a way to cultivate standards of aesthetic and moral judgment, and believed that the humanities could offer the moral guidance once provided by religion. Greenlaw wrote that "the service of literature, rightly conceived, is akin to the service of religion. . . . Our materials are human lives, instruments to be played upon by spirits of the dead, by living spirits incarnate in poetry and music and art, by the deeper music of humanity." The New Humanists' position with regard to religion was similar to that of natural and social scientists in the late nineteenth century: they maintained that humanistic scholarship supported religious values, but the line between supporting religion and replacing it was thin and easily crossed. Some humanists, such as T. S. Eliot, argued that humanism made sense only in the context of Christian theology. But for others, such as Irving Babbitt, humanism could serve as a substitute for religion. Although he presented humanism as compatible with Christian idealism, Babbitt privately looked upon the Christian Church as a competitor rather than compatriot. He hoped to forge an alternative idealist philosophy from classical thought and Eastern religions. He maintained that his humanist philosophy could better meet the intellectual demands of the modern era than the Christian religion because it was "experimental."[13]

Increasingly, scholars in literature, the arts, and to some extent philosophy and history argued that science had failed to reconstruct religion or offer a secular alternative to it. They concluded from this failure that spiritual and moral issues lay outside the realm of science, and that their disciplines could better address those concerns. They maintained that the humanities should be at the center of collegiate education because they offered moral guidance. This common belief helped some of the disciplines, particularly in literature and the arts, surmount the internal disputes that had divided them in the late nineteenth century. In addition, it united faculty in the modern and classical languages, the arts, history, and philosophy and offered them a common identity as humanists.

Literary scholars most actively promoted the modern humanities as the source of unity and moral guidance in higher education. In the 1910s scholars in the classical and modern languages began to claim that their disciplines provided the only true antidote to specialization. Scholars in various areas of language and literature presented their aims as holistic rather than specialized, striving to understand all of civilization rather than to analyze bits of it. In an address at the University of Chicago, Richard Green Moulton, head of the department of general literature, explained that knowledge had become so specialized that scholars were losing sight of the unity of "life," or human experience. "What defines this Life," he maintained, "is its synthetic character, and for this reason it is incompatible with specialization." He argued that although the sciences could not overcome specialization, literature could. "Many sciences touch Life, but by their constitution as sciences they can deal with only one aspect of Life at a time. . . . Hence the medium for this study of Life reverts from science to literature." Literature, "besides being the natural organ for the integration of thought, has in this one case a specific function: it serves as the only possible science and practical art of Life." Moulton believed that the study of literature, not science, would provide the unity that religion had once offered.[14]

Literature professors sympathetic to this humanistic ideal emphasized the moral and spiritual benefits of literary study. "The student of literature," wrote Nelson Glenn McCrea, professor of Latin at Columbia, "will find in its masterpieces, as he will not find in any of the natural sciences or in any of the social sciences, the imaginative portrayal of the inner life of man himself in connection with the problems that eternally imperil his happiness." Professors of literature presented their subject in moral and spiritual terms. Greenlaw defined literature as "the record of the human spirit in its search for the interpretation of life." Scholars presented literature as the best way to teach students values. "In the study of the literature of a particular people," wrote George Barton Cutten, president of Acadia

University, "we meet the noblest values of the race. Permeated as is all literature with inspiring deeds, finest emotions, and worthy aspirations, it becomes the source of our highest ideals." As these examples show, while social scientists were trying to shed moralism, literary scholars were elevating it to their raison d'être.[15]

Literature professors presented the study of literature as a spiritual experience. In his autobiography, William Lyon Phelps of Yale looked backed on his literary education and described it in religious terms. He remembered reading Carlyle's essay "The Hero as Man of Letters" as a "spiritual" event exciting him to a state of "mental ecstacy." He described reading Tennyson's poem *Maud* as a "profound spiritual experience," equivalent to a religious conversion. "I shall always be grateful to this poem," Phelps wrote, "for it was the means of my conversion; I escaped from the gall of bitterness and the bond of Philistine iniquity, into the kingdom of light." Reading *Maud,* Phelps understood for the first time the joys of "pure poetry" and the role of the poet as "the interpreter . . . of the beauty of nature and the passions of man." As a professor of literature in the early twentieth century, Phelps hoped his students would appreciate literature as a means to spiritual growth and an avenue to greater self-understanding.[16]

Faculty who promoted the study of literature in the university emphasized the inspirational value of the artist "speaking" directly to the student through literature. For example, Frank Aydelotte, who advocated transforming the standard freshman English class from a composition course to a literature course, compared the poet to a prophet. "The business of the poet is to say the most serious and the truest things about life that his divine vision reveals to him. His business is to tell us the truth, to show us the way of life." Poets, he explained, were particularly effective prophets because of the beauty of their writing. Literature not only contained important moral lessons, but was also a "pleasure" to read. Students, then, would happily imbibe its lessons.[17]

According to this view, literature was an especially effective moral teacher because it joined lofty content with compelling form. McCrea discussed the dual importance of content and form.

> Like all the fine arts, literature provides us with noble pleasure; but it finds its chief function as criticism and interpretation of life. Its content, therefore, is the supremely important element. . . . The object of language is to convey thought and feeling from one mind to another without loss of moving power . . . the supremely

important thing is the human life that is thus adequately expressed . . . the style is an inseparable part and not, as it were, a garment which may be donned or doffed.

Literature allowed students to understand and empathize with others. It brought them into "many-sided intimacy with [their] fellow beings," broadening their minds and enlarging their sympathies.[18]

As faculty in the 1920s began to focus on developing students' aesthetic sense and inculcating moral values, the conflicts between those teaching classical languages and literature and those teaching modern languages and literature subsided. The notion of a tradition of great works spanning ancient Greece to modern Western civilization connected the two fields. Scholars teaching classical languages and English, French, German, Italian, and Spanish literature now seemed to share educational goals and interests. Charles H. Grandgent of Harvard commented on the change. He noted that the "Ancients and the Moderns" had been "rivals" and "sometimes bitter opponents" for many decades. "Of a sudden, however, their attitude has changed, each of the two parties having perceived in the other its natural ally." Universities began to require that students majoring in modern literature have some knowledge of classical literature, and vice versa. In 1921, for example, the language division at Harvard proposed such a requirement, explaining that "the history of literature is continuous, and that every well-educated person should have a general acquaintance with the masterpieces of the great literatures. This idea underlies the study of the Humanities, or *Litterae Humaniores,* and this study, in turn, has been an essential part of a liberal education since the days of Pericles." The Harvard literature faculty used the prestige of history—the great tradition of the liberal arts—to support its innovative curriculum in literature. This new curriculum and the resuscitated conception of the humanistic liberal arts united scholars in the classics and the modern languages.[19]

The spread of the humanistic ideal increased the influence of literary scholars at the expense of philologists. Humanists argued that philological courses were too specialized and called for new classes that would highlight the moral and aesthetic value of literature. Humanists first introduced their courses in the undergraduate curriculum. In the late nineteenth century, even departments where philologists predominated had offered a few literature and "cultural" courses to college students. In the early twentieth century the number of these classes grew. In the 1910s departments such as University of Michigan's department of English language and literature changed their core surveys from historical courses to "reading appreciation" classes. Classical and modern language departments began to offer classes that used translations. As Herbert Weir Smyth of the Harvard Classics Department explained, "The courses in question offer to non-classical students the opportunity to imbibe something of the spirit of ancient life and literature; and thereby avert from 'the humanities' even the suspicion of being only a specialized branch of study." By 1930 departments such Harvard's English department and Columbia's department of Romance philology and French offered no philological courses at the undergraduate level.[20]

Philologists' influence in graduate study eventually diminished as literature was established on the undergraduate level. Humanists pushed for more literary instruction on the graduate level to adequately prepare students to teach undergraduates. The scholarly interests of graduate students shifted to reflect the humanistic conception of their disciplines. By 1929 Grandgent was lamenting that linguistics had become the weakest part of the modern language program at Harvard. He noted that graduate students preferred research in "letters" over philological work. He felt there was a disturbing indifference to the intrinsic interest of language. The tyranny of philology that Babbitt had complained about had been undercut by the expansion of undergraduate literature instruction.[21]

The humanistic ideal also helped define the role of university arts instruction. Scholars in the visual arts and music echoed the moralism of their colleagues in literature. Edward Robinson, the director of the Metropolitan Museum of Art, praised art education as the "most liberalizing of liberal studies, all the more valuable because of its remoteness from the practical, of prime importance for its broadening effect upon the mind and its refining influence on the character." Art, Robinson continued, represented the "highest expression of a race or an individual." The purpose of art instruction in the college, explained Holmes Smith of Washington University, was to communicate to students the "value of artistic culture." The "duty of the college art instructor" was "to cultivate in the minds of his students a catholic receptivity to all that is sincere in artistic expression; to open up avenues of thought in the minds of those whose lives would otherwise be barren of artistic sympathy; to cull the best from the experience of the past, and, by its help, to impart to his hearers some of his own enthusiasm; for their lives cannot fail to touch at some point the borderlands of the magic realm of art." Instruction in art, according to this view, broadened students' experiences and made them receptive to the best expression of the values of their culture.[22]

The new identification with the humanities ended disputes about the purpose of the arts in the university. Instead of arguing for university-sponsored professional arts training, faculty in music and the visual arts increasingly championed their subjects as a form of cultural education. This conception aligned the study of music and art with the study of literature. For example, Walter R. Spalding, professor of music at Harvard, explained that just as the English department did not primarily aim to produce poets, the music department did not exist to prepare professional musicians. Instead, he saw the music department as developing students' understanding and appreciation of great music as an expression of the highest values of civilization. It would also help advance American culture by creating a discerning and receptive audience for future musical "genius."[23]

Faculty's justification for instruction in the performing and visual arts echoed the New Humanists' arguments in favor of the study of literature. Edward Dickinson of Oberlin emphasized the spiritual and aesthetic rather than the technical aspects of music training:

> With all the scientific aspects of the art with respect to material, structure, psychological action, historical origins and developments and relations, of which the college, as an institution of exact learning, may take cognizance, music must be accepted and taught just because it is beautiful and promotes the joy of life, and the development of the higher sense of beauty and the spiritual quickening that issues therefrom must be the final reason for its use.

Dickinson maintained that the history and appreciation of music were now generally accepted as the backbone of the curriculum in college music departments. These courses could stand alone or be combined with training in performance, composition, and theory. "But there seems to be universal conviction that if the college accept music in any guise, they must use it as a means of enlarging comprehension and taste on the part of their young people." Making the explicit comparison with literature, Dickinson concluded by feigning amazement that there had ever been any disagreement about the purpose of arts instruction: "it seems incredible that a college should employ literature and the fine arts except with fixed intention to bear upon the mind of youth according to the purpose of those [great artists] who made them what they are in the spiritual development of humanity." The humanist program offered a compelling rationale for the expansion of college art instruction.[24]

Faculty in the arts eagerly portrayed their subjects as an essential element of modern humanistic education. They maintained that students who studied literature should also study the visual arts. "Associating literature with the other arts," wrote A. E. Duddy of Montana State College, "will open up for the student new vistas of knowledge, and better than that, give him a new idea of the significance of art principles as they apply in the world of affairs. For at no former time have [*sic*] the breadth of beauty been more needed in the world." New graduate programs, such as Yale's "History, the Arts and Letters," were designed to prepare faculty to teach the arts in a broadly humanistic context.[25]

Art instruction, its proponents pointed out, fulfilled the basic mission of the collegiate education as well as, or better than, instruction in more traditional subjects. "It is the function of art to discipline the emotions, to train the taste, to awaken a sense of beauty, to provide a release for the individual from the tedium and complexity of our modern civilization." The modern humanities provided a clear rationale for the inclusion of art instruction in the college. Advocates of the arts could put aside questions about the propriety of the university training professional artists and present the art as part of the liberal humanistic tradition.[26]

Faculty in history and philosophy also presented their fields as integral to the modern humanities by emphasizing the unifying potential and moralism of their disciplines. Carlton H. Hayes of Columbia believed that history, if it could shake off the false influence of science, could provide the intellectual unity that had been lost in the late nineteenth century. "The college instructor in history," he wrote, is "gradually admitting that history, for all practical purposes, can not be treated as closely akin to zoology and mathematics. . . . He is discovering that history is not only past politics, but also past society in its broadest aspects: religion, economics, art, philosophy,—what man has thought and said as well as what he has done." With this broad mission, Hayes asserted, "history is now science rather than a science; it is almost synonymous with knowledge." Hayes believed that this synthetic concept aligned history with the humanities, not with the natural and social sciences. Increasingly, faculty associated science with specialization and the humanities with synthesis and unity.[27]

Similarly, some philosophers dissociated philosophy from the specialized sciences and claimed for it a synthetic function. William Montague, professor of philosophy at Columbia, maintained that philosophy should not be considered one of the sciences but rather a discipline devoted to unifying the specialized sciences. "Philosophy, when considered in its relation to science, may be defined as the attempt to formulate a coherent theory of the world as a whole in distinction from the attempt on the part of each science to explain some particular phase of the world." The true aim of philosophy, according to Montague, was "to give a bird's-eye view of the field of knowledge and to interpret reflectively the bearing of that knowledge upon human life and human conduct." Montague, like Hayes, was opposed to overspecialization within his own discipline and in the college curriculum as a whole. He thought that philosophy, viewed as a synthetic rather than a specialized subject, could again provide the unity that moral philosophy had provided in the antebellum college.[28]

Historians and philosophers who viewed their disciplines as related to literature rather than to the sciences also emphasized moral training. For example, Woodrow Wilson argued that history was different from science because its primary value was moral training. In the sciences, Wilson explained,

> the subject-matter itself is non-moral, whereas the subject-matter of life is saturated with moral imputations, and all those studies which concern themselves with life should constitute a training in moral perception. The facts of history may escape our memory, but the morals of history, the operations of character, the play of motive, the distinction of integrity, may leave their lasting impression upon us.

As social scientists began to define their disciplines as nonmoral, historians committed to moral education could reply that history was not a science. They could claim that their true compatriots in the university were scholars in literature and the arts who recognized that their subject matter had "a moral content as well as an intellectual."[29]

In philosophy, Frank Thilly of Cornell wrote that "the study of philosophy has a high cultural value," echoing the language of Matthew Arnold. It helps the student to "see things in their right relations, to acquire the proper intellectual and volitional attitude toward his world through understanding of its meaning and appreciation of its values; in short, it strengthens him in his struggle to win his soul, to become a person." Philosophy, according to this conception, offered students an avenue for intellectual and moral growth. Montague wrote that philosophy "is the effort to bring about in our moral and intellectual life the same sort of unification and harmony which religion brings about in our moral and emotional life." Philosophers such as Montague and Thilly believed that they and their colleagues should forge a modern substitute for the Christian synthesis taught in antebellum moral philosophy courses.[30]

The humanistic position did not come to dominate in history and philosophy as it did in literature and the arts. In these disciplines, faculty who allied themselves with the humanities had to coexist with powerful colleagues who still defined their field in scientific terms. Nonetheless, as this "holistic" conception of the humanities became widely accepted within universities, philosophers and historians who espoused it also gained legitimacy and found secure positions within university departments of philosophy and history. For example, Montague, who viewed philosophy as a moralistic and synthetic subject, had a prosperous career in the philosophy department at Columbia, which was dominated by more scientifically oriented scholars. Montague's humanism united him with faculty in literature, and his attention to the moral welfare of undergraduates won him the respect and support of university administrators.[31]

Through their common focus on the limits of science instruction, the value of synthesis, and the importance of morality, professors in the languages, literature, the arts, history, and philosophy came to see themselves as part of a common enterprise. They strengthened their identity as part of the humanities by stressing the connections among the disciplines. Franklin B. Snyder, an English professor at Northwestern University, argued that literature faculty should tie "as closely as possible the three subjects of history, philosophy and literature." He maintained that there was a natural union between them: "we know that literature *is* history, plus a sort of beauty which ensures permanence to the record; we know that it *is* philosophy, expressed not in abstract scientific terminology, but in concrete image and colorful phrase." Seeing themselves as part of a broader enterprise, faculty in literature, the arts, philosophy, and history self-consciously sought to incorporate references to other subjects in their courses. Humanistically oriented historians introduced lectures about art, literature, and ideas into courses that had been dominated by politics, economics, and war. Philosophers discussed ideas in the context of their "cultural milieu." Faculty in literature, in music, and in the visual arts related their subjects to other forms of art. "The study of the history of music," explained Thomas W. Surette of Harvard, "obviously means the study of other forms of human expression during any given period; of philosophy, art, literature and the general social situation. It means a view of human life in the large." From these references, faculty helped establish the humanities as a set of related disciplines with a common mission within the university.[32]

Humanists also reinforced the ties between their disciplines with historical references. "The Greeks," they noted, "developed the major forms of literature, history, art and philosophy." Scholars in the humanities emphasized the common origins of their subjects in Greek thought and the classical tradition of the liberal arts. They called for a modern revival of a liberal arts education based in the humanities. Although, as historian Bruce A. Kimball has argued, the modern humanists did not fully adopt the classical philosophy of the liberal arts, particularly its dogmatic epistemology, they did share enough of its tenets—attention to morality, interest in preparing citizens for social leadership, and reliance on selected texts to articulate values—to plausibly claim a historical tie. The modern humanists maintained that their subjects could revitalize liberal arts education, thereby restoring order and moral purpose to colleges.[33]

As scientists increasingly emphasized specialization and value-neutrality, and scholars in literature and the arts successfully united around their new common identity as humanists, university presidents and deans began praising the inspirational value of literature and the arts. Humanists, by claiming the mantle of moral training, took on a responsibility valued by university administrators, trustees, and alumni. Consequently, the humanities, like the social sciences a few decades earlier, began to receive more institutional support.

The growth of art instruction provides an important example of this improved patronage. Most of the universities under study had begun offering some art instruction in the middle or late nineteenth century. Only a few, however, had stable departments of fine arts and music before the 1920s. During this period, university administrators began to tout the moral influence of the arts. For example, in his 1920–21 annual report, President Burton of the University of Michigan announced the creation of a new fellowship in the creative arts. The fellowship brought an artist to campus for a year, not to teach, but to serve as "an inspiration to students." Burton believed that art could be "an important factor in the character that the true university strives to build in its members." Burton was not disappointed in the first recipient of the fellowship, Robert Frost. In his next annual report, Burton reported that Frost's "presence, his active participation in University life, and his particularly inspiring personality have been of incalculable value." To corroborate his assessment, he quoted a letter from a student: "'no single influence at Michigan has been . . . more significant or more beneficial that the presence of Robert Frost . . . we are very certain . . . that the Frost stability, the Frost honesty, the stray, quiet spirit of the man, is leaving its mark on the student body, and this is exactly the kind of influence that Michigan wants to see upon all her sons and her daughters.'" University presidents, always eager to demonstrate their school's commitment to character formation, borrowed the moralistic language of the humanists and paid them back with increased resources for their subjects.[34]

The increased interest in the humanities also brought in outside funding for the arts. At Columbia, for example, the department of fine arts floundered for several decades without adequate support. It was finally given a stable foundation when merchant and art connoisseur Hugo Reisinger gave Columbia $100,000 to establish a professorship of the history of art. As a result of this gift, S. Butler Murray was hired as an assistant professor in 1921. Murray steadily built a strong undergraduate and graduate program in the history of art. In 1925 the Carnegie Corporation began to give money to promote leadership in the arts. It awarded fellowships to prospective college arts teachers and grants to universities to improve their art instruction. Under this program, Yale, which had approved a bachelor of arts in fine arts in 1919–20, received $150,000 to establish a professorship in the history of art. Frederick P. Keppel, the president of Carnegie who had initiated the support for the arts, praised art instruction as a way to reach "those students to whom the dominant appeal is through the sensibilities and emotions rather than through the intellect" and "to enrich and inspire college life and to continue its influence thereafter." Keppel brought from Columbia, where he had been dean of the college, to Carnegie a belief in the power of the arts to uplift individuals and society.[35]

In 1925 Keppel could report that college courses in art had grown from practically "zero" a decade earlier to a respectable, if not yet satisfactory, amount. The enlarged art programs were part of the growing importance of the humanities in the undergraduate curriculum. The humanities, however, only slowly displaced the sciences as the backbone of the liberal arts college. In 1930 the majority of college orientation courses still aimed to teach students the "scientific method" and to familiarize them with the problems of contemporary society through the study of the social sciences. Over the next decade, this situation began to change. Through the influence of John Erskine, Henry Seidel Canby, Mortimer Adler, and Robert Hutchins, "great books" courses in the humanities replaced "citizenship" courses in the social sciences as the model core curriculum.[36]

Literature professor John Erskine introduced the "great books" class as Columbia University's general honors course in 1920. The honors course was a two-year sequence introducing students to "the masterpieces in literature, poetry, in history, in philosophy, and in science." The course was conceived as an antidote to the specialization of the university curriculum. Erskine also saw it as an important opportunity to develop students' character. He thought the course would moderate their "egotism" and broaden their sympathies. He believed that the masterpieces of literature contained "noble" characters and important moral lessons that could cure the shallowness and selfishness of contemporary culture. In 1937 Columbia University used Erskine's general honors course as the model for its new required humanities orientation class for freshmen. The new great books program supplemented the social science–sponsored "Contemporary Civilization" course, the first year of which had been redesigned as a historical survey of Western culture. In the 1930s and 1940s university educators looked to literature, art, philosophy, and history, rather than the biological and social sciences, to provide unity and values in the college curriculum.[37]

The shift from the sciences to the humanities as the source of moral guidance repeated changes that had occurred in the study of religion. As scientific studies of religion had failed to validate its cognitive aspects, scholars had emphasized the emotional and aesthetic value of religion. They had maintained that religion expressed "spiritual truths" even if those truths could not be expressed as "factual truths" acknowledged by science. Efforts to find secular sources of moral authority had resulted in similar conclusions. Scientists had disavowed any moral purpose, maintaining that values could not be validated as a form of "objective" knowledge. Humanists, on the other hand, maintained that art powerfully communicated moral values. This associated morality with the emotional appeal of beauty, rather than with the cognitive authority of knowledge.[38]

EIGHT

Administrative Order

By the end of the first decade of the twentieth century criticism of higher education had become so commonplace, one educator quipped, that "nobody has a good word to say for the college." After decades of belittling the old-style college, a new note of nostalgia entered public discourse about higher education. Commentators missed the unity, moral purpose, and high ideals of the classical college. They perceived the new universities as chaotic and materialistic, and their students as selfish and undisciplined. This criticism escalated over the next decade, growing as universities' various efforts to keep knowledge and morality united in a modern form of moral education failed.[1]

Some critics of higher education argued that the practices of the modern research university should be rejected completely. The most prominent example of this extreme was the Protestant fundamentalists who repudiated religious liberalism and the institutions that supported it, wanting to ground education in the authority of the Bible. Others were more moderate, hoping to solve some of the problems created by university reform without completely rejecting modern practices. Moderates were often associated with "liberal arts" colleges, where they tried to selectively adopt some of the reforms instituted by universities, while retaining the more intimate environment of the traditional college. A group of administrators and faculty within the research universities also joined the chorus of moderate critics. They became convinced that their institutions had lost track of essential educational goals and would have to make significant changes to reclaim them. Drawing on the ideas of their colleagues in liberal arts colleges, this last group led a campaign for a second wave of university reform—the collegiate reforms of the 1910s and 1920s.[2]

Although electives allowed universities to offer a comprehensive curriculum, students no longer recapitulated the whole chain of knowledge in their personal education. As a consequence, critics of universities argued that students lost any sense that the different areas of knowledge were related. "The lack of unity in the intellectual appeal of the university of today," wrote President Marion LeRoy Burton of the University of Michigan, "accounts in a measure for our dissatisfaction with educational standards. . . . Students have imagined that the universe, in some mysterious way, is actually departmentalized, just as a university is. They have not sensed the unity of all knowledge." Yale historian George Adams feared university reforms were demolishing the "unity, unity of place and unity of work, common tasks, common interests, common purposes and ideals" that had characterized the American college.[3]

The rejection of the standardized curriculum of the classical college was the most obvious reason for the loss of unity and moral purpose. "In the earlier days every student pursued the traditional classical course in the College of Liberal Arts," explained Burton. ". . . Then came the elective principle in its unadulterated form and made our students adepts in scattering and smattering. It brought real enrichment of the curriculum, but at the serious loss of continuity, correlation, and concentration." Electives, which epitomized both the university reform movement and disunity, came under attack.[4]

A sharp change in attitude toward electives was evident in the educational literature of the day. A survey of college and university presidents conducted in 1901, for example, concluded that "the elective system is a fixture so far as our colleges are concerned. The tendency is more and more toward free election." By 1920 this trend seemed reversed. "The American college," wrote one educator in 1922, "is moving in the other direction—away from the freedom of individual impulse and toward a freedom of humane control." Schools now were trying "to rescue students from the dangers of a random election of studies." This change was a response to fears that the effect of electives on the college was the fragmentation of intellectual life and the loss of values in education.[5]

College education, according to critics, had become simply a "multitude of disconnected parts," with no connection to an overarching philosophy of life. Burton used a vivid image to portray the gravity of the situation: "At present the dazed undergraduate is suddenly ushered into the gross anatomy laboratory of knowledge and vigorous groups of specialists hurl at him the heart, lungs, and other vital organs of the body of knowledge." The student is supposed to "fashion these disjecta membra into a harmonious living organism." But "it cannot be done by this method." Universities could not provide a unified conception of knowledge simply by offering instruction in all its branches. Edwin Greenlaw of the University of North Carolina wrote that "we can not gain unity merely through offering our courses in Sanskrit, butter-making and photo-play writing in an institution directed by the same president and faculty, employed by the same board of trustees; we can not dodge the problem by offering courses in all possible crafts and knowledges and then throw on immature students the responsibility for choice." Comprehensive institutions, offering courses in all areas of knowledge, could not be equated with a comprehensive curriculum. Institutional unity, critics asserted, meant nothing if individual students experienced only a small portion of the whole.[6]

Opponents challenged the late nineteenth-century notion that electives accorded intellectual and moral benefits to students. They said that students did not select a course of study that best developed their own talents and that the responsibility of self-selection did not help develop students' character. They maintained that university reformers had wrongly assumed that students understood their own educational needs, and claimed that few students used electives to any advantage. The growth of the curriculum presented students with a dizzying "variety of courses . . . offered in every branch of study." This vast number of choices subjected the student "to a dozen misleading chances." Under these circumstances, students were incapable of designing "a suitable course of work." "The student, both by excess and deficiency, may pursue a course which has little to commend it either as a medium of general knowledge or as a preparation for special work."[7]

Critics of electives also argued that students selected their courses for the wrong reasons. Emil Wilm of Harvard argued that students picked "snap" courses that required little work, or else they took a course because their friends were in it or because they liked the instructor or because of "a number of other considerations" unrelated "to the student's scholarship or future welfare." Consequently, "the student's course is . . . frequently a rope of sand, with no relation of any study or stage to any other; and the possibility of finding a way thru the curriculum with a minimum expenditure of energy often affects disastrously the student's habits of study, and often results in the complete arrest of his intellectual development soon after entering college." Nicholas Murray Butler of Columbia noticed that the "rapid growth of the elective system" produced a "noticeable laxity in the control and discipline" of students. "As a result," he believed, "the period of college residence is not always as well spent as it should be in acquiring habits of industry and application and in promoting mental and moral growth." Far from providing good intellectual and ethical training, self-selection encouraged laziness and dissipation.[8]

Educators felt that free election of classes created two kinds of problems: haphazard courses of study and overspecialization. Most undergraduates "sampled" a variety of classes with no overarching plan. President Lowell of Harvard wrote, "The ordinary student is too apt to treat courses as Cook's tourists do the starred pictures in foreign galleries, as experiences to be checked-off and forgotten. To have taken a course is by no means always equivalent to possessing any real command of a subject." Elective systems encouraged superficiality. "The college student of today," wrote Butler, ". . . is permitted to sprawl over so large and so varied an area of intellectual interest that he loses the discipline in concentration, in hard work and in the mastery of some relatively small field that comes from pursuing a better and older method." Most college students, left to their own devices, developed no strong intellectual interests and, as a consequence, enrolled in classes merely to amass the requisite number of credits to graduate.[9]

At the opposite end of the spectrum was the problem of overspecialization. Educators worried that students would pursue a narrow area of study "without knowledge of other fields." Woodrow Wilson, for example, warned that overspecialization would make college students narrow and unable to consider things beyond their small sphere of experience. He maintained that the college should "regeneralize each generation as it came on, to give it a view of the stage as a whole before it was drawn off to occupy only a little corner of the stage and forget the rest, to forget the plot as a whole in the arrangement of a portion of it." Wilson associated specialization with self-interest and a broad education with service to others. Arthur Hadley of Yale also viewed specialization as a threat to the formation of "conceptions of duty based on considerations other than those of self-interest" and to the development of disinterested public sentiment.[10]

At the turn of the century disciplinary divisions and specialization became a common subject of concern among university administrators and faculty. Although most university officials still viewed academic disciplines as "arbitrary division[s] of the field of knowledge," they increasingly relied on subject-oriented departments as the most practical way to organize the growing faculty. Academics recognized specialization, like departmental organization, as a necessary outgrowth of and instrument for intellectual progress. But they also feared that specialization was segregating scholars within the university and isolating the university from the larger community. Rather than administrative conveniences, departments seemed to become worlds unto themselves.[11]

Specialization sped the growth of departments, and course offerings ballooned in all the universities under study. In its first twenty years Johns Hopkins University grew from six departments to twenty-four. The University of California's courses were listed in fewer than thirty pages in its 1890 *Register*. Twenty years later they spread over more than 200 pages. Such growth forced universities to drop one of their symbols of the ideal of the unity of truth. Long after they had abandoned the traditional curriculum, universities continued to list departments in the course catalogue according to their "logical" relations. Thus, modern languages came after ancient languages, and chemistry followed physics, which followed mathematics. These systems implied that all knowledge was related and could be integrated into a unified intellectual system. The expansion of course offerings made these organizational schemes too cumbersome, and in the 1910s and 1920s they were generally replaced by the more convenient alphabetical listings.[12]

Some educators felt that the highly specialized courses causing this growth were inappropriate for undergraduates. Chauncy S. Boucher, dean of the Colleges of Arts, Literature, and Science at University of Chicago, thought that universities should cut out many of their classes.

> A critical examination of the courses announced in any one of two dozen departments in a single college in the early 1900s would show that perhaps half of the courses in any department could not be justified on any ground, save one—they offered the instructors opportunities to pursue pet hobbies in a very limited part of a field—and that the course offerings of the department were not properly related and balanced.

He also reproached departments for designing their introductory courses to prepare students to take advanced courses in that field. "It seemed that nearly every department framed its curriculum as though the intellectual sun rose and set within its boundaries, as though every worthy student must desire to specialize in that department, and as though that department had a lifelong vested interest in every student who elected its introductory course." Many university administrators felt that faculty were tempted to advance "the interest of [their] department rather than that of the institution as a whole" and to think only "about the teaching of a particular subject to the neglect of the full development of the student as a complex human being." The increasing specialization of knowledge, some educators feared, proceeded at the cost of students' education.[13]

The elective system produced conditions that permitted the increasing number and specialization of college classes, but it was faculty research interests that fueled the process. Once research was identified as an essential concomitant to university teaching, professors' research interests became more professionalized and more specialized. Research became an important part of professors' identity and one of the prime determinants of their standing within the academy. Faculty frequently taught classes that drew directly on their original research. University reformers initially encouraged this practice, believing that professors would pass on to students their enthusiasm for their subjects and that such courses would help students develop the "mental discipline" of an original investigator.

But disapproval of specialized classes raised questions about the benefits of combining research and teaching. In 1910 John F. Woodhull of Columbia Teachers College argued that specialization was hurting universities and turning students away from highly specialized subjects, such as physics. He contended that defenders of specialization relied on an outmoded pedagogical theory that assumed that the intellectual skills developed through the study of one subject prepared students to study all other subjects. This view challenged one of the central tenets of university reformers: that it was more important for students to assimilate scientific habits of thought than to learn particular information.[14]

Criticism of electives and specialization cut at the underlying assumption of university reformers: free inquiry would automatically lead to what was true and good. Now educators began to question the universal benefits of freedom. Butler's changing attitude toward the ideal of freedom reflected the growing dissatisfaction with American higher education. When he took over the presidency of Columbia in 1901, he was known as an enthusiastic champion of the recent changes at Columbia and other universities. Over time, however, he tempered his support of university ideals. In 1910 he still identified "freedom of the spirit" as "the essence of a university's life." But he proposed that the needs for a "common morality, common sense, common loyalty, and a decent respect for the opinions of mankind" imposed limits on this freedom. As the decade progressed, the balance of Butler's rhetoric shifted from freedom to restraint.[15]

By 1920 Butler had become an outspoken opponent of the views that had sustained university reform.

> The decline in educational power is primarily the result of a widely influential and wholly false philosophy of education. . . . It has been dinned into our ears that all subjects are of equal value, and that it matters not what one studies but how he studies it. This doctrine has destroyed the standard of value in education,

and in practical application is making us a widely instructed but
an uncultivated and undisciplined people.

He charged that the rejection of "any fixt principle of knowledge" in the
name "of finding the truth" was, in fact, a celebration of ignorance.[16]

Butler came to view open and free inquiry and the educational reforms based on it as destructive forces in American life. He called for a
revived commitment to universal truths and values. "There can be no cure
for the world's ills and no abatement of the world's discontents until faith
and the rule of everlasting principle are again restored and made supreme
in the life of men and nations," he wrote in his 1920 annual report. The
"millions of man-made gods" and "myriads of personal idols," which Butler saw as the outcome of the "false" scholarly and educational practices
that had come to dominate American universities, "must be broken up
and destroyed, and the heart and mind of man brought back to a comprehension of the real meaning of faith and its place in life." Butler, who had
made his career fighting the narrowness of the college of his youth, ended
up a nostalgic admirer of its discipline and devotion to Christian ideals.[17]

The new nostalgia for the classical college centered on its clear moral
purpose. Critics of the university praised the older college for its attention
to the development of students' character. For example, Clarence Birdseye, a lawyer and author of several books on higher education, argued that
the "older colleges . . . concentrated upon the individual student and his
development for the largest possible future usefulness. . . . The institution
itself was humble and unimportant. The production of useful citizens was
its great end, and severe mental and moral discipline lay at the very basis
of its conception of training for citizenship." The modern university, in
contrast, seemed to have become amoral. Critics charged that university
reforms had destroyed traditional forms of moral education without creating adequate replacements. The modern university, they believed, did not
give adequate attention to students' moral education. "Colleges give too
little attention to the physical and spiritual education of the young men,"
wrote Otis E. Randall of Brown University. "The average professor feels
that his tasks are completely done when he has, through the medium of
the lecture, recitation or laboratory, contributed his part toward the intellectual development of the young men." Undergraduates' morals were no
longer scrutinized. "The college," explained Alexander Smith of the University of Chicago, "has given up its attempt to form the character of its
students by the enforcement of strict regulations. The student is no longer
guarded against all temptation to form bad habits. He is no longer fur-

nished with exercises and customs calculated to produced good habits." According to these critics, concern for students' character seemed to have dropped out of the educational agenda of the modern university.[18]

Much of the specific criticism of university education was motivated by the general sense that it had lost its moral purpose. Assaults on electives, specialization, and faculty research all repeatedly returned to the same question: did these practices undermine the students' moral training? Critics challenged universities to demonstrate that they graduated students with "force of character sufficient to encourage honesty and righteousness whenever and wherever found, and . . . the courage to frown upon dishonesty and unmanliness in [their] fellow men." University leaders had to face this challenge at the same time as they had to acknowledge their own failing efforts to reconstruct religious education or replace it with a scientific substitute.[19]

Despite the nostalgia for the classical college, no university leader in the early twentieth century considered establishing a standardized curriculum, abolishing advanced instruction, and abandoning research. Instead, they sought to offset the ill effects of the late nineteenth-century reforms with a series of administrative changes. They modified the elective system to reduce the arbitrariness of the average student's education. Although this second round of curricular reforms was intended to offer some form of "general" education that would provide unity and moral guidance, it really addressed more particular problems, such as lack of student initiative and planning.[20]

A major premise of the second wave of reform in higher education was that the college was a distinct entity within the university, with educational aims and practices different from graduate and professional schools. Ernest DeWitt Burton, president of University of Chicago, explained that "graduate and undergraduate work are largely different in character and deserve each to be developed, not on lines of compromise between them, but each according to its own character and requirements." This position, which helped fuel a revival of interest in smaller liberal arts colleges, also inspired the second wave of university reform.[21]

In defining the special mission of the college, critics of the university offered an updated version of the antebellum ideal of unity. The purpose of the college was defined partly in contradistinction to other forms of education: a college education was supposed to be broad rather than spe-

cialized, "liberal" rather than professional, relevant but not "narrowly vocational." The college aimed to develop the "whole" student, not just the
intellect. "The function of the college," wrote Randall, "is to prepare men
to meet efficiently the duties of life and therefore [it] must furnish something more than intellectual training." The development of students' values and character was essential. The purpose of a college education was
"to establish character, and make that character more efficient through
knowledge; to make moral character more efficient through mental discipline." The college was supposed to transform the parochial, self-
interested youth into a cosmopolitan, disinterested adult. The aim of the
college, summarized William Nitze of University of Chicago, "is to hu-
manize the individual, to emancipate him intellectually and emotionally
from his prejudices and conventions by giving him a wider horizon, a
sounder judgment, a firmer and yet more tolerant point of view." The
ideal college graduate would serve society "loyally, intelligently, and
broad-mindedly, with an increasing understanding of its aims and purposes."[22]

Although university reformers of the late nineteenth century had
maintained that freedom of the university would shape such graduates,
by the 1910s the leaders of collegiate reform disagreed. They argued that
electives and the freedom of the university failed to shape students' character and asserted that the solution lay in the colleges adopting their own
unique practices. With regard to the curriculum, they sought to bolster
the college by limiting self-selection of classes and by instituting other
curricular reforms, such as honors programs and general exams.

University officials portrayed the aims of curricular reforms as two-
fold: to restore unity and moral purpose to college education and to promote a higher level of scholarship among undergraduates. Educators
assumed that these goals were compatible. They thought students' anti-
intellectualism was a response to the disorder and triviality of the college
curriculum. Like the university reformers, they believed that improving
student scholarship would have moral as well as intellectual benefits. "In-
dolence and general dissipation of mental power," maintained Charles
Fordyce of the University of Nebraska, were responsible for many moral
failings. "Laziness weakens one morally as well as mentally; a loafer is
incapable of ethical growth because his mental fibre is too dormant to
assimilate moral nourishment." In practice, however, curricular changes
addressed only the second goal, student scholarship.[23]

Yale's experience illustrates the process of collegiate reform at many
major research universities in this period: critics pressed for extensive

changes intended to provide unity and moral guidance, but after a long period of negotiation, they settled for more limited reforms that simply helped structure the undergraduate curriculum. The administration at Yale for several years considered proposals for a common freshman course for all students in the college and in the Sheffield School of Science, before deciding on a curriculum for all the first-year students. "The problem of shaping the course of study in the Freshman year was a difficult one because we had to satisfy several conflicting demands," President Hadley explained. The graduates wanted a uniform curriculum "common to all students" that would provide a "common groundwork of education." Instructors were split by school and department: the engineers wanted students to take mechanics, the chemists chemistry, "and so on down the line." In addition to departmental particularism, no two members of the faculty "felt exactly alike on the various questions at issue." The resulting compromise required freshmen to take English and European history, and to select three courses from the following areas: mathematics, natural science, modern languages, ancient languages, or engineering.[24]

After overcoming the initial resistance to revising the college curriculum, Yale officials suggested more far-reaching reforms. Yale secretary Anson Phelps Stokes lobbied for a "systematic course of instruction covering the present condition of the various fields of knowledge and indicating their interrelation." He also favored required instruction in American history and government "so that every student will go out intelligently prepared to meet the responsibilities of citizenship," and a required series of lectures for freshmen "designed to give a clearer idea of the purposes and ideals of education and the outlines of a philosophy of life." Phelps wanted the college curriculum to be ordered but "flexible." He advocated a series of alternative courses of study that students would select after their freshman year. These courses would ensure that students had a broad education, but one that prepared them for further study in their chosen profession.[25]

Yale did adopt additional reforms of the undergraduate curriculum in the 1920s. These changes, however, were not as extensive as those proposed by Phelps or other critics of university education. Yale instituted "group study" plans, similar in effect to concentration and distribution requirements but with more effort to correlate related subject areas. It changed the required European history course into a broader thematic course on the development of Western civilization. Yale also experimented with a voluntary series of lectures, orienting students to the college and introducing them to the various fields of study, such as "Science," "Social

Science," and "The Study of Literature." In addition, it attempted to develop a voluntary social science orientation course. These efforts represented acceptable compromises between more extensive reforms advocated by Phelps and the need for freedom to pursue specialized study. Even these more modest reforms of the 1920s faced difficulties in practice, and most were dismantled by the end of the decade.[26]

Although several of the universities in this study instituted some required course work, none attempted to establish an extensive core curriculum that significantly limited electives. The failure to establish a more extensive core curriculum was often blamed on faculty's desire to protect their own subjects. William C. Trow of the University of Cincinnati wrote that

> each professor is a specialist and because of natural interest and aptitude, and training sees his specialty out of its proper perspective. If a colleague suggests such faculty action as might possibly cut down his enrollment, far from viewing the matter from the point of view of society as a whole and its relation to individual student development, he considers it as a personal affront, swells with pride of his accumulated years of scholarship, and brings down about the ears of his unfortunate victim all the bombast of Lecture I, of his introductory course.

Turf battles made it extremely difficult to substantially reduce electives by establishing a common curriculum.[27]

Although some faculty supported a unified and morally significant curriculum in principle, they did not agree on what subjects constituted the essential elements of the curriculum. After reviewing educators' attitudes about the various fields of knowledge, Charles H. Judd of University of Chicago concluded that a required general curriculum was impractical because of lack of consensus about which subjects should be required. "One comes back after searching for essentials with a more vivid realization than ever that we live in an individualistic age. . . . The day of cores is either passed or has not come." Despite the criticism of electives, few universities could abandon the basic principle of election.[28]

Faculty also resisted core curricula because they did not want to teach general education courses. Most natural and social scientists had come to believe that offering general education for undergraduates was not in the interest of their disciplines. Becoming a principal subject in the college curriculum meant less specialization, less attention to research, and less intellectual freedom. Given these conditions, scientists preferred to concentrate on professional and advanced instruction rather than on general undergraduate education. Although faculty in the humanities were mostly willing to assume responsibility for general education, their colleagues in other disciplines were often unwilling to have students locked into required classes of language, literature, and philosophy.

Most important, faculty resisted plans for a required, coordinated curriculum because they had begun to lose faith in the ideal of the unity of truth. As Alexander Meiklejohn, president of Amherst College, recognized, his contemporaries had come to view "the unity of knowledge" as a "myth." "Knowing," they believed, "is a number of relatively separate investigations. No one man can be acquainted with all these lines of inquiry. And if he were, he could not make them into a single meaning, a unitary scheme of understanding." When none of the efforts to find a modern substitute for moral philosophy succeeded, educators like Meiklejohn protested and deplored the situation, but others accepted it as the price of intellectual progress.[29]

In the 1910s and 1920s no major university implemented a "coordinated" curriculum, made up largely of required courses. In proposing to modify the curriculum, university officials accepted "the obvious fact that the rigid curriculum of fifty years ago has been laid aside forever." Despite the rhetoric calling for a new intellectual unity, collegiate reformers were willing to settle for changes that fell short of this ideal. Later efforts at curricular reform demonstrated that this assessment was realistic. For example, President Hutchins's efforts to institute a uniform curriculum at University of Chicago in the 1930s were unsuccessful—an indication that the compromises of the 1910s and 1920s probably represented the limits of change.[30]

University officials settled for a more modest goal when restricting electives: reducing the chaos of the average college student's course of study. Rather than jettisoning freedom, educators tried to temper it with basic principles and guidelines. A. Lawrence Lowell, Charles Eliot's successor at Harvard, led this effort. "We must," he declared at his inaugural, "construct a new solidarity to replace that which is gone. The task before us is to frame a system which, without sacrificing individual variation too much, or neglecting the pursuit of different scholarly interests, shall produce an intellectual and social cohesion." Lowell's revision of the elective system consisted of the introduction of concentration and distribution requirements.[31]

The curricular reforms at Harvard were among the most influential. In 1910 Harvard introduced the practice of requiring students to select a major area of study and to sample a range of subjects. The concentration requirement commanded students to take at least six courses, four of them advanced, in one department or area of study. The distribution requirement directed students to take another six classes, dispersed among four areas: (1) language, literature, fine arts, and music; (2) natural sciences; (3) history and political and social sciences; (4) philosophy and mathematics. Students were instructed to select the six courses among three areas outside their major area. In addition, they had to take rhetoric, and a foreign language if they did not pass the language examinations at admission. After 1919 physical education and hygiene were added to the required courses. Students were expected to draw up a course plan by the end of their freshman year, which had to be approved by a faculty adviser.[32]

Lowell supplemented concentration and distribution requirements with additional reforms modeled after practices at Cambridge and Oxford, such as academic honors, general examinations, tutorials, and reading periods. First, he instituted academic honors to try to offset the disdain he perceived among students for intellectual achievements. He also promoted general examinations as a means to improve student scholarship. To graduate, students would have to pass not only a requisite number of classes but also an examination demonstrating broad knowledge in their major discipline. The division of history, government, and economics gave the first general examinations in 1915–16. By 1921–22 all divisions except natural sciences and mathematics required general examinations. Lowell thought that the major benefit of general examinations was that students would be required to master a broader range of material than could be required in a single class. He decided that students needed more help to prepare for the examinations and created a system of tutors for divisions that required examinations. Tutors were supposed to help students use independent reading to draw connections between what they learned in individual classes. The reading period—three weeks at the end of the term when classes would not meet and students would instead be given a list of readings to complete on their own—was also designed to encourage independent scholarship on the part of students.[33]

Concentration and distribution requirements were intended to allay some of the troubling aspects of student behavior under the elective system. They made it more difficult for students to pick their classes randomly or to select only the easiest courses. They did not, however, create a common course of study or unify the curriculum in any significant way. Indeed, the primary effect of these requirements was to encourage specialization among Harvard undergraduates. Studies of students' selection of courses under free electives showed that most students took a smattering of introductory courses, sampling a wide range of subjects. Based on his studies of students who succeeded in professional schools, Lowell concluded that specialization in college correlated with later accomplishments. Therefore, he emphasized the importance of concentration, strengthening departmental divisions, rather than the importance of a general education. His other reforms had a similar effect. He equated serious scholarship with independent work in a particular field of study. This model of scholarly achievement was closer to that expected of contemporary graduate students than to that of students in the classical college.[34]

The introduction of concentration and distribution requirements became one of the most widespread and enduring reforms of the 1910s and 1920s. Other universities also instituted reading periods, and many considered requiring some form of general examinations. The expense and difficulty of administering examinations and of hiring tutors, however, ensured that these programs were praised more than imitated. Some universities established honors programs in their stead and gave the honors students more freedom by allowing them to pursue independent study in their major field. Honors programs, then, encouraged better work habits and respect for scholarship, while reinforcing specialization. A brief, but important, exception to this pattern was Columbia's general honors program, the two-year "great books" sequence designed by John Erskine. Within a decade of its adoption, however, Columbia replaced the general honors program with departmental honors.[35]

Universities responded to criticism that they had destroyed the unity of college education by reducing the chaos of college study and encouraging better scholarship among students. They did not, however, succeed in reinstituting a synthetic view of knowledge and a unified philosophy of life. To do this would have required a more radical departure from the scholarly and educational practices that had developed since the 1870s. After failing to create a modern source of moral training, faculty were more willing to abandon the principle of unity than to stray too far from the principle of freedom and the practice of specialized scholarship.

Curricular changes constituted only one aspect of the collegiate reform movement. Over the 1910s and 1920s educators gradually shifted their attention from curricular to extracurricular forms of moral guidance. One of the indications of the transition was the discussion of the role of faculty.

Although university administrators had always been concerned with the morality of their faculty, they began to consider character as the sole source of faculty's moral influence. In discussing the impact of the faculty on the development of student morality, educators stopped talking about what faculty taught—the content of their classes—and focused instead on the potency of their personalities. This emphasis on professors' personal influence on students led to greater scrutiny of the quality of the professorate and the effectiveness of their teaching.

Americans were generally proud of the rapid development of scholarship in the late nineteenth century. Leading universities boasted of their distinguished faculty, now dominated by Ph.D.s and dotted with internationally renowned scientists and authors. Smaller institutions scrambled to catch up; they required their new faculty to have graduate degrees and preferred to hire products of leading universities rather than their own former students. In the early twentieth century, however, a note of doubt crept into the generally laudatory discussion of the quality of university faculty. In 1906, for example, Andrew West, professor of Latin and dean of the Graduate School at Princeton, presented a paper at the annual meeting of the Association of American Universities, in which he stated that the overall quality of faculty had declined. "The decline of the old college ideal . . . has been profoundly influencing the character of our supply of professors. Less and less emphasis has been placed on the general make-up of the man, and more and more on his specialized knowledge." As a consequence, West maintained, fewer faculty were "men of all-round ability—men who are able to see, and fit to solve, larger questions with the moderation of wisdom." In the discussion of West's paper, Ira Remsen, president of Johns Hopkins, took exception to his portrayal of university faculty and accused him of romanticizing the past. "We may talk of those good old days in our colleges when . . . every professor was just the kind of professor we want; but I doubt whether this will bear investigation." Indeed, Remsen thought the opposite was true: "I believe our professors are just as good men, just as much interested in the welfare of their students and the formation of character, as they were formerly. On the whole, I believe the race of professors is improving."[36]

In 1906 West's views about the declining quality of college faculty were idiosyncratic and could be dismissed by Remsen and other university administrators. Over the next two decades, however, the tone of public discussion changed. Remsen's optimism was soon drowned out by a chorus of complaints about the quality of university teaching and the character of professors. These complaints were a response to increased attention to the personal influence of faculty.

Around 1910, in discussing the problems that college students face, Daniel Abercrombie, principal of Worcester Academy, concluded that "the greatest need of the average boy is the friendship and guidance of a fine personality rather than instruction by a professional expert simply." In his report for 1923–24, Yale president James Rowland Angell maintained that "Yale's greatness will not be measured by the number of courses that are offered, but by the character of its teaching and the inspiration of its teachers." A few years later Dean Ernest Wilkins of Chicago asserted that "the quality of the teaching is the measure of the success of the college. If the teaching is good, the college is a good college." Nicholas Murray Butler wrote that "the important thing about a college is its spirit, its clearness of aim, its steadiness of purpose, and the opportunity which it affords for direct personal contact between teacher and student." The necessity of an inspiring and sympathetic faculty had become a frequent refrain of university leaders.[37]

Given their failing efforts to ground moral training in the curriculum, university educators now minimized the connection between academic subjects and morality. Otis Randall, for example, argued that universities needed to do more to shape the character of students, but he acknowledged that the curriculum could not fulfill this function. "There are no courses of study yet devised nor are there likely to be, which in themselves are going to build character in our young men." In the absence of such classes, Randall turned to the faculty. "Character building in the young man is accomplished by indirect and subtle influences. . . . The great contributions toward character building are made by those teachers who through the influence of their own lives and characters, who by their personal touch and magnetism are able to mould the life of the young man." Charles Fordyce agreed with Randall that an instructor's personal influence was more important to the moral development of students than the subject he taught. "A teacher's power is infinitely more in what he is, than what he teaches. . . . It is this contact of student life with that of the faculty that counts for more than all else in the morals of our institutions. Really the strongest lessons we teach are the lessons we do not teach, but those that emanate from our personality." Without a clear connection between one or more subjects of instruction and moral training, university educators concerned about character development began to place greater emphasis on the personal qualities of faculty.[38]

The growing acceptance of objectivist conceptions of science also contributed to the new emphasis on the personality of the instructor. According to the new objectivism, the investigator's research had no moral implications. Edward Pace of Catholic University explained the distinction between value-free research and value-laden teaching. "The researcher's aim is to get at the truth hitherto unknown. As to the form which that when discovered shall present, he has no concern. . . . Whatever the event, provided only it be true, the researcher accepts it without regard to its import for human interests or values." The teacher "endeavors to fashion a growing personality upon the ideal of life as he conceives it." The purpose of education was to shape the student's character as well as intellect. The teacher's task, unlike the researcher's, had moral relevance. Therefore, the teacher "cannot be indifferent as to results" of his teaching. "Because it is the pattern which his own life more and more fully reproduces," explained Pace, "he may not be contented with a manner of teaching whose results are at variance with his inmost convictions." The professor could not "brush the question of values aside." For educators who believed that universities must be responsible for the moral development of their students, the notion of value-free knowledge forced attention away from the content of courses and toward the character of the instructors.[39]

Academic freedom also drew attention to the instructor's personal influence. Universities committed themselves to allowing faculty freedom to pursue and teach the "truth" as they could best identify it in their own academic disciplines. As a consequence, they could not demand that the faculty hold a certain set of views, as colleges did when they required teachers to take religious tests, but they could require "moral character." Harvard philosopher William Ernest Hocking noted that academic freedom raised particular problems in regard to moral education. Hocking believed that, because people are dogmatic about their own moral views, direct moral instruction was inevitably taught in an "authoritative" manner. But, he said, a university could not exercise "such authority without disloyalty to its ideal of free examination and skeptical inquiry." Hence, efforts to teach moral values directly tended to violate universities' commitment to freedom.[40]

Hocking concluded that universities could influence students' morality indirectly through the example of their faculty. He maintained that "the personal transmission of value is the most effective and only completely pertinent way." He noted, however, that this "imposes upon the university a tremendous responsibility regarding the quality of the teaching staff." Hocking applauded academic freedom and the abolition of religious tests.

But he felt that universities must take seriously their right to scrutinize faculty character. He argued that "if the training of values through personal transmission is at all right—we have to consider some immediate response between the university and faculty members, which says to them, 'I believe in you; I believe in the kind of values which you are likely to transmit without knowing it.' And this is, of course, a new definition of competence in the staff of the university!" Hocking, and others concerned about the moral training of college students, maintained that universities should pay more attention to the personal character of their teaching staff as they paid less attention to the content of professors' ideas.[41]

According to this logic, the teaching staff rather than curriculum became the linchpin of a student's moral education. For faculty to play this crucial role, university leaders maintained that, in addition to giving evidence of sound scholarship and upright character, they had to be able to reach out to their students. They needed to have the "personality traits" that students admired: a "cheerful disposition," "friendly manner," "sense of humor," and a "broad type of mind." They should also have a good understanding of human nature and the psychology of college students. "To instruct, to persuade, to control men," explained President John G. Hibben of Princeton, "there must be an understanding of their nature and disposition, and the success or failure of most persons will be determined by their ability to deal with men." Finally, faculty had to be engaged in the vital issues of their day and be able to relate their subjects to these issues. The Harvard student council defined "inspirational" teaching as "practical in the largest sense . . . tinged with thought, with mental vigor, with philosophy, in such a way that the material of the subject is made to throw light upon things that really matter to the student—upon the fundamental problems of living." Summarizing the sentiment of much of the literature on college teaching, Harvard students called for professors who dispensed "wisdom" rather than mere "knowledge."[42]

Many university leaders who trumpeted the importance of the personal influence of faculty found that the existing teaching staff of colleges and universities fell short of their ideal. For example, Charles Fordyce celebrated the teacher as the only secure source of moral guidance. But when he discussed the typical American professor, he concluded sadly that "many of our instructors not only lend nothing to the uplift of the moral atmosphere of the institutions served, but rather detract from it." Such feelings of disappointment were common among educators who emphasized the professor rather than the course of study. As they placed greater stress on faculty character, commentators tended to agree with West rather than with Remsen: the modern university professor, whatever his strength as a scholar, was not as good a "man" as his early nineteenth-century predecessor.[43]

Observers of university education maintained that many faculty were so preoccupied with their research that they neglected their teaching and had little impact on students. "Too many professors," wrote Randall, "live in their laboratories and libraries. They know and care too little about outside matters which do not bear directly upon their line of work." Universities often hired men who, though eminent in their own discipline, were uninterested in or unsuited to teaching. "Colleges," Randall explained, "are too frequently looking for specialists, men who through investigation or publication have won for themselves wide reputation, men who have become so completely absorbed in their special line of work that they have lost touch with student life and are absolutely ignorant of the temper, tendency and aspiration of young men." Research distracted professors and removed them from students, both physically and emotionally.[44]

Far from exciting students' interest in their disciplines, investigator-instructors seemed to deaden their subject matter. "Young doctors of philosophy, fresh from the prolonged study of some remote nook of science or literature," Carl Holliday of the University of Montana maintained, "have been turned loose on freshmen and sophomores and have bored them to desperation with minutiae." The specialization of teaching "has filled the soul of the undergraduate with unutterable weariness." Holliday believed that colleges needed to return to an older model of scholarship. "We need men with the broad, genial outlook of the old fashioned professor of natural philosophy rather than so many undergraduate specialists in entomology, ecology, embryology, bacteriology, and heaven knows how many other 'ologies.'" Generalists, with interests in several areas of knowledge, made more "affectionate" and "contagious" college professors. Students needed instructors who would explain the connections between various areas of knowledge and help them make sense of the whole.[45]

Most commentators agreed that few faculty had the strong personality needed to be inspiring teachers. Critics outside the modern university gave particularly harsh assessments of university teaching. One wrote, "It is notorious that the colleges . . . lack men of force and inspiration. There is something negative about the modern species. A group of young men sit under his instruction, but too often he can not dominate or inspire them by his personality because he has none." Another agreed with this negative assessment, stating that "our schools and colleges have altogether too few men who are well-trained, broadly and deeply, and who have enough personal power and magnetism to thrill and inspire susceptible young men and women." Modern scholars, such critics maintained, were too remote from other people and from important daily issues to understand their students.[46]

The inability of faculty to excite their students meant that indirect moral training—based on imitation of faculty role models—would be doomed to failure. "The absence of a means of communication and this lack of sympathetic appreciation of his students on the part of an instructor," noted V. T. Thayer of Ohio State, "is one explanation for the fact that college students can attend college four years without experiencing any fundamental transformation in their outlook upon life." Robert C. Angell of University of Michigan agreed that lack of inspirational teaching undercut the influence of faculty.

> The failure of the students to respond more readily to intellectual stimulation is in some measure due to the personality and point of view of the faculty. No one can deny that professors are interested in their fields of study; but many believe that frequently they have little ability in, or enthusiasm for, imparting their knowledge and interest to immature undergraduates. Many professors have devoted themselves so completely to research in some narrow field that they have not the familiarity with present-day realities which must form the basis for sympathetic contact.[47]

In addressing the quality of teaching, commentators focused on two causes for poor instruction: the priority given to training and hiring researchers, and the absence of any formal instruction in teaching techniques and educational psychology. First, they reprimanded universities for hiring talented researchers rather than gifted teachers. They maintained that by basing hiring and promotion decisions on research accomplishments, universities robbed students of the opportunity for a vital education. They concluded that faculty should be hired on the basis of teaching ability rather than research or that research and teaching should be separated rather than combined in the same position.[48]

Educators thought the research ideal contributed to poor teaching in several ways. They argued that by giving priority to research, universities distorted graduate study. William James's article "The Ph.D. Octopus," published in 1903, is an early, and famous, example of what became a common theme in discussions of university education: how graduate education could cramp and distort intellectual life. Critics charged that graduate schools aimed to make every student into a researcher. They encouraged immediate specialization. Graduate students responded to such pressure by losing all interest in subjects outside their own small ken. Their academic programs left them no time for leisurely reading or social contact. The research they were encouraged to pursue was often so narrow as to be trivial. By the end of graduate school, their advanced education had dulled their intellect and deadened their creativity.[49]

Critics argued that overspecialization in graduate school was one cause of poor undergraduate teaching. F. J. Kelly of University of Minnesota, for example, asserted that a change was needed "in the essential spirit which dominates graduate schools." Graduate schools valued "intensive specialization and capacity for independent investigation." But the "undergraduate-college teacher, on the other hand, requires the broadest possible training." One suggested reform would include explicit training in educational methods in graduate programs. Proponents of this change pointed out that the vast majority of Ph.D.s became college teachers. They blamed poor teaching on lack of training: "the average university professor is a poor teacher because he has never been trained in the technique of teaching." Faculty in education schools led the call for required instruction in educational psychology, pedagogy, and supervised teaching in graduate programs. Some argued that all graduate programs should include formal instruction in education as well as in the subject matter. Others argued for the development of a two-track system of graduate education: one for students who would become primarily researchers and the other for future college teachers. The second track would emphasize teaching, problems facing higher education, and broad knowledge of an area of scholarship, rather than an original contribution to research.[50]

Since administrators at leading universities had themselves emphasized the importance of faculty role models, they could not ignore the ensuing critique of university teaching. In their annual reports during the 1920s, administrators at universities such as Harvard, Yale, Johns Hopkins, University of Chicago, and University of California discussed problems of quality of teaching and graduate training. Although they were more temperate than their critics outside the research university, these leaders agreed that the quality of teaching and graduate education needed to be improved. In keeping with their desire for faculty role models, they were particularly concerned that undergraduates did not have enough personal contact with their instructors and that the contact they did have was not "inspirational" enough.[51]

Just as in the case of the curriculum, the problem of the lack of faculty "inspiration" was defined in broad terms, but the solutions were relatively narrow and administrative. For example, in 1920 President of Burton of University of Michigan defined the goal of "inspirational" teaching as "the actual awakening of a student until he has a faint glimpse of what it means to be alive today in America." He believed that students needed to be "stabbed and pricked and goaded into a fine realization of their real possibilities." Teaching had to "set free" students' "actual potentialities . . . if civilization is to be preserved." In short, "inspirational" teaching was supposed to fulfill the traditional moral goals of higher education: to prepare students to live "properly" so that they could make the world a better place.[52]

Despite these lofty goals, universities were unwilling to radically change their practices regarding the hiring and promotion of professors or the training of future faculty. Although they now acknowledged that research and teaching were separate and sometimes in conflict, university leaders did not want to elevate teaching as the primary criterion for faculty positions. Instead, they made minor adjustments. Some universities, such as Yale and Columbia, made teaching the primary qualification for hiring and promotion of instructors specifically hired to teach freshmen. Others provided voluntary instructional material about teaching techniques. The University of Chicago, for example, in 1924 formed a committee on the quality of instruction in elementary classes, consisting of students and faculty. The committee created a self-assessment guide for effective teaching, which it distributed to faculty teaching lower division students. The guide outlined and rated the various qualities that the committee thought were essential to successful teaching.[53]

Universities' response to demands for changes in graduate programs were similarly moderate. President Lowell of Harvard suggested that the narrowness attributed to graduate students resulted from "a lack of association with other scholars pursuing different subjects" rather than from "the necessary limitation of their studies." He proposed that a dormitory or hall be set aside for the use of graduate students. "The broadening of interest and the stimulation of thought by the intellectual atmosphere of such a place," he asserted, "could hardly fail to be of the highest value to all of them." University leaders did not want to significantly change graduate instruction, particularly the emphasis on research. Gordon J. Laing, dean of the University of Chicago Graduate School, thought that the quality of research conducted in graduate school had to be improved; he therefore rejected pleas for relaxing research requirements. He did, however, agree that students, especially in fields where research positions were scarce, should be required to have "some degree of familiarity with modern methods of presentation and with chief problems of the college curriculum today." Universities were willing to add instruction in teaching techniques but were unwilling to shift the emphasis of graduate education away from research.[54]

Without leadership from university administrators, faculty in the various disciplines were left to consider the problem of graduate education on their own. Professors in literature most actively debated the need for reforming graduate studies. Among literature faculty, proposals to broaden graduate training and reduce the emphasis on research received considerable support. This interest grew out of efforts, discussed in chapter 7, to turn literature into a secular source of moral training. Faculty who saw literature as the basis of a humanistic education also tended to criticize specialization and value inspirational teaching. Their efforts shifted graduate education away from philological training, which they saw as narrowly specialized, to historical subjects and literary criticism. They did not, however, eliminate research as the prime focus of Ph.D. programs.[55]

Instead of reconsidering the research ideal, university administrators looked for new ways to provide the personal guidance that students needed. They responded to the problem by establishing "student advising" as one of the specialized functions of the university. Harvard formalized a system of freshman advisers in 1910. Under this program, all faculty were assigned up to four students each. Students were required to meet with their advisers at the beginning of their freshman year to set up a program for the year, and again at the end of the year to plan a program for their subsequent years. Faculty advisers could make exceptions to distribution and concentration requirements if students had a good plan of study and could authorize changes in students' original course of study.[56]

Harvard's system of faculty advisers was designed to help students create more rational courses of study without eliminating the elective system. Others universities followed Harvard's example and set up student advising programs. Some of these programs emphasized the importance of personal as well as academic advice. Yale, for example, established a system of faculty advisers when it created its common freshman-year program. Yale's program, unlike Harvard's, was voluntary. Only faculty with an interest in students were expected to serve. Roswell P. Angier, dean of freshmen, wanted the adviser "to get as intimately acquainted with his men as temperaments and circumstances permit. Advice to and influence over the boy are thus, in a way, incidental results of unforced personal tie." Advisers had no role in disciplining students; they were not required to fill out forms or make formal reports. They were encouraged to do the job as they thought best and were provided with a sum of money to cover expenditures for socializing with students. The University of Michigan also established a voluntary program of faculty advisers, designed in part so that students could become "intimately" acquainted with at least one faculty member. Its advisers were supposed to meet with students socially and informally twice a month.[57]

University administrators viewed advising as a solution to the problem of moral guidance. David Starr Jordan wrote,

> It is now generally recognized that the most pressing problem of higher education in America is the care of underclassmen, the freshmen and sophomores. Training in personal habits must be effected by some positive method, requiring action and vigilance. In brief, the college must furnish its lower classmen with advisers of some kind, men who come near the students, men whom the students can trust, and who at the same time are in touch with the highest ideals the University teachers represent.

Designated advisers would ensure that students had some personal contact with faculty role models.[58]

Administrators wrote enthusiastically about their student advising programs, which became one of the most widely adopted reforms of the early twentieth century. A study conducted by the Association of American Colleges in 1928 found that approximately 75 percent of the 281 colleges surveyed had faculty advisers. Most used faculty advisers to help students schedule their courses and to counsel students on personal and vocational matters. Despite the popularity of the programs, critics pointed out that the problems that made faculty poor teachers—their narrow specialization and lack of interest in students—also made them poor advisers. Percy Marks, an English professor, thought that the "advisory system is excellent in theory," but that in practice the "average professor" was too "rigidly dignified" to make students confide in him. "If the professors could simply learn to take a little human interest in the boys," Marks thought, "the problem would be easily solved." Joseph A. Bursley, dean of students at University of Michigan, who praised faculty advising, admitted that it was difficult to find "men who are interested in the personal side of student life and who can afford to give the time and thought which proper handling of the problem requires." He also noted that some students did not "realize the advantages to be gained by a close relationship between the older and younger members of the community," and therefore did not use their services.[59]

Because of the difficulty in finding adequate faculty advisers, some universities used deans or other officers hired primarily to serve students' needs. For example, University of Chicago, in response to a survey of the quality of teaching, published in 1909, established a system in which each department designated one faculty member as its student adviser. This system turned out to be unsatisfactory because a departmental adviser often viewed "the performance of his duties as a troublesome annoyance. . . . Students have reported many times to the Deans that the average departmental adviser gives but perfunctory service and considers the extent of his duties to be to list some course numbers on a sequence blank." To strengthen the advising system, Chicago hired deans to counsel lower division students and limited departmental advising to juniors and seniors.[60]

Universities also supplemented faculty advisers by hiring specialized student-support staff, such as vocational counselors and health advisers, and they created new administrative positions to oversee the growing student-service programs. In 1919, for example, Yale created the position of the dean of students. President Hadley reported that the new dean "will deal with all the collective problems of public morals and public order which confront the University as a whole." The dean of students was to "help student *morale* in every way" and was to be "primarily an adviser rather than a disciplinary officer." Deans of students were part of a new field that emerged in higher education in the early twentieth century, known then as "personnel technique." One new expert in the field, Adam Leroy Jones, explained that it addressed a range of subjects, such as "the wise selection of . . . students, the provision made for adjusting them to the life and work of the college, the attention given to their health, their economic needs, to their intellectual demands, and to their moral and religious life as well as their instruction." Jones acknowledged that these issues had previously been the care of the faculty, but stated that as universities had grown, their problems had become more complex, demanding the help of experts.[61]

Administrators in charge of student affairs tried to find ways to give students additional guidance. One of the most common new programs, in addition to faculty advisers, was freshman orientation. The Association of American Colleges reported that 60 percent of the 281 colleges it surveyed in 1928 had some form of freshman orientation. The University of Chicago, University of Michigan, University of California, and Yale all instituted freshman orientation programs in the 1920s. These programs aimed to introduce students to "the whole academic, social and moral environment" of the college. University administrators assumed that student failures, both personal and academic, resulted from their ignorance of college life. Freshman orientation activities explained the complex curriculum to students, discussed study habits, introduced the students to religious and other extracurricular activities, and warned them away from the "traps" of college life that led to moral dissipation. The programs tried to compensate for some of the chaos of the modern university and to provide proper advice before freshmen came under the more questionable guidance offered by upperclassmen.[62]

Freshman orientation programs were designed as part of a growing program of student services overseen by a dean or other administrative officer. The development of these student services illustrates the evolution away from the conviction that teaching the "truth" always had both moral and intellectual value and toward the notion that moral guidance was one function of a university education—one that, like other functions, could be best fulfilled through specialized programs.

University leaders' commitment to student services reflected their growing belief that the moral value of a university education resided in the community life of students, not in their formal education. By the early twentieth century students at most American universities and colleges had developed an elaborate array of extracurricular activities. Observers of higher education agreed that, while students cared little about their classes, they were ardently interested in these activities. Although educators hoped to increase student interest in academic subjects, they appreciated the "spirit" that students displayed in their own endeavors and maintained that these activities, if properly directed, could develop student morality. As a result, university administrators began increasingly to regulate the activities of students. By the 1920s they were attempting to shape students' community life by building dormitories and by instituting selective admission policies. "Student life" replaced the classroom and the chapel as the locus of the moral mission of the university. This institutional arrangement reflected the intellectual division between fact and value, and reduced morality to campus morale.[63]

University educators who had argued that morality could be better taught through personal influence than through formal instruction also believed in the intangible but powerful influence of the university "community." They thought that successful colleges created a strong group identity among their students. President Burton of the University of Michigan called this group identity the "university atmosphere" and maintained that it could provide "a strong sense of united effort and of common aims." Educators argued that a strong group identity could serve as the most effective moral influence on students.[64]

University leaders believed that group identity was a powerful moral tool because it was pervasive and inclusive. President Lowell of Harvard explained that students' morality could be influenced by "personal contact, or indirectly by the creation of good traditions." He pointed out, however, that "direct personal contact of an intimate character is not possible with a large number of students enjoying the freedom of college life." The good influence of an upright and inspiring individual would have only limited impact in the university as a whole. "To influence a large number of men," he continued, the college "must form a community, with common sentiments, aspirations, and interests. In short, they must have a strong consciousness of being bound together by common ties. They must have *esprit de corps.*" Educators believed that they could shape students' character by fostering a positive group ethos in the university.[65]

Seeking to mold a student community, university leaders turned their attention to the area of university life in which students expressed the greatest interest: extracurricular activities. Educators began to advocate a "paternalist" approach to student activities, thus adopting an attitude similar to that of their predecessors in the classical college. In the antebellum college, students had organized literary societies, debating clubs, and semiformal athletic contests between different classes. Although students had initiated and run these activities, college faculty had felt that it was their duty to oversee all aspects of students' lives and, therefore, had regulated all activities to ensure that they served moral ends. All activities that might foster immorality were forbidden.

The variety and organization of student activities expanded rapidly during the first wave of university reform. In the late nineteenth century students established fraternities and sororities, eating and other social clubs, intercollegiate athletic competitions, student newspapers, yearbooks, humor magazines, dramatic societies, and other group activities. The university ideal of freedom encouraged the growth of these activities. The new universities gave students more personal independence and rejected policies that required students to live either in dormitories or in their parents' home. Schools that did not embrace the ideal of freedom often tried to block activities that they felt were morally suspect, such

as baseball and theater, but they found that competition for students
and increased student wealth made such resistance difficult. As these colleges gradually adopted other university reforms, such as electives, they
dropped their opposition to these student activities. By the beginning of
the twentieth century most American colleges and universities had elaborate student-run organizations.[66]

With the exception of religious organizations, university reformers in
the late nineteenth century left the development of extracurricular activities to students. Athletic contests, for example, were arranged and run by
students. Student captains coached the teams, students formed athletic
associations to raise money for the teams, student managers arranged for
transportation and equipment. As collegiate athletics became more popular, alumni also became involved and raised money to hire coaches, buy
equipment, and build facilities. Other activities followed the same pattern.
Students took charge of dramatic events and publications. They organized
their own fraternities and clubs. When students received assistance,
it came from alumni rather than the university administration. Consequently, university reformers did not concern themselves greatly with extracurricular activities.[67]

Given freedom and independence, students did not always use their
activities for moral ends. Controversies regarding intercollegiate athletics
first drew attention to the shortcomings of student-managed activities. In
the 1880s and 1890s administrators faced a variety of questions about the
conduct of college sports, such as the brutality of football and the use
of professional players on college baseball teams. University leaders were
uncertain how to respond to these crises: some maintained that students
controlled their own activities and that athletic events were beyond the
purview of the faculty and administration, others wanted the faculty to
impose rules regulating athletic contests, while still others created com-
mittees of students, alumni, and faculty to settle problems. Although
university officials acknowledged that there were abuses in intercollegiate
sports, they also defended athletics in principle, arguing that a strong
body strengthened the mind and that sportsmanship inculcated manly
virtues. In this period university officials were drawn into one area of extracurricular activities, but they only hesitatingly and ineffectively tried to
regulate it.[68]

By the early twentieth century collegiate reformers recognized that to
exploit the moral potential of extracurricular activities, they would have to
take a more active interest in student activities. University officials rejected
student control and adopted the principle of institutional regulation of

intercollegiate athletics. In 1905 a group of colleges and universities agreed to form the National Collegiate Athletic Association (NCAA). Although initially weak, the NCAA successfully instituted new rules regulating football, student eligibility, recruitment of athletes, and other controversial matters. The organization's successes, however, did not diminish the amount of attention paid to athletics. Collegiate reformers had come to view intercollegiate sports and other student activities as a central feature of the college experience, one that could be reformed to serve higher purposes.[69]

In their discussions of college sports, university leaders bemoaned practices commonly found on their campuses. They argued that amateur sports had been overtaken by commercialism and professionalism. They complained about professional coaches who were paid as much as the university president and who resorted to unethical tactics to win a game. They castigated these coaches for their aggressive recruiting tactics and excessive practice schedules. They reproached newspapers for showering attention on student sports stars. They lamented that students neglected their studies to attend games and worried that on weekend trips to away games, the students smoked, drank, and mixed too freely with members of the opposite sex. They thought that mania about sports distorted people's values, mistakenly convincing students, alumni, and the public that the most important thing about a university was a winning football team.[70]

At the same time that university leaders excoriated the conduct of intercollegiate athletics, they insisted that athletics had important moral benefits. University of Chicago's famous football coach, Amos Alonzo Stagg, frequently spoke of the moral value of college sports. Athletics, Stagg asserted, "employs leisure in wholesome and beneficial ways; takes a man's mind and directs it along wholesome lines, and keeps it off the unwholesome; it curtails his animal spirits as to stop expression in explosive ways that are immoral." Stagg maintained that he had opted for a career in coaching rather than the ministry because he believed he could have stronger moral influence as a coach. He thought of athletics as "one of the strongest forces now in operation to counteract the tremendous moral let-down in the relations of both men and women." Although Stagg had a vested interest in defending athletics, his views on the moral benefits of sports were widely shared among university educators. Indeed, in the early twentieth century, educators who doubted the moral value of athletics were considered "iconoclastic."[71]

Educators believed that students who participated in athletics developed desirable attributes: cooperation with a team, service and self-sacrifice, respect for rules, discipline, hard work, loyalty, confidence, self-control, stamina, and courage. They emphasized that athletics promoted masculine virtues, and they associated physical strength with strength of character. Although relatively few college students actually played college sports, athletics could benefit student spectators as well as players. University officials pointed out that athletics helped build group loyalty and allowed students to become interested in something higher than themselves. A committee of the American Association of University Professors explained that football "creates a strong sense of common interest" and promotes a "common bond of loyalty" among students. Sports, then, contributed to the powerful group identity that educators believed had moral benefits.[72]

University leaders insisted that they could reap the positive moral fruits of athletics if they could reform how sports were played on their campuses. Despite the limited effects of previous reform measures, educators proposed numerous changes in college athletics. They wanted the university administration to have more control over athletics. They replaced coaches hired by alumni-student athletic associations with "faculty coaches" hired by the university. They proposed that the NCAA change eligibility rules so students would not be able to play throughout their college career. They wanted more students participating on teams and suggested that universities field more than one team in a sport and create additional programs in "minor" sports, such as tennis, golf, and swimming. They also tried to increase student interest in intramural sports.[73]

By instituting changes in athletics, university educators hoped that they could reshape students' community life to make it a force for moral improvement. In the 1920s educators tried out new policies designed to elevate the moral value of other extracurricular activities. They felt that fraternities were often a "powerful source of moral misbehavior" and wanted to improve their influence. They realized that students respected and emulated members of prominent fraternities. Educators hoped that the new student affairs officers could persuade fraternities to take academics and community service more seriously. Administrators proposed that fraternities hire university-appointed proctors to live in their houses and university-approved chaperones for dances and other social events. They also tried to limit the influence of fraternities by forbidding freshmen to join. Universities also considered plans that would limit the number of activities in which individual students could participate. These programs tried to prevent fraternity members from dominating the important positions in student organizations and to keep individuals from spending too much time on extracurricular activities.[74]

University officials recognized that it was almost impossible to mold the social lives of students when they lived outside the college. Regulating extracurricular activities alone could not create the desired community spirit. In the 1910s and 1920s university leaders perceived a need to create a physical community for students, and they began to try to raise money to build dormitories. Late nineteenth-century university reformers had paid little attention to student housing. They had argued that one of the reasons for the weakness of the antebellum colleges had been that they spent their money on dormitories rather than faculty, libraries, and laboratories. They in turn had reversed these priorities. As student enrollments had grown, few of the leading universities had built enough dormitories. Instead, students had lived in private boarding houses, fraternities and sororities, or other clubs. When collegiate reformers began to emphasize the importance of community spirit, they realized that their universities did not offer students a cohesive community. Students lived in a variety of communities, which were often stratified by wealth, hostile to one another, and largely independent of university authority.[75]

In the 1920s renewed interest in the community life of students and expanding enrollments pushed dormitories into the forefront of university concerns. University presidents regularly discussed the beneficial influence of dormitories. Butler, for example, claimed that college residences provided "the largest amount of carefully ordered and stimulating influence that can be brought to bear upon the daily life of growing and expanding youth. . . . Indeed, it has been often said that the college gives more through its opportunities which attach to residence, than through its opportunities which attach to instruction." University officials believed that they would be able to effectively form students' character if they controlled their living environment.[76]

Educators portrayed dormitories as a moral necessity rather than simply a practical arrangement. "The problem of the college," explained President Lowell, "is a moral one, deepening the desire to develop one's own mind, body and character; and this is much promoted by living in surroundings and an atmosphere congenial to the object." He considered student residences "a social device for a moral purpose." The moral value of dormitories was closely associated with the creation of community spirit. Lyman Wilbur, president of Stanford, wrote that "when students are housed together there is developed a strong cooperative sense of loyalty and enthusiasm called 'college spirit' which has a profound effect upon the development of the character of the students and upon the welfare of the institution." Educators believed that by building dormitories for their students they could also build a close-knit student community and use peer pressure to encourage high moral standards.[77]

In addition to promoting group identity, educators thought that dormitories would offer an opportunity for more intimate relations between adult role models and students than the classroom provided. University officials expected that adults—ideally, faculty members—would live in the student residences. By living in a group with students, these adults would win their friendship and respect and would be able to furnish moral counsel. "Once a group is established," Robert C. Angell explained, "the sympathetic guidance of an older person is invaluable in establishing and maintaining high moral standards." University officials thought they could ensure that the community values in their colleges were healthy by selecting appropriate role models to live in student residences.[78]

University educators discussed what kind of living arrangements would best achieve these moral aims. They agreed that the dormitories should be relatively small, housing around two hundred students. They hoped that the dormitory would replicate the role of the old college class and would be small enough so that all the students could know each other. They believed such a group would be ideal for developing the desired "esprit de corps" and moral discipline. As Kerr D. MacMillan, president of Wells College, explained, "a group of two hundred can be known, observed, regulated and guided as the individual cannot be when his interests and loyalties are divided as they generally are to-day." Each dormitory should have a resident "dean" or "master" and several resident faculty members. The dormitories should have a "home-like atmosphere" and provide students with clean, well-lighted, and well-ventilated rooms and wholesome food.[79]

Not all universities could afford to house the majority of their students in these ideal arrangements. University presidents commonly appealed to donors for help in financing residence halls. Harvard and Yale were fortunate to receive large gifts from the Standard Oil fortune of Yale graduate Edward S. Harkness to build student residences that fit the prescribed model. Both institutions established a series of dormitories, called "houses" at Harvard and "colleges" at Yale. Students lived in their selected house or college from their sophomore to senior years (freshmen lived together in separate dormitories). University officials hoped that students would develop identities as members of a particular house/college.

They encouraged intramural athletic competitions between residence halls and other activities that would foster community spirit. Administrators also hoped that these houses would break down what they considered to be pernicious social divisions that developed among students when they lived in private residences. By building university-run housing, educators tried to replace the existing student culture with what they expected would be a more morally uplifting community life.[80]

As university educators lost faith in the possibility of formal moral education, they tried to harness the power of student peer relations for moral purposes. The desire to mold student social life drew university officials' attention to the kinds of students that attended their university. In the 1920s universities began to discuss the importance of more carefully selecting future students. Rising enrollments after World War I made restrictive admissions feasible at universities such as Harvard, Yale, Columbia, Stanford, Chicago, Johns Hopkins, and Michigan. University leaders did not view increased student applications primarily as an opportunity to raise academic standards. Instead, they lobbied for new admissions procedures that would take into consideration a new criterion for selecting students: character.[81]

Before the 1920s university admission policies had been designed to determine students' academic preparation. Universities had used various means to measure students' preparation, including administering their own examinations on subjects required for admission, accepting subject examinations given by the College Entrance Examination Board, and examining students' grades in secondary school. By the early 1920s educators at leading universities had come to believe that adequate academic preparation did not necessarily ensure that an individual was appropriate "material" for their college. "The colleges," explained President C. C. Little of University of Michigan, "have begun to look for factors more general and less tangible than the student's ability in elementary French or plane geometry. They have begun to admit that he has a personality, a general 'something' of immense importance in determining his potential value as a student." University leaders wanted to change admission policies so that they considered applicants' "character" and "native abilities" as well as their scholarly achievements.[82]

Educators maintained that they should broaden the criteria for admission because colleges aimed to develop students' character as well as intellect. "If the purpose of the college is to prepare students for leadership by developing all the qualities of mind and character and personality," explained the Harvard Student Council Committee on Education, "then the admission standards must test character and personality, as well as mental power." Dean Wilkins at University of Chicago agreed that the mission of the college was to graduate future leaders. Leadership required intellectual ability, physical health, and strong morals. A student who had the intellectual and physical attributes but lacked the moral ones was potentially dangerous, because he might use his "powers for anti-social ends—might be no leader, but a slacker or a traitor to society." Wilkins argued that colleges should only admit students who "possessed" or showed "promise of possessing" all qualities associated with leadership, especially moral character.[83]

To determine applicants' personal qualities, university administrators proposed new admissions procedures that would supplement subject examinations and high school records with new sources of information. Universities adopted a variety of measures: IQ tests to determine students' "potential"; elaborate questionnaires, such as Stanford's "Personal Rating Blank," which asked about students' "industry," "judgment and common sense," "reliability," "initiative," "co-operation," "leadership," and "physical vitality"; required character references from teachers and other members of the community in which the prospective student lived; and personal interviews. Educators realized that these additional sources of information were "subjective" and looked forward to the development of rating scales similar to IQ tests that would measure the "temperament and character" of potential students.[84]

University leaders' new emphasis on screening applicants' personal qualities reflected their changing assumptions about character development. They seemed to have lost faith in the view that schooling inculcated morality. Instead, they spoke about how education could help develop moral traits in students who had the capacity for them, but maintained that it could not make students who lacked potential into moral adults. This betrayed an increased acceptance of the view that personal traits, including morals, were inherent rather than acquired. The new character requirements also reflected universities' reliance on peer culture as the most important potential moral influence in the college and indicated that many university leaders felt that at least some of their current students did not possess the desired moral traits.[85]

University officials used selective admissions and character requirements to keep "undesirables" off their campuses. In theory, these restrictions prevented young people who had "character flaws" that might corrupt the community life of the college, or who had "personality traits" that inhibited success in college, from enrolling in universities. In practice, the new admissions policies allowed elite universities to discriminate against ethnic minorities, particularly Jews. At schools such as Harvard, the decision to expand the criteria for admission and limit the size of the undergraduate population was closely tied to efforts to solve the "Jewish problem." In the 1920s many of the leading universities and colleges decided that rising numbers of Jewish students upset the social life of their institutions and sought ways to restrict their matriculation. The new admissions practices—making character a requirement for all students—provided a means that did not explicitly target a single group. Hence, they served to mask anti-Semitism.[86]

Nonetheless, the new admissions policies were not simply a cover for anti-Semitism; they were part of a broader agenda aimed at shaping the community life of students. Given the assumptions of university officials in the 1920s, these two goals easily merged. Common prejudices allowed university administrators to believe, even though evidence did not support it, that Jewish students were more deceitful and less honorable than their Protestant counterparts. In addition, the value that educators placed on a cohesive student community supported social prejudice. Although educators reasoned that strong group identity was good because it could be used to enforce moral norms, they often fell into discussing "school spirit" as an end in itself. Since they viewed campus unity as good, they thought that things that interfered with it, such as a diverse student population, were bad.[87]

Community cohesiveness and school spirit easily slipped from being means to moral influence to being ends in themselves. University officials were limited in the extent to which they could interfere in students' social lives. They wanted to reshape student culture, but they could not do things that would risk alienating students from campus activities. Students had to care about and be involved in the social life of the college in order to maintain "school spirit." So educators' efforts to regulate student life were restricted by their desire to maintain esprit de corps. For example, university officials believed that intramural sports were better suited to moral ends than intercollegiate athletics and hoped to transfer students' loyalty from the latter to the former. They tried to interest students in intramural sports, but they did not dare eliminate intercollegiate athletics because, despite all the scandals associated with them, they did build student spirit. By settling on group cohesiveness as the best source of moral influence, university officials came to equate morality with morale.[88]

Student-service professionals would never have the power to define moral norms that the president and faculty of the classical college had exercised. They devoted themselves to facilitating social bonds among students. They discovered that imposing their own standards of behavior risked alienating students from campus-sponsored social life. Regulating extracurricular activities meant reaching a compromise between the demands of morale and those of morality. The subsequent history of fraternities and athletics indicates that morale often won.

By the 1920s university leaders thought that the moral education of students would be achieved largely outside the classroom. They maintained that morality was learned by example and not precept. They tried to provide students with proper moral influence: first, by providing designated adult role models for students, and second, by trying to shape the norms of student peer culture. Both these efforts rested on the assumption that the moral value of higher education depended on the personal relations found in the community life of the campus.

Educators' reliance on the indirect moral value of social relations reflected the separation of morality and knowledge. University leaders tacitly recognized that they could not find a way to institutionalize the ideal of the unity of truth and maintain a commitment to the ideal of free inquiry. Without institutional support, the ideal of unity no longer seemed plausible. Over the twentieth century leaders of research universities strengthened their institutions' commitment to the advancement of knowledge, but they were never able to recapture university reformers' faith in the power of knowledge to elevate individuals and the world.

CONCLUSION

In the sixty years surrounding the turn of the twentieth century, American higher education was transformed through two reform movements. The first and most important, university reform, tried to recreate higher education by institutionalizing the ideal of open inquiry. Drawing on ideas about science, university reformers in the late nineteenth century believed that freedom could provide a superior form of mental training. Under the banner of freedom, reformers instituted a variety of changes: electives, laboratory training, seminars and lectures, and support for original research. These changes produced unanticipated developments, such as the proliferation of independent departments and specialization of courses. The second movement, collegiate reform, tried to offset some of the effects of the earlier university reforms and to strengthen the unity and moral purpose of undergraduate education. It also spawned its own specialization: new administrative structures responsible for student services.

In this transition from the classical college to the modern university, the older ideal of the unity of truth was largely gutted. The ideal lingered on in educational rhetoric: universities boasted that they offered instruction in all areas of knowledge and educated the "whole" student. The old triad—the good, true, and beautiful—was updated as service and character, research and objective knowledge, and culture and art. Universities still encompassed all elements of the old ideal, but each element was now pursued as an independent goal. Unity had given way to fragmentation; diverse and specialized programs were loosely held together under a single administrative structure.

While the second and third elements of the triad, the true and the beautiful, formally expanded through the development of academic disciplines in natural and social sciences and arts and literature, the first, the good, diminished appreciably. In the natural and social sciences, the service ideal encompassed only technical expertise and vocational training. Character development, to the extent that it remained in the curriculum, was affiliated with the humanities and the arts. Attention to morality shifted away from the course of study to extracurricular influences. In this change, morality became identified with behavior rather than belief. As university officials equated morality with student morale, the ideal of character eventually lost much of its association with Protestant morality. The cult of personality, which historians have attributed to business culture and consumerism, also found its way into higher education in the early twentieth century.[1]

The division between knowledge and morality was formally elaborated in two philosophical movements that gained wide acceptance in the United States in the 1930s. The first of these, logical positivism, asserted that value statements were meaningless in science. Morality, therefore, lay outside the realm of scientific knowledge. The second, emotivist ethics, maintained that ethical judgments were distinguished by their emotional rather than their cognitive meaning. The intellectual and institutional changes of the preceding half-century—the spread of objectivism among natural and social scientists, the development of the modern humanities, and the relegation of morality to extracurricular activities—helped prepare Americans for logical positivism and emotivist ethics. By the 1920s academics had already accepted the central premises of these philosophies: that science excluded values and that morality was determined by feeling rather than intellect. Hence, logical positivism and emotivist ethics made "sense" to American intellectuals. They readily accepted the major tenets of these philosophies, even if they did not fully understand their intricacies.[2]

The separation of fact and value became both a powerful and a problematic concept in twentieth-century intellectual life. It has often been invoked as a normative guide for scholars. Its normative status is reinforced by the structure of modern higher education, which makes the separation of morality and knowledge seem a "natural" part of intellectual life. Nonetheless, the notion of value-free scholarship has been challenged from its inception. In recent decades, it has been attacked by scholars in disciplines ranging from the philosophy and history of science to postmodern literary criticism. There is a deep ambivalence about the separation of knowledge and morality.

This ambivalence has clear roots in the developments discussed in this book. Universities never renounced their traditional moral aims. Educators continued to believe that universities should prepare their students to live "properly" and contribute to the betterment of society. Contemporary interest in multicultural education indicates that this is still an important imperative in universities today. But universities no longer have a basis from which to judge moral claims. The Protestant synthesis that provided moral guidance up until the late nineteenth century did not survive the adoption of modern standards of scholarship or increased cultural diversity. Despite the hopes of its early advocates, scientific inquiry never produced authoritative intellectual standards for determining what it means to live "properly" or how to identify what constitutes social "betterment." Without a means of adjudicating moral claims, contemporary debates about what college students should learn seem to be reduced to "politics."

The irony is that the eventual separation of knowledge and morality began with efforts to define more reliable ways of knowing, in part so that scholars could provide more authoritative guidance on moral questions. In the late nineteenth century university educators embraced a model of science that presented successful inquiry as beginning with open questioning and leading to consensus among researchers. Based on this notion of science, educators adopted the ideal of free inquiry and viewed agreement as a distinguishing feature of true knowledge. Although the ideals of freedom and agreement seemed compatible in technical and specialized scholarship, free inquiry when applied to moral issues produced conflict. For a variety of institutional and professional reasons, the desire of faculty and university leaders to avoid conflict eventually prevailed over their desire to maintain a close tie between knowledge and morality. Eventually scholars decided that moral concerns fell outside the realm of scientific scholarship.

Scholars hoped that the distinction between fact and value would lead to more reliable knowledge as measured by greater agreement. The subsequent history of academic disciplines in the twentieth century indicates that this hope was illusory. We should then reevaluate whether agreement is the proper standard by which to identify "truth." If universities can learn to tolerate more conflict, we may be able to define cognitive standards by which we can address moral questions. Since it has proved impossible to completely separate fact and value, we should begin to explore ways to reintegrate them.

NOTES

Introduction

1. Charles W. Eliot, "The Elements of a Liberal Education," *Educator Journal* 8 (1908): 499; Samuel Eliot Morison, *Three Centuries of Harvard, 1636–1936* (Cambridge, 1936), chap. 14.

2. Josiah Quincy, *A History of Harvard University,* 2 vols. (Boston, 1860 [1840]), 1:49–50, 2:646.

3. Quincy, *History of Harvard,* 1:48. For the 1884 seal, see Harvard University, *Record of the Commemoration, November 5 to 8th, 1886, on the Two Hundred and Fiftieth Anniversary of the Founding of Harvard College* (Cambridge, 1887), frontispiece.

4. Robert N. Proctor, *Value-Free Science? Purity and Power in Modern Knowledge* (Cambridge, 1991).

5. David A. Hollinger, *In the American Province: Studies in the History and Historiography of Ideas* (Bloomington, Ind., 1985); Thomas Bender, *New York Intellect: A History of Intellectual Life in New York City, from 1750 to the Beginnings of Our Own Time* (Baltimore, 1987); John Higham and Paul K. Conkin, eds., *New Directions in American Intellectual History* (Baltimore, 1979).

6. For relevant histories of philosophy, see Elizabeth Flower and Murray Murphey, *A History of Philosophy in America,* 2 vols. (New York, 1977); James Kloppenberg, *Uncertain Victory: Social Democracy and Progressivism in European and American Thought, 1870–1920* (New York, 1986); Bruce Kuklick, *The Rise of American Philosophy: Cambridge, Massachusetts, 1860–1930* (New Haven, 1977); Kuklick, *Churchmen and Philosophers: From Jonathan Edwards to John Dewey* (New Haven, 1985); Gerald E. Myers, *William James: His Life and Thought* (New Haven, 1986); Steven C. Rockefeller, *John Dewey: Religious Faith and Democratic Humanism* (New York, 1991); Marcus G. Singer, ed., *American Philosophy* (New York, 1985); Alan P. F. Sell, *The Philosophy of Religion, 1875–1980* (New York, 1988); Guy W. Stroh, *American Ethical Thought* (Chicago, 1979); Morton White, *Science and Sentiment in America* (New York, 1972); Daniel J. Wilson, *Science, Community, and the Transformation of American Philosophy* (Chicago, 1990).

7. This list of journals is not complete.

8. Douglas Sloan, "The Teaching of Ethics in the American Undergraduate Curriculum, 1876–1976," in *Ethics Teaching in Higher Education,* ed. Daniel Cal-

lahan and Sissela Bok (New York, 1980), pp. 1–57. Although he focuses on lower schools, B. Edward McClellan also discusses moral education in college and universities in *Schools and the Shaping of Character: Moral Education in America, 1607–Present* (Bloomington, Ind., 1992).

9. For examples of the standard account of the history of American higher education, see Richard Hofstadter and Walter P. Metzger, *The Development of Academic Freedom* (New York, 1955); Frederick Rudolph, *The American College and University: A History* (New York, 1962); and John S. Brubacher and Willis Rudy, *Higher Education in Transition: A History of American Colleges and Universities, 1636–1968,* rev. ed. (New York, 1968).

10. For examples of revisionist work, see James Axtell, "The Death of the Liberal Arts College," *History of Education Quarterly* 9 (1971): 339–52; Natalie A. Naylor, "The Ante-Bellum College Movement: A Reappraisal of Tewksbury's Founding of American Colleges and Universities," *History of Education Quarterly* 13 (1973): 261–74; James McLachlan, "The American College in the Nineteenth Century: Toward a Reappraisal," *Teacher's College Record* 80 (1978): 287–306; David B. Potts, "American Colleges in the Nineteenth Century: From Localism to Denominationalism," *History of Education Quarterly* 11 (1971): 363–80; and Potts, "Curriculum and Enrollments: Some Thoughts Assessing the Popularity of Antebellum Colleges," *History of Higher Education Annual* 1 (1981): 88–109; Martin Finkelstein, "From Tutor to Specialized Scholar: Academic Professionalization in Eighteenth and Nineteenth Century America," *History of Higher Education Annual* 3 (1983): 123–44; Jurgen Herbst, "American Higher Education in the Age of the College," *History of Universities* 7 (1988): 37–59; Colin Bradley Burke, *American Collegiate Populations: A Test of the Traditional View* (New York, 1982); Mark A. Noll, *Princeton and the Republic, 1768–1822: The Search for a Christian Enlightenment in the Era of Samuel Stanhope Smith* (Princeton, 1989); Louise L. Stevenson, *Scholarly Means to Evangelical Ends: The New Haven Scholars and the Transformation of Higher Learning in America, 1830–1890* (Baltimore, 1986); J. David Hoeveler, Jr., *James McCosh and the Scottish Intellectual Tradition: From Glasgow to Princeton* (Princeton, 1981); and J. Bruce Leslie, *Gentlemen and Community: The College in the "Age of the University," 1865–1917* (State College, Pa., 1992).

11. Some recent scholarship on the modern university addresses a different set of concerns. It has focused on the relationship between the university and the new business-industrial order that came to dominate the nation's economy and politics in the late nineteenth and early twentieth centuries. This scholarship finds a close relationship between higher education and the corporate economy. The tone of some of this scholarship is "disappointed": it implies that universities betrayed their mission by aligning themselves with the interests of corporations. This book does not challenge the conclusions of this scholarship. It does, however, indicate that university leaders assumed that establishing close ties to industry was part of their mission. These leaders did not see universities as "ivory towers" promoting "pure" research. They assumed that all knowledge had practical implications and that material progress was closely related to moral progress. Thus, they understood their support for material advancement as part of their traditional moral mission.

For examples of this scholarship, see Burton J. Bledstein, *The Culture of Professionalism: The Development of Higher Education in America* (New York, 1976); and Clyde W. Barrows, *Universities and the Capitalist State: Corporate Liberalism and the Reconstruction of American Higher Education, 1894–1928* (Madison, Wis., 1990).

12. Laurence Veysey, *The Emergence of the American University* (Chicago, 1965). For a discussion of Veysey's book and later scholarship, see John R. Thelin, "Retrospective: Laurence Veysey's *The Emergence of the American University*," *History of Education Quarterly* 27 (1987): 517–23.

13. George M. Marsden, "The Soul of the American University: An Historical Overview," in *The Secularization of the Academy*, ed. George M. Marsden and Bradley J. Longfield (New York, 1992), pp. 9–45; Marsden, *The Soul of the American University: From Protestant Establishment to Established Nonbelief* (New York, 1994). See also Marsden's earlier essay, "The Collapse of American Evangelical Academia," in *Faith and Rationality: Reason and Belief in God*, ed. Alvin Plantinga and Nicholas Wolterstorff (Notre Dame, Ind., 1983), pp. 219–64; Van Harvey, "On the Intellectual Marginality of American Theology," in *Religion and Twentieth-Century American Intellectual Life*, ed. Michael J. Lacey (Cambridge, 1989), pp. 172–92; James Tunstead Burtchaell, "The Decline and Fall of the Christian College," parts 1 and 2, *First Things* (1991): 16–29 and 30–38; Robert S. Shepard, *God's People on the Ivory Tower: Religion in the Early American University* (Brooklyn, 1991); Henry C. Johnson, Jr. "'Down from the Mountain': Secularization and the Higher Learning in America," *Review of Politics* 54 (1992): 551–88.

14. James Turner, *Without God, Without Creed: The Origins of Unbelief in America* (Baltimore, 1985).

15. Ronald L. Numbers, "Science and Religion," in *Historical Writings on American Science: Perspectives and Prospects*, ed. Sally Gregory Kohlstedt and Margaret W. Rossiter (Baltimore, 1986); James R. Moore, *The Post-Darwinian Controversies: A Study of the Protestant Struggle to Come to Terms with Darwin in Great Britain and America, 1870–1900* (New York, 1979); David C. Lindberg and Ronald L. Numbers, eds., *God and Nature: Historical Essays on the Encounter between Christianity and Science* (Berkeley, 1986); Lindberg and Numbers, "Beyond War and Peace: A Reappraisal of the Encounter between Christianity and Science," *Church History* 55 (1986): 338–54; John Hedley Brooke, *Science and Religion: Some Historical Perspectives* (New York, 1991).

16. George H. Daniels, *American Science in the Age of Jackson* (New York, 1976); Theodore Dwight Bozeman, *Protestants in an Age of Science: The Baconian Ideal and Antebellum Religious Thought* (Chapel Hill, N. C., 1977); and Herbert Hovencamp, *Science and Religion in America, 1800–1860* (Philadelphia, 1978). For an example of recent scholarship on ideas about science in the late nineteenth century, see Albert Moyer, *A Scientist's Voice in American Culture: Simon Newcomb and the Rhetoric of the Scientific Method* (Berkeley, 1992).

17. Dorothy Ross, "The Development of the Social Sciences," in *The Organization of Knowledge in Modern America, 1860–1920*, ed. Alexandra Oleson and John Voss (Baltimore, 1979), pp. 107–38; Ross, *The Origins of American Social Science*

(New York, 1991); Thomas L. Haskell, *The Emergence of Professional Social Science: The American Social Science Association and the Nineteenth-Century Crisis of Authority* (Urbana, Ill., 1977); Mary O. Furner, *Advocacy and Objectivity: A Crisis in the Professionalization of American Social Science, 1865–1905* (Lexington, Ky., 1975); L. L. Bernard and Jessie Bernard, *Origins of American Sociology* (New York, 1943); David M. Ricci, *The Tragedy of Political Science: Politics, Scholarship, and Democracy* (New Haven, 1984); Jurgen Herbst, *The German Historical School in American Scholarship: A Study in the Transfer of Culture* (Ithaca, N. Y., 1965); Albert Somit and Joseph Tanehaus, *The Development of American Political Science: From Burgess to Behaviorism* (Boston, 1967); Raymond Seidelman and Edward J. Harpham, *Disenchanted Realists: Political Science and the American Crisis, 1884–1984* (Albany, 1985); Bernard Crick, *The American Science of Politics: Its Origins and Conditions* (London, 1959); Robert C. Bannister, *Sociology and Scientism: The American Quest for Objectivity, 1880–1940* (Chapel Hill, N. C., 1987)..

18. Sloan, "The Teaching of Ethics," p. 1.

19. *The Tercentenary of Harvard College: A Chronicle of the Tercentenary Year, 1935–1936* (Cambridge, 1937).

Chapter One

1. Josiah Cooke, "The Nobility of Knowledge," *Popular Science Monthly* 5 (1874): 621.

2. There is disagreement about the degree to which Puritans relied on their reason to understand the divine will. For an interpretation that emphasizes their reliance on the intellect, see Perry Miller, *The New England Mind: The Seventeenth Century* (Cambridge, 1982 [1939]). For an interpretation that stresses distrust of reason, see John Morgan, *Godly Learning: Puritan Attitudes towards Reasoning, Learning and Education, 1560–1640* (New York, 1986). On Harvard, see Samuel Eliot Morison, *The Founding of Harvard College* (Cambridge, 1963 [1935]).

3. Elizabeth Flower and Murray G. Murphey, *A History of Philosophy in America*, 2 vols. (New York, 1977), 1:chap. 1; Frederick Rudolph, *Curriculum: A History of the American Undergraduate Course of Study since 1636* (San Francisco, 1977), chap. 2; Lawrence A. Cremin, *American Education: The Colonial Experience, 1607–1783* (New York, 1970), chap. 6; Miller, *The New England Mind*, chap. 6.

4. Margo Todd, *Christian Humanism and the Puritan Social Order* (New York, 1987), chaps. 2 and 3; Cremin, *American Education: The Colonial Experience*, chap. 2; Flower and Murphey, *A History of Philosophy*, 1:chap. 1; Miller, *The New England Mind*, pp. 161–62; Norman Fiering, *Moral Philosophy at Seventeenth-Century Harvard: A Discipline in Transition* (Chapel Hill, 1981), pp. 22–52.

5. Norman S. Fiering, "President Samuel Johnson and the Circle of Knowledge," *William and Mary Quarterly* 3rd ser., 28 (1971): 199–236, especially 220, 221, 227. See also Flower and Murphey, *A History of Philosophy*, 1:81–99.

6. Fiering, *Moral Philosophy*, pp. 6–7; Fiering, "President Samuel Johnson," p.

201. See also Richard Warch, *School of the Prophets: Yale College, 1701–1740* (New Haven, 1973), chaps. 8 and 9.

7. Flower and Murphey, *A History of Philosophy,* 1:215–38. On the ideas and influence of Scottish common-sense philosophy, see Douglas Sloan, *The Scottish Enlightenment and the American College Ideal* (New York, 1971); Mark A. Noll, *Princeton and the Republic, 1768–1822: The Search for a Christian Enlightenment in the Era of Samuel Stanhope Smith* (Princeton, 1989); Daniel Walker Howe, *The Unitarian Conscience: Harvard Moral Philosophy, 1805–1861* (Middletown, Conn., 1988); D. H. Meyer, *The Instructed Conscience: The Shaping of the American National Ethic* (Philadelphia, 1972); Theodore Dwight Bozeman, *Protestants in an Age of Science: The Baconian Ideal and Antebellum American Religious Thought* (Chapel Hill, 1977), pp. 4–23; Herbert Hovencamp, *Science and Religion in America, 1800–1860* (Philadelphia, 1978), chaps. 1 and 2; J. David Hoeveler, Jr., *James McCosh and the Scottish Intellectual Tradition from Glasgow to Princeton* (Princeton, 1981); George M. Marsden, "Everyone's Own Interpreter?: The Bible, Science, and Authority in Mid-Nineteenth-Century America," in *The Bible in America: Essays in Cultural History,* ed. Nathan O. Hatch and Mark A. Noll (New York, 1982), pp. 79–100..

8. John Hedley Brooke, *Science and Religion: Some Historical Perspectives* (Cambridge, 1991), chap. 6; Ronald L. Numbers, "Science and Religion," in *Historical Writing on American Science: Perspectives and Prospects,* ed. Sally Gregory Kohlstedt and Margaret W. Rossiter (Baltimore, 1985), pp. 66–70; Robert V. Bruce, *The Launching of Modern American Science, 1846–1876* (New York, 1987), p. 122; George H. Daniels, *American Science in the Age of Jackson* (New York, 1968), p. 52; Jon H. Roberts, *Darwinism and the Divine in America: Protestant Intellectuals and Organic Evolution, 1859–1900* (Madison, Wis., 1988), pp. 8–24. In antebellum America, scholars frequently distinguished between natural theology (evidence of God in the natural world) and natural religion (evidence of God in human nature), but for the purpose of this brief discussion, these will be considered together under the rubric of natural theology. Howe, *Unitarian Conscience,* p. 95.

9. Francis Wayland, *The Elements of Moral Science,* rev. and improved ed. (New York, 1865), p. 125; Charles Kingsley, "The Study of Physical Science: A Lecture to Young Men," *Popular Science Monthly* 4 (1872): 456.

10. Bowen quoted in Howe, *The Unitarian Conscience,* p. 2. See also Meyer, *The Instructed Conscience;* Wilson Smith, *Professors and Public Ethics: Studies of Northern Moral Philosophers before the Civil War* (Ithaca, N. Y., 1956); and David Hogan, "Moral Authority and the Antinomies of Moral Theory: Francis Wayland and Nineteenth-Century Moral Education," *Educational Theory* 40 (1990): 95–119.

11. A. P. Peabody, *Christianity and Science* (New York, 1874), p. 2; Wayland, *The Elements of Moral Science,* pp. 132–33.

12. Wayland, *The Elements of Moral Science,* pp. 133–34; "The Logical Relations of Religion and Natural Science," *Princeton Review* 3 (1860): 580; Howe, *The Unitarian Conscience,* pp. 70–71.

13. Francis Wayland, *Elements of Intellectual Philosophy,* 9th ed. (Boston, 1857),

p. 407; Wayland, *The Elements of Moral Science,* p. 126; Meyer, *The Instructed Conscience,* p. 24.

14. Cornelius Conway Felton, "Characteristics of the American Colleges," *American Journal of Education* 9 (1860): 122; George P. Schmidt, *The Old Time College President* (New York, 1930), chap. 7; Donald G. Tewksbury, *The Founding of American Colleges and Universities before the Civil War, with Particular Reference to the Religious Influences Bearing upon the College Movement* (New York, 1932). Relying largely on these works, historians of education have often depicted the antebellum college as narrowly sectarian and repressive in its piety. See, for example, the chapter "The Great Retrogression" in Richard Hofstadter, *The Development of Academic Freedom* (New York, 1955), pp. 209–22. More recent scholarship has challenged this view and depicted the colleges as "broadly Christian." See Natalie A. Naylor, "The Ante-Bellum College Movement: A Reappraisal of Tewksbury's Founding of American Colleges and Universities," *History of Education Quarterly* 13 (1973): 261–74; David B. Potts, "American Colleges in the Nineteenth Century: From Localism to Denominationalism," *History of Education Quarterly* 11 (1971): 363–80; James McLachlan, "The American College in the Nineteenth Century: Toward a Reappraisal," *Teachers College Record* 80 (1978): 287–306. For a synthesis of the work on the religious nature of the antebellum college, see William Ringenberg, *The Christian College: A History of Protestant Higher Education in America* (Grand Rapids, 1984), chap. 2..

15. F. A. P. Barnard to E. C. Herrick, 28 June 1838, F. A. P. Barnard Papers, Columbia University; Rudolph, *Curriculum,* pp. 147–48; Barnard's annual report for 1886–87, reprinted in *The Rise of a University,* ed. William F. Russell, 2 vols. (New York, 1937), 1:59. Most colleges did not require faculty to take religious oaths, but piety and character were important considerations in hiring. There were several cases of faculty being fired for improper religious views, and schools frequently refused to hire faculty who were not members of "standard" Protestant churches. For example, Columbia refused to hire the respected chemist Wolcott Gibbs because he was a Unitarian. See Frederick Rudolph, *The American College and University: A History* (New York, 1962), pp. 69–74; and Bruce, *Launching,* pp. 228–30.

16. I use the masculine pronoun purposefully in this sentence; most college students were male in this period. Wayland, *The Elements of Moral Science,* p. 45; J. W. Richard quoted in Edmund E. Lacy, "The Conflict of Thought over the Role of Religion in Higher Education, 1865–1910" (Ph.D. diss., University of Illinois, 1969), p. 136.

17. "Original Papers in Relation to a Course of Liberal Education," *American Journal of Science and Arts* 15 (1829): 312–13. For a brief overview of systems that attempted to "map out" the unity of truth, see Nicholas Fisher, "The Classification of Sciences," in *Companion to the History of Modern Science,* ed. R. C. Olby et al. (London, 1990), pp. 853–68.

18. J. R. Loomis, "Collegiate System of the United States" (1862), quoted in Lacy, "The Conflict of Thought," p. 152. On the contents and purpose of the moral philosophy course, see Meyer, *The Instructed Conscience;* Smith, *Professors and*

Public Ethics; Douglas Sloan, "Harmony, Chaos, and Consensus: The American College Curriculum," *Teachers College Record* 83 (1971): 246–47; C. H. Smith, "Faculty Participation in Student Religious Life," in *Two Centuries of Christian Activity at Yale, 1701–1901,* ed. James B. Reynolds et al. (New York, 1901), pp. 160–61; Ralph Henry Gabriel, *Religion and Learning at Yale: The Church of Christ in the College and University, 1757–1957* (New Haven, 1958), pp. 110–13; Howe, *The Unitarian Conscience,* pp. 74–75; Ringenberg, *The Christian College,* pp. 67–68..

19. Fiering, "President Samuel Johnson," p. 226; Rudolph, *Curriculum,* chap. 2; Bruce A. Kimball, *Orators and Philosophers: A History of the Idea of Liberal Education* (New York, 1986), chap. 4; Howard Miller, *The Revolutionary College: American Presbyterian Higher Education, 1707–1837* (New York, 1976), pp. 86–94, 179–83, 271–83; Francis Wayland, *Thoughts on the Present Collegiate System in the United States* (Boston, 1842), p. 80.

20. George Ticknor, "Remarks on Changes Lately Proposed or Adopted, in Harvard University" (1825), reprinted in *The Colleges and the Public, 1787–1862,* ed. Theodore Rawson Crane (New York, 1963), pp. 79–80.

21. Rudolph, *Curriculum,* p. 76; David B. Tyack, *George Ticknor and the Boston Brahmins* (Cambridge, 1967), chap. 3.

22. "Original Papers," pp. 299–300; Rudolph, *Curriculum,* pp. 66–67; Gabriel, *Religion and Learning,* chap. 6; Brooks Mather Kelley, *Yale: A History* (New Haven, 1974), p. 161. Traditionally, historians have viewed the Yale report as a regressive document, but revisionist scholarship on the antebellum college has drawn attention to its progressive aspects. See Sloan, "Harmony, Chaos, and Consensus," p. 244; Jack C. Lane, "The Yale Report of 1828 and Liberal Education: A Neorepublican Manifesto," *History of Education Quarterly* 27 (1987): 325–38.

23. "Original Papers," p. 308.

24. Ibid., p. 301.

25. Ibid., pp. 308–9.

26. Ibid., pp. 318–19.

27. Rudolph, *Curriculum,* pp. 67–94; Jurgen Herbst, "American Higher Education in the Age of the College," *History of Universities* 7 (1988): 37–59; Colin Bradley Burke, *American Collegiate Populations: A Test of the Traditional View* (New York, 1982), chap. 1.

28. Josiah Quincy, *The History of Harvard University,* 2 vols. (Boston, 1860), 2:452–53. On the ill effects of founding large numbers of schools, see "College Education," *North American Review* 55 (1842): 306–7.

29. Wayland, *Thoughts,* pp. 12–13.

30. Henry P. Tappan, *University Education* (New York, 1851), pp. 50 and 68.

31. Wayland, *Thoughts,* p. 81.

32. Ibid., p. 83; Tappan, *University Education,* p. 53.

33. Tappan, *University Education,* pp. 52–53; Wayland, *Thoughts,* pp. 84–88.

34. Rudolph, *Curriculum,* pp. 109–15; Francis Wayland, *Report to the Corporation of Brown University, On Changes in the System of Collegiate Education, Read March 28, 1850,* in *American Higher Education: A Documentary History,* ed. Rich-

ard Hofstadter and Wilson Smith, 2 vols. (Chicago, 1961), 2:478–87. For Tappan's ideas on the relationship of the college and the university and his evaluation of Wayland's program at Brown, see Tappan, *University Education,* pp. 43–76.

35. Joseph Henry, "On the Importance of the Cultivation of Science: Letter to the Committee of Arrangements of the Farewell Banquet to Professor Tyndall," in *A Scientist in American Life: Essays and Lectures of Joseph Henry,* ed. Arthur P. Moella et al. (Washington, D.C., 1980), p. 106; Bruce, *Launching,* pp. 271–312; George M. Fredrickson, *The Inner Civil War: Northern Intellectuals and the Crisis of the Union* (New York, 1965), pp. 209–15..

36. Frank Wigglesworth Clarke, "American Colleges vrs. American Science" (1876), in *Science in America: Historical Selections,* ed. John C. Burnham (New York, 1971), p. 228. See also Simon Newcomb, "Exact Science in America," *North American Review* 119 (1874): 288–308; Albert Moyer, *A Scientist's Voice in American Culture: Simon Newcomb and the Rhetoric of Scientific Method* (Berkeley, 1992), pp. 83–84.

37. Clarke, "American Colleges," pp. 234–35.

38. Ibid., pp. 231–33. Antebellum reformers did not question the spiritual aims of the college. For the most part, they simply assumed that their reforms would not upset the place of religion in the college. Tappan did recognize that the substitution of a few large universities for the multitude of smaller colleges would upset denominational control of schools. Henry Tappan, "University: Its Constitution and Its Relations, Political and Religious," in *American Higher Education,* ed. Hofstadter and Smith, 2:533.

39. Clarke, "American Colleges," pp. 231–32.

40. Alexander Winchell, *Reconciliation of Science and Religion* (New York, 1877), p. 227.

41. Hovencamp, *Science and Religion;* Bozeman, *Protestants in an Age of Science;* Numbers, "Science and Religion," pp. 66–70; Jon H. Roberts, *Darwinism and the Divine in America: Protestant Intellectuals and Organic Evolution, 1859–1900* (Madison, Wis., 1988), pp. 24–30.

42. See Winchell, *Reconciliation,* pp. 222–26, for a synopsis of these conflicts and their later reconciliation. On the Darwinian conflict, see James R. Moore, *The Post-Darwinian Controversies: A Study of the Protestant Struggle to Come to Terms with Darwin in Great Britain and America, 1870–1900* (New York, 1979); and Numbers, "Science and Religion," pp. 70–77, for a discussion of the literature on the relationship between Darwinian theory and religion.

43. James Thompson Bixby, "Science and Religion as Allies," *Popular Science Monthly* 9 (1876): 691; Joseph LeConte, *Religion and Science: A Series of Sunday Lectures on the Relation of Natural and Revealed Religion; or Truths Revealed in Nature and Scripture* (New York, 1891 [1873]), p. 14. See also Winchell, *Reconciliation.* Another factor in the focus on the problem of design in debates about the compatibility of evolution and Christianity might also have been that in earlier conflicts over scientific theories, such as the nebular hypothesis, religious thinkers had accustomed themselves to nonliteral interpretation of the Bible. Ronald L.

Numbers, *Creation by Natural Law: Laplace's Nebular Hypothesis in American Thought* (Seattle, 1977), p. 103; Roberts, *Darwinism and the Divine,* p. 212.

44. Charles Hodge, *What is Darwinism?* (New York, 1874), pp. 177, 173. On Hodge, see Jonathan Wells, *Charles Hodge's Critique of Darwinism: An Historical-Critical Analysis of Concepts Basic to the Nineteenth Century Debate* (Lewiston, N. Y., 1988); and Moore, *The Post-Darwinian Controversies,* pp. 203–4..

45. James R. Moore, *The Post-Darwinian Controversies,* chap. 10; George P. Fisher, "The Alleged Conflict of Natural Science and Religion," *Princeton Review* 12 (July 1883): 34.

46. George Frederick Wright, "Recent Works Bearing on the Relation of Science to Religion: No. IV—Concerning the True Doctrine of Final Cause or Design in Nature," *Bibliotheca Sacra* 34 (1877): 363–68.

47. E. L. Youmans, "The Progress of Theology," *Popular Science Monthly* 5 (1874): 114. See also W. Stanley Jevons, "Evolution and the Doctrine of Design," *Popular Science Monthly* 5 (1874): 98–103; and reviews of William Woods Smyth, *The Bible and The Doctrine of Evolution, Popular Science Monthly* 4 (1874): 503–4.

48. Youmans, "Progress of Theology," p. 114.

49. Frederick Temple, *The Relations between Religion and Science* (New York, 1903 [1884]), lecture 7, pp. 193–221; Tess Cosslett, *Science and Religion in the Nineteenth Century* (New York, 1984), pp. 190–92.

50. John Burroughs, "Science and Theology," *Popular Science Monthly* 30 (1886): 145; and Burroughs, "The Natural *Versus* the Supernatural," *Popular Science Monthly* 31 (1887): 2.

51. Noah Porter, *The Old Chapel and the New,* part 2 (New Haven, 1876), p. 37; Porter, *Agnosticism: A Doctrine of Despair* (New York, 1880), p. 6; Daniel Greenleaf Thompson, "Science in Religious Education—Part II," *Popular Science Monthly* 30 (1887): 459. John Tyndall, in his presidential address before the British Association for the Advancement of Science in 1874, presented this opinion most forcefully: "The impregnable position of science may be described in a few words. All religious theories, schemes, and systems, which embrace notions of cosmogony, or which otherwise reach into its domain, must, in so far as they do this, submit to the control of science, and relinquish all thought of controlling it." Tyndall's speech, of course, elicited outcries from defenders of religion, but it was reprinted and defended by E. L. Youmans in *Popular Science Monthly.* John Tyndall, "Inaugural Address before the British Association," *Popular Science Monthly* 5 (1874): 653–86; E. L. Youmans, "Tyndall's Address," *Popular Science Monthly* 5 (1874): 747–48. See also John LeConte, "Modern Biological Inquiry," *Popular Science Monthly* 8 (January 1876): 299.

52. E. L. Youmans, review of Joseph LeConte, *Religion and Science, Popular Science Monthly* 4 (1874): 502.

53. John William Draper, *History of the Conflict between Religion and Science* (New York, 1898 [1874]), p. vi.

54. Ibid., pp. x–xi, 217–18, 353. Readers did not miss Draper's message to Protestant churches. See John Fiske, "Draper on Science and Religion," in *The Unseen*

World and Other Essays (Boston, 1876), p. 142. Moore, in *The Post-Darwinian Controversies,* treats Draper's book as an anti-Catholic tract. This is one of the weakest parts of an otherwise excellent book. In his zeal to establish harmonious relations between religion and science, Moore tries to discredit Draper by criticizing his work as if it were a work of historical scholarship rather than analyzing it as a primary source..

55. Donald Fleming, *John William Draper and the Religion of Science* (Philadelphia, 1950), pp. 134–35.

56. LeConte, *Religion and Science,* pp. 227, 230–31.

57. Ibid., pp. 261, 231.

Chapter Two

1. On the relationship between Darwinism and the rejection of Baconianism, see John Hedley Brooke, *Science and Religion: Some Historical Perspectives* (New York, 1991), pp. 286–87. On the transformation of the philosophy of science, see Larry Laudan, "Why Was the Logic of Discovery Abandoned?" in *Science and Hypothesis: Historical Essays on Scientific Methodology* (Dordrecht, Holland, 1981), pp. 181–91. The development of the progressivist conception of science was closely related to the development of pragmatism. As the following discussion indicates, William James, Charles Peirce, and John Dewey all participated in the debates over Darwinism and helped articulate the progressivist conception of science. I do not want to conflate pragmatism and progressivist ideas about science both because pragmatism is a broader theory of knowledge and because some proponents of a progressivist view of science, such as James Mark Baldwin, did not consider themselves pragmatists. On pragmatism and evolution, see Max H. Fisch, "Evolution in American Philosophy," *Philosophical Review* 56 (1947): 357–73; James Collins, "Darwin's Impact on Philosophy," *Thought* 34 (1959): 185–248; Philip P. Wiener, *Evolution and the Founders of Pragmatism* (Cambridge, 1949); Cynthia E. Russett, *Darwinism in America: The Intellectual Response, 1865–1912* (San Francisco, 1976), chap. 3. For a comparison of the philosophy of Peirce, James, and Dewey, see Morton White, *Science and Sentiment in America* (New York, 1972), chaps. 7, 8, 11. James considered Baldwin's genetic logic to be in full accordance with pragmatism; William James, *The Meaning of Truth* (Cambridge, 1978), p. 236n.2. Baldwin was critical of the pragmatic conception of truth; J. M. Baldwin, "The Limits of Pragmatism," *Psychological Review* 11 (1904): 30–60.

2. Edward Everett, "Character of Lord Bacon," *North American Review* 16 (1823): 300. On Reid's philosophy of science, see Larry Laudan, "Thomas Reid and the Newtonian Turn of British Methodological Thought," in *Science and Hypothesis,* pp. 86–110. I do not mean to imply that the American version of Baconianism accurately describes Bacon's own ideas or that the simplified version of Baconianism described below fully reflects Reid's philosophy of science.

3. Barbara J. Shapiro, *Probability and Certainty in Seventeenth-Century England: A Study of the Relationships between Natural Science, Religion, History, Law, and Literature* (Princeton, 1982); Ian Hacking, *The Emergence of Probability: A Philosophical Study of Early Ideas about Probability, Induction and Statistical Inference*

(New York, 1975); Laudan, "Thomas Reid and the Newtonian Turn of British Methodological Thought"; Larry Laudan, "The Epistemology of Light: Some Methodological Issues in the Subtle Fluids Debate," in *Science and Hypothesis,* pp. 111–40.

4. John W. F. Herschel, *Preliminary Discourse on the Study of Natural Philosophy,* new ed. (London, 1851 [1830]), pp. 104, 164; Laudan, "Why Was the Logic of Discovery Abandoned?"; Richard Yeo, "An Idol of the Marketplace: Baconianism in Nineteenth-Century Britain," *History of Science* 23 (1985): 267–77; John Losee, *A Historical Introduction to the Philosophy of Science,* 2nd ed. (New York, 1980), chaps. 9, 10; David Oldroyd, *The Arch of Knowledge: An Introductory Study of the History of the Philosophy and Methodology of Science* (New York, 1986), chap. 4..

5. For a brief description of Mill's and Comte's philosophy of science, see Losee, *A Historical Introduction to the Philosophy of Science,* chap. 10; and Larry Laudan, "Towards a Reassessment of Comte's 'Méthode Positive'" in *Science and Hypothesis,* pp. 141–61. For a discussion of the impact of positivism in the United States, see Charles D. Cashdollar, *The Transformation of Theology, 1830–1890: Positivism and Protestant Thought in Britain and America* (Princeton, 1989).

6. William Whewell, *The Philosophy of the Inductive Sciences,* parts 1 and 2 (London, 1967 [1840]); Menachem Fisch, *William Whewell, Philosopher of Science* (New York, 1991), chap.4; Larry Laudan, "William Whewell on the Consilence of Inductions," in *Science and Hypothesis,* pp. 163–79.

7. On American Baconianism, see George H. Daniels, *American Science in the Age of Jackson* (New York, 1968); Robert V. Bruce, *The Launching of American Science, 1846–1876* (New York, 1987); Theodore Dwight Bozeman, *Protestants in an Age of Science* (Chapel Hill, 1977); and Herbert Hovencamp, *Science and Religion in America, 1800–1860* (Philadelphia, 1978), chap. 2. The following account of the Baconian ideal in the United States is largely derived from these sources.

8. Bruce, *The Launching of American Science,* pp. 67–69; Nathan Reingold, "Joseph Henry on the Scientific Life: An AAAS Presidential Address of 1850," in *Science, American Style* (New Brunswick, N.J., 1991); Albert Moyer, *A Scientist's Voice in American Culture: Simon Newcomb and the Rhetoric of Scientific Method* (Berkeley, 1992), chaps. 1, 3.

9. Charles Peirce, "The Fixation of Belief," *Popular Science Monthly* 12 (1877): 2. See also Alexander Winchell, *Reconciliation of Science and Religion* (New York, 1877), p. 135n.1. Richard Yeo also notes that in Britain, despite the serious reassessment of Bacon's conception of science before 1860, public rejection of Bacon became common only in the late nineteenth century. He explains this "asymmetry" in Bacon's reputation by distinguishing between different "rhetorical" uses of Bacon and referring to the rising professional confidence of scientists in the late nineteenth century. While I do not dispute Yeo's explanation, I emphasize the importance of the debates over evolution as the context for the rejection of Baconianism in the United States. Yeo, "Idol of the Marketplace," pp. 280–87. On the methodological criticism of Darwin, see David L. Hull, *Darwin and His Critics: The Reception of Darwin's Theory of Evolution by the Scientific Community* (Cambridge, 1973); and Hull, "Charles Darwin and Nineteenth Century Philosophies of Sci-

ence," in *Foundations of Scientific Method: The Nineteenth Century,* ed. Ronald N. Giere and Richard S. Westfall (Bloomington, Ind., 1973); Alvar Ellegård, *Darwin and the General Reader: The Reception of Darwin's Theory of Evolution in the British Periodical Press, 1859–1872* (Goteborg, 1958); Ellegård, "The Darwinian Theory and Nineteenth-Century Philosophies of Science," *Journal of the History of Ideas* 18 (1957): 383–86; Cashdollar, *The Transformation of Theology, 1830–1890,* p. 191. By the beginning of the twentieth century, Protestant fundamentalists were the main proponents of the Baconian method. See George Marsden, *Fundamentalism and American Culture: The Shaping of Twentieth-Century Evangelicalism, 1870–1925* (New York, 1980), chap. 6..

10. Rudolph Virchow, *Freedom of Science in the Modern State* (London, 1878); also published as "The Liberty of Science in the Modern State," *Popular Science Monthly* suppl. 10 (1878): 296–307. See also Ernst Haeckel, *Freedom of Science and Teaching,* with prefatory note by T. H. Huxley (London, 1878; New York, 1879); for additional commentary on Virchow's speech, see E. L. Youmans, "The Liberty of Science and Education," *Popular Science Monthly* 13 (1878): 106–11; W. K. Clifford, "Virchow on the Teaching of Science," *Popular Science Monthly* suppl. 13 (1878): 73–85; John Tyndall, "Virchow and Evolution," *Popular Science Monthly* 14 (1879): 266–90.

11. Virchow, "The Liberty of Science in the Modern State," pp. 297 and 307 (emphasis in original).

12. Haeckel, *Freedom of Science and Teaching,* pp. 64, 63.

13. The former was a more common response among English evolutionists. For example, T. H. Huxley in his introduction to the Virchow-Haeckel dispute defended Virchow's views on science but criticized his interpretation of evolution.

14. Hull, "Charles Darwin and Nineteenth-Century Philosophies of Science," pp. 119–25.

15. Bruce Kuklick, *The Rise of American Philosophy, Cambridge, Massachusetts 1860–1930* (New Haven, 1977), pp. 71–77; A. Hunter Dupree, *Asa Gray, American Botanist, Friend of Darwin* (Baltimore, 1988 [1959]), chap. 15. On the range of philosophic positions in the public discussions of science, see William E. Leverette, Jr., "E. L. Youmans' Crusade for Scientific Autonomy and Respectability," *American Quarterly* 17 (1965): 12–32.

16. Parke Godwin, "The Sphere and Limits of Science," *Popular Science Monthly* 3 (1873): 106–7.

17. E. L. Youmans, "Mr. Godwin's Letter," *Popular Science Monthly* 3 (1873): 116.

18. Jevons reiterates this point throughout *The Principles of Science: A Treatise on Logic and Scientific Method,* 2nd rev. ed., (New York, 1877 [1873]), especially pp. 456, xxix. On Jevons, see Margaret Schabas, *A World Ruled by Number: William Stanley Jevons and the Rise of Mathematical Economics* (New York, 1990); and W. B. Mays, "Jevons' Conception of Scientific Method," *The Manchester School* 30 (1962): 223–49.

19. David Starr Jordan, "The Stability of Truth," *Popular Science Monthly* 50 (1897): 646; Moyer, *A Scientist's Voice in American Culture,* p. 229. For examples

of praise for Jevons, see Josiah P. Cooke, *The Credentials of Science, The Warrant of Faith* (New York, 1888), pp. 125–26; Daniel C. Gilman, "Notes on Education" (1875), p. 9, Gilman Papers, Johns Hopkins University; and Winchell, *Reconciliation*, p. 135n.1. For examples of universities that assigned Jevons's books in philosophy courses in the late nineteenth century, see *Columbia College Handbook of Information 1890–91*, p. 13; *The Harvard University Catalogue, 1890–91*, p. 75; *University of Chicago Annual Register, 1892–93*, p. 38; *Calendar of the University of Michigan, 1890–91*, p. 57; *The Leland Stanford Junior University Registrar, 1891–92*, p. 47; *Catalogue of Yale University, 1890–91*, p. 37; *University of California: Biennial Report of the President, 1890*, p. 48; *The Johns Hopkins University of Baltimore Register for 1890–91*, p. 88. These course catalogues are part of the collection of the Cubberly Library at Stanford University. They are also available in the archives of the respective universities. Throughout this study, the catalogues are cited simply by title, year, and page..

20. Cooke, *The Credentials of Science*, p. 209.

21. Jevons, *Principles of Science*, p. 504.

22. T. W. Richards, "The New Outlook in Chemistry," *Science* n. s. 26 (1907): 297.

23. John Dewey, *Studies in Logical Theory* (1903), in *John Dewey: Middle Works*, ed. Jo Ann Boydston et al., 15 vols. (Carbondale, Ill., 1976–83), 2:315.

24. W. B. Carpenter, "Darwin on the Origin of Species" (1860), in Hull, *Darwin and His Critics*, p. 89; Hull, *Darwin and His Critics*, chap. 5; Ellegård, *Darwin and the General Reader*, chap. 10; Michael T. Ghiselin, *The Triumph of the Darwinian Method* (Berkeley, 1969), pp. 49–61. Not all critics of Baconianism accepted all of the tenets of the progressivist conception of science. For example, Simon Newcomb was a critic of Baconianism who believed that scientific knowledge was not certain knowledge, but a method that relied on hypothesis and verification. He did not, however, reject natural law or adopt the view of science as a form of functional adaptation. On Newcomb's view of science, see Moyer, *A Scientist's Voice in American Culture*.

25. John Dewey, "The Influence of Darwinism on Philosophy" (1909), in *The Middle Works*, 4:3.

26. William James, *Principles of Psychology* (Cambridge, 1981 [1890]), pp. 960–61 (emphasis in original).

27. George M. Beard, "The Scientific Study of Human Testimony, Part III," *Popular Science Monthly* 8 (1878): 328–38; John Dewey, *How We Think* (1910), in *The Middle Works*, 6:191.

28. William James, "Humanism and Truth" (1904), in *The Meaning of Truth*, pp. 206–7.

29. H. Hoffding, "The Influence of the Conception of Evolution on Modern Philosophy," in *Darwin and Modern Science*, ed. A. C. Seward (Cambridge, 1909), p. 456; William James, *Pragmatism* (Cambridge, 1978 [1907]), p. 94. See also C. Lloyd Morgan, "Mental Factors in Evolution," in *Darwin and Modern Science*, ed. Seward, pp. 424–45; Dewey, "The Influence of Darwinism on Philosophy"; Charles A. Ellwood, "The Influence of Darwin on Sociology," *Psychological Re-*

view 16 (1909): 188–94; J. E. Creighton, "Darwin and Logic," *Psychological Review* 16 (1909): 170–87; J. Mark Baldwin, "The Influence of Darwin on the Theory of Knowledge and Philosophy," *Psychological Review* 16 (1909): 207–18; Baldwin, "Darwinism and Logic: A Reply to Professor Creighton," *Psychological Review* 16 (1909): 431–36; Baldwin, *Darwin and the Humanities* (Baltimore, 1909).

30. Charles S. Peirce, "The Order of Nature," *Popular Science Monthly* 13 (1878): 213; Baldwin, "The Influence of Darwin," pp. 208–9; see also James, *Pragmatism*, pp. 83–84..

31. Dewey, *How We Think*, p. 188.

32. James, *Pragmatism*, p. 32 (emphasis in original).

33. John Dewey, "Is Logic a Dualistic Science?" (1890), in *John Dewey: The Early Works*, ed. Jo Ann Boydston et al., 5 vols. (Carbondale, Ill., 1969–72), 3:80. James disagreed with Dewey on this point. Dewey argued that scientific inquiry was simply a more controlled and exact form of common-sense inquiry. James said that scientific inquiry, because it denied the reality of secondary qualities, was different from common-sense inquiry (*Pragmatism*, p. 91). As a result, James did not share Dewey's view that science was a better form of inquiry; he argued that it was different, and better in some circumstances. James seems to have been ambivalent about science, although he did say that if the pragmatic method was adopted, philosophy and science "would come much nearer together" (ibid., p. 31). For more on James's attitude toward science, see David A. Hollinger, "William James and the Culture of Inquiry," in *In The American Province: Studies in the History and Historiography of Ideas* (Bloomington, Ind., 1985), pp. 3–22. For an example of a contemporary intellectual who disagreed with using practicality as a standard for judging the success of science, see Thorstein Veblen, "The Place of Science in Modern Civilization" (1906), in *The Place of Science in Modern Civilization* (New York, 1919), pp. 1–31.

34. Charles S. Peirce, "The Marriage of Religion and Science," *Open Court* 7 (1893): 3559.

35. Charles S. Peirce, "Deduction, Induction, and Hypothesis," *Popular Science Monthly* 13 (1878): 476; Thomas C. Chamberlin, "The Ethical Nature of Scientific Study—Address at the Dedication of Stephenson Hall of Science, Lawrence University, June 20, 1899," Chamberlin Papers Addenda, University of Chicago.

36. James, *Principles*, pp. 1235–36.

37. John Dewey, "Some Stages of Logical Thought" (1900), in *The Middle Works*, 1:155–56. This emphasis on distrust of senses was part of a move to distinguish science from common sense and to emphasize the need for expertise in science. For parallel developments in British views of science, see Richard Yeo, "Scientific Method and the Rhetoric of Science in Britain, 1830–1917," in *The Politics and Rhetoric of Scientific Method*, ed. John Schuster and Richard Yeo (Dordrecht, Holland, 1986), p. 272.

38. James, *Principles*, p. 191. On the failure of late nineteenth-century philosophers to justify their views on progress, see Larry Laudan, "Peirce and the Trivialization of the Self-Correcting Thesis," in *Foundations of Scientific Method: The Nineteenth Century*, ed. Ronald N. Giere and Richard S. Westfall (Bloomington,

Ind., 1973). On the importance of consensus as a sign of scientific truth, see William Eamon, "From the Secrets of Nature to Public Knowledge: The Origins of the Concept of Openness in Science," *Minerva* 23 (1985): 321.

39. Thorstein Veblen, "The Evolution of the Scientific Point of View," *University of California Chronicle* 10 (1908): 412, 395–96..

40. Ibid., p. 394. For more on Darwin's philosophy of science, see Hull, "Charles Darwin and Nineteenth-Century Philosophies of Science"; and David L. Hull, "Metaphysics of Evolution," *British Journal for the History of Science* 3 (1976): 309–37; Ghiselin, *Triumph of the Darwinian Method;* and reviews of Ghiselin's book: Frank N. Egerton, "Darwin's Method or Methods?" *Studies in History and Philosophy of Science* 2 (1971): 281–86; and Michael Ruse, "The Darwinian Industry," *History of Science* 12 (1974): 43–58. See also Michael Ruse, "Darwin's Debt to Philosophy: An Examination of the Influence of the Philosophical Ideas of John F. W. Herschel and William Whewell on the Development of Charles Darwin's Theory of Evolution," *Studies in History and Philosophy of Science* 6 (1975): 159–81; Ellegård, "The Darwinian Theory."

41. Bruce Kuklick, *Churchmen and Philosophers: From Jonathan Edwards to John Dewey* (New Haven, 1985), p. 194.

42. James R. Moore, *The Post-Darwinian Controversies: A Study of the Protestant Struggle to Come to Terms with Darwin in Great Britain and America, 1870–1900* (New York, 1979), chaps. 10–12. See also Jon H. Roberts, *Darwinism and the Divine in America: Protestant Intellectuals and Organic Evolution, 1859–1900* (Madison, Wis., 1988), chap. 5.

43. See chapter 1.

44. The distinction between the natural and supernatural realm was not new. It was part of popular writing about religion and science, as well as of more philosophically grounded discussions of the subject. The Kantian distinction between the phenomenal world and the noumenal realm was introduced to American intellectuals largely through the work of Sir William Hamilton. Kuklick, *The Rise of American Philosophy,* pp. 16–20. See James Turner, *Without God, Without Creed: The Origins of Unbelief in America* (Baltimore, 1985), for a discussion of the long history of tensions between rationalism and pietism.

45. Lawrence Johnson, "The Chains of Species: Science and Religion," *Popular Science Monthly* 5 (1874): 314; J. Lawrence Smith, "Speculation in Science," *Popular Science Monthly* 3 (1873): 745; Leverette, "E. L. Youmans' Crusade for Scientific Autonomy and Respectability," p. 26.

46. Joseph Henry, "On the Importance of the Cultivation of Science," *Popular Science Monthly* 2 (1873): 649. See also Simon Newcomb, "The Course of Nature: An Address before the American Association for the Advancement of Science at St. Louis," *Popular Science Monthly* suppl. 13–20 (1878): 481.

47. Charles F. Deems, "Science and Religion," extract from the opening address at the inauguration of Vanderbilt University, *Popular Science Monthly* 8 (1876): 449. See also "God and Nature—By the Lord Bishop of Carlisle," *Popular Science Monthly* 17 (1880): 27.

48. Kuklick, *Churchmen and Philosophers,* chap. 11; Claude Welch, *Protestant*

Thought in the Nineteenth Century: Volume One, 1799–1870 (New Haven, 1972), chap. 11; William R. Hutchison, *The Modernist Impulse in American Protestantism* (New York, 1972), pp. 43–48; Turner, *Without God, Without Creed,* pp. 161–63, 195–96.

49. Deems, "Science and Religion," p. 441; Parke Godwin, "The Sphere and Limits of Science—Letter to the Editor," *Popular Science Monthly* 3 (1873): 108.

50. George Frederick Wright, "Recent Works Bearing on the Relation of Science and Religion: No. II—The Divine Method of Producing Living Species," *Bibliotheca Sacra* 33 (July 1876): 480..

51. D. G. Hart, "Poems, Propositions, and Dogma: The Controversy over Religious Language and the Demise of Theology in American Learning," *Church History* 57 (1988): 310–21; Hans W. Frei, *The Eclipse of Biblical Narrative: A Study in Eighteenth-and Nineteenth-Century Hermeneutics* (New Haven, 1974), chap. 12; Hutchison, *The Modernist Impulse,* pp. 84–87.

52. Agnostics drew upon the ideas of theologians, particularly Henry Longueville Mansel, who argued that reason was incapable of proving anything about the nature or existence of God. Mansel supplemented this negative appraisal of rational religion with a defense of revelation. Agnostics agreed with Mansel that reason was not a source of knowledge about God but ignored his defense of Christianity. For them, the incomprehensibility of the supernatural realm provided a platform for criticizing established religion and defending the independence of science. Bernard Lightman, *The Origins of Agnosticism: Victorian Unbelief and the Limits of Knowledge* (Baltimore, 1987); George P. Fisher, "The Alleged Conflict of Natural Science and Religion," *Princeton Review* 12 (1883): 46; Herbert Spencer, "The Study of Sociology," *Popular Science Monthly* 2 (1872): 162; Richard Hofstadter, *Social Darwinism in American Thought* (Boston, 1955), pp. 30–35.

53. E. L. Youmans, "Mr. Godwin's Letter," *Popular Science Monthly* 3 (1873): 119; Lightman, *Origins of Agnosticism,* p. 87. On Christian reaction to agnosticism, see James McCosh, *Criteria of Diverse Kinds of Truth as Opposed to Agnosticism, Being a Treatise on Applied Logic* (New York, 1884); Jacob Gould Shurman, *Agnosticism and Religion* (New York, 1896).

54. John Dewey, "Ethics and Physical Science" (1887), in *The Early Works,* 1:206. See also D. H. Meyer, "American Intellectuals and the Victorian Crisis of Faith," in *Victorian America,* ed. Daniel Walker Howe (Philadelphia, 1976), p. 64.

55. Josiah Cooke, "The Nobility of Knowledge," *Popular Science Monthly* 5 (1874): 621; James Thomas Bixby, "Science and Religion as Allies," *Popular Science Monthly* 9 (1876): 701.

56. Charles S. Peirce, "Illustrations of the Logic of Science—Part I: The Fixation of Belief," *Popular Science Monthly* 12 (1877): 8.

57. Ibid.

58. Ibid., pp. 10–11.

59. Frank Wigglesworth Clarke, "Scientific Dabblers," *Popular Science Monthly* 2 (1872): 598; Francis Galton, "On the Causes which Operate to Create Scientific Men," *Popular Science Monthly* 3 (May 1873): 69; Daniel Greenleaf Thompson, "Science in Religious Education—Part II," *Popular Science Monthly* 31 (1887):

457; Winchell, *Reconciliation,* p. 29; Newcomb, "The Course of Nature," pp. 482–84; John Burroughs, "The Natural *Versus* the Supernatural," *Popular Science Monthly* 31 (1887): 1; R. S. Woodward, "The Progress of Science," *Popular Science Monthly* 59 (1901): 516–17; William Henry Hudson, "Veracity," *Popular Science Monthly* 53 (1898): 206–7..

60. Simon Newcomb, "The Course of Nature," *Popular Science Monthly* suppl. 13–20 (1878): 483. Some writers recognized that science could also be dogmatic and that intolerance was a human flaw not restricted to theologians, but this was a minority view. See Fisher, "The Alleged Conflict of Natural Science and Religion," p. 35; and Joseph LeConte, "Science and Mental Improvement," *Popular Science Monthly* 13 (1878): 101.

61. Henry Ward Beecher, "The Progress of Thought in the Church," *North American Review* 135 (1882): 108; Hutchison, *The Modernist Impulse;* Martin E. Marty, *Modern American Religion, Volume One: The Irony of It All, 1893–1919* (Chicago, 1986), chaps. 2–4; Lloyd J. Averill, *American Theology in the Liberal Tradition* (Philadelphia, 1967); Kenneth Cauthen, *Impact of Religious Liberalism* (New York, 1962).

62. Minot J. Savage, "After Orthodoxy—What?" *North American Review* 170 (1900): 585.

63. Charles Peirce, "Illustrations of the Logic of Science: Fifth Paper—The Order of Nature," *Popular Science Monthly* 13 (1878): 216–17.

64. Glenn C. Altschuler, *Andrew D. White: Educator, Historian, Diplomat* (Ithaca, N. Y., 1979), chap. 12; Andrew Dickson White, *Autobiography of Andrew White,* 2 vols. (New York, 1905); White, "Scientific and Industrial Education in the United States," *Popular Science Monthly* 5 (1874): 170–90; White, "The Warfare of Science," *Popular Science Monthly* 8 (1876); White, *The Warfare of Science* (New York, 1876); White, *A History of the Warfare of Science with Theology in Christendom,* 2 vols. (New York, 1896).

65. White, *The Warfare of Science,* p. 8; John William Draper, *History of the Conflict between Religion and Science* (New York, 1898 [1874]).

66. White, *The Warfare of Science,* pp. 145–46.

67. White, *History,* 1:ix. White's association of science and theology with "epochs in the evolution of human thought" reflects the influence of August Comte among liberal Protestants. See Charles D. Cashdollar, *The Transformation of Theology, 1830–1890: Positivism and Protestant Thought in Britain and America* (Princeton, 1989).

68. Ibid., 1:xii. Ronald Numbers also pointed out that White introduced the distinction between religion and theology only in 1896, and that this distinction did not really change his analysis of the relationship of religion and science. But Numbers does not explore why White made this distinction. Numbers is interested only in placing White in the same historiographical tradition as Draper. He treats the works of White and Draper as inaccurate works of history, rather than as instructive primary sources. See Ronald Numbers, "Science and Religion," in *Historical Writing on American Science: Perspectives and Prospects,* ed. Sally Gregory Kohlstedt and Margaret W. Rossiter (Baltimore, 1985), p. 61.

69. For optimistic predictions about the end of the conflict, see Daniel Coit Gilman, "Prospects of Science in the United States at the Beginning of the Twentieth Century," *University Record* (University of Chicago) 8 (1903): 31; and Woodward, "The Progress of Science," p. 521. Of course, more orthodox religious thinkers were not willing to concede that religion could survive apart from theology. R. M. Wenley, philosophy professor at the University of Michigan, realized this and argued that the distinction between theology and religion was an inadequate solution to the conflict between religion and science. But even he admitted that the distinction had "eased or disguised the conflict in recent years." R. M. Wenley, "Science and Philosophy," *Popular Science Monthly* 59 (1901): 361..

70. Ira Remsen, "Pseudo-Science," manuscript address, n.d., Ira Remsen Papers, Johns Hopkins University.

Chapter Three

1. Frederick A. P. Barnard, 1866 Annual Report, in *The Rise of a University: The Later Days of Old Columbia College; Selections from the Annual Reports of Frederick A. P. Barnard, Vol.I,* ed. William F. Russell (New York, 1937), p. 339. On the prestige of science, see Nathan Reingold, *Science, American Style* (New Brunswick, N.J., 1991), chaps. 4–7.

2. Frederick A. P. Barnard, 1870 Annual Report, in *The Rise of a University,* pp. 66–155; John Fulton, *Memoirs of Frederick A. P. Barnard* (New York, 1896), pp. 382–84. Barnard's concern with declining enrollment was shared by other educators; see Laurence Veysey, *The Emergence of the American University* (Chicago, 1965), p. 5.

3. Charles W. Eliot, "Inaugural Address" (1869), in *Educational Reform: Essays and Addresses* (New York, 1898), p. 2. In his inaugural speech, Eliot was careful to promise that the growth of modern studies would not come at the expense of classical studies. Eliot's diplomacy was understandable given that his nomination to the presidency was almost rejected because of a fear that, as a scientist, Eliot would not protect the classics. Charles W. Eliot to G. J. Brush, 21 May 1869, G. J. Brush Correspondence, Yale University Archives. See also Samuel Eliot Morison, *Three Centuries of Harvard* (Cambridge, 1936), pp. 327–28; and Henry James, *Charles W. Eliot,* 2 vols. (Boston, 1930), 1:196–97. At other times Eliot was more candid in acknowledging that the classics' *relative* position in colleges and universities would have to suffer as modern subjects were introduced with full equality. Eliot, "What Is a Liberal Education?" in *Educational Reform,* p. 90. For an example of the contemporary interest in scientific education, see *The Culture Demanded by Modern Life; A Series of Addresses and Arguments on the Claims of Scientific Education,* ed. with introduction by E. L. Youmans (New York, 1867); and Daniel C. Gilman, "On the Growth of American Colleges and Their Present Tendency to the Study of Science," *Proceedings of the American Institute of Instruction* (1871): 96–115. See also Cornell University, *Annual Report to the Board of Trustees* (1881), frontispiece; and Frederick Rudolph, *The American College and University* (New York, 1962), p. 266. For historical criticism of Barnard's study,

see Colin Bradley Burke, *American Collegiate Populations: A Test of the Traditional View* (New York, 1982), chap. 2; and David Potts, "Curriculum and Enrollments: Some Thoughts Assessing the Popularity of the Antebellum Colleges," *History of Higher Education Annual* 1 (1981): 88–109..

4. Frederick A. P. Barnard, *Annual Report of the President* (Columbia University, 1882), p. 30. See also Eliot, "Inaugural Address," p. 2; Gilman, "On the Growth of American Colleges," p. 101; James B. Angell, "Inaugural Address, University of Michigan, June 28, 1871," in *Selected Addresses* (New York, 1912), pp. 10–11; A. D. White, "Scientific and Industrial Education in the United States," *Popular Science Monthly* 5 (1874): 188; Rudolph, *The American College and University,* p. 266. Eliot's, Angell's, and White's advice to the trustees of Johns Hopkins University indicate that in the mid–1870s they were still thinking of comprehensive instruction as the key feature of a university. See Hugh Hawkins, "Three University Presidents Testify," *American Quarterly* 11 (1959): 99–119.

5. As president of the University of Alabama in 1853, Barnard opposed the efforts of reformers to introduce electives. See Fulton, *Memoirs,* chap. 8; R. Freeman Butts, *The College Charts Its Course* (New York, 1939), pp. 125–28. Barnard developed his argument in favor of electives in his 1871 president's report and continued to push for a more liberal elective system throughout his term as president. In addition to his defense of electives as necessary, given the popular demand for science and the proliferation of subjects, he also argued that the rising age of college students made the disciplinary aspects of the old college course less important. *Annual Report of the President* (Columbia College, 1871), pp. 25–50; Fulton, *Memoirs,* chaps. 15, 16. See also F. A. P. Barnard to Hamilton Fish, 22 May 1880, Hamilton Fish Collection, Columbia University.

6. Eliot and Gilman each supported different means to diversifying and deepening instruction: Eliot supported electives, while Gilman advocated multiple undergraduate degree programs and graduate programs. Offering different degree programs was a continuation of antebellum reform efforts. Some reformers distrusted this course of action because they assumed that the classics would be in a privileged position. For example, White, in his advice to the Johns Hopkins University trustees, explained, "I should hope . . . that you would not fall into the error of making any separation between the students in various courses. I mean by that to express my hope that so far as classical students or scientific students or technological students are pursuing the same studies, they will stay together; and that no special separation will be made between them either during their courses or at graduation. . . . I think it of very great importance to place all good studies on a full equality" (A. D. White to JHU Trustees, 13 March 1874, Daniel Coit Gilman Papers, Johns Hopkins University). In practice, most universities combined the two approaches, first offering alternative degree programs and then gradually adding electives until the separate programs were meaningless. On the origins of graduate programs, see Richard J. Storr, *The Beginning of the Future: A Historical Approach to Graduate Education in the Arts and Sciences* (New York, 1973); Nathan Reingold, "Graduate School and Doctoral Degree: European Models and Ameri-

can Realities," in *Science American Style* (New Brunswick, N.J., 1991); and Robert Kohler, "The Ph.D. Machine: Building on the Collegiate Base," *Isis* 81 (1990): 638–62.

7. John Dewey, "Science as Subject-Matter and as Method" (1901), in *John Dewey: Middle Works,* ed. Jo Ann Boydston et al., 15 vols. (Carbondale, Ill., 1976–83), 6:78. See also Albert Moyer, *A Scientist's Voice in American Culture: Simon Newcomb and the Rhetoric of Scientific Method* (Berkeley, 1992), p. 92. The new emphasis on "scientific thinking" is identified by Bruce Kimball as the emergence of the "liberal-free ideal" in education. Although Kimball traces this ideal to the Enlightenment, he thinks it influenced American higher education only after the Civil War. See Bruce A. Kimball, *Orators and Philosophers: A History of the Idea of Liberal Education* (New York, 1986), chap. 5..

8. H. B. Hutchins, "Thinking Ahead—Some Results and Problems That Come of it—Address at the University of Minnesota Commencement, 1914," Henry Burns Hutchins Papers, University of Michigan.

9. David Starr Jordan, "The American University System, Past and Present," in *The Trend in the American University* (Palo Alto, 1929), p. 82. George E. Peterson, *The New England College in the Age of the University* (Amherst, 1964), discusses the impact of "university values" on colleges.

10. Josiah P. Cooke, *The Credentials of Science, the Warrant of Faith* (New York, 1888), p. 157.

11. John M. Coulter, "Mission of Science in Education, An Address Delivered at the Annual Commencement of the University of Michigan, June 21, 1900" (Ann Arbor, 1900), pp. 5–6; Thomas C. Chamberlin, "The Scientific and the Non-Scientific," undated manuscript, Thomas C. Chamberlin Papers, University of Chicago. See also David Starr Jordan, "Science in the High School," *Popular Science Monthly* 36 (1890): 721–27; Ira Remsen, "Laboratory Methods of Science," n.d., Ira Remsen Papers, Johns Hopkins University; Henry A. Rowland, "The Physical Laboratory in Modern Education," Gilman Papers; Thomas C. Chamberlin, "Programme of the Department of Geology" (University of Chicago, May 1894), Chamberlin Papers.

12. James B. Angell, "The Old College and the New University—University of Chicago Founder's Day Address, July 1, 1899," *University Record* 4 (1899): 79; Frederick Rudolph, *Curriculum: A History of American Undergraduate Course of Study since 1636* (San Francisco, 1977), pp. 130, 224; Lincoln Blake, "The Concept and Development of Science at the University of Chicago, 1890–1905" (Ph.D. diss., University of Chicago, 1966), chap. 4; F. H. Gerrish to J. B. Angell, 19 February 1875, and Ira Remsen to Angell, 18 August 1875, James Burrill Angell Papers, University of Michigan.

13. Angell, "The Old College and the New University," p. 79; W. T. Sedgwick, "Educational Value of the Methods of Science," *Educational Review* 5 (1893): 250.

14. Daniel C. Gilman, "The Johns Hopkins University, 1876–1891," p. 70, Gilman Papers; Frank H. Foster, *The Seminary Method of Original Study in the Historical Sciences* (New York, 1888). See also Daniel C. Gilman, *Annual Report of the President* (Johns Hopkins University, 1886), pp. 12–13.

15. G. H. Palmer, "The New Education," *Andover Review* 4 (1885): 398.

16. Ibid., pp. 393, 397.

17. Ibid., p. 398.

18. James B. Angell, "The Old and New Ideal of Scholars—Baccalaureate Address, 1905," manuscript, J. B. Angell Papers. See also Hugh Hawkins, "University Identity: The Teaching and Research Functions," in *The Organization of Knowledge in Modern America, 1860–1920,* ed. Alexandra Oleson and John Voss (Baltimore, 1979)..

19. R. H. Chittenden, "The Position That Universities Should Take in Regard to Investigation—A Discussion before the American Society of Naturalists, New Haven, December 25, 1899," *Science* n. s. 11 (1900): 54; Ira Remsen, "Colleges and Universities," undated manuscript, Remsen Papers; Robert A. McCaughy, "The Transformation of American Academic Life: Harvard University, 1821–1892," *Perspectives in American History* 8 (1974): 289. C. O. Whitman's negotiations with W. R. Harper, president of the University of Chicago, indicate how faculty got universities to commit resources for research as conditions of the employment. C. O. Whitman to W. R. Harper, 15 January 1892, W. R. Harper Papers, University of Chicago; cf. also Harper's correspondence with A. A. Michelson and John U. Nef, Harper Papers.

20. James Playfair McMurrich, "Present-Day Conditions and the Responsibilities of the University," *Science* n. s. 25 (1907): 644; Chittenden, "The Position," p. 53.

21. D.C. Gilman, *Annual Report of the President* (Johns Hopkins University, 1883), p. 7; N. M. Butler, *Annual Report of the President* (Columbia University, 1902), p. 26. Because of the prestige associated with scientific discoveries, research rapidly became the most important consideration in hiring. N. M. Butler to J. M. Cattell, 12 November 1914, James McKeen Cattell Papers, Columbia University; W. R. Harper, "Annual Report of the President, 1892," manuscript, Special Collections, University of Chicago; D.C. Gilman, *Annual Report of the President* (Johns Hopkins University, 1876), p. 21. Only gradually, after articulating the ideal of faculty research, did university administrators adopt practices that helped facilitate such research. See Roger Geiger, *To Advance Knowledge: The Growth of American Research Universities, 1900–1940* (New York, 1986), pp. 67–77.

22. David Starr Jordan, "Science and the Colleges," *Popular Science Monthly* 42 (1893): 726; Harper, "Annual Report of the President, 1892."

23. Daniel C. Gilman, "The Characteristic of a University—An Address before the Phi Beta Kappa Society of Harvard University, July 1, 1886," in *University Problems* (New York, 1898), p. 87.

24. Information derived from the *Yale College Catalogue* (1870–71). Of the 61 instructors, 37 were designated professors; 13, lecturers or instructors; 7, tutors; and 4, assistants or demonstrators. Twenty-four of them taught mathematics or a scientific subject; 1, history or social science; 1, philosophy and psychology; 2, English; 2, a modern foreign language; 7, Greek or Latin; 1, another classical language; 7, miscellaneous; 3, law; 8, medicine; and 5, theology. Charles W. Eliot, "The New Education," *Atlantic Monthly* (February 1869): 207–10. For an assess-

ment of Yale's reputation in the sciences in 1870, see Brooks Mather Kelley, *Yale: A History* (New Haven, 1974), p. 248. Sheffield's preeminence continued throughout the decade. Robert V. Bruce, *The Launching of American Science, 1846–1876* (New York, 1987), p. 328..

25. Irving Fisher to Arthur T. Hadley, 6 December 1898, Arthur T. Hadley Papers, Yale University. Sheffield's growth is chronicled in Russell H. Chittenden, *History of the Sheffield Scientific School of Yale University, 1846–1922* (New Haven, 1928), chaps. 5–10. In academic year 1895–96, the Yale University catalogue listed 206 officers concerned with instruction. Seventy-eight were professors; 14, assistant professors; 8, tutors; 67, lecturers and instructors; and 39, assistants and demonstrators. Sixty-eight of the 206 were listed as teaching mathematics or one of the natural and applied sciences; 11, history or the social sciences; 7, philosophy and/or psychology; 6, English; 14, modern foreign languages; 15, Greek and/or Latin; 2, other classical languages; 18, miscellaneous; 26, law; 8, theology; and 31, medicine.

26. Noah Porter, *American Colleges and the American Public* (New Haven, 1871); Porter "Inaugural Address," in *Addresses at the Inauguration of Professor Noah Porter, as President of Yale College, Wednesday, October 11, 1871* (New York, 1871), pp. 26–65; Veysey, *The Emergence,* chap. 1. Timothy Dwight tried to convince Daniel Gilman not to leave Yale in 1863. He predicted a more liberal atmosphere after President Woosley retired because Porter would be his likely replacement. "If it should be Mr. Porter . . . surely there will both large-mindedness and sympathy enough for all your wishes" (Dwight to Daniel Coit Gilman, 13 June 1863, Gilman Papers). Louise L. Stevenson, *Scholarly Means to Evangelical Ends: The New Haven Scholars and the Transformation of Higher Learning in America, 1830–1890* (Baltimore, 1986).

27. Porter, *American Colleges,* pp. 269, 271.

28. Ibid., p. 98 (emphasis in original).

29. Timothy Dwight, "Yale College—Some Thoughts Respecting Its Future: A Series of Articles Originally Printed in July and October 1870 and April, July, and October 1871, *New Englander*" (New Haven, 1871), p. 88.

30. Ibid., p. 7.

31. Timothy Dwight, "Inaugural Address," in *Addresses at the Induction of President Dwight as President of Yale College, Thursday July 1, 1886* (New Haven, 1886), p. 20. For an account of Dwight's accomplishments as president, see George Wilson Pierson, *Yale College* (New Haven, 1952), chap. 5; Kelley, *Yale,* p. 134.

32. William Graham Sumner, "Our Colleges before the Country" (1884), in *War and Other Essays,* ed. Albert G. Keller (New Haven, 1911), pp. 355–73.

33. Ibid., pp. 368, 369, 371.

34. A. T. Hadley, "The Relation of Science to Higher Education in America," *Science* n. s. 37 (1913): 779.

35. Eliot, "The New Education," p. 216; Nicholas Murray Butler, "Five Evidences of an Education," *Educational Review* 22 (1901): 327; and *Annual Report of the President* (Columbia University, 1902), p. 52.

36. Jordan, "Science and the Colleges," p. 721; Nicholas Murray Butler, "The

American College and the American University," in *The Meaning of Education,* rev. and enlarged ed. (New York, 1907), pp. 144–45. Because they thought all phenomena were interconnected, many late nineteenth-century intellectuals believed that divisions of knowledge were artificial. As inquiry progressed, they expected the underlying unity to be revealed. See, for example, John Dewey, "Ethical Principles Underlying Education" (1897), in *John Dewey: The Early Works,* ed. Jo Ann Boydston et al., 5 vols. (Carbondale, Ill., 1969–72), 5:68; and Dewey, "Renan's Loss of Faith in Science" (1893), in *The Early Works,* 4:12–13; Thomas C. Chamberlin, "Conditions of a Wholesome, Ethical, and Religious Atmosphere in a University" (28 January 1897), Chamberlin Papers; Henry S. Pritchett, *What Is Religion? and Other Student Questions; Talks to College Students* (New York, 1906), p. 25. See also D. H. Meyer, "American Intellectuals and the Victorian Crisis of Faith," in *Victorian America,* ed. Daniel Walker Howe (Philadelphia, 1976), pp. 74–75..

37. Gilman, "The Characteristics of a University," pp. 96–97; W. J. Herdman, "The Methods of Science Applied to Christianity," in *Religious Thought at the University of Michigan* (Ann Arbor, 1893), p. 124.

38. Marion Talbott, *More than Lore* (Chicago, 1936), p. 32; Robert M. Wenley, "Science and Philosophy," *Popular Science Monthly* 59 (1901): 362.

39. John Dewey, "The Significance of the Problem of Knowledge" (1897), in *The Early Works,* 5:20–21; David Starr Jordan, "The College of the Twentieth Century: An Address to Young Men" (Boston, 1903), p. 56; Clyde W. Votow, "Courses in Religion: Moral and Religious Instruction in the College," *Religious Education* 5 (1910): 295–96.

40. John Dewey, "My Pedagogic Creed" (1897), in *The Early Works,* 5:93; Nicholas Murray Butler, "Scholarship and Service" (1902), in *Scholarship and Service* (New York, 1921), p. 11.

41. Nicholas Murray Butler, "The Building of Character" (1905), in *Scholarship and Service,* p. 203; Charles W. Eliot, "Resemblances and Differences among American Universities," *Science* n. s. 22 (1905): 774.

42. Benjamin Ide Wheeler to Charles Eliot, 14 March 1899, Charles W. Eliot Papers, Harvard University.

43. Arthur T. Hadley to Reverend Lyman Abbott, 22 May 1905, Arthur Twining Hadley Presidential Records, Yale University; William Rainey Harper, "Waste in Higher Education," in *The Trend in Higher Education* (Chicago, 1905), p. 113.

44. Palmer, "The New Education," p. 398; Francis Greenwood Peabody, *The Religion of an Educated Man* (New York, 1903), pp. 53–54. See also David A. Hollinger, "Inquiry and Uplift: Late Nineteenth-Century American Academics and the Moral Efficiency of Scientific Practice," in *The Authority of Experts: Studies in History and Theory,* ed. Thomas L. Haskell (Bloomington, Ind., 1984), pp. 150–51.

45. Remsen, "Scientific Investigation and Progress," pp. 14–15. Although educational leaders generally discussed the moral qualities of scientific inquiry as evidence of the compatibility of science with religion, David Hollinger has shown how the emphasis on scientific morality could be used to supplant religion. David

A. Hollinger, "Justification by Verification: The Scientific Challenge to the Moral Authority of Christianity in Modern America," in *Religion and Twentieth-Century American Intellectual Life,* ed. Michael J. Lacey (New York, 1989), pp. 116–35. See chapter 6 for more extensive discussion of secularizing tendencies..

46. Charles W. Eliot, "Religion in the Schools" (1886), manuscript, Eliot Papers; David Starr Jordan, *The Foundation Ideals of Stanford University* (Stanford, 1915), p. 19; "Religious Work Programme," *Columbia Alumni News* 4 (28 March 1913): 413–14. See also James B. Angell, "The Spiritual Opportunities for Secular Education, Address at the Convention of the Congregational Brotherhood, Detroit 1907," manuscript, J. B. Angell Papers. For a variety of contemporary views on the relationship between religion and morality, see "A Modern 'Symposium': The Influence upon Morality of a Decline in Religious Belief," reprinted from *Nineteenth-Century,* published in *Popular Science Monthly* suppl. 1 (1877): 46–62, 124–33; William Henry Hudson, "The Moral Standard," *Popular Science Monthly* 50 (1896): 1–13; Crawford Howell Toy, "Ethics and Religion," *Popular Science Monthly* 36 (1890): 727–44; Nicholas Murray Butler, "Religious Instruction and Its Relation to Education," in *Principles of Religious Education* (New York, 1900), pp. 14–15; and George Herbert Palmer, *The Field of Ethics* (Boston, 1901), lectures 4 and 5.

47. William Rainey Harper, *Religion and the Higher Life* (Chicago, 1904), p. 34; Charles W. Eliot to Daniel Coit Gilman, 2 December 1893, Gilman Papers.

48. Charles W. Eliot, "The New Education: Its Organization, Part II" (typescript, Eliot Papers; published in *Atlantic Monthly* [March 1869]), pp. 16–17 ; Eliot, "Inaugural Address, October 19, 1869," in *Educational Reform,* p. 7. Eliot had been trained as a chemist and like many other scientists had become impatient with the natural theology tradition. He wanted scientific investigation to be free from theological concerns. Hugh Hawkins, *Between Harvard and America: The Educational Leadership of Charles W. Eliot* (New York, 1972), p. 20.

49. Eliot, "Inaugural Address . . . 1869," p. 6. Throughout his career, Eliot displayed a certain hostility toward organized Christianity and its leaders. Before becoming president he wrote, "A really learned minister is almost as rare as a logical sermon" (quoted in Hawkins, *Between Harvard and America,* p. 123). After becoming president, he continued to be hostile to traditional religion. In 1883 he wrote an article implying that most ministers, because of their training, were intellectually dishonest. Charles W. Eliot, "On the Education of Ministers" (1883), in *Educational Reform,* pp. 61–86. He also said that theology had caused "more bigotry and more cruelty" than any other subject studied. Charles W. Eliot, "The Elements of a Liberal Education," *The Educator Journal* 8 (1908): 504–5. But Eliot softened these later statements by providing an alternative and, in his view, more acceptable conception of religion.

50. *Annual Report of the President of Harvard College, 1874–75,* p. 22; George Hunston Williams, ed., *The Harvard Divinity School, Its Place in Harvard University and in American Culture* (Boston, 1954), pp. 134–47; William Wallace Fenn, "The Theological School, 1869–1928," in *The Development of Harvard University,*

since the Inauguration of President Eliot, 1869–1929, ed. Samuel E. Morison (Cambridge, 1930), pp. 463–71.

51. Charles W. Eliot, "The Theological Curriculum," *The American Journal of Theology* 3 (April 1899): 331.

52. Charles W. Eliot to Francis G. Peabody, 20 August 1879, Eliot Papers; *Annual Report of the President of Harvard College, 1878–79,* p. 22..

53. *Annual Report of the President of Harvard College, 1877–78,* pp. 36–37.

54. Williams, *The Harvard Divinity School,* pp. 145–47, 166–71; C. W. Eliot to W. Robertson Smith, 25 February and 19 April 1880, and Eliot to Adolf Harnack, 2 February 1893, Eliot Papers.

55. C. W. Eliot to E. E. Hale, 4 February 1909, Eliot Papers; Eliot, "On the Education of Ministers"; Eliot, "The Theological Curriculum"; Charles W. Eliot, "The Harvard Divinity School," *Harvard Graduates Magazine* (September 1905): 209–11; Eliot, "More Harvard Graduates for the Ministry," in *The Ministry as a Profession* (Cambridge, 1907); Eliot, "Municipal Misgovernment—Address at Harvard Divinity School, Alumni Dinner, June 26, 1907," Eliot Papers; Eliot, "Religion in the Schools"; Hawkins, *Between Harvard and America,* p. 131.

56. Courtland Palmer to C. W. Eliot, 5 January and 27 February 1885, Eliot Papers; Charles W. Eliot, "What Place Should Religion Have in a College?" paper read before the Nineteenth Century Club of New York, 3 February 1886, Eliot Papers; James McCosh, *Religion in a College: What Place It Should Have* (New York, 1886). On state universities and the ideal of nonsectarian Christianity, see Bradley J. Longfield, "From Evangelicalism to Liberalism: Public Midwestern Universities in Nineteenth-Century America," in *The Secularization of the Academy,* ed. George M. Marsden and Bradley Longfield (New York, 1992), pp. 46–73.

57. Eliot, "What Place," p. 4.

58. Charles W. Eliot, "President Eliot's Address at President Faunce's Inauguration" (Brown University, 17 October 1899), Eliot Papers; Eliot, "What Place," p. 4.

59. Eliot, "What Place," p. 6.

60. Ibid., pp. 8–10.

61. Ibid., p. 12.

62. Ibid., p. 14.

63. Charles W. Eliot, "The Aims of Higher Education" (1891), in *Educational Reform,* p. 235; Eliot, "Municipal Misgovernment," p. 2. See also Eliot to George W. Quick, 19 November 1904, Eliot Papers.

64. J. A. Smith, "The Colleges and Universities of the West," *Proceedings of the Western Baptist Education Convention* (1871): 43, quoted in Edmund E. Lacy, "The Conflict of Thought over the Role of Religion in American Higher Education, 1865–1910" (Ph.D. diss., University of Illinois, 1969), pp. 69–70.

65. McCosh, *Religion in a College,* pp. 12, 17, 7.

66. Noah Porter, *American Colleges and the American Public* (New Haven, 1870), pp. 207, 214; Porter, Baccalaureate Address (1886), manuscript, Noah Porter Papers, Yale University; George Maguon, "The Making of a Christian College," *Education* 11 (1891): 336.

67. Andrew Dickson White, "Scientific and Industrial Education in the United States," *Popular Science Monthly* 5 (1874): 187–88; John Bascom, "Atheism in Colleges," *North American Review* 132 (1881): 39.

68. Andrew Dickson White to the Johns Hopkins University trustees, 13 March 1874, Gilman Papers; Daniel C. Gilman to Reverdy Johnson, 30 January 1875, Gilman Papers; Charles W. Eliot, "Congratulatory Address," in *Addresses at the Inauguration of Daniel C. Gilman, as President of the Johns Hopkins University, February 22, 1876* (Baltimore, 1876), p. 8. The trustees had already indicated their preference for nondenominationalism; see Reverdy Johnson to Daniel C. Gilman, 4 January 1875, Gilman Papers. See also Hugh Hawkins, "Three Presidents Testify," *American Quarterly* 10 (1959): 106–7..

69. Daniel C. Gilman, "The Future of the Johns Hopkins University," *The Independent* 48 (1888): 1366. See also *Annual Report of the President* (Johns Hopkins University, 1886), pp. 64–66; and Daniel C. Gilman, "Resignation, February 22, 1902," manuscript, Gilman Papers; Hugh Hawkins, *Pioneer: A History of the Johns Hopkins University, 1874–1889* (Ithaca, N. Y., 1960), pp. 68–69; D. G. Hart, "Faith and Learning in the Age of the University: The Academic Ministry of Daniel Coit Gilman," in *The Secularization of the Academy,* pp. 107–45.

70. *The Founding Grant* (with amendments; Stanford University, 1971 [1885]), p. 6; David Starr Jordan, *The Care and Culture of Men: A Series of Addresses on Higher Education* (San Francisco, 1896), pp. 113–14; Armando Trindade, "Roman Catholic Worship at Stanford University, 1891–1971" (Ph.D. diss., Stanford University, 1971), p. 42.

71. "Editorial," *Educational Review* 1 (1891): 63–64; Frederick T. Gates to William R. Harper, 17 February 1890, Harper Papers.

72. *The Decennial Publications of the University of Chicago; Vol. I: The President's Report* (Chicago, 1903), p. xxii; Thomas Wakefield Goodspeed, *A History of the University of Chicago: The First Quarter-Century* (Chicago, 1916), chaps. 1–3; "Articles of Incorporation of the University of Chicago, State of Illinois, Tenth of September, 1890," University Presidents' Papers, University of Chicago. Harper's determination to make Chicago nonsectarian upset some people involved in the founding of the university. They felt that he was undermining religious training at the school. See T. W. Goodspeed to W. R. Harper, 10 May 1889, A. H. Strong to W. R. Harper, 23 December 1890, and E. Nelson Blake to W. R. Harper, 1 January 1891, Correspondence of John D. Rockefeller and His Associates, University of Chicago.

73. William Rainey Harper, "Why Are There Fewer Students for the Ministry?" in *The Trend in Higher Education,* p. 201; *Official Bulletin* (University of Chicago, 1891), p. 2; W. R. Harper to T. W. Goodspeed, 23 September and 1 October 1890, Correspondence of J. D. Rockefeller and Associates; G. W. Northrup to W. R. Harper, 3 and 7 December 1888, 10 September 1890, 16 February and 28 April 1891, University Presidents' Papers; E. Nelson Blake to W. R. Harper, 1 January 1891, Correspondence of J. D. Rockefeller and Associates; T. W. Goodspeed to W. R. Harper, 17 April 1891, University Presidents' Papers.

74. *Decennial Publications of the University of Chicago; Vol. I,* pp. lxxiv, lxxvi;

President's Report (University of Chicago, 1907–8), pp. 15–20. This agreement was reached after Harper's death, but records indicate that he was a driving force in pushing for church recognition of reforms at the divinity school. See "Report of the Commission of Affairs of the Divinity School of the University of Chicago, June 15, 1908," University Presidents' Papers. In 1923 President Judson renewed efforts to make the divinity school independent of the Northern Baptist Convention; Henry P. Judson to President Burton, 16 February 1923, University Presidents' Papers. See James P. Wind, *The Bible and the University: The Messianic Vision of William Rainey Harper* (Atlanta, 1987), pp. 116–18..

75. J. H. George to W. R. Harper, 19 January 1905, University Presidents' Papers; *Decennial Publications; Vol. I*, p. lxxvi; "Affiliated Schools of Divinity," in *President's Report* (University of California, 1886), pp. 26–27; Wallace Stearns and the Committee of Six, "Religious and Moral Education in the Universities and Colleges of the United States," *Religious Education* 1 (1907): 221–22; John Wright Buckman, "Changing Ideals in Theological Education," *Religious Education* 4 (1909): 237–38; J. B. Angell to N. M. Butler, 6 February 1893, J. B. Angell Papers; "Ann Arbor Federation for Students in Religion," *Religious Education* 5 (1910): 525; C. C. Hall, "Annual Survey of Progress," in *Proceedings of the Second Annual Convention of the Religious Education Association* (Chicago, 1904), p. 98; Daniel Coit Gilman, "Present Aspects of College Training," *North American Review* 136 (1883): 540; Francis W. Kelsey, "The Problem of Religious Education in State Universities," in *Proceedings of the Fifth Annual Convention of the Religious Education Association* (Chicago, 1908), p. 141.

76. Seth Low to Reverend Reese F. Aslop, 19 March 1894, and Low to Melvil Dewey, 18 January 1896, Seth Low Papers, Columbia University; Nicholas Murray Butler, "From Kings College to Columbia University," *Educational Review* 28 (1904): 504–5; and Butler, "Making Liberal Men and Women," in *Scholarship and Service,* p. 16. The minister of St. Anne's convinced Low that he need not quit the vestry; Low to Aslop, 21 March 1894, Low Papers. During his presidency Low avoided associating himself with religious organizations. He declined invitations to serve on boards or become an honorary member of associations, pleading that he had not "allowed my name to stand where it did not carry with it the man it stands for." There is evidence, however, that Low allowed his name to be used by religious organizations before he was president and by nonreligious organizations while president. Low to Reverend W. H. P. Faunce, 8 December 1893; Low to W. F. C. Morsell, 19 December 1890; Low to Caleb T. Rowe, 10 January 1894; Low to Reverend John W. Kramer, 2 November 1893; Low to Reverend Reese F. Aslop, 13 April 1891; Low to Henry M. Brooks, 6 June 1894; Low to Theodore C. Mitchell, 23 April 1894; all in Low Papers.

77. Arthur T. Hadley, "The Public Conscience" (1905), in *Baccalaureate Addresses and Other Talks on Kindred Themes* (New York, 1907), pp. 203–4; Hadley to Dr. Lockhart, 21 December 1908, Hadley Papers.

78. Arthur T. Hadley to Reverend W. Douglas Mackenzie, 17 February 1909, Hadley Papers; Anson Phelps Stokes, "University Schools of Religion," *Religious Education* 9 (1914): 330. See also A. T. Hadley to E. L. Curtis, 5 December 1906;

George P. Fisher to Hadley, 21 June 1901; Hadley to Reverend E. P. Parker, 23 March 1909; Hadley to George B. Stevens, 8 February 1905; Hadley to George Adam Smith, 28 November 1905; Hadley to Reverend James Barton, 2 June 1904; Edward L. Curtis to Hadley, 11 January 1910; Curtis to Hadley, 15 February 1907; Hadley to John R. Mott, 16 April 1909; Hadley to Charles F. Thwig, 2 December 1908; all in Hadley Papers. See also Roland Herbert Bainton, *Yale and the Ministry; A History of Education for the Christian Ministry at Yale from the Founding in 1701* (New York, 1957), chap. 15..

79. Henry S. Pritchett, "The Relations of Christian Denominations to Colleges, An Address before the Conference of the Education of the Methodist Episcopal Church, South, at Atlanta, Ga., 20 May 1908" (n.p., n.d.), p. 4. On the Carnegie Foundation's decision, see Ellen Condliffe Lageman, *Private Power for the Public Good: A History of the Carnegie Foundation for the Advancement of Teaching* (Middletown, Conn., 1983).

80. Charles W. Eliot, "Address at the Formal Opening of the Laboratory of the Rockefeller Institute for Medical Research," *Science* n. s. 24 (July 1906): 3. See also Albert Coe, "Annual Survey of Progress in Religious and Moral Education," *Religious Education* 4 (1909): 12–13. It is generally accepted that during the late nineteenth and early twentieth centuries, denominational institutions declined from a majority to a minority of colleges and universities. But it seems that Carnegie's decision to exclude denominational schools reflected rather than hastened this change. See Mark Noll, "Introduction," in William C. Ringenberg, *The Christian College: A History of Protestant Higher Education in America* (Grand Rapids, 1984), p. 1; Earl McGrath, "The Control of Higher Education in America," *Educational Record* 17 (April 1936): 264–65; David B. Potts, "American Colleges in the Nineteenth Century: From Localism to Denominationalism," *History of Education Quarterly* 11 (1971): 374.

Chapter Four

1. *Annual Report of the President* (Columbia College, 1871), pp. 6–7, 50–52; *Annual Report of the President* (Columbia College, 1872), p. 4; and *Annual Report of the President* (Columbia College, 1877), pp. 19–20.

2. To determine changes in courses related to religion and philosophy, I examined the University of California's course catalogues from 1870 to 1915, and the other schools' catalogues at five-year intervals, and entered all relevant courses into a data base. Unless otherwise noted, all information about particular courses is derived from this source. "Dean of the College Report," in *Annual Report of the President of Harvard College, 1872–73,* p. 40.

3. G. Stanley Hall, "Letter to the Editor of the *Nation*" (1876), in William James, *Essays in Philosophy* (Cambridge, 1978), pp. 245–46; also Hall, "Philosophy in the United States," *Mind* 4 (1879): 89–105. See Daniel J. Wilson, *Science, Community, and the Transformation of American Philosophy* (Chicago, 1990), for discussion of changes in philosophy in the late nineteenth and early twentieth centuries.

4. William James, "The Teaching of Philosophy in Our Colleges," in *Essays in Philosophy,* p. 3.

5. Ibid., p. 5. See, for example, John Dewey, "Inventory of Philosophy Taught in American Colleges" (1886), in *John Dewey: The Early Works,* ed. Jo Ann Boydston et al., 5 vols. (Carbondale, Ill., 1969–72), 5:116–21.

6. A. P. Peabody to C. W. Eliot, 30 March 1875, Charles W. Eliot Papers, Harvard University. For an extensive discussion of these changes at Harvard University, see Bruce Kuklick, *The Rise of American Philosophy, Cambridge, Massachusetts, 1860–1930* (New Haven, 1977). For similar developments at the University of Michigan, California, and Columbia, see Dewitt H. Parker and Charles B. Vibbert, "The Department of Philosophy," in *The University of Michigan: An Encyclopedic Survey,* ed. Wilfred B. Shaw, 4 vols. (Ann Arbor, 1951), 2:668–79; Elmo A. Robinson, "One Hundred Years of Philosophy Teaching in California (1857–1957)," *Journal of the History of Ideas* 20 (1959): 369–84; and John Herman Randall, Jr., "The Department of Philosophy," in *A History of the Faculty of Philosophy, Columbia University,* ed. John Herman Randall, Jr. (New York, 1957), pp. 104–10..

7. James B. Angell to James R. Angell, 22 November 1891, James Rowland Angell Papers, Yale University.

8. Daniel C. Gilman to Reverend Jonas Miller, 5 January 1876, Daniel Coit Gilman Papers, Johns Hopkins University.

9. Daniel C. Gilman to Reverend Atwater, 15 April 1876, Gilman to C. R. Bliss, 4 February 1876, Gilman to Reverend Atwater, 4 April 1876, Gilman Papers.

10. Daniel C. Gilman to George S. Morris, 12 December 1877, Gilman Papers.

11. Daniel C. Gilman to Andrew D. White, 24 September 1882, and Gilman to George S. Morris, 15 May 1883, Gilman Papers. Gilman publicly quoted Hall's remarks about psychology's relationship to Christianity. See Daniel C. Gilman, "The Benefits Which Society Derives from Universities" (Baltimore, 1885), p. 23. Scholars who have examined Gilman's decision to keep Hall and dismiss Peirce and Morris have concluded that it is impossible to know with certainty why he made the decision. But they agree that Hall's statements about his desire to reconcile religion and science played an important part in his success at Hopkins. His self-promotion, the close relations of psychology and biology, the potential practical applications of psychology, Morris's relatively retiring personality, and Peirce's troubled relations with colleagues and questionable marital history are also cited as reasons for Gilman's decision. Gilman's choice has been carefully scrutinized because, in retrospect, the Hall appointment seems to have been a mistake and because Peirce's dismissal ruined his professional career. But without benefit of hindsight, Gilman's ultimate choice was perfectly consistent with his statements about what he was looking for in a philosophy professor. Historians have also questioned Hall's sincerity regarding religion. It is likely that Hall exaggerated his own religious respectability in order to get the position at Hopkins. But Hall was an early promoter of the psychology of religion, which, as is discussed below, was seen as a way to make religion intellectually respectable. Hugh Hawkins, *Pioneer: A History of the Johns Hopkins University, 1874–1889* (Ithaca, N. Y., 1960), pp. 188–202; Max H. Fisch, "Peirce at Johns Hopkins University," in *Peirce, Semeiotics, and Pragmatism,* ed. Kenneth Laine Ketner and Christian J. W. Kloesel

(Bloomington, Ind., 1986); Dorothy Ross, *G. Stanley Hall: The Psychologist as Prophet* (Chicago, 1972), chap. 8; R. M. Wenley, *The Life and Work of George Sylvester Morris* (New York, 1917), pp. 147–57.

12. Ira Remsen to Daniel C. Gilman, 22 April 1889, Gilman to E. H. Griffen, 9 May 1889, and memo entitled "Dean," Gilman Papers. See also D. H. Hart, "Faith and Learning in the Age of the University: The Academic Ministry of Daniel Coit Gilman," in *The Secularization of the Academy,* ed. George M. Marsden and Bradley J. Longfield (New York, 1992), pp. 120–24..

13. *President's Report* (University of California, 1882–84), p. 19; Robinson, "One Hundred Years," pp. 373–74; Howison to Reverend Minot J. Savage, 25 January 1902, George H. Howison Papers, University of California, Berkeley. See also Josiah Royce, *The Religious Aspect of Philosophy* (New York, 1958 [1885]), p. x. For more on Howison, see John Wright Buckham and George Malcolm Stratton, *George Holmes Howison, Philosopher and Teacher* (Berkeley, 1934).

14. For examples of these philosophers' understanding of the relationship between philosophy and religion, see Royce, *The Religious Aspect of Philosophy;* and George S. Morris, *Philosophy and Christianity* (New York, 1975 [1883]). For more information on idealism in the United States in the late nineteenth century, see Herbert W. Schneider, *A History of American Philosophy,* 2nd ed. (New York, 1963), chap. 7; and Elizabeth Flower and Murray G. Murphey, *A History of Philosophy in America,* 2 vols. (New York, 1977), 2:chap. 8.

15. J. B. Angell to G. H. Howison, 29 February 1896; H. C. King to Angell, 11 May 1895; G. H. Palmer to Angell, 31 March, 22 May 1895, 30 January 1896; Angell to Howison, 25 May 1895; Howison to Angell, 8 June 1895; James Orr to Angell, n.d. (22 August 1895); Angell to R. M. Wenley, 16 October 1895; all in James B. Angell Papers, University of Michigan. On the professionalization of philosophy, see Kuklick, *The Rise of American Philosophy,* p. 565; Bruce Kuklick, *Churchmen and Philosophers* (New Haven, 1985), part 3; and Wilson, *Science, Community, and the Transformation of American Philosophy.*

16. George M. Duncan to Mr. Judd, 14 April 1904, E. W. Scripture to Arthur T. Hadley, 14 August, 9 November, 4 December 1902, Arthur T. Hadley Papers, Yale University Archives. George M. Duncan, then head of the philosophy department, also wrote numerous letters to Hadley about the department's problems in 1903; see Hadley Papers. On specialization and scientism in philosophy, see Kuklick, *The Rise of American Philosophy;* and Wilson, *Science, Community, and the Transformation of American Philosophy.*

17. The decline of religious and moral concerns among Harvard philosophers is discussed in Kuklick, *The Rise of American Philosophy,* part 5. In addition, during this period, philosophers developed more naturalistic approaches to ethics and religion. See Guy W. Stroh, *American Ethical Thought* (Chicago, 1979); and Allan P. F. Sell, *The Philosophy of Religion 1875–1980* (New York, 1988).

18. Several of Yale's course offerings in religion were cross-listed with the divinity school. C. H. Smith commented on these changes in 1901: "A comparison of these courses with those which formed a prominent part of the ancient curriculum

shows the far wider range now given to religious instruction, and the important change which has taken place in its character, it being now biblical instead of theological" (C. H. Smith, "Faculty Participation in Student Religious Life," in *Two Centuries of Christian Activity at Yale, 1701–1901,* ed. James B. Reynolds et al. [New York, 1901], p. 162). For information about biblical instruction at Yale and Johns Hopkins, see Sanders's and Adams's contributions to "Bible Study in College," *Biblical World* n. s. 5 (1895): 206–7, 288..

19. Abstract of an address by Emil Hersh, "The Human Side of Religion," *University Record* (University of Chicago) 1 (17 April 1896): 65; Adams, "Bible Study in College," p. 28; Henry W. Bowden, *Church History in the Age of Science: Historiographical Patterns in the United States, 1876–1918* (Chapel Hill, 1971), p. 26; "Teaching the Bible in Colleges," Report of the Subcommittee of the Department of Universities and Colleges of the Religious Education Association, *Religious Education* 11 (1916): 323; *Yale University Catalogue* (1894–95), p. 80.

20. Clyde W. Votow, "Courses in Religion: Moral and Religious Instruction in the College," *Religious Education* 5 (1910): 300.

21. Henry Ward Beecher, "The Progress of Thought in the Church," *North American Review* 135 (1882): 100. See also William R. Hutchison, *The Modernist Impulse in American Protestantism* (Cambridge, 1976); Kenneth Cauthen, *The Impact of American Religious Liberalism* (New York, 1962); and Frank Hugh Foster, *The Modern Movement in American Theology* (New York, 1939).

22. Beecher, "The Progress of Thought," pp. 110 and 117.

23. Charles A. Briggs, "The Theological Crisis," *North American Review* 153 (1891): 91; Charles W. Eliot, "The Religion of the Future, An Address before the Harvard Summer Theological School, July 21, 1909," typescript, Eliot Papers.

24. See, for example, Henry S. Pritchett, *What Is Religion? and Other Student Questions* (Boston, 1906), p. 32; William Rainey Harper, "Religious Belief among College Students," in *Religion and the Higher Life* (Chicago, 1904), p. 134.

25. Charles W. Eliot to William C. Sturgis, 13 August 1909, Eliot Papers.

26. Phillips Brooks, "Orthodoxy," in *Essays and Addresses,* ed. John Cotton Brooks (New York, 1895), p. 193.

27. William Rainey Harper, "Religion and the Higher Life," in *Religion and the Higher Life,* p. 17; Pritchett, *What Is Religion,* p. 18; Raymond Knox, *Religion and the American Dream* (New York, 1934), pp. 38–39; James B. Angell, "Relation of American Colleges to Christianity, Evangelical Alliance, Detroit, Nov. 1, 1877," manuscript, J. B. Angell Papers. See, for example, R. Heber Newton, "Religion and Religions," *North American Review* 178 (1904): 555–56.

28. John M. Coulter, "Christianity and Science," pp. 9–10, typescript, John M. Coulter Papers, University of Chicago. In emphasizing liberals' efforts to use the new university to reconstruct religion, I am departing from Henry C. Johnson, Jr.'s interpretation of the secularization of higher education. Johnson argues that liberals, because they rejected doctrines and defined religion in emotional and psychological terms, wanted to be independent of the university. Although I agree that the result of liberalism was to privatize religion, I argue that liberals hoped

to create modern, nondogmatic doctrine, but failed in their efforts. See Henry C. Johnson, Jr., "'Down from the Mountain': Secularization and the Higher Learning in America," *Review of Politics* 54 (1992): 578–85..

29. William Rainey Harper to J. D. Rockefeller, 8 January 1891, Correspondence of John D. Rockefeller and His Associates, University of Chicago. A. H. Strong's daughter was in a class Harper was teaching at Vassar College. Strong read his daughter's notebook and discovered some views he considered heretical. The situation was complicated by the fact that Baptists in Chicago were trying to get Rockefeller to donate money to resurrect the old University of Chicago. They were proposing Harper, whom Rockefeller respected, as the president of the new school. Strong, on the other hand, wanted Rockefeller to donate his money to a start a Baptist graduate school in New York City, which he hoped to lead. Harper presented his views in a moderate fashion. Although Strong was not completely satisfied with Harper's explanation, he dropped his charges against him. See G. W. Northrup to William Rainey Harper, 1 January 1889, University Presidents' Papers, University of Chicago; F. T. Gates to Harper, 5 January 1889, W. R. Harper Papers, University of Chicago; A. H. Strong to Harper, 8 January 1889, Correspondence of J. D. Rockefeller and Associates. For information about the competition among Baptists for Rockefeller's donation, see Thomas Wakefield Goodspeed, *A History of the University of Chicago, The First Quarter-Century* (Chicago, 1916), chap. 1. See also Grant Wacker, *Augustus Strong and the Dilemma of Historical Consciousness* (Macon, 1985), pp. 50–56; James P. Wind, *The Bible and the University: The Messianic Vision of William Rainey Harper* (Atlanta, 1987), pp. 106–8.

30. W. R. Harper to J. D. Rockefeller, 8 January 1891, Correspondence of J. D. Rockefeller and Associates.

31. F. T. Gates to H. L. Morehouse, 6 February 1891, H. L. Morehouse to W. R. Harper, 2 February 1891, Correspondence of J. D. Rockefeller and Associates.

32. W. R. Harper to H. L. Morehouse, 7 February 1891, Correspondence of J. D. Rockefeller and Associates. This principle was raised many times as Baptists complained about the liberal teaching at the university and theological seminary. See, for example, T. W. Goodspeed to (E. N.) Blake, 7 November 1909, University Presidents' Papers.

33. "Articles of Agreement between the Baptist Theological Union Located at Chicago and the University of Chicago," University Presidents' Papers; *The Decennial Publications of the University of Chicago; Vol. I: The President's Report* (Chicago, 1903), p. 509; William Rainey Harper, "What Can Universities and Colleges Do for the Religious Life of Their Students?" in *The Aim of Religious Education: The Proceedings of the Third Annual Convention of the Religious Education Association* (Chicago, 1905), pp. 110–11.

34. Clyde W. Votow, "Courses in Religion: Moral and Religious Instruction in the College," *Religious Education* 5 (1910): 302; Raymond C. Knox, *Religion and The American Dream* (New York, 1934), pp. 37–38.

35. Harper, "What Can Colleges and Universities Do," pp. 111–12.

36. Both Harper and Eliot thought that students' declining interest in the min-

istry was due in part to their view of religion as dogmatic and out of step with modern thinking. See William Rainey Harper, "Why Are There Fewer Students for the Ministry?" in *The Trend in Higher Education* (Chicago, 1905), pp. 205–6; and Charles W. Eliot, "On the Education of Ministers," in *Educational Reform* (New York, 1908), pp. 61–86; Benjamin Bacon, "College Courses of Bible Study," in *Proceedings of the Second Annual Convention of the Religious Education Association* (Chicago, 1904), p. 134. See also W. C. Bitting, "The Next Step Forward," in *Proceedings of the First Annual Convention of the Religious Education Association* (Chicago, 1903), pp. 26–27; Arthur Holmes, "University Students' Taste in Bible Study," *Religious Education* 6 (1911): 412..

37. Sanders, "Bible Study in the College," pp. 206–7; Bacon, "College Courses of Bible Study," pp. 132–33.

38. Morris Jastrow, Jr., "Recent Movements in the Historical Study of Religions in America," *Biblical World* n. s. 1 (1893): 24. For contemporary overviews of the science of religion, see Morris Jastrow, Jr., *The Study of Religion* (New York, 1902); Louis Henry Jordan, *Comparative Religion: Its Genesis and Growth* (Edinburgh, 1905), pp. ix, 7–8; and Jordan, *Comparative Religion: Its Adjuncts and Allies* (London, 1915). For historical accounts, see Eric J. Sharpe, *Comparative Religion: A History,* 2nd ed. (La Salle, Ill., 1986), chaps. 1–5; Claude Welch, *Protestant Thought in the Nineteenth Century,* 2 vols. (New Haven, 1985), 2:chaps. 3 and 4; Bowden, *Church History in the Age of Science,* chaps. 1–5; Ernest W. Saunders, *Searching the Scriptures: A History of the Society of Biblical Literature, 1880–1980* (Chico, Calif., 1982), chaps. 1–2; Robert S. Shepard, *God's People in the Ivory Tower: Religion in the Early American University* (Brooklyn, N. Y., 1991); Murray G. Murphey, "On the Scientific Study of Religion in the United States, 1870–1980," in *Religion and Twentieth-Century American Intellectual Life,* ed. Michael J. Lacey (New York, 1989), pp. 136–71; and D. G. Hart, "American Learning and the Problem of Religious Studies," in *The Secularization of the Academy,* pp. 195–233.

39. Sir James George Frazer, *The Golden Bough,* abridged ed. (New York, 1922 [1890]); Sir Edward Burnett Tylor, *Religion in Primitive Culture,* introduction by Paul Radin (Gloucester, Mass., 1970 [1871]); Emile Durkheim, *The Elementary Forms of the Religious Life,* trans. Joseph Ward Swain (New York, 1915 [1912]); Max Weber, *The Protestant Ethic and the Spirit of Capitalism,* trans. Talcott Parsons (New York, 1958 [1904]); Weber, *The Sociology of Religion,* trans. Ephraim Fishoff (New York, 1963 [1922]). See also John W. Burrows, *Evolution and Society* (Cambridge, 1968).

40. G. Stanley Hall, "The Moral and Religious Training of Children," *Princeton Review* 10 (1882): 26–48; Edwin Diller Starbuck, *The Psychology of Religion* (New York, 1899); James Leuba, "Studies in the Psychology of Religious Phenomena— Conversion," *American Journal of Psychology* 7 (1896): 195–225; Leuba, *A Psychological Study of Religion* (New York, 1912); William James, *The Varieties of Religious Experience* (Cambridge, 1985 [1902]); George Albert Coe, *The Psychology of Religion* (Chicago, 1916); James Bissett Pratt, *The Religious Consciousness: A Psychological Study* (New York, 1920); Edward Scribner Ames, *The Psychology of Religious Experience* (Boston, 1910). See also Benjamin Beit-Hallahmi, "Psychol-

ogy of Religion, 1880–1930: The Rise and Fall of a Psychological Movement," *Journal of the History of the Behavioral Sciences* 10 (1974): 84–90; Howard J. Booth, *Edwin Diller Starbuck: Pioneer in the Psychology of Religion* (Washington, D.C., 1981); Claude Welch, *Protestant Thought in the Nineteenth Century, Vol. Two, 1870–1914* (New Haven, 1985), chap. 3; and Murphey, "On the Scientific Study," pp. 140–42. James Pratt was particularly successful in combining his interest in comparative religion and the psychology of religion. Sharpe, *Comparative Religion,* pp. 114–16..

41. Starbuck, *Psychology,* p. 1.

42. George A. Coe, "My Own Little Theatre," in *Religion in Transition,* ed. Vergilus Ferm (New York, 1937), p. 95.

43. Ibid., pp. 97–98; Edward Scribner Ames, *Beyond Theology: The Autobiography of Edward Scribner Ames,* ed. Van Meter Ames (Chicago, 1959), p. 57.

44. James, *Varieties,* pp. 34, 67 (emphasis in original).

45. Edwin D. Starbuck, "The Feelings and Their Place in Religion," *American Journal of Religious Psychology and Education* 1 (1904): 169; Jean Ellen Harrison, "The Influence of Darwinism on the Study of Religions," in *Darwin and Modern Science,* ed. A. C. Seward (Cambridge, 1909), pp. 495–96.

46. Edwin D. Starbuck to David Starr Jordan, 14 November 1897, David Starr Jordan Papers, Stanford University; William James, "Preface," in Starbuck, *Psychology,* p. ix; James to Frances R. Morse, 12 April 1900, in *Letters of William James,* ed. Henry James, Jr., 2 vols. (Boston, 1920), 2:127.

47. Jastrow, "Recent Movements," pp. 31–32.

48. Ames, *Beyond Theology,* p. 210, quoting himself from "Christianity and Scientific Thinking," in *Modern Trends in World-Religions,* ed. A. E. Haydon (Chicago, 1934), pp. 26, 28.

49. James Leuba, "Introduction to a Psychological Study of Religion," *Monist* 11 (1901): 213–14; Harrison, "The Influence of Darwinism," pp. 494–511; William James to Henry W. Rankin, 16 June 1901, in *Letters of William James,* 2:149.

50. James, *Varieties,* p. 30. See also Leuba, "Introduction," pp. 195–225.

51. James, *Varieties,* pp. 41, 49 (emphasis in original).

52. Ibid., pp. 210, 266, 299.

53. George A. Coe, *The Psychology of Religion,* p. 241.

54. James, *Varieties,* pp. 342, 300.

55. Ibid., pp. 340, 359, 335.

56. Ibid., p. 335.

57. Ibid., p. 402.

58. Pratt, *The Religious Consciousness,* p. 31.

59. Jastrow, *The Study of Religion,* pp. 19–20; Emerton quoted in Bowden, *Church History,* p. 108.

60. Jerry Wayne Brown, *The Rise of Biblical Criticism in America, 1800–1870* (Middletown, Conn., 1969).

61. John William Stewart, "The Tethered Theology: Biblical Criticism, Common Sense Philosophy and the Princeton Theologians, 1812–1869" (Ph.D. diss., University of Michigan, 1990); Mark A. Noll, *Between Faith and Criticism: Evan-*

gelicals, Scholarship, and the Bible in America (San Francisco, 1986), chap. 1; Saunders, *Searching the Scriptures,* chap.1; Thomas H. Olbricht, "Intellectual Ferment and Instruction in the Scriptures: The Bible in Higher Education," in *The Bible and Instruction in the Scriptures: The Bible in Higher Education,* ed. David L. Barr and Nicholas Piediscalzi (Chico, Calif., 1982), pp. 97–119; Wind, *The Bible and the University;* Hans W. Frei, *The Eclipse of the Biblical Narrative: A Study in Eighteenth- and Nineteenth-Century Hermeneutics* (New Haven, 1974)..

62. Olbricht, "Intellectual Ferment," pp. 101–2.

63. Harper quoted in Wind, *The Bible and the University,* p. 60. Wind maintains that Harper's understanding of science was inductive. I think that Harper's rhetoric about science was closer to the progressivist position than to the Baconian.

64. Thayer quoted in Olbricht, "Intellectual Ferment," p. 102.

65. William Rainey Harper, "The Bible and the Monuments" (n.d.), manuscript, Harper Papers; Herbert Willett, "Historical Study of the Bible," in *Religious Education Association, Proceedings of the First Annual Convention* (Chicago, 1903).

66. Hutchison, *Modernist Impulse,* chap. 3.

67. Roy A. Harrisville, *Benjamin Wisner Bacon: Pioneer in American Biblical Criticism* (Missoula, Mont., 1976).

68. Frank C. Porter, "The Bearing of Historical Studies on the Religious Use of the Bible," *Harvard Theological Review* 2 (1909): 253; Saunders, *Searching the Scriptures,* p. 28; Roy A. Harrisville, *Frank Chamberlain Porter: Pioneer in American Biblical Interpretation* (Missoula, Mont., 1976).

69. Porter, "The Bearing of Historical Studies," pp. 257, 259, 254.

70. Richard G. Moulton, "The Study of Literature and the Integration of Knowledge," *University Record* 3 (1917): 93–94. On Moulton, see David Norton, *A History of the Bible as Literature, Volume Two: From 1700 to the Present Day* (Cambridge, 1993), chap. 7. See also David S. Reynolds, *Faith in Fiction: The Emergence of Religious Literature in America* (Cambridge, 1981), chap. 5. For information on a different view of biblical criticism in this period, see D. G. Hart, *Defending the Faith: J. Gresham Machen and the Crisis of Conservative Protestantism in Modern America* (Baltimore, 1994), chap. 2.

71. Ephraim Emerton, "The Study of Church History," *Unitarian Review and Religious Magazine* 19 (1883): 18.

72. Jastrow, *The Study of Religion,* p. 312.

73. Frank K. Sanders to Arthur T. Hadley, 28 March 1900, Hadley to Sanders, 23 August 1900, Hadley Papers. On student interest in the science of religion, see Shepard, *God's People in the Ivory Tower,* chap. 3.

74. Frank K. Sanders to Arthur T. Hadley, 16 August, 28 November 1900, 17 January 1901, 21 June (1903), Hadley Papers.

75. *University of Chicago, Annual Register* (1893–94), p. 77.

76. J. H. Barrows to W. R. Harper, 19 October 1895, University Presidents' Papers. In 1898 the University of Chicago began to tabulate and publish the numbers of students enrolled in courses. University of Chicago had an elaborate system of categorizing courses, in which a full-credit course was called a "major course." The university listed how many students in their last two years (senior college students)

took major courses in each department. Students elected nineteen and a half major courses in the Semitic language and literature, biblical and patristic Greek, and comparative religion departments combined. Students elected more than three hundred courses in the English department. In later years the figures were similar. See *President's Report* (University of Chicago, 1897–98), p. 71. On divinity student enrollment, *President's Report* (University of Chicago, 1907–8, p. 15) stated: "The Department of Semitic Languages and Literature, the Department of Biblical and Patristic Greek, and the Department of Comparative Religion are University departments under the Faculties of Arts, Literature, and Science, but offer instruction also to Divinity students—and in fact their classes are very largely supplied from the Divinity School." See also Shepard, *God's People in the Ivory Tower,* pp. 42–50..

77. *University of Chicago Annual Register* (1897–98), p. 275. For example, in 1901–2 senior college students enrolled in 85 major courses in literature in English, compared with 248 in English, 313 in history, and 178 in sociology. *Decennial Publications; Vol. I,* pp. 89–90; *University of Chicago Annual Register* (1903–4), p. 310.

78. *President's Report* (University of California, 1898–1900), p. 186.

79. *President's Report* (University of California, 1904–6), pp. 26–27; *Register* (University of California, 1908–9), pp. 41–42.

80. R. G. Moulton to W. R. Harper, 12 October 1896, University Presidents' Papers; Laura Wild, "The Equipment of a Department of Biblical Literature," *Religious Education* 10 (1915): 345.

81. Holmes, "University Students' Taste," p. 410.

82. Ibid., pp. 410–11.

83. Holmes "haphazardly" selected some answers to report in full. Ibid., pp. 411–12.

84. Walter S. Athearn, "Religion in the Curriculum," *Religious Education* 8 (1913): 433; Saunders, *Searching the Scriptures,* p. 102. The question about the devotional aspect of courses on religion has haunted religious studies throughout the twentieth century. In research universities, the tendency has been to separate religious practice from the academic study of religion, but there is still no consensus about the goals and limitations of courses in religious studies. See Paul Ramsey and John F. Wilson, eds., *The Study of Religion in Colleges and Universities* (Princeton, 1970); and Claude Welch, *Graduate Education in Religion* (Missoula, Mont., 1971).

85. William Rainey Harper, "Editorial," *Biblical World* n. s. 9 (1897): 3.

86. Harrison S. Elliot, "Voluntary Bible Study: Its Place in the Religious Education of Students," *Religious Education* 7 (1913): 713–14.

87. Shepard, *God's People in the Ivory Tower,* pp. 4–6; Beit-Hallahmi, "Psychology of Religion," pp. 87–89.

88. James B. Angell to (A. Caswell), 18 February 1872, and Angell to Caswell, 27 September 1871, J. B. Angell Papers; despite his initial misgivings, Angell later publicly defended voluntary chapel. See James B. Angell, "Religious Life in Our State Universities," *Andover Review* 8 (1890): 366. A study in 1908 indicated that 12 out of 19 state colleges and universities had voluntary rather than compulsory

chapel services. The figure for nonsectarian private schools was 11 out of 33, and for denominational schools it was 6 out of 72. Overall, 29 schools had voluntary prayers, and 95 had compulsory prayers. A study in 1912 of 116 institutions found that 107 had daily chapel services; of these 39 were voluntary and 68 compulsory. Henry F. Cope, "Ten Years Progress in Religious Education," *Religious Education* 8 (1913): 138. The universities included in this study were leaders in the development of voluntary chapel..

89. Wm. Richardson to Charles W. Eliot, 24 July 1869, Eliot Papers; Samuel Eliot Morison, *Three Centuries at Harvard, 1636–1936* (Cambridge, 1936), p. 366; F. A. P. Barnard, in *The Rise of a University: The Later Days of Old Columbia College; Selections from the Annual Reports of Frederick A. P. Barnard,* ed. William Russell (New York, 1937), pp. 242–46.

90. G. H. Palmer to Charles W. Eliot, 25 May 1882, Eliot Papers.

91. David Starr Jordan, *The Care and Culture of Men: A Series of Addresses on Higher Education* (San Francisco, 1896), pp. 18–19; "Chaplain's Report," in *President's Report* (University of Chicago, 1897–98), p. 201; William Faunce, "Annual Report of Progress" in *Religious Education Association, Proceedings of the Third Annual Convention* (Chicago, 1905), p. 18.

92. Morison, *Three Centuries,* p. 366; Francis G. Peabody to Charles W. Eliot, 10 June 1886, Eliot Papers; *Annual Report of the President* (Columbia University, 1891), pp. 13–14.

93. *President's Annual Report* (Columbia University, 1891), pp. 13–14; W. R. Harper to F. T. Gates, 10 October 1892, Correspondence of J. D. Rockefeller and Associates; E. D. Burton to (F. T. Gates), 18 December 1892, University Presidents' Papers; *President's Annual Report* (Columbia University, 1896), pp. 26–27.

94. "Report of the Pacific Coast Conference of the Religious Education Association," *Religious Education* 9 (1914): 602.

95. Charles W. Eliot to George Wigglesworth, 12 November 1908, Eliot Papers.

96. "Chaplain's Report" (n.d.), Jordan Papers; "University Meetings," in *President's Report* (University of California, 1910–12), pp. 367–70; "Aids to Moral and Religious Culture," in *University of Michigan Calendar, 1909–1910,* pp. 57–58; A. T. Hadley to J. C. Jones, 14 October 1901, Hadley Papers. See also "The University Church," *Yale University Bulletin, 1910–1911,* pp. 608–9; W. R. Harper to Charles Henderson, 25 September 1899, Harper Papers; "Religious Agencies of the University," in *President's Report* (University of Chicago, 1910–11), pp. 145–46; "Report of the Religious Work Committee, 1910–1911," Columbia University Christian Association Correspondence and Documents, Columbiana Collection, Columbia University (henceforth cited as CACU).

97. *Annual Report of the President of Harvard University, 1895–96,* p. 12; *President's Report* (Columbia University, 1906), pp. 2–3; A. P. Stokes, "Present Condition of Religious Life at Yale," in *Two Centuries of Christian Activity at Yale,* p. 126.

98. W. E. Hocking, "The Religious Function of State Universities," *University of California Chronicle* 10 (1908): 465; *Annual Report of the President of Harvard University, 1895–96,* pp. 12–13; James B. Angell to Charles W. Eliot, 9 November 1895, J. B. Angell Papers. Eliot thought the figure was inadequate and hoped to

raise it by securing an endowment for the chapel. Charles W. Eliot to George Wigglesworth, 22 July 1908, Eliot Papers. For a sense of faculty salaries at this time, see *The Development of Harvard University since the Inauguration of President Eliot, 1869–1929,* ed. Samuel E. Morison (Cambridge, 1930), p. xli; and Seymour E. Harris, *Economics of Harvard* (New York, 1970), pp. 140–46..

99. The University of Chicago report "Religious Agencies of the University" discusses the activities of the Christian Union, which is described as "the official board under which the various religious and philanthropic activities of the University are co-ordinate." It also discusses the activities of the Young Men's Christian Association, the Young Women's Christian League, the Evangelistic Band, and the University of Chicago Settlement. *President's Report* (University of Chicago, 1910–11), pp. 145–48. Roy S. Wallace, graduate secretary of the Phillips Brooks House at Harvard, described the role of the Phillips Brooks House Association in "The Religious Life of Students," in *Religious Education Association, Proceedings of the Third Annual Convention,* pp. 113–14. Frederick Rudolph, *The American College and University* (New York, 1962), chap. 18.

100. "President Dwight's Address," in *Dwight Hall, Yale University, Its Origin, Erection, and Dedication* (New Haven, 1887), p. 18.

101. "Earl Hall Report," in *President's Annual Report, Columbia University* (1915), p. 233; Hocking, "The Religious Function of State Universities," pp. 463–64. Educators in the late nineteenth and early twentieth centuries viewed campus architecture as a significant determinant and symbol of the school's educational philosophy. For a pioneer study of the subject, see Helen Lefkowitz Horowitz, *Alma Mater: Design and Experience in the Women's Colleges from Their Nineteenth Century Beginnings to the 1930s* (New York, 1984).

102. *President's Report* (Columbia University, 1895), p. 45; *President's Report* (Columbia University, 1900), p. 68.

103. Nicholas Murray Butler to Seth Low, 21 September 1903, Seth Low Papers, Columbia University; *President's Report* (Columbia University, 1906), pp. 2–3.

104. John D. Rockefeller to president and trustees of the University of Chicago, 13 December 1910, quoted in John D. Rockefeller, Jr., to Mr. Ryerson, 20 February 1922, University Presidents' Papers; John Casper Branner, *One of Mrs. Stanford's Ideals* (Palo Alto, 1917), p. 5.

105. Hocking, "The Religious Function of State Universities," p. 464; Henry Pratt Judson, "Education and Social Progress" (n.d.; c. 1905–10), University Presidents' Papers. The emphasis on social ethics in universities was part of the broader interest in the social gospel. For more on the social gospel, see Charles Hopkins, *The Rise of the Social Gospel in American Protestantism, 1865–1915* (New Haven, 1940); and Henry F. May, *Protestant Churches in Industrial America* (New York, 1949).

106. Clyde W. Votow, "Religion in Public School Education," in *Religious Education Association, Proceedings of the Fifth Annual Convention* (Chicago, 1908), pp. 166–67; Charles W. Eliot, "What Unitarian Parents Can Teach Their Children" (Boston, 1904), p. 9.

107. Harper, "Bible Study and Religious Life," in *Religion and the Higher Life,* p. 169; Pritchett, *What Is Religion,* pp. 74–75.

108. F. N. Scott, "Christianity and the Newspaper," in *Religious Thought at the University of Michigan,* ed. Martin L. D'Ooge et al. (Ann Arbor, 1893), pp. 77–78; David Starr Jordan, *The Call of the Twentieth Century, An Address to Young Men* (Boston, 1903), pp. 72–73. This problem was not unique to the Christian modernism in universities. A common criticism of liberal Christianity in general was that it lost its distinctly Christian character and became too submerged in general culture. See Hutchison, *The Modernist Impulse,* chap. 6..

109. C. W. Eliot to Edwin A. Alderman, 8 August 1902, Eliot Papers; *President's Report* (University of Chicago, 1904–5), pp. 28–29.

110. "Chapel Assembly," *The University of Chicago Weekly* (1901): 742, clipping in University Presidents' Papers.

111. Ernest D. Burton to (F. T. Gates), 18 December 1892, University Presidents' Papers.

112. Despite money spent on chapel services at Harvard, officials in charge of religious services reported relative declines in student attendance at chapel services. See "Appleton Chapel and Phillips Brooks House," in *Annual Report of the President of Harvard University, 1907–08,* p. 227; "Aids to Moral and Religious Culture," in *University of Michigan Calendar, 1893–94,* p. 33; *University of Michigan Calendar, 1894–95,* p. 32; *University of Michigan Calendar, 1895–96,* p. 30; *President's Report, University of Michigan* (1890–91), p. 29. See also "The Problem of College Chapel," *Educational Review* 46 (1913): 177–87; *The Leland Stanford Junior University Register* (1900–1901), p. 157. The enrollment at Hopkins was 520 in 1896–97. "Report of the General Secretary of the YMCA, 1896–97," Gilman Papers; *The Johns Hopkins University Annual Report* (1897), p. 5. From the existing YMCA reports these figures seem typical. For example, in 1902–3, 15 students attended daily prayers on the average. "Report of the YMCA Secretary, 1902–3," Records of the Office of the President, Johns Hopkins University; "Annual Report of the YMCA at Columbia College, Feb. 15, 1895," CACU. Student enrollment at Columbia in 1894–95 was 1,943. *Annual Report of the President* (Columbia University, 1895), p. 3. In 1910–11, the "Religious Work Committee of the YMCA" tried to improve chapel attendance "at least one day a week." It invited prominent ministers and faculty to talk, asked fraternities to encourage their members to attend, and had the student newspaper publicize the meetings. These efforts resulted in some short-term improvements, but did not solve the attendance problem. "Report of the Religious Work Committee, 1910–11," CACU; Clifford Brown, general secretary of Earl Hall, to the International Committee of the YMCA, 23 April 1914, CACU.

113. William Rainey Harper, "Sixteenth Quarterly Address," pp. 382–83; Charles Henderson to W. R. Harper, 12 August 1896, University Presidents' Papers; Richard J. Storr, *Harper's University: The Beginnings* (Chicago, 1966), p. 187.

114. Arthur T. Hadley, "Inaugural Address" (New Haven, 1899), pp. 39–41; Arthur T. Hadley to O. R. Houston, 3 May 1904, and Hadley to Mrs. C. W. Com-

fort, 11 June 1909, Hadley Papers; C. H. Smith, "Faculty Participation in Student Religious Life," in *Two Centuries of Christian Activity*, p. 169. In the same volume, A. P. Stokes defended the requirement on devotional grounds (p. 119).

115. A. P. Stokes, "Present Condition of Religious Life at Yale," in *Two Centuries of Christian Activity*, p. 121; Smith, "Faculty Participation," p. 170; Brooks Mather Kelley, *Yale: A History* (New Haven, 1974), p. 387; Bradley J. Longfield, "'For God, for Country, and for Yale': Yale, Religion, and Higher Education between the World Wars," in *The Secularization of the Academy*, pp. 151–58..

116. Jerome D. Green to Mrs. Noble, 9 March 1906, Eliot Papers; Chaplain Knox, "Addresses by Dr. Harry Emerson Fosdick," *Columbia Alumni News* 8 (1916): 187; H. N. Sibley to H. E. Fosdick, 9 November 1920, CACU.

117. Henry Wright, "Recent Epochs of College Life," in *Two Centuries of Christian Activity*, p. 110.

118. C. Howard Hopkins, *History of the Y.M.C.A in North America* (New York, 1951), chap. 7; Charles W. Eliot to Reverend Addison Foster, 12 September 1902; and Charles W. Eliot to Arthur L. Thayer, 8 November 1907, Eliot Papers.

119. Howard J. Booth, *Edwin Diller Starbuck* (Washington, D.C., 1981), p. 68; *The Leland Stanford Junior University Register* (1891–92), p. 24; J. R. Mott to A. A. Stagg, 20 October 1892, University Presidents' Papers.

120. "The Organization of Religious Work in the University in the Year of 1892–3" (memo, n.d.), and Charles Henderson to F. T. Gates, 20 December 1892, University Presidents' Papers.

121. "The Organization of Religious Work," and Charles Henderson to William R. Harper, 18 May 1896, University Presidents' Papers.

122. A. O. Lovejoy to F. J. Goodnow, 11 March 1916, and Goodnow to Lovejoy, 11 March 1916, Presidents' Records.

123. Report of the Columbia University Christian Association (1913–14), and "Corrected Report of the Sub-Committee [on religious work]" (1916), CACU.

124. Clarence Prouty Shedd, *The Church Follows Its Students* (New Haven, 1938), p. 63.

Chapter Five

1. Mary Pickering, *Auguste Comte: An Intellectual Biography* (New York, 1993); Charles Cashdollar, *The Transformation of Theology, 1830–1890: Positivism and Protestant Thought in Britain and America* (Princeton, 1989); Richmond Laurin Hawkins, *Auguste Comte and the United States, 1816–1853* (Cambridge, 1936); and Hawkins, *Positivism in the United States, 1853–1861* (Cambridge, 1938).

2. Stow Persons, *Free Religion* (New Haven, 1947); Bernard Lightman, *The Origins of Agnosticism: Victorian Unbelief and the Limits of Knowledge* (Baltimore, 1987); James Turner, *Without God, Without Creed: The Origins of Unbelief* (Baltimore, 1985); Frank Smith, *Robert G. Ingersoll: A Life* (Buffalo, 1990).

3. Freeman quoted in Robert Church, "The Development of the Social Sciences as Academic Disciplines at Harvard, 1869–1900" (Ph.D. diss., Harvard University, 1965), p. 80. On Fiske, see also Milton Berman, *John Fiske: The Evolution of a Popularizer* (Cambridge, 1961), chap. 4.

4. William R. Hutchison, *The Modernist Impulse in American Protestantism* (Cambridge, 1976); Kenneth Cauthen, *The Impact of American Religious Liberalism* (New York, 1962); Claude Welch, *Protestant Thought in the Nineteenth Century,* 2 vols. (New Haven, 1985), vol. 2; Cashdollar, *Transformation of Theology,* chap. 10; A. D. Rogers, *John Merle Coulter: Missionary in Science* (Princeton, 1944); and David N. Livingstone, *Nathaniel Southgate Shaler and the Culture of American Science* (Tuscaloosa, 1987).

5. C. R. Mann, "Physics in the College Course," *Educational Review* 34 (1910): 480, 479..

6. Henry Pritchett, "The College of Freedom and the College of Discipline," *Atlantic Monthly* 102 (1908): 604.

7. Edward L. Nicholas, "Physical Science and Religious Citizenship," *Religious Education* 8 (1913): 425; David Hollinger, "Inquiry and Uplift: Late Nineteenth-Century American Academics and the Moral Efficacy of Scientific Practice," in *The Authority of Experts: Studies in History and Theory,* ed. Thomas Haskell (Bloomington, Ind., 1984), pp. 142–56; Hollinger, "Justification by Verification: The Scientific Challenge to the Moral Authority of Christianity in Modern America," in *Religion and Twentieth-Century American Intellectual Life,* ed. Michael J. Lacey (New York, 1989), pp. 116–35. Hollinger emphasizes the use of the scientific ethic as a challenge to religion. But there is evidence that the notion of the scientists as particularly moral predates the late nineteenth-century conflict between religion and science, and may be a holdover from the image of scientists as discoverers of God's works. See Keith R. Benson, "From Museum Research to Laboratory Research: The Transformation of Natural History into Academic Biology," in *The American Development of Biology,* ed. Ronald Rainger, Keith R. Benson, and Jane Maienschein (Philadelphia, 1988), p. 51. For other discussions of university reformers' association of science and ethics, see Daniel J. Kevles, *The Physicists: The History of a Scientific Community in Modern America* (New York, 1978), chap. 2; and John C. Burnham, *How Superstition Won and Science Lost: Popularizing Science and Health in the United States* (New Brunswick, N.J., 1987), pp. 22–23.

8. Jesse Macy, "The Scientific Spirit in Politics," *American Political Science Review* 11 (1917): 6; T. C. Chamberlin, "Programme of the Department of Geology" (May 1894), Thomas C. Chamberlin Papers, University of Chicago; Robert Kohler, "The Ph.D. Machine: Building on the Collegiate Base," *Isis* 81 (1990): 640; Larry Owens, "Pure and Sound Government: Laboratories, Playing Fields, and Gymnasia in the Nineteenth-Century Search for Order," *Isis* 76 (1985): 191–94.

9. Macy, "The Scientific Spirit in Politics," pp. 6–7; Randolph Bourne, "The College: An Undergraduate View," *Atlantic Monthly* 108 (1911): 673; Burnham, *How Superstition Won,* pp. 168–69.

10. Franklin H. Giddings, *The Principles of Sociology* (New York, 1896), p. 358; Robert A. Nisbet, *History of the Idea of Progress* (New York, 1980); T. J. Jackson Lears, *No Place of Grace: Anti-Modernism and the Transformation of American Culture, 1880–1920* (New York, 1981); Charles E. Rosenberg, "Science and Social Values in Nineteenth-Century America: A Case Study in the Growth of Scientific

Instititutions," in *Science and Values: Patterns of Tradition and Change,* ed. Arnold Thackray and Everett Mendelsohn (New York, 1974), pp. 21–42.

11. In the late nineteenth century, there was a debate about the value of "pure" versus applied science. The best known defense of "pure" science was Henry Rowland's address, "A Plea for Pure Science," *Popular Science Monthly* 24 (1883): 30–44. Rowland, however, did not deny or oppose the applicability of scientific knowledge to human problems. Rather, he protested limiting scientific research to those areas that promised immediate material profit. His position was not far from that of most university reformers, who used the terms *practical* and *applied* broadly to mean "public service." The failure to recognize the broad use of these terms has opened pragmatists and American intellectuals in general to the inaccurate charge of crass materialism. On the philosophy of science and liberal Christian thought, see chapters 2 and 3. On Rowland, and the issue of pure versus applied science, see Kevles, *The Physicists,* pp. 45–50. See also Richard A. Overfield, *Science with Practice: Charles E. Bessey and the Maturing of American Botany* (Ames, Iowa, 1993), especially chaps. 2 and 3..

12. *Annual Report of the President* (Johns Hopkins University, 1886), pp. 63–64; Edward Bellamy, *Looking Backward, 2000–1887* (Boston, 1888). On utopianism in the late nineteenth and early twentieth centuries, see Howard P. Segal, *Technological Utopianism in American Culture* (Chicago, 1985).

13. David Starr Jordan, *Leading Men of Science* (New York, 1910), p. 3; Giddings, *The Principles of Sociology,* p. 357; Rosenberg, "Science and Social Values," p. 26.

14. Kevles, *The Physicists,* chap. 5; Robert C. Bannister, *Sociology and Scientism: The American Quest for Objectivity, 1880–1940* (Chapel Hill, 1987); Thomas L. Haskell, *The Emergence of Professional Social Science: The American Social Science Association and the Nineteenth-Century Crisis of Authority* (Urbana, Ill., 1977).

15. Herbert Maule Richards, "Zoology," in *Columbia University Lectures on Science, Philosophy, and Art, 1907–1908* (New York, 1908), pp. 5–6; Samuel C. Mitchell, "Character and Culture: Should All Subjects of the College Curriculum Aim at Character Formation or at Scholarship?" *Religious Education* 5 (1910): 107; Robert J. Richards, *Darwin and the Emergence of Evolutionary Theories of Mind and Behavior* (Chicago, 1987); Paul F. Boller, Jr., *American Thought in Transition: The Impact of Evolutionary Naturalism, 1865–1900* (New York, 1981 [1969]); Cynthia Eagle Russet, *Darwin in America: The Intellectual Response, 1865–1912* (San Francisco, 1976); Richard Hofstadter, *Social Darwinism in American Thought,* rev. ed. (Boston, 1955); Robert C. Bannister, *Social Darwinism: Science and Myth in Anglo-American Social Thought* (Philadelphia, 1979); George W. Stocking, Jr., "Lamarckianism in American Social Science, 1890–1915," in *Race, Culture, and Evolution,* Phoenix ed. (Chicago, 1982), pp. 234–69; Carl N. Degler, *In Search of Human Nature: The Decline and Revival of Darwinism in American Thought* (New York, 1991).

16. T. C. Chamberlin, "The Teaching of Geology," in *College Teaching: Studies in Methods of Teaching in the College,* ed. Paul Klapper (New York, 1920), p. 144;

Gregg Mitman, *The State of Nature: Ecology, Community, and American Social Thought, 1900–1950* (Chicago, 1992); Andrew Kirby, "The Great Desert of the American Mind: Concepts of Space and Time and Their Historiographic Implications," in *The Estate of Social Knowledge,* ed. JoAnne Brown and David K. Van Keuren (Baltimore, 1991), pp. 23–43.

17. Albion Small to William Rainey Harper, 14 July 1892, William Rainey Harper Papers, University of Chicago; Albion Small, "The Province of Sociology" (manuscript), University Presidents' Papers, University of Chicago; Robert Flint, *Philosophy as Scientia Scientiarum and A History of Classifications of the Sciences* (London, 1904), pp. 328–38; Bannister, *Sociology and Scientism,* p. 36..

18. John S. Flagg, "Anthropology: A University Study," *Popular Science Monthly* 51 (1897): 510, 512; Roland B. Dixon, "Anthropology," in *The Development of Harvard University, since the Inauguration of President Eliot, 1869–1929,* ed. Samuel Eliot Morison (Cambridge, 1930), p. 203. Also see David K. Van Keuren, "From Natural History to Social Science: Disciplinary Development and Redefinition in British Anthropology, 1860–1910," in *The Social Estate of Knowledge,* pp. 45–66.

19. Richards, *Darwin and the Emergence of Evolutionary Theories;* Arthur T. Hadley, "Ethics as a Political Science" (1892–93), in *The Education of the American Citizen* (New York, 1901), pp. 105–6; Hadley, "The Influence of Charles Darwin upon Historical and Political Thought," *Psychological Review* 16 (1909): 143–51.

20. Clyde Votow, "Courses in Religion: Moral and Religious Instruction in the College," *Religious Education* 5 (1910): 298.

21. Ernest Gale Martin, "Memorandum on the Relationship of Physiology to the School of Biology," in *Annual Report of the President of Stanford University, 1922–23,* p. 13.

22. John Coulter, "Christianity and Science," pp. 8–9, John M. Coulter Papers, University of Chicago; George J. Fisher, "The Ethical Value of Physical Training," in *The Materials of Religious Education: Proceedings of the Fourth Annual Convention of the Religious Education Association* (Chicago, 1907), pp. 199–200; Coulter, "The Biological Background of Religious Education," (manuscript), pp. 12–13, Coulter Papers.

23. George Barton Cutten, "Moral Influences of the Curriculum," *Religious Education* 9 (1914): 527.

24. Edward McNall Burns, *David Starr Jordan: Prophet of Freedom* (Stanford, 1953); John C. Burnham, "New Perspectives on the Prohibition 'Experiment' of the 1920's," in *Paths into American Culture: Psychology, Medicine, and Morals* (Philadelphia, 1988), pp. 170–84; Charles Rosenberg and Carroll Smith Rosenberg, "Pietism and Social Action: Some Origins of the American Public Health Movement," in *No Other Gods: On Science and American Social Thought* (Baltimore, 1976), pp. 109–22.

25. John D'Emilio and Estelle Freedman, *Intimate Matters: A History of Sexuality in America* (New York, 1988), pp. 150–56, chap. 9; David J. Pivar, *Purity Crusade: Sexual Morality and Social Control, 1868–1900* (Westport, Conn., 1973); John C. Burnham, "Medical Inspection of Prostitutes in America in the Nineteenth Century: The St. Louis Experiment and Its Sequel" and "The Progressive

Era Revolution in American Attitudes toward Sex," in *Paths into American Culture,* pp. 138–49 and 150–69; Allan M. Brandt, *No Magic Bullet: A Social History of Venereal Disease in the United States since 1880* (New York, 1985), chap. 1.

26. Frederick J. E. Woodbridge, "The University and the Public," *Educational Review* 48 (1915): 121; Barbara Gutmann Rosenkrantz, *Public Health and the State: Changing Views in Massachusetts, 1842–1936* (Cambridge, 1972); Judith Walzer Leavitt, *The Healthiest City: Milwaukee and the Politics of Health Reform* (Princeton, 1982); Burnham, *How Superstition Won,* pp. 50–53, 61; W. Bruce Fye, "Growth of American Physiology, 1850–1900," in *Physiology in the American Context, 1850–1940,* ed. Gerald L. Geison (Bethesda, Md., 1987), pp. 57–58..

27. Charles W. Eliot, "Three Results of the Scientific Study of Nature; Speech Given at New York Museum, December 22, 1877" (manuscript), Charles W. Eliot Papers, Harvard University.

28. Loeb quoted in Philip Pauly, *Controlling Life: Jacques Loeb and the Engineering Ideal in Biology* (New York, 1987), pp. 139–40. On hereditarian views among social scientists, see works cited in note 15, above.

29. Douglas Sloan, "The Teaching of Ethics in the American Undergraduate Curriculum, 1876–1976," in *Ethics Teaching in Higher Education,* ed. Daniel Callahan and Sissela Bok (New York, 1980), pp. 8–13; Gladys Bryson, "Sociology Considered as Moral Philosophy," *Sociological Review* 24 (1932): 26–36; Bryson, "The Comparable Interests of the Old Moral Philosophy and the Modern Social Sciences," *Social Forces* 11 (1932): 19–27; Bryson, "The Emergence of the Social Sciences from Moral Philosophy," *International Journal of Ethics* 42 (1932): 304–23; Jurgen Herbst, "From Moral Philosophy to Sociology: Albion Woodbury Small," *Harvard Educational Review* 29 (1959): 117–32.

30. Dorothy Ross, "The Development of the Social Sciences," in *The Organization of Knowledge in Modern America, 1860–1920,* ed. Alexandra Oleson and John Voss (Baltimore, 1979), pp. 109–10; and Ross, *The Origins of American Social Science* (New York, 1991); Haskell, *The Emergence of Professional Social Science;* Mary O. Furner, *Advocacy and Objectivity: A Crisis in the Professionalization of American Social Science, 1865–1905* (Lexington, Ky., 1975), chap. 1; L. L. Bernard and Jessie Bernard, *Origins of American Sociology* (New York, 1943), part 8.

31. On ties to religion, see Susan E. Henking, "Protestant Religious Experience and the Rise of American Sociology: Evidence from the Bernard Papers," *Journal of the History of the Behavioral Sciences* 28 (1992): 325–39.

32. David M. Ricci, *The Tragedy of Political Science: Politics, Scholarship, and Democracy* (New Haven, 1984), p. 65; Raymond J. Cunningham, "'Scientia Pro Patria': Herbert Baxter Adams and Mugwump Academic Reform at Johns Hopkins, 1876–1901," *Prospects* 15 (1990): 109–44; Thomas Bender, "E. R. A. Seligman and the Vocation of Social Science," in *Intellect and Public Life: Essays on the Social History of Academic Intellectuals in the United States* (Baltimore, 1993), pp. 49–77; Barry D. Karl, *Charles E. Merriam and the Study of Politics* (Chicago, 1974); Steven J. Diner, *A City and Its Universities: Public Policy in Chicago, 1892–1919* (Chapel Hill, 1980).

33. For examples of the assumption that objectivity always meant "value-free"

and of the view that disputes between social scientists divided into camps of "advocacy" versus "objectivity," see Furner, *Advocacy and Objectivity;* Peter Novick, *The Noble Dream: The 'Objectivity Question' and the American Historical Profession* (New York, 1988). Biologists have not been presented in the same way. I think this is because, ever since the 1920s, biologists have not been significantly divided over this issue. They have successfully presented themselves as "objective" even after this term came to mean "value-free." Hence, historians are not tempted to read this debate back into the pre–1920 period. Social scientists, on the other hand, have vigorously debated the issue of value-neutrality since World War I..

34. For the following discussion of the history of economics, I draw on Ross, *The Origins of American Social Science;* Furner, *Advocacy and Objectivity;* Paul Bernard, "The Making of the Marginal Mind" (Ph.D. Diss., University of Michigan, 1990); William J. Barber, ed., *Breaking the Academic Mould: Economists and American Higher Learning in the Nineteenth Century* (Middletown, Conn., 1988); and Jurgen Herbst, *The German Historical School in American Scholarship: A Study in the Transfer of Culture* (Ithaca, N. Y., 1965).

35. William Graham Sumner, "What Makes the Rich Richer and the Poor Poorer?" (1887), in *The Challenge of Facts and Other Essays,* ed. Albert Galloway Keller (New Haven, 1914), p. 75.

36. John Stuart Mill, *A System of Logic Ratiocinative and Inductive; Being a Connected View of the Principles of Evidence and the Methods of Scientific Investigation* (1843), in *Collected Works of John Stuart Mill,* ed. J. M. Robson, 32 vols. (Toronto, 1963–91), 8:878.

37. Ibid., 8:876, 943.

38. William Graham Sumner, "Sociology" (1881), in *War and Other Essays,* ed. Albert Galloway Keller (New Haven, 1911), p. 191.

39. Richard T. Ely, "Ethics and Economics," *Science* n. s. 7 (1886): 530.

40. Richard Mayo-Smith, "Methods of Investigation in Political Economy," *Science* n. s. suppl. 8 (1886): 84.

41. Ibid.; Henry Carter Adams, "Another View of Economic Laws and Methods," *Science* n. s. suppl. 8 (1886): 104.

42. Henry Carter Adams, "Economics and Jurisprudence," *Science* n. s. suppl. 8 (1886): 17.

43. Ely, "Ethics and Economics," p. 531. On the religious background of the historical economists, see Ross, *The Origins of American Social Science,* pp. 101–3. Many of the first generation of social scientists were active in the social gospel movement.

44. Simon Newcomb, "Can Economists Agree upon the Basis of Their Teachings?" *Science* n. s. 8 (1886): 25; Newcomb, "Aspects of the Economic Discussion," *Science* n. s. 7 (1886): 541. See also Sumner, "Sociology," pp. 168–72, 191–92; Arthur T. Hadley, "Economic Law and Methods," *Science* n. s. 8 (1886): 47.

45. Newcomb, "Aspects of the Economic Discussion," p. 540.

46. Mayo-Smith, "Methods of Investigation in Political Economy," pp. 81, 82.

47. Ibid., p. 86.

48. Edward Bemis to J. L. Laughlin, 27 February 1892, Harper Papers.

49. Karl Pearson, *The Grammar of Science* (Gloucester, Mass., 1969 [1892, 1900, 1911]), pp. 86–87.

50. Ibid., pp. 13, 9 (emphasis in original). On Dunbar, see Church, "The Development of the Social Sciences," pp. 130–34. Hadley, influenced by Sumner's evolutionism, was more comfortable with the language of evolutionary science and even in 1886 spoke in terms of proposing and verifying hypotheses. Hadley, "Economic Laws and Methods," p. 47..

51. Ross, *The Origins of American Social Science,* pp. 157, 327.

52. Margaret Schabas, *A World Ruled by Number: William Stanley Jevons and the Rise of Mathematical Economics* (New York, 1990); Schabas, "Mathematics and the Economics Profession in Late Victorian England," in *The Estate of Social Knowledge,* pp. 67–83; Bernard, "The Making of the Marginal Mind," chaps. 5, 6; Ross, *The Origins of American Social Science,* pp. 118–22, 172–86.

53. Edward Bemis to William Rainey Harper, 21 February 1892, Harper Papers; Irving Fisher to Arthur T. Hadley, 21 December 1908, Arthur Twining Hadley Papers, Yale University Archives; Ross, *The Origins of American Social Science,* pp. 193–94.

54. Frank J. Goodnow, "The Work of the American Political Science Association" (1904), in *Readings in Political Science,* ed. Raymond Garfield Gettell (Boston, 1911), p. 3; Henry Jones Ford, "Present Tendencies in American Politics," *American Political Science Review* 14 (1920): 5.

55. Westel Woodbury Willoughby, "The Individual and the State," *American Political Science Review* 8 (1914): 2; Macy, "The Scientific Spirit in Politics," p. 7; A. Lawrence Lowell, "The Physiology of Politics," *American Political Science Review* 4 (1910): 14.

56. James Bryce, "The Relation of Political Science to History and Practice," *American Political Science Review* 3 (1909): 18.

57. Charles A. Beard, "The Study and Teaching of Politics," *Columbia University Quarterly* 12 (1910): 270; Lowell, "The Physiology of Politics," p. 3.

58. Macy, "The Scientific Spirit in Politics," p. 9; Lowell, "The Physiology of Politics," p. 14; Albert Shaw, "Presidential Address," *American Political Science Review* 1 (1907): 186.

59. Albion Small, "The Era of Sociology," *American Journal of Sociology* 1 (1895): 6–7; Giddings, *The Principles of Sociology,* p. 351.

60. Giddings, *The Principles of Sociology,* pp. 351–52; Albion Small, "The Significance of Sociology for Ethics," *Decennial Publications of the University of Chicago* 4 (1903): 119.

61. C. H. Cooley, "A Primary Culture for Democracy," *Michigan Alumnus* 25 (1919): 293.

62. John M. O'Donnell, *The Origins of Behaviorism: American Psychology, 1870–1920* (New York, 1985), p. 7; Jill G. Morawski, "Assessing Psychology's Moral Heritage through Our Neglected Utopias," *American Psychologist* 37 (1982): 1082–95.

63. Clyde W. Barrows, *Universities and the Capitalist State: Corporate Liberalism and the Reconstruction of American Higher Education, 1894–1928* (Madison, Wis.,

1990), pp. 44–50; Margaret W. Rossiter, "Philanthropy, Structure, and Personality: or, The Interplay of Outside Money and Inside Influence," in *Science at Harvard University: Historical Perspectives,* ed. Clark A. Elliott and Margaret Rossiter (Bethlehem, Pa., 1992), pp. 13–27..

64. D.C. Gilman, *The Benefits Which Society Derives from Universities* (Baltimore, 1885), pp. 19–21. On the Johns Hopkins biology program, see Jane Maienschein, *Transforming Traditions in American Biology, 1880–1915* (Baltimore, 1991). On the development of academic biology, also see Philip Pauly, "The Appearance of Academic Biology in Late Nineteenth-Century America," *Journal of the History of Biology* 17 (1984): 396–97; Jane Maienschein, "Whitman at Chicago, Establishing a Chicago Style of Biology?" in *The American Development of Biology,* pp. 151–84; Benson, "From Museum Research to Laboratory Research," in *The American Development of Biology,* pp. 49–86; Fye, "Growth of American Physiology, 1850–1900"; and Alejandra C. Laszlo, "Physiology of the Future: Institutional Styles at Columbia and Harvard," in *Physiology in the American Context, 1850–1940,* pp. 67–96. Although I think that biology's perceived tie to medicine increased the resources devoted to biology in the university, I am not arguing that university administrators accurately assessed biology's relationship to medicine. This is a subject of dispute among historians of science. For a guide to literature on the relationship between medicine and biology, see John Harley Warner, "Science in Medicine," in *Historical Writing on American Science: Perspectives and Prospects,* ed. Sally Gregory Kohlstedt and Margaret W. Rossiter (Baltimore, 1985).

65. T. W. Galloway, "The Teaching of Biology," in *College Teaching,* p. 86.

66. Alan W. C. Menzies, "General Hygiene as a Required College Course," *Science* n. s. 35 (1912): 609.

67. G. Stanley Hall, "Relation of the Church to Education," *Pedagogical Seminary* 15 (1908): 193–94; Alfred Worcester to the Committee on Instruction, 20 January 1927, in "Minutes and Committee Reports, 1903–1943" (Harvard University, Faculty of the Arts and Sciences, Committee on Instruction); *Annual Report of the President of Harvard University, 1918–1919,* pp. 240–41; Burton Bledstein, *The Culture of Professionalism: The Middle Class and the Development of Higher Education in America* (New York, 1976), pp. 152–57; Sloan, "Teaching of Ethics," p. 25; *University of Chicago, Annual Register* (1901–2), pp. 154, 219, 326; *University of Michigan Calendar, 1901–02,* pp. 102–3; *Yale University Catalogue* (1901–2), p. 162; *Register* (University of California, 1902–3), p. 272; *Catalogue, 1901–02* (Columbia University), p. 152; *Catalogue, 1901–02* (Harvard University), p. 404; *The Leland Stanford Junior University Register* (1901–2), pp. 104, 150; *President's Report, University of Michigan* (1920–21), p. 44; *Report of the President of Yale University, 1920–1921,* p. 373; *President's Report* (University of Chicago, 1920–21), p. 49.

68. Daniel J. Kevles, *In the Name of Eugenics: Genetics and the Uses of Human Heredity* (Berkeley, 1985), p. 69.

69. A. D. White to Johns Hopkins University trustees, 13 March 1874, Daniel Coit Gilman Papers, Johns Hopkins University.

70. H. B. Adams to W. R. Harper, 1 May 1891, Harper Papers; Cunningham,

"Scientia Pro Patria," pp. 115, 118; D.C. Gilman, "Commemorative Address," *Science* n. s. 15 (1902): 326. Gilman, however, rejected a proposed merger of the ASSA with Johns Hopkins University because he thought the university should not assume the association's role as agitator for social reform. Nonetheless, he thought the university should sponsor research related to social problems and should cooperate with the ASSA and other reform groups. See Daniel Coit Gilman to F. A. Sanborn, 27 November 1878; "Mr. Gilman's Social Remedies" (typescript, 30 October 1893); Gilman, "Address to JHU Alumni" (typescript, 1894); all in Gilman Papers. See also Haskell, *The Emergence of Professional Social Science,* chap. 7..

71. Gilman, "Address to JHU Alumni," Gilman Papers; D.C. Gilman, "Present Aspects of College Training," *North American Review* 136 (1883): 536. Gilman had reservations about Ely because of Simon Newcomb's opposition to him and perhaps also because of Ely's radicalism. On Ely's position at Hopkins, see William J. Barber, "Political Economy in the Flagship of Postgraduate Studies: The Johns Hopkins University," in *Breaking the Academic Mould,* pp. 210–23. Sociology, though supported by Gilman, did not become an important department at Johns Hopkins during the early twentieth century. See Luther L. Bernard, "The Teaching of Sociology in the United States," *American Journal of Sociology* 15 (1909): 183.

72. F. A. P. Barnard, "Annual Report, 1882," in *The Rise of the University, Volume One: The Later Days of Columbia College; Selections from the Annual Reports of Frederick A. P. Barnard, President of Columbia College,* ed. William F. Russell and Edward C. Elliott (New York, 1937), p. 358; Ralph Gordon Hoxie et al., *A History of the Faculty of Political Science, Columbia University* (New York, 1955), p. 29. See also F. A. P. Barnard, *Annual Report of the President* (Columbia College, 1877), pp. 18–19.

73. Anna Haddow, *Political Science in American Colleges and Universities, 1636–1900* (New York, 1939), pp. 206–7.

74. Frank L. Tolman, "The Study of Sociology in Institutions of Higher Learning in the United States," parts 1–4, *American Journal of Sociology* 7–8 (1902): 809–26, 90–101, 104–6, 108–10, 115–20, 263–64, 268, 534–36. See also Bernard, "The Teaching of Sociology in the United States"; *Register* (University of California, 1907–9), p. 237; Benjamin Ide Wheeler, "The Place of the State University in American Education," *School and Society* 7 (30 March 1918): 362.

75. *University of Michigan Calendar, 1900–01,* political science courses 5 and 22.

76. On Carver's activism, see Abbot Lawrence Lowell Presidential Papers, Harvard University. Eliot invited Thorstein Veblen to lecture in Carver's course on methods of social reform. Charles W. Eliot to Thorstein Veblen, 13 November 1905, Eliot Papers. Under these conditions, even the conservative Dunbar recognized the importance of contemporary social and political concerns in the development of academic social science. Charles Franklin Dunbar, "The Academic Study of Political Economy," *Quarterly Journal of Economics* 5 (1891): 398–99.

77. *Annual Report of the President* (Columbia University, 1902), pp. 56–57. On Adler, see Horace L. Freiss, *Felix Adler and Ethical Culture,* ed. Fannia Weingartner (New York, 1981).

78. Orrin Leslie Elliot, *Stanford University: The First Twenty-five Years* (Stanford, 1937), pp. 117–18; *Annual Report of the President of Stanford University, 1923–24*, pp. 131–32; Bernard, "The Teaching of Sociology," p. 187..

79. Eliot quoted in Lawrence T. Nichols, "The Establishment of Sociology at Harvard: A Case of Organizational Ambivalence and Scientific Vulnerability," in *Science at Harvard University*, p. 194. On Eliot's support for social ethics, see Charles W. Eliot to Alfred T. White, 14 May 1905, Eliot Papers. Also see Church, "The Development of the Social Sciences," p. 33 and passim; Byrd L. Jones, "A Quest for National Leadership: Institutionalization of Economics at Harvard," in *Breaking the Academic Mould*, pp. 95–131; and Paul Buck, ed., *Social Sciences at Harvard, 1860–1920* (Cambridge, 1965).

80. Arthur T. Hadley, "Ethics as a Political Science," p. 100; Irving Fisher to Hadley, 17 May 1904, Hadley Papers; David B. Potts, "Social Ethics at Harvard, 1881–1931: A Study in Academic Activism," in *Social Sciences at Harvard*, pp. 203–24.

81. Ernest H. Wilkins, "Initiatory Courses for Freshmen: Report by Committee G, on Increasing the Intellectual Interest and Raising Intellectual Standards of Undergraduates," *Bulletin of the American Association of University Professors* 8 (1922): 29.

82. *Annual Report of the President of Harvard University, 1922–23*, p. 7; Ernest Gale Martin, "Memorandum on the Relationship of Physiology to the School of Biology," in *Annual Report of the President of Stanford University, 1922–23*, p. 13.

83. *Annual Report of the President of Stanford University, 1922–23*, pp. 19–20.

84. *Annual Report of the President of Stanford University, 1923–24*, p. 128; *Annual Report of the President of Stanford University, 1922–23*, pp. 5–6; *Annual Report of the President of Stanford University, 1924–25*, pp. 165–66; *Annual Report of the President of Stanford University, 1927–28*, pp. 234–35.

85. Roswell Parker Angier, "The Organization of Freshman Year," *Association of American Universities, Proceedings of the Annual Conference* 23 (1921): 75–76. Mr. Robertson reported on the University of Chicago's efforts at general education in *President's Report* (University of Chicago, 1924–25), pp. 21–22; Russell Thomas, *A Search for a Common Learning: General Education, 1800–1960* (New York, 1962), p. 76; Chauncy S. Boucher, "Progressive Developments in the College," *University of Chicago Magazine* 22 (1930): 184–85.

86. Ernest H. Wilkins (dean of the Colleges of Arts, Literature, and Science), "Report," in *President's Report* (University of Chicago, 1924–25), pp. 21–22.

87. Wilkins, "Initiatory Courses," pp. 18–20; Donald G. Paterson, "Evaluation of Orientation Course at University of Minnesota," *Educational Record* 8 (1927): 99. See also American Economics Association, "Round Table Conference on the Teaching of Elementary Economics," *American Economic Review Supplement* 12 (1922): 182–83; and Gregg Mitman, "Evolution as Gospel: William Patten, the Language of Democracy, and the Great War," *Isis* 81 (1990): 457.

88. H. Hawkes, in Angier, "The Organization of Freshman Year," p. 74; Wilkins, "Initiatory Courses," p. 14; Herbert Hawkes, "Curriculum Revision at Columbia College," *Educational Record* 10 (1929): 34–35. Columbia's "Introduction to Con-

temporary Civilization" course is often misrepresented as primarily a "Western Civilization" history course or a "great books" literature/philosophy course. It was, in fact, more of a social science and contemporary events course. Columbia did develop an introductory history course, aimed at explaining the development of modern "European civilization," but "Introduction to Contemporary Civilization" was more concerned with the nature of human society and political and social reform. Compare Wilkins, "Initiatory Courses," with Carlton H. Hayes, "History in the College Course," *Educational Review* 41 (1911): 224–27. Columbia also developed a "great books" course at the same time as it introduced "Introduction to Contemporary Civilization." This two-year program was Columbia's general honors course. Unlike "Introduction," it was elective. See John Erksine, "General Honors at Columbia" (education suppl.), *New Republic* 32 (25 October 1922): 13. General honors was discontinued in 1929 and replaced with departmental honors. In 1937 "Introduction to Contemporary Civilization" was redesigned and made more like a great books course. See Gilbert Allardyce, "The Rise and Fall of the Western Civilization Course," *American Historical Review* 87 (1982): 695–725, for an example of an author who treats "Introduction to Contemporary Civilization" primarily as a history class..

89. Wilkins, "Initiatory Courses," pp. 10–12, 25–28; Clayton C. Hall, "Statesmanship and the Universities," *Forum* 48 (1912): 712.

90. Samuel P. Capen, "The New Task of the Colleges," *School and Society* 12 (1920): 151–52. There was some disagreement about the new emphasis on the importance of the social sciences. The biggest opposition came from humanists (see chapter 7). Another group of faculty, emphasizing the ideal of scientific mental training, wanted formal instruction in methods of scientific inquiry. The AAUP committee investigating orientation courses in 1922, for example, favored the orientation course established at Johns Hopkins, "Introduction to College Work." This class was designed to help students acquire the proper habits of intellectual inquiry, "habits of definiteness in ideas and accuracy in statement, a sense of the difference between the plausible and the proved, an appreciation of the contrast between the patient, critical and circumspect methods of genuine science and the casual observation and hasty generalization of the untrained mind." The Hopkins course reflected the values of the earlier university reformers: the purpose of higher education was to train students to think scientifically. The difference between the recommendations of the AAUP and the policies of the universities reflected the differences between the first wave of university reform and the newer changes aimed at strengthening the college (see chapter 8). Advocates of the second wave of reform did not reject the ideal of scientific mental training. Most of the schools surveyed stated that a secondary goal of their orientation course was to train students "in thinking." Also, University of Chicago and Columbia University, both influenced by Dewey, introduced elective courses in "reflective thinking." But this was not the main goal of the new curricular reforms. These aimed to restore some of the lost unity to the college education and to provide more tangible character education. By the time the AAUP issued its report, the dominant discussion was not over the best form of mental discipline, but over what subjects could provide

unity and moral direction. The notion that colleges should teach students to think independently was generally taken for granted. Wilkins, "Initiatory Courses," pp. 20, 29. Bruce Kimball, *Orators and Philosophers: A History of the Idea of Liberal Education* (New York, 1986), pp. 182–83, argues that even the most forceful advocates of a "traditional" liberal arts education in the twentieth century really accepted the model of free inquiry..

91. Roger L. Geiger argues that the social sciences' pattern of professionalization and acceptance into the university inverted that of the natural sciences: it preceded rather than followed intellectual developments. See Roger L. Geiger, *To Advance Knowledge: The Growth of American Research Universities, 1900–1940* (New York, 1986), pp. 27–29, 149–60.

92. David Starr Jordan, "Standeth God within the Shadow" (New York, 1901), p. 8; Jordan, "The Ethics of Dust" (Richmond, Ind., 1888), p. 17.

93. David Starr Jordan, "The Foundation Ideals of Stanford University" (Stanford, 1915), p. 20; letters to the director of the Liberal Congress of Religion are in the David Starr Jordan Papers, Stanford University.

94. David Starr Jordan, "The Hopes of Japan," in *The Voice of the Scholar; With Other Addresses on the Problems of Higher Education* (San Francisco, 1903), p. 272. Jordan's biographer reported that "he once told a student gathering that if he was not brought up in the Christian faith, he would have chosen to be a follower of Shintoism" (Burns, *David Starr Jordan,* p. 183). Jordan's description of Shintoism should not be taken as accurate.

95. *The Leland Stanford Junior University Register* (1891–92), p. 52.

96. *The Leland Stanford Junior University Register* (1892–93), pp. 60–61.

97. *The Leland Stanford Junior University Register* (1895–96), p. 72.

98. *The Leland Stanford Junior University Register* (1897–98), pp. 71–72.

99. Elliot, *Stanford University,* p. 117; David Starr Jordan, *The Days of a Man: Being Memories of a Naturalist, Teacher, and Minor Prophet of Democracy,* 2 vols. (Yonkers-on-Hudson, N. Y., 1922), 1:407–8; and Jordan, *The Religion of a Sensible American* (Boston, 1909).

100. William James, *The Varieties of Religious Experience* (Cambridge, 1985 [1902]), p. 81.

101. *The Aims of Religious Education: The Religious Education Association Proceedings of the Third Annual Convention* (Chicago, 1905), pp. 40, 43; Coulter, "The Biological Background of Religious Education," pp. 10–11.

102. T. C. Chamberlin, "The Ethical Nature of True Scientific Study: Dedication of Stephenson Hall of Science, Lawrence University, June 20, 1899," Chamberlin Papers.

103. See, for example, Coulter, "The Biological Background of Religious Education."

104. Albion Small quoted in Vernon K. Dibble, *The Legacy of Albion Small* (Chicago, 1975), pp. 239–40.

105. *The University of Chicago, Annual Register* (1892–93), p. 50; Small, "The Significance of Sociology for Ethics."

106. Small quoted in Dibble, *The Legacy,* pp. 61–62.

107. On late nineteenth-century philosophy, see chapter 4. Also see Guy W. Stroh, *American Ethical Thought* (Chicago, 1979), chap. 5; Herbert W. Schneider, *A History of American Philosophy,* 2nd ed. (New York, 1963), chap. 7; Bruce Kuklick, *Josiah Royce: An Intellectual Biography* (Indianapolis, 1985); Kuklick, *The Rise of American Philosophy: Cambridge, Massachusetts, 1860–1930* (New Haven, 1977), chap. 26; Elizabeth Flower and Murray G. Murphey, *A History of Philosophy in America,* 2 vols. (New York, 1977), 2:chaps. 8, 12. John Herman Randall, Jr. "The Department of Philosophy," in *A History of the Faculty of Philosophy, Columbia University* (New York, 1957), p. 114, discusses idealism and its ties to religion..

108. Sloan, "The Teaching of Ethics," p. 22; John Dewey and James Tufts, *Ethics,* in *The Middle Works of John Dewey, 1899–1924,* ed. Jo Ann Boydston et al., 15 vols. (Carbondale, Ill., 1978), 5:181–83. On Dewey's moral philosophy, see Steven C. Rockefeller, *John Dewey: Religious Faith and Democratic Humanism* (New York, 1991), chap. 9; Stroh, *American Ethical Thought,* chaps. 4, 6.

109. Dewey and Tufts, *Ethics,* p. 8.

110. Mitchell, "Character and Culture," pp. 105–6.

Chapter Six

1. Robert Flint, *Philosophy as Scientia Scientiarum and A History of Classifications of the Sciences* (London, 1904), p. 4; Hugo Münsterberg, "The Scientific Plan of the Congress," in *Congress of Arts and Science: Universal Exposition, St. Louis, 1904,* ed. Howard J. Rogers, 8 vols. (Boston, 1905–7), 1:92.

2. "Universal Exposition at Saint Louis 1904—Congress of Arts and Science" (published pamphlet, n.d.), Charles W. Eliot Papers, Harvard University. On the congress, see George Haines and Frederick Jackson, "A Neglected Landmark in the History of Ideas," *Mississippi Valley Historical Review* 34 (1947–48): 201–26; A. W. Coats, "American Scholarship Comes of Age: The Louisiana Purchase Exposition 1904," *Journal of the History of Ideas* 22 (1961): 404–17; Matthew Hale, Jr., *Human Science and Social Order: Hugo Münsterberg and the Origins of Applied Psychology* (Philadelphia, 1980), pp. 93–97.

3. Albion Small to William Rainey Harper, 24 January 1903, and Harper to N. M. Butler, 3 January 1903, University Presidents' Papers, University of Chicago.

4. John Dewey, letter to the editor, *Science* n. s. 18 (1903): 276–77.

5. Münsterberg, "The Scientific Plan," p. 97; Hugo Münsterberg, letter to the editor, *Science* n. s. 18 (1903): 561.

6. Münsterberg, "The Scientific Plan," pp. 128, 130; Frank W. Blackmar, "Sociology," in *Congress of Arts and Science,* 5:786. On James's view of the congress, see Haines and Jackson, "Neglected Landmark," p. 212; and Bruce Kuklick, *The Rise of American Philosophy* (New Haven, 1977), p. 209.

7. *Annual Report of the President* (Columbia University, 1908), pp. 17–18; Columbia University, *Lectures on Science, Philosophy, and Art, 1907–1908* (New York, 1908).

8. Dixon Ryan Fox, ed. and introd., *A Quarter Century of Learning, 1904–1929* (New York, 1931), p. 2.

9. Rexford G. Tugwell, "Experimental Economics," in *The Trend of Economics,* ed. Rexford G. Tugwell (New York, 1924), p. 394.

10. William Coleman, *Biology in the Nineteenth Century: Problems of Form, Function, and Transformation* (New York, 1971), chap. 7; Garland Allen, *Life Science in the Twentieth Century* (New York, 1978 [1975]), pp. xv–xxiii, chap. 1; Garland Allen, "The Transformation of a Science: T. H. Morgan and the Emergence of a New American Biology," in *The Organization of Knowledge in Modern America, 1860–1920,* ed. Alexandra Oleson and John Voss (Baltimore, 1979), pp. 174–75; Jane Maienschein, *Transforming Traditions in American Biology, 1880–1915* (Baltimore, 1991); Sharon E. Kingsland, "The Battling Botanist: Daniel Trembly MacDougal, Mutation Theory, and the Rise of Experimental Evolutionary Biology in America, 1900–1912," *Isis* 82 (1991): 479–509..

11. Raymond Pearl, "Trends in Modern Biology," *Science* n. s. 56 (1922): 584; Edmund B. Wilson, "Biology," in *A Quarter Century of Learning, 1904–1929,* p. 256; Philip Pauly, *Controlling Life: Jacques Loeb and the Engineering Ideal in Biology* (New York, 1987), pp. 73–75; Allen, "The Transformation of a Science," p. 179; and Allen, *Thomas Hunt Morgan: The Man and His Science* (Princeton, 1978), pp. 35–46.

12. Ralph S. Lillie, "The Philosophy of Biology: Vitalism Versus Mechanism," *Science* n. s. 40 (1914): 844; Wilson, "Biology," p. 259. J. S. Haldane was one of the few leading biologists who advocated the opposite, "vitalist" position. See, for example, J. S. Haldane, "The New Physiology," *Science* n. s. 44 (1916): 619–31.

13. Edmund Wilson, "Biology," in Columbia University, *Lectures on Science,* p. 5; Francis Carter Wood, "Research Institutes and Their Value," *Science* n. s. 55 (1922): 657–60; Alan Cruetz, "From College Teacher to University Scholar: The Evolution and Professionalization of Academics at the University of Michigan" (Ph.D. diss., University of Michigan, 1981), pp. 252–73; Hamilton Cravens, "The Role of Universities in the Rise of Experimental Biology," *Science Teacher* 44 (1977): 33–37.

14. A. N. Whitehead, "The Organization of Thought," *Science* n. s. 44 (1916): 409; F. W. Clarke, "The Interrelations of Pure and Applied Chemistry," *Science* n. s. 43 (1916): 258.

15. Edmund B. Wilson, "Science and a Liberal Education," *Science* n. s. 42 (1915): 626. See Edwin G. Conklin, "Biology and Human Life," *Science* n. s. 68 (1928): 463–69, for an example of a public discussion of biology that emphasizes social and moral value. For discussion of personal motives of biologists in the 1920s and 1930s, see Ronald Rainger, "Introduction," in *The Expansion of American Biology,* ed. Ronald Rainger et al. (New Brunswick, N.J., 1991); and Gregg Mitman, *The State of Nature: Ecology, Community, and American Social Thought, 1900–1950* (Chicago, 1992).

16. Mary O. Furner, *Advocacy and Objectivity: A Crisis in the Professionalization of the American Social Sciences, 1865–1905* (Lexington, Ky., 1975), pp. 278–312. During the late nineteenth century the institutional practices of universities encouraged ambitious faculty to form separate disciplines. Before departmental structure was formalized in the twentieth century, universities often considered

each full professor as the head of his department. Therefore, when a president promoted or hired a new full professor, he formed a new department. In this context, faculty who defined their subjects as distinct and separate from existing studies gained promotion more easily. Creutz, "From College Teacher," pp. 190–91; Charles Camic and Yu Xie, "The Statistical Turn in American Social Science: Columbia University, 1890–1915," *American Sociological Review* 59 (1994): 773–805. For information about social scientists' turn to "scientism" beginning in the 1910s and becoming dominant in the 1920s, see Edward A. Purcell, *The Crisis of Democratic Theory: Scientific Naturalism and the Problem of Value* (Lexington, Ky., 1973), chaps. 1–3; Dorothy Ross, "Social Science and the Idea of Progress," in *The Authority of Experts*, ed. Thomas L. Haskell (Bloomington, Ind., 1984), pp. 165–70; and Ross, "The Development of the Social Sciences," in *The Organization of Knowledge*, pp. 125–30; Douglas Sloan, "The Teaching of Ethics in the American Undergraduate Curriculum, 1876–1976," in *Ethics Teaching in Higher Education*, ed. Daniel Callahan and Sissela Bok (New York, 1980), pp. 14–19; Robert C. Bannister, *Sociology and Scientism: The American Quest for Objectivity, 1880–1940* (Chapel Hill, 1987); John M. O'Donnell, *The Origins of Behaviorism, American Psychology, 1870–1920* (New York, 1985); Albert Somit and Joseph Tanenhaus, *The Development of American Political Science: From Burgess to Behaviorism* (New York, 1982 [1967]), parts 2 and 3; George W. Stocking, Jr., "The Scientific Reaction against Cultural Anthropology, 1917–1920," in *Race, Culture, and Evolution*, Phoenix ed. (Chicago, 1982), pp. 270–307..

17. Albion Small to William Rainey Harper, 24 January 1903, University Presidents' Papers; Charles A. Ellwood, "How History Can Be Taught from a Sociological View," *Education* 30 (1909–10): 300.

18. Franklin Giddings, "Sociology as a University Study," *Political Science Quarterly* 6 (1891): 636–37; Henrika Kuklick, "Boundary Maintenance in American Sociology: Limitations to Academic 'Professionalization'," *Journal of the History of the Behavioral Sciences* 16 (1980): 201–16.

19. Robert F. Hoxie, "Sociology and Other Sciences," *American Journal of Sociology* 12 (1907): 751–53 (emphasis in original).

20. Jessie Bernard, "The History and Prospects of Sociology in the United States," in *Trends in American Sociology*, ed. George Lundberg et al. (New York, 1929), pp. 47–48.

21. Wesley C. Mitchell, "Economics," in *A Quarter Century of Learning, 1904–1929*, pp. 40, 56–57.

22. Charles E. Merriam, "Progress in Political Research," *American Political Science Review* 20 (1926): 8.

23. F. Stuart Chapin, "The Elements of Scientific Method in Sociology," *American Journal of Sociology* 20 (1914): 371.

24. Read Bain, "Trends in American Sociological Theory," in *Trends in American Sociology*, p. 106. For an important discussion of social scientists who resisted the turn to objectivism, see Mark C. Smith, *Social Science in the Crucible: The American Debate over Objectivity and Purpose, 1918–1941* (Durham, N. C., 1994).

25. Stuart A. Rice, *Quantitative Methods in Politics* (New York, 1969 [1928]),

pp. 3–4; JoAnne Brown, "Mental Measurements and the Rhetorical Force of Numbers," in *The Estate of Social Knowledge,* ed. JoAnne Brown and David K. Van Keuren (Baltimore, 1991), p. 137.

26. Raymond Taylor Bye, "Some Recent Developments of Economic Theory," in *The Trend of Economics,* pp. 285–86; Frederick Cecil Mills, "On Measurement in Economics," in *The Trend of Economics,* pp. 37–70. Less sophisticated social scientists treated statistics as if they were statements of absolute law. See Dorothy Ross, *The Origins of American Social Science* (New York, 1991), p. 405..

27. For an example of a justification of the survey method, see Charles A. Ellwood, "The Present Condition of the Social Sciences," *Science* n. s. 46 (1917). See also Martin Bulmer, *The Chicago School of Sociology* (Chicago, 1984).

28. Mills, "On Measurement in Economics," p. 37.

29. Robert M. MacIver, "Sociology," in *A Quarter Century of Learning, 1904–1929,* pp. 62–91, describes this attitude but is critical of it.

30. Franklin Giddings, "Exact Methods in Sociology," *Popular Science Monthly* 56 (1899): 146–47. See also George E. Vincent, "The Province of Sociology," *American Journal of Sociology* 1 (1896): 490–91; Lester Ward, "Contemporary Sociology," *American Journal of Sociology* 7 (1902): 476–77; Anthony Oberschall, "The Institutionalization of American Sociology," in *The Establishment of Empirical Sociology,* ed. Anthony Oberschall (New York, 1972), p. 219.

31. Henry Rogers Seager, "Economics," in Columbia University, *Lectures on Science,* pp. 5, 14.

32. Frank Albert Fetter, "The Teaching of Economics," in *College Teaching: Studies in Methods of Teaching in College,* ed. Paul Klapper (Yonkers-on-Hudson, N.Y., 1920), p. 238; Wesley Clair Mitchell, "Economics," in *A Quarter Century of Learning, 1904–1929,* p. 51.

33. A. Gordon Dewey, "On Methods in the Study of Politics, I," *Political Science Quarterly* 38 (1923): 638.

34. George A. Lundberg, "The Logic of Sociology," in *Trends in American Sociology,* p. 404; Willford I. King, "Round Table Conference on the Relation between Economics and Ethics," *American Economic Review Supplement* 12 (1922): 200.

35. Frank Knight, in "Round Table Conference on the Relation between Economics and Ethics," p. 193; Albert Benedict Wolfe, "Functional Economics," in *The Trend of Economics,* p. 452; Lundberg, "The Logic of Sociology," p. 419. Smith, *Social Science in the Crucible,* discusses the ideas of the minority of social scientists who reject objectivisms. He sees this group as emerging with special force in the 1920s, while I see it as having to take a more defensive position.

36. George Soule, "Economics—Science and Art," in *The Trend of Economics,* p. 359. By clarifying that objectivists did not reject "practical" aims, I would like to avoid drawing too sharp a dichotomy between them and their predecessors. On this danger, see John G. Gunnell, "Continuity and Innovation in the History of Political Science: The Case of Charles Merriam," *Journal of the History of the Behavioral Sciences* 28 (1992): 133–42.

37. William Bennet Munro, "Physics and Politics—An old Analogy Revised," *American Political Science Review* 22 (1924): 8–9. For some examples, see Tugwell,

"Experimental Economics," p. 387; and Charles Ellwood, "The Present Condition of the Social Sciences," *Science* n. s. 46 (1917): 469.

38. Bye, "Some Recent Developments," p. 290..

39. W. Y. Elliot, "The Possibility of a Science of Politics: With Special Attention to Methods Suggested by William B. Munro and George E. G. Catlin" in *Methods in Social Science: A Case Book,* ed. Stuart A. Rice (Chicago, 1931), pp. 70–94; George E. G. Catlin, "Reply to Elliot," in *Methods in Social Science,* pp. 92–93; Wesley Clair Mitchell, "The Prospects of Economics," in *The Trend of Economics,* pp. 32–33. For a discussion of the range of social scientists' views on the question of means and ends, see Read Bain and Joseph Cohen, "Trends in Applied Sociology," in *Trends in American Sociology,* pp. 365–71.

40. Bain, "Trends in American Sociological Theory," p. 104.

41. James Rowland Angell, "The Effect of the War on Education," *Association of American Universities, Proceedings of the Annual Conference* 20 (1918): 69; Mr. Lloyd of University of Michigan, comments on "The Future Place of the Humanities in Education," *Association of American Universities, Proceedings of the Annual Conference* 20 (1918): 103.

42. I am using the term *objectivism* rather than *positivism* or *scientism.* In the historical literature, these terms are often used interchangeably. I prefer to use *positivism* to refer to the philosophy of science associated with Mill and Comte. *Scientism* is often used to imply that there is one model of science and that social scientists are placing more emphasis upon it. I am arguing that the model of science, not the degree of commitment to it, changed. *Objectivism* is also a contemporary term used by sociologists and behavioral psychologists. I think the term highlights the redefinition of *objectivity,* away from a broad empiricism and toward the notion of value-free.

43. Charles A. Ellwood, "Objectivism in Sociology," *American Journal of Sociology* 22 (1916): 289. Ellwood is critical of this new objectivism. Mitchell, "Economics," p. 52; Bain, "Trends in American Sociological Theory," p. 73.

44. Wolfe, "Functional Economics," p. 451. Wolfe was a critic of objectivism.

45. Ralph S. Lillie, "The Universities and Investigation," *Science* n. s. 41 (1915): 555; Lundberg, "The Logic of Sociology," p. 406.

46. Daniel Coit Gilman, "Faculty Hiring" (manuscript, c. 1881), Gilman Papers, Johns Hopkins University; Stanford University, *Ninth Annual Report of the President of the University, Year Ending 1912,* p. 6.

47. *President's Report, University of Chicago, 1892–1902,* pp. xxi–xxii.

48. H. P. Judson to John P. Hubble, 29 June 1909, University Presidents' Papers.

49. David Starr Jordan to H. P. Judson, 6 October 1909, University Presidents' Papers; Joseph Dorfman, *Thorstein Veblen and His America* (New York, 1934), p. 295; Robert J. Richards, *Darwin and the Emergence of Evolutionary Theories of Mind and Behavior* (Chicago, 1987), pp. 495–501; Kerry W. Buckley, *Mechanical Man: John Broadus Watson and the Beginnings of Behaviorism* (New York, 1989), pp. 123–32; David Cohen, *J. B. Watson: The Founder of Behaviorism* (London, 1970), pp. 145–67.

50. Jordan did not fully succeed in redefining the Ross case. Most observers

continued to see Ross as the victim of Jane Stanford's capricious power. Because of this, colleagues helped Ross salvage his academic career. David Starr Jordan to James B. Angell, 4 December 1900, J. B. Angell Papers, University of Michigan. On the Ross case, see Richard Hofstadter and Walter P. Metzger, *The Development of Academic Freedom in the United States* (New York, 1955), pp. 436–45; and Furner, *Advocacy and Objectivity,* pp. 235–59..

51. *President's Report, University of Chicago, 1892–1902,* p. xxiii; Andrew F. West, "The Changing Conception of the 'Faculty' in American Universities," *Proceedings of the Seventh Annual Conference of the American Association of Universities* (1906): 66–67.

52. John Dewey, "Academic Freedom" (1902), in *The Middle Works, 1899–1924,* ed. Jo Ann Boydston et al., 15 vols. (Carbondale, Ill., 1976–83), 2:58–59.

53. West, "The Changing Conception," pp. 66–67; *Annual Report of the President* (Columbia University, 1915), pp. 21–22. See also N. M. Butler to James McKeen Cattell, 15 May 1916, James Mckeen Cattell Papers, Columbia University.

54. *Annual Report of the President of Harvard University, 1916–1917,* pp. 17–21.

55. American Association of University Professors, "General Report of the Committee on Academic Freedom and Academic Tenure" (n.p., 1915), pp. 19–25.

56. For an account of the World War I academic freedom cases, see Carol S. Gruber, *Mars and Minerva: World War I and the Uses of the Higher Learning in America* (Baton Rouge, 1975), pp. 163–212; Josiah Royce, *The Philosophy of Loyalty* (New York, 1908). For examples of the interest in citizenship at universities, see the Yale Lectures on the Responsibilities of Citizenship, published annually beginning in 1909. In 1910 Columbia established the Richard Watson Gilder Fund for the Promotion of Good Citizenship (announcement in Lowell Papers, Harvard University). See also Clarence F. Birdseye, "The Official Standard of the College: Shall It Be Constructive Citizenship or a Marking System Diploma?" *American College* 2 (1910): 97–105, 205–14, 277–84, 366–72.

57. "Joint Report of the Columbia University Committee on Education and the Special Committee on the State of Teaching" (excerpt), *AAUP Bulletin* 4 (February–March 1918): 12; Arthur O. Lovejoy, letter to the editor, *Nation* 106 (4 April 1918): 401. See also "The Professors in Battle Array," *Nation* 106 (7 March 1918): 255; "Report of Committee on Academic Freedom in Wartime," *AAUP Bulletin* (February–March 1918): 29–47.

58. Minutes of Board of Trustees, Johns Hopkins University, 21 June 1894, Herbert Baxter Adams Papers, Johns Hopkins University; Henry Pratt Judson to Albion Small, 19 June 1915, University Presidents' Papers.

59. See, for example, Abraham Flexner to Henry Pratt Judson, 16 May 1915, University Presidents' Papers.

60. Whitman and Harper quoted in Jane Maienschein, "Whitman at Chicago, Establishing a Chicago Style of Biology?" in *The American Development of Biology,* ed. Ronald Rainger et al. (Philadelphia, 1988), pp. 163–64.

61. *Presidents' Report* (University of California, 1924–26), pp. 252–53; *Reports Made to the President of Yale University, 1924–1925,* p. 41; *Annual Report of the*

President of Harvard University, 1926–1927, p. 83; George Herbert Mead, "The Teaching of Science in College" (1906), in *Selected Writings: George Herbert Mead,* ed. Andrew J. Reck (Chicago, 1964), p. 60; Robert V. Bruce, *The Launching of American Science, 1846–1876* (New York, 1987), p. 327. Daniel Kevles discusses how nonbiological sciences became increasingly removed from public concerns during this period. Daniel Kevles, "The Physics, Mathematics, and Chemistry Communities," in *The Organization of Knowledge,* p. 153..

62. Nicholas Murray Butler, "Education after the War," *Educational Review* 57 (1919): 71–72.

63. *Annual Report of the President of Harvard University, 1922–23,* p. 7; "Report of the Committee on Improving Instruction in Harvard College" (1903), p. 9, Harvard University Archives; *Annual Report of the President of Harvard University, 1915–1916,* pp. 18–19.

64. *Annual Report of the President of Harvard University, 1925–1926,* pp. 11–12; Committee on Choice of Electives, "Studies of the Freshman Year in Harvard College" (n.d.), Lowell Papers.

65. "Report of the Harvard Student Council Committee on Education" (reprinted from the *Harvard Advocate* [April 1926]), p. 33, Lowell Papers.

66. Ibid.

67. T. W. Galloway, "The Teaching of Biology," in *College Teaching,* p. 99; Frederick E. Brasch, "The Teaching of the History of Science," *Science* n. s. 42 (1915): 759. See also C. Riborg Mann, "College Methods and Administration: The College Laboratory," *Education* 27 (1906): 208; Arnold Thackray, "The Pre-History of an Academic Discipline: The Study of the History of Science in the United States, 1891–1941," *Minerva* 18 (1980): 455–56.

68. James M. Anders, "Research Method of Teaching Science," *General Magazine and Historical Chronicle* 31 (1929): 484; C. G. MacArthur, "The Scientific Teaching of Science," *Science* n. s. 52 (1920): 347–51; Joel H. Hildebrand, "The Early Training of Scientists," *Science* n. s. 55 (1922): 355–58.

69. See, for example, the report of the Stanford School of Biology, in *Annual Report of the President of Stanford University, 1928–1929,* p. 262.

70. Charles Tabor Fitts and Fletcher Harper Swift, "The Construction of Orientation Courses for College Freshmen," *University of California Publications in Education* 2 (1930): 168, 209–10; Mary Ann Dzuback, *Robert M. Hutchins: Portrait of an Educator* (Chicago, 1991), p. 122.

71. *Annual Report of the President of Stanford University, 1928–29,* p. 262.

72. *Report of the President of Yale University, 1922–23,* p. 5; *Reports to the President of Yale University, 1925–26,* pp. 18–19; *President's Report* (University of Chicago, 1927–28), p. xix; Russell M. Story, "News and Notes: The Content of the Introductory Course in Political Science," *American Political Science Review* 20 (1926): 419. See also A. B. Wolfe, "Shall We Have an Introductory Course in Social Science," *Journal of Political Economy* 2 (1914): 254; "Round Table Conference on the Teaching of Elementary Economics," *American Economic Review Supplement* 12 (1922): 177–85. Under pressure from the Hutchins administration, Uni-

versity of Chicago did design general social science classes in the 1930s. After several years of floundering, faculty found a format that worked. This led to the highly successful "Soc 2" seminar in the 1940s. Dzuback, *Robert M. Hutchins,* p. 123; David E. Orlinsky, "Chicago General Education in Social Sciences, 1931–92: The Case of Soc 2," in *General Education in the Social Sciences: Centennial Reflections on the College of the University of Chicago,* ed. John J. MacAloon (Chicago, 1992), pp. 115–25..

73. W. E. Mosher, "Orientation Courses" (Reports of Round Table Conferences at the APSA), *American Political Science Review* 20 (1926): 410; Frank G. Bates, "Instruction in Political Science on Functional Rather Than Descriptive Lines" (Reports of Round Table Conferences at the APSA), *American Political Science Review* 21 (1927): 405; *Stanford University President's Annual Report, 1934–35,* pp. 308–9.

74. A. L. Lowell to Richard Cabot, 16 December 1920, Lowell to John F. Moore, 12 March 1920, Cabot to Lowell, 27 March 1920, Lowell to Cabot, 9 March 1920, and Cabot to Lowell, 8 March 1920, Lowell Papers; Lawrence T. Nichols, "The Establishment of Sociology at Harvard," in *Science at Harvard University,* ed. Clark A. Elliott and Margaret Rossiter (Bethlehem, Pa., 1992); Steven J. Diner, "Department and Discipline: The Department of Sociology at the University of Chicago, 1892–1920," *Minerva* 13 (1975): 544; Paul John Plath, "The Fox and the Hedgehog: Liberal Education at the University of Chicago" (Ph.D. diss., University of Illinois at Urbana-Champaign, 1989), pp. 191–93; Robert C. Angell, "The Department of Sociology," in *The University of Michigan: An Encyclopedic Survey,* ed. Wilfred B. Shaw (Ann Arbor, 1951), p. 728; Seymour Martin Lipset, "The Department of Sociology," in *A History of the Faculty of Political Science Columbia University,* ed. Ralph Gordon Hoxie (New York, 1955), pp. 287–88.

75. David Starr Jordan et al., "To What Extent Should the University Investigator Be Relieved from Teaching? *The Association of American Universities, Proceedings of the Annual Conference* 7 (1906): 23, 44. See also Hugh Hawkins, "University Identity: The Teaching and Research Functions," in *The Organization of Knowledge,* pp. 285–308.

76. On criticism of faculty, see chapter 8. On faculty response, see, for example, C. E. Kenneth Mees, "The Production of Scientific Knowledge," *Science* n. s. 46 (1917): 519–28; Ralph S. Lillie, "The Universities and Investigation," *Science* n. s. 41 (1915): 553–66; and Gordon J. Laing (dean of the Graduate School of Arts and Letters, University of Chicago), "Report," in *President's Report* (University of Chicago, 1926–27).

77. G. S. Hall et al., "How Can Universities Be Organized to Stimulate More Work for the Advancement of Science," *Association of American Universities, Proceedings of the Annual Conference* 18 (1916): 35; John C. Merriam, "The Function of Educational Institutions in Development of Research," *University of California Chronicle* 23 (1920): 142.

78. *President's Report, University of Michigan* (1920–21), p. 53; Robert Kohler,

"The Ph.D. Machine: Building on the Collegiate Base," *Isis* 81 (1990): 638–62; Roger Geiger, *To Advance Knowledge: The Growth of American Research Universities, 1900–1940* (New York, 1986), pp. 61–67, 147–49..

79. *Annual Report of the President of Stanford University, 1928–29,* p. 3; *Reports to the President of Yale University, 1924–25,* p. 41; *President's Report* (University of California, 1924–26), p. 253; *Annual Report of the President of Harvard University, 1926–27,* p. 83; *President's Report* (University of California, 1928–30), p. 106; University of Chicago, *The President's Report, 1928–29,* p. 5; Ellen Condliffe Lagemann, *The Politics of Knowledge: The Carnegie Corporation, Philanthropy, and Public Policy* (Middletown, Conn., 1989), chap. 3; Geiger, *To Advance Knowledge,* pp. 149–60; Ross, *The Origins of American Social Science,* pp. 401–2; Martin Bulmer and Joan Bulmer, "Philanthropy and Social Science in the 1920s: Beardsley Ruml and the Laura Spelman Rockefeller Memorial, 1922–29," *Minerva* 19 (1981): 347–407.

Chapter Seven

1. The claims of the humanities to age and venerability were not completely spurious: most of the academic disciplines classed among the humanities were committed to recovering and preserving the past; in addition, classical languages, rhetoric, and philosophy had dominated the curriculum of the eighteenth-century and antebellum American college. The development of a distinctive identity for the humanities also was related to changes in the position of the arts outside the university. For the discussion of the development of the humanities, I have drawn on Laurence Veysey, "The Plural Organized Worlds of the Humanities," in *The Organization of Knowledge in Modern America, 1860–1920,* ed. Alexandra Oleson and John Voss (Baltimore, 1979), pp. 51–106; Bruce Kuklick, "The Emergence of the Humanities," *South Atlantic Quarterly* 81 (1990): 194–206; Bruce A. Kimball, *Orators and Philosophers: A History of the Idea of Liberal Education* (New York, 1986); Gerald Graff, *Professing Literature: An Institutional History* (Chicago, 1987); Arthur N. Applebee, *Tradition and Reform in the Teaching of English: A History* (Urbana, Ill., 1974); Kenneth Cmiel, *Democratic Eloquence: The Fight over Popular Speech in Nineteenth-Century America* (New York, 1990); Kermit Vanderbilt, *American Literature and the Academy: The Roots, Growth, and Maturity of a Profession* (Philadelphia, 1986); John Henry Raleigh, *Matthew Arnold and American Culture* (Berkeley, 1961); Jo McMurty, *English Language, English Literature: The Creation of an Academic Discipline* (Hamden, Conn., 1985); James Turner, "Secularization and Sacralization: Speculations on Some Religious Origins of the Secular Humanities Curriculum, 1850–1900," in *The Secularization of the Academy,* ed. George M. Marsden and Bradley Longfellow (New York, 1992), pp. 74–106; Thomas Nevin, *Irving Babbitt: An Intellectual Study* (Chapel Hill, 1984); and J. David Hoeveler, Jr., *The New Humanism: A Critique of Modern America, 1900–1940* (Charlottesville, Va., 1977).

2. Peter Novick, *The Noble Dream: The "Objectivity Question" and the American Historical Profession* (New York, 1988); John Higham, *History: Professional Scholarship in America,* rev. ed. (Baltimore, 1989).

3. (Committee on Choice of Electives, Harvard College), "Studies of the Freshman Year in Harvard College" (n.d.), Abbot Lawrence Lowell Papers, Harvard University. This report associated philosophy with history and political science.

4. John Higham, "The Schism in American Scholarship," in *Writing American History:Essays on Modern Scholarship* (Bloomington, Ind., 1972), pp. 3–24..

5. Matthew Arnold, *Culture and Anarchy and Other Essays,* ed. Stefan Collini (New York, 1993 [1869]), p. 145, and see chap. 1, "Sweetness and Light," and chap. 4, "Hebraism and Hellenism."

6. Ibid., pp. 201, 61, 62.

7. Ibid., pp. 60, 78.

8. The moralism of faculty at the reform-oriented universities was not that different from that of their colleagues at institutions that resisted reform. David A. Jolliffe, "The Moral Subject in College Composition: A Conceptual Framework and the Case of Harvard, 1865–1900," *College English* 51 (1989): 163–73; Sybil Gordon Kantor, "The Beginnings of Art History at Harvard and the 'Fogg Method'," in *The Early Years of Art History in the United States,* ed. Craig Hugh Smyth and Peter M. Lukehart (Princeton, 1993), pp. 161–74; Mary Ann Stankiewicz, "Virtue and Good Manners: Towards an Art History Instruction," in *The Early Years of Art History,* pp. 183–93; Louise L. Stevenson, *Scholarly Means to Evangelical Ends: The New Haven Scholars and the Transformation of Higher Learning in America, 1830–1890* (New Haven, 1986), pp. 127–37.

9. Irving Babbitt, *Literature and the American College* (Boston, 1908), pp. 65, 63.

10. Edwin Greenlaw, "A New Humanism," *English Journal* 13 (1924): 240–41.

11. Norman Foerster, *Humanism and America: Essays on the Outlook of Modern Civilization* (New York, 1930), p. x.

12. Louis Trenchard More, "The Pretensions of Science," in *Humanism and America,* pp. 3–4.

13. Greenlaw, "A New Humanism," p. 245; Irving Babbitt, "Humanism: An Essay at Definition," in *Humanism and America,* pp. 37, 44–45. The New Humanists were uniformly critical of liberal Christian movements. The New Humanists who were religious wanted to return to church movements that defended religious orthodoxy. Thus, Babbitt's variant of humanism was the one promoted in public and nonsectarian universities. As such, New Humanism clearly represented a rejection of both moral education grounded in the science of religion and secular scientific substitutes.

14. Richard Green Moulton, "The Study of Literature and the Integration of Knowledge," *University Record* 3 (1917): 90–91.

15. Nelson Glenn McCrea, "Literature and Liberalism," *Columbia University Quarterly* 19 (1916): 25; Edwin Greenlaw, "English in Modern Education: Aims and Methods," *School and Society* 5 (21 April 1917): 453; George Barton Cutten, "The Moral Influence of the Curriculum," *Religious Education* 9 (1914): 526.

16. William Lyon Phelps, *Autobiography with Letters* (New York, 1939), pp. 138, 144–45.

17. Frank Aydelotte, "English as Training in Thought," *Education Review* 43 (1912): 364.

18. McCrea, "Literature and Liberalism," pp. 24–25.

19. Charles H. Grandgent, "The Modern Languages," in *The Development of Harvard University since the Inauguration of President Eliot, 1869–1929,* ed. Samuel Eliot Morison (Cambridge, 1930), p. 65; "Announcement of Plans for the Reading in the Bible, Shakespeare, Ancient and Modern Authors Required of Those Who Concentrate in Ancient or Modern Languages, Feb. 1921," Lowell Papers..

20. W. R. Humphreys, "The Department of English Language and Literature," in *The University of Michigan: An Encyclopedic Survey,* ed. Wilfred B. Shaw, 4 vols. (Ann Arbor, 1942–58), 2:553–55; Herbert Weir Smyth, "The Classics," in *The Development of Harvard University,* p. 61; Charles H. Grandgent, "The Modern Languages," in *The Development of Harvard University,* p. 74; Norman L. Torrey, "Romance Philology and French," in *A History of the Faculty of Philosophy, Columbia University,* ed. Dwight C. Miner (New York, 1957), pp. 208–9. This pattern was common in all the histories of individual language and literature departments at Columbia University, University of Michigan, and Harvard University.

21. Grandgent, "The Modern Languages," pp. 104–5; Babbitt, *Literature and the American College,* p. 141.

22. "The Fine Arts in American Education," *Association of American Colleges Bulletin* 12 (1926): 67–68; Holmes Smith, "The Teaching of Art," in *College Teaching: Studies in Methods of Teaching in the College,* ed. Paul Klapper (Yonkers-on-Hudson, N. Y., 1920), pp. 494–95.

23. Walter R. Spalding, "Music," in *The Development of Harvard University,* p. 115.

24. Edward Dickinson, "The Teaching of Music," in *College Teaching,* pp. 474, 469.

25. A. E. Duddy, "The New Synthesis: An Approach through the Study of English," *Educational Review* 59 (1920): 323; George Kubler, "Arts at Yale University," in *The Early Years of Art History,* pp. 69–70.

26. Duddy, "The New Synthesis," p. 323.

27. Carlton H. Hayes, "History in the College Course," *Educational Review* 41 (1911): 218.

28. William P. Montague, "Philosophy in the College Course," *Educational Review* 40 (1910): 489–90.

29. Woodrow Wilson, "Position and Importance of the Arts Course as Distinct from the Professional and Semi-Professional Courses," *Association of American Universities, Proceedings of Annual Conference* 11 (1910): 76.

30. Frank Thilly, "The Teaching of Philosophy," in *College Teaching,* p. 305; Montague, "Philosophy in the College Course," p. 491.

31. John Herman Randall, Jr., "The Department of Philosophy," in *A History of the Faculty of Philosophy, Columbia University,* pp. 123–24.

32. Franklin B. Snyder, "Teaching Literature to Undergraduates," *School and Society* 17 (1923): 711; Thomas Whitney Surette, "Music in the Liberal College," in *The Effective College,* ed. Robert Lincoln Kelly (New York, 1928), p. 174.

33. "Announcement of Plans for the Reading in the Bible," Lowell Papers; Kimball, *Orators and Philosophers.*

34. *President's Report, University of Michigan* (1920–21), pp. 53–54, 127–28; *President's Report, University of Michigan* (1921–22), pp. 90–91. On support for the arts, see William Bell Dinsmoor, "The Department of Fine Arts and Archaeology," in *A History of the Faculty of Philosophy, Columbia University;* and Bruce M. Donaldson, "The Department of Fine Arts," in *The University of Michigan: An Encyclopedic Survey,* pp. 575–79..

35. Dinsmoor, "The Department of Fine Arts," pp. 256–57; Ellen Condliffe Lagemann, *The Politics of Knowledge: The Carnegie Corporation, Philanthropy, and Public Policy* (Middletown, Conn., 1989), pp. 110–11; *Report of the President of Yale University, 1919–20,* p. 195; Frederick P. Keppel, "The Place of the Arts in American Education," *Bulletin of the Association of American Colleges* 11 (1925): 101–2.

36. Keppel, "The Place of the Arts," p. 100. On the growth of the arts, see also Lura Beam, "The Place of Art in the Liberal College," *Bulletin of the Association of American Colleges* 13 (1927): 265–88; Edwin Litchfield Turnbull, "Music an Important Factor in the Modern University," *Johns Hopkins Alumni Magazine* 7 (1919): 231–40.

37. *Annual Report of the President* (Columbia University, 1920), pp. 22–23; John Erksine, "General Honors at Columbia" (educational suppl.), *New Republic* 32 (25 October 1922): 13; Joan Shelly Rubin, *The Making of Middlebrow Culture* (Chapel Hill, 1992), pp. 164–78. On orientation courses, see Charles Tabor Fitts and Fletcher Harper Swift, "The Construction of Orientation Courses for College Freshmen," in *University of California Publications in Education* 2 (1930): 148–250; Mary Ann Dzuback, *Robert Maynard Hutchins: A Portrait of an Educator* (Chicago, 1991), p. 117; Daniel Bell, *Reforming of General Education: The Columbia College Experience in Its National Setting* (New York, 1966), p. 21.

38. David Hollinger, "The Knower and the Artificer," *American Quarterly* 39 (1987): 37–55.

Chapter Eight

1. Alexander Smith, "The Rehabilitation of the College and the Place of Chemistry in It," *Science* n. s. 30 (1909): 457.

2. For an example of conservative Protestant criticism, see Albert Clarke Wyckoff, "The College Class Room vs. the Christian Pulpit," *Biblical Review* 2 (1917): 586–604. See also Virginia Lieson Bereton, *Training God's Army: The American Bible School, 1880–1940* (Bloomington, Ind., 1991); George E. Peterson, *The New England College in the Age of the University* (Amherst, 1964); J. Bruce Leslie, *Gentlemen and Community: The College in the "Age of the University," 1865–1917* (State College, Pa., 1992).

3. *President's Report, University of Michigan* (1921–22), pp. 184–85; George B. Adams, "Memo not published," 15 May 1909, Arthur Twining Hadley Papers, Yale University.

4. *President's Report, University of Michigan* (1921–22), p. 184.

5. E. D. Phillips, "The Elective System in American Education," *Pedagogical Seminary* 8 (1901): 218; Karl Young, "Hope for the College" (educational suppl.),

New Republic 32 (25 October 1922): 8; R. Freeman Butts, *The College Charts Its Course* (New York, 1939), chap. 14; Frederick Rudolph, *Curriculum: A History of the Undergraduate Course of Study since 1636* (San Francisco, 1977), chap. 6; Russell Thomas, *The Search for a Common Learning: General Education, 1800–1960* (New York, 1962), pp. 61–68..

6. Alexander Meiklejohn, "The Unity of the Curriculum" (educational suppl.), *New Republic* 32 (25 October 1922): 2; M. L. Burton, "The Undergraduate Course" (educational suppl.), *New Republic* 32 (25 October 1922): 10; Edwin Greenlaw, "English in Modern Education: Aims and Methods," *School and Society* 5 (1917): 452.

7. John Bascom, "American Higher Education," *Educational Review* 34 (1907): 136–37.

8. Emil C. Wilm, "Colleges and Scholarship," *Educational Review* 43 (1912): 67; *Annual Report of the President* (Columbia University, 1904), p. 20.

9. *Annual Report of the President of Harvard University, 1908–09*, p. 15; Nicholas Murray Butler, "Is American Higher Education Improving?" *Educational Review* 54 (1917): 178.

10. *President's Report, University of Michigan* (1926–27), p. 9; Woodrow Wilson, "Position and Importance of the Arts Course as Distinct from the Professional and Semi-Professional Courses," *Proceedings of the Annual Conference, Association of American Universities* 11 (1910): 75; Arthur T. Hadley, "The Problems Which Confront Our Colleges at the Opening of the Twentieth Century," *Education* 20 (1900): 588.

11. *Annual Report of the President* (Columbia University, 1909), p. 33. See also William Rainey Harper, "Twenty-fifth Convocation Statement" (1 October 1898), University Presidents' Papers, University of Chicago; John Higham, "The Matrix of Specialization," in *The Organization of Knowledge in Modern America, 1860–1920*, ed. Alexandra Oleson and John Voss (Baltimore, 1979), p. 12. See, for example, John Dewey, "Academic Freedom" (1902), in *The Middle Works*, ed. Jo Ann Boydston et al., 15 vols. (Carbondale, Ill., 1976), 2:64. The growing independence of departments sustained the new view of disciplines held by younger scientists: that disciplines were independent modes of inquiry rather than arbitrary divisions of unified knowledge. University administrators were not yet willing to accept this view.

12. *Annual Report of the President* (Johns Hopkins University, 1877), p. 27; *University Register, 1916–17* (Johns Hopkins University), pp. 208–81; *Register* (University of California, 1890–91), pp. 37–65; *Register* (University of California, 1910–11), pp. 3–214. See also Alan Cruetz, "From College Teacher to University Scholar: The Evolution and Professionalization of Academics at the University of Michigan, 1841–1900" (Ph.D. diss., University of Michigan, 1981), p. 190. Colleges with a prescribed curriculum did not list the individual courses in their catalogues. Instead, they laid out all the classes the freshmen were to take, and then those of the sophomores, and so forth. When electives were introduced, catalogues continued in this way, listing all the electives open to each group of students. As electives grew, this became cumbersome, and catalogues began to list classes by

subject departments. The order of the departments generally reflected the structure of the old required curriculum. The catalogue began with mathematics or ancient languages and worked its way "up" to philosophy, or else it began with philosophy and proceeded through the humanities and social sciences back to mathematics and the natural sciences. With the exception of Columbia, which went directly from year-based listings to alphabetical listings of departments in 1892–93, departments were listed in "logical" order until the multiplication of departments in the twentieth century made this impossible..

13. *President's Report* (University of Chicago, 1928–29), p. 33; *Annual Report of the President of Harvard University, 1913–1914,* p. 20.

14. John F. Woodhull, "What Specialization Has Done for Physics Instruction," *Science* n. s. 31 (1910): 19.

15. *Annual Report of the President* (Columbia University, 1910), p. 23.

16. *Annual Report of the President* (Columbia University, 1920), p. 18; Nicholas Murray Butler, "Concerning Some Matters Academic," *Educational Review* 49 (1915): 396.

17. *Annual Report of the President* (Columbia University, 1920), p. 25. See, for example, Butler, "Is American Higher Education Improving?" p. 177; and Nicholas Murray Butler, *Across the Busy Years: Recollections and Reflections,* 2 vols. (New York, 1939), 1:63; Butts, *The College Charts Its Course,* p. 399; Rudolph, *Curriculum,* p. 207. Butler is still remembered primarily as a builder of the modern research university rather than as a critic of it. See, for example, Daniel Bell, *The Reforming of General Education: The Columbia College Experience in Its National Setting* (New York, 1966), pp. 17–18.

18. Clarence F. Birdseye, "The Official Standard of the College: Shall It Be Constructive Citizenship or a Marking System Diploma?" *American College* 2 (1910): 100; Otis E. Randall, "Character Building in College," *Education* 35 (1914–15): 624; Alexander Smith, "The Rehabilitation of the American College and the Place of Chemistry in It," *Science* n. s. 30 (1909): 458.

19. M. L. Crossely, "The Function of a College Education?" *Education* 33 (1912–13): 134.

20. Butts, *The College Charts Its Course,* pp. 247–48; Thomas, *The Search for a Common Learning,* p. 69.

21. Adopting the ideal of free inquiry, the American university made no significant distinction between graduate and undergraduate instruction. Under these conditions, the college seemed to lack a unique mission, existing only to pass students on to professional or advanced academic training. *President's Report* (University of Chicago, 1922–23), p. xvi. See also Thomas Lindsey Blayney, "The Modern Languages as Cultural College Disciplines," *Educational Review* 41 (1911): 480–81; Henry Aaron Yeomans, *Abbot Lawrence Lowell, 1856–1943* (Cambridge, 1948), p. 65.

22. Randall, "Character Building in College," p. 620; LeBaron Russell Briggs, *School, College, and Character* (Boston, 1901), p. 133; William A. Nitze, "The Teaching of Romance Languages," in *College Teaching: Studies in Methods of Teaching in the College* (New York, 1920), p. 424.

23. Charles Fordyce, "College Ethics," *Education* 33 (1912–13): 76. See also David Levine, *The American College and the Culture of Aspiration, 1915–1940* (Ithaca, N.Y., 1986), chap. 5..

24. *Report of the President of Yale University, 1919–20,* pp. 3–6; C. M. Bakewell to Arthur T. Hadley, 9 December 1914, Hadley Papers; Anson Phelps Stokes, "University Reorganization Problems and Policies," *Yale Alumni Weekly* 28 (1919): 429–30; George Wilson Pierson, "The Elective System and the Difficulties of College Planning, 1870–1940," *Journal of General Education* 4 (1950): 167–68. Yale's new curriculum was possible because World War I upset usual university routines and because Yale was given several large gifts. Both these events made change seem possible and more pressing. Yale's difficulties are all the more significant because the Yale faculty was relatively open to restricting student choice. Because of its late adoption of university reforms, Yale never allowed free electives. In 1901 it adopted a system of controlled choices, allowing freshmen to pick their courses from eight subjects and sophomores to choose from fifteen. In 1911 it modified this system to ensure greater distribution of subject matter in the first two years of college. No course was required of everyone. See Clive Day, "A New Course of Study in Yale College," *Educational Review* 41 (1911): 371–81.

25. Stokes, "University Reorganization," p. 434. Yale students also supported more extensive revision of the curriculum. See "Report on Educational Organization by the Student Council of Yale College, 1927–1928."

26. *Report of the President of Yale University, 1920–21,* p. 266; *Reports to the President of Yale University, 1921–22,* pp. 161–62, 184–85; *Report of the President of Yale University, 1922–23,* pp. 4–5, 85–86; *Reports to the President of Yale University, 1928–29,* pp. 18–19.

27. William C. Trow, "Dangers of the Doctorate," *Educational Review* 69 (1925): 35–36. See also Frederick Jones Kelly, *The American Arts College: A Limited Survey* (New York, 1925), pp. 36–37. See chapters 6 and 7 for a discussion of orientation courses that were instituted in this period.

28. Charles Hubbard Judd, "Individualism in the Choice of Studies," *University of Chicago Magazine* 3 (1911): 175.

29. Alexander Meiklejohn, "The Unity of the Curriculum" (educational suppl.), *New Republic* 32 (25 October 1922): 3, 2. For a summary of the discussion of curricular reform until the end of the 1920s, see Carte V. Good, *Teaching in College and University: A Survey of the Problem and Literature of Higher Education* (Baltimore, 1929), chap. 4.

30. "Reorganization of Undergraduate Instruction: Report of a Sub-committee of the Advisory Board" (Stanford University), in *Annual Report of the President of the University, for the year ending in 1920,* p. 15. On Hutchins, Mary Ann Dzuback, *Robert Maynard Hutchins: A Portrait of an Educator* (Chicago, 1991).

31. A. Lawrence Lowell, "Inaugural Address" (1909), in *At War with Academic Traditions in America* (Cambridge, 1934), p. 35. See also Frederick P. Keppel, *The Undergraduate and His College* (New York, 1917), p. 21.

32. "Rules for the Choice of Electives" (n.d.), and George L. Meylan to A. L. Lowell, 10 June 1919, Abbot Lawrence Lowell Papers, Harvard University.

33. *Annual Report of the President of Harvard University, 1919–20,* pp. 100–102; Yeomans, *Abbot Lawrence Lowell,* pp. 137, 145–64. See also *Reports to the President of Yale University, 1929–30,* pp. 32–33; *President's Report* (University of Chicago, 1927–28), p. xix; *President's Report, University of Michigan* (1923–24), p. 178; *Report of the President of Yale University, 1923–24,* pp. 61–62; *Annual Report of the President of Stanford University, 1921–22,* pp. 56–57; *President's Report* (University of California, 1924–26), pp. 253–54; Veysey, "Stability and Experiment," p. 12; Levine, *The American College,* pp. 108–9..

34. See also Yeomans, *Abbot Lawrence Lowell,* pp. 121–59; A. L. Lowell, "College Rank and Distinction in Life" (1903), in *At War,* pp. 12–26; and William T. Foster, *Administration of the College Curriculum* (Boston, 1911), chap. 11. The modest nature of these changes is in part attributable to the similarities between Lowell's and Eliot's educational philosophies. Despite Lowell's posture as a critic of Eliot's reforms, they shared many assumptions about intellectual inquiry. Lowell agreed that "there is no such thing today" as "a body of knowledge common to all educated men" and thought that none was needed. Method of inquiry was more important than content. "The object of a liberal education," he echoed Eliot, "is not so much knowledge as an attitude of mind and familiarity with processes of thought." Lowell held onto the notion that education should inculcate "scientific" habits of thought. Lowell, "Culture" (1915), in *At War,* p. 117; and *Annual Report of the President of Harvard University, 1908–09,* p. 10. Nathan Reingold has also commented on how efforts to improve the college often relied on standards of scholarship appropriate to graduate schools. See Nathan Reingold, "Graduate School and Doctoral Degree: European Models and American Realities," in *Science, American Style* (New Brunswick, N.J., 1991), p. 186.

35. Lewis M. Terman, "The Independent Study Plan at Stanford University," *School and Society* 24 (14 July 1926): 96–98; *Annual Report of the President of Stanford University, 1921–22,* pp. 55–57; *Annual Report of the President of Harvard University, 1924–25,* p. 44; *President's Report* (University of Chicago, 1927–28), p. xix; *President's Report, University of Michigan* (1925–26), p. 61; Edward H. Kraus and Lloyd S. Woodburne, "The Administration and Curriculum of the College of Literature, Science, and the Arts," in *The University of Michigan: An Encyclopedic Survey,* ed. Wilfred B. Shaw, 4 vols. (Ann Arbor, 1942–58), 2:430–31; Frederick S. Jones, in *Report of the President of Yale University, 1923–24,* pp. 61–62. On the general honors program at Columbia, see *Annual Report of the President* (Columbia University, 1920), pp. 22–23. The program was replaced by departmental honors in 1929. Herbert Hawkes, "Curriculum Revision at Columbia College," *Educational Record* 10 (1929): 34–35. Laurence Veysey, "Stability and Experiment," p. 12, reports that at least ninety-three universities had adopted honors programs by 1927.

36. Leslie, *Gentlemen and Community,* chap. 7; Andrew F. West, "The Changing Conception of the 'Faculty' in American Universities," *Association of American Universities, Proceedings of the Annual Conference* 7 (1906): 71–72 (see 74 for Remsen's discussion of West's address).

37. Daniel Abercrombie, "The Responsibility of the College for the Freshman"

(New England Association of Colleges' Symposium on College Freshmen), *Education* 30 (1909–10): 647–48; *Report of the President of Yale University, 1923–24*, p. 7; Ernest H. Wilkins, *The Changing College* (Chicago, 1927), p. 48; Nicholas Murray Butler, "Introduction," in *College Teaching*, p. xiii.

38. Randall, "Character Building in College," p. 626; Fordyce, "College Ethics," pp. 77–78. Also see Kelly, *The American Arts College*, p. 44, for a discussion of the relationship between the rejection of required courses and the emphasis on the quality of teaching..

39. Edward A. Pace et al., "The Training of the College Teacher," *Educational Record* 7 (1926): 136.

40. William Ernest Hocking, "Can Values be Taught?" in *The Obligation of Universities to the Social Order: Addresses and Discussion as a Conference of Universities under the Auspices of New York University* (New York, 1933), p. 341.

41. Ibid., pp. 341–42.

42. Guy E. Snavely, "Who Is a Great Teacher," *Association of American Colleges Bulletin* 15 (1929): 68–70; Max Mason, "The College within the University," in *The Effective College*, ed. Robert Lincoln Kelly (n.p., 1928), p. 28; President Hibben's paper in "The Type of Graduate Scholar," *Association of American Universities, Proceedings of the Annual Conference* 15 (1913): 26; "Report of the Harvard Student Council Committee on Education" (reprinted from the Harvard *Advocate* [April 1926]), pp. 47–48, Lowell Papers. See also Milton H. Reuben, "An Undergraduate's View of College Education," *Educational Review* 43 (1915): 48–55; M. L. Burton, *President's Report, University of Michigan* (1920–21), pp. 167–68; Paul Klapper, "General Principles of College Teaching," in *College Teaching*, p. 60; Keppel, *The Undergraduate and His College*, chap. 12.

43. Fordyce, "College Ethics," p. 77.

44. Randall, "Character Building in College," p. 626.

45. Carl Holliday, "Our 'Doctored' Colleges," *School and Society* 2 (1915): 783–84.

46. William O. Stevens, "Mark Hopkins or the Ph.D.," *Educational Review* 59 (1920): 227; Nathan G. Goodman, "More about Ph.D.'s," *School and Society* 24 (2 October 1926): 429. Criticism of faculty was a prominent feature of general assessment of higher education. See, for example, Percy Marks, *Which Way Parnassus?* (New York, 1926), chap. 5; Clarence Cook Little, *The Awakening College* (New York, 1930), chap. 8. Some commentators supported their negative assessment of faculty with student surveys. See, for example, C. C. Crawford, "Defects and Difficulties in College Teaching," *School and Society* 28 (27 October 1926); and Kelly, *The American Arts College*, pp. 91–92.

47. V. T. Thayer, "The University as a Training School for College and University Teachers," *Association of American Universities, Proceedings of the Annual Conference* 28 (1926): 41; Robert Cooley Angell, *The Campus: A Study of Contemporary Undergraduate Life in the American University* (New York, 1928), pp. 36–37. Although most critics blamed faculty for their inability to "inspire" students and thereby transform them in positive ways, some commentators placed the blame on students. See, for example, Randolph Bourne, "The College: An Undergraduate

View," *Atlantic Monthly* 108 (1911): 669; and John R. Effinger, "A Secondary Function of the College," in *The Effective College,* p. 14.

48. Randall, "Character Building in College," p. 18. See, for example, Frederick M. Foster, "The Training of College Teachers," *School and Society* 12 (20 November 1920): 477–78; Herbert F. Davison, "The Puzzled Professor," *School and Society* 15 (20 May 1922): 559–60; Stevens, "Mark Hopkins or the Ph.D.," pp. 226–35; Edward A. Pace, "Does Research Interfere with Teaching?" in *The Effective College,* pp. 124–25; Charles E. Persons, "The Introductory Course in Economics," *Educational Review* 53 (1917): 355; R. H. Edwards, J. M. Artman, and Galen M. Fisher, *Undergraduates: A Study of Morale in Twenty-Three American Colleges and Universities* (New York, 1928), pp. 310–39; Klapper, "General Principles of College Teaching," pp. 46–48; Wilkins, *The Changing College,* pp. 50–51..

49. William James, "The Ph.D. Octopus" (1903), in *Memories and Studies* (Boston, 1911), pp. 329–47. James's major issue in "Ph.D. Octopus" was the problem of the Ph.D. becoming a requirement for college teaching. He was most concerned with the increasing regimentation of academic hiring, in which the credential was more important than the individual. In this context, he discussed how the Ph.D. program could stifle intellectual interest. James reiterated this theme in "A Great French Philosopher at Harvard" (1910), in *Essays in Philosophy,* ed. John J. McDermott (Cambridge, 1978), pp. 166–71. For examples of other critiques of graduate education, see Floyd W. Reeves, "A Critical Summary and Analysis of Current Efforts to Improve College Teaching," *Phi Delta Kappan* 11 (1928): 65–71; Hibben, "The Type of Graduate Scholar," pp. 23–31; Nathan G. Goodman, "More about Ph.D.'s," *School and Society* 24 (2 October 1926): 429–30; Marks, *Which Way Parnassus,* pp. 76–92; F. J. Kelly, "The Training of College Teaching," *Journal of Educational Research* 16 (1927): 332–41. For an account of contemporary summary of the debates about graduate education, see Good, *Teaching in College and University,* pp. 365–77.

50. Kelly, "The Training of College Teaching," p. 335; Foster, "The Training of College Teachers," p. 478. See also Paul Klapper, "The College Teacher and His Professional Status," *Educational Administration and Supervision* 11 (1925): 74; A. J. Klein, "Administrative Procedures for Improving College Teaching," in *Problems of College Education: Studies in Administration, Student Personnel, Curriculum and Instruction,* ed. Earl Hudelson (Minneapolis, 1928), pp. 102–7; M. E. Haggerty, "The Improvement of College Instruction," *School and Society* 27 (14 June 1928): 25–36; Clyde M. Hill, "The College President and the Improvement of College Teaching," *Educational Administration and Supervision* 15 (1929): 212–22; E. S. Evenden, "The Improvement of College Teaching," *Teachers College Record* 29 (1928): 587–96; C. D. Bohannan, "Improvement of College Instruction," *Phi Delta Kappan* 10 (1928): 161–73; Reeves, "A Critical Summary," pp. 65–71; Wilkins, *The Changing College,* pp. 62–64; Good, *Teaching in College and University,* pp. 69–74; Sidney E. Mezes, "Professional Training for College Teaching," in *College Teaching,* pp. 31–42.

51. See Roswell Parker Angier, "The Organization of the Freshman Year," *Association of American Universities, Proceedings of the Annual Conference* 23 (1921):

63–77; *Report of the President of Yale University, 1919–1920,* pp. 57–58; *Report of the President of Yale University, 1922–23,* pp. 5–11; *Report of the President of Yale University, 1923–24,* p. 7; *Reports to the President of Yale University, 1929–30,* pp. 65–67; *Annual Report of the President of Harvard University, 1924–25,* pp. 19, 45–46; *President's Report* (University of Chicago, 1925–26), pp. 24–25; *President's Report* (University of Chicago, 1929–30), p. 5; Chauncy S. Boucher, "Progressive Developments in the Colleges," *University of Chicago Magazine* 2 (1930): 181–87; *President's Report, University of Michigan* (1925–26), p. 114; *President's Report, University of Michigan* (1926–27), pp. 2–6; *President's Report, University of Michigan* (1928–29), p. 34; *President's Report* (University of California, 1926–28), p. 79; *Annual Report of the President* (Johns Hopkins University, 1929–30), p. 6..

52. *President's Report, University of Michigan* (1920–21), pp. 167–68.

53. Angier, "The Organization of the Freshman Year," pp. 65–66; Percy T. Walden (dean of freshmen), in *Reports to the President of Yale University, 1925–26,* pp. 16–17; N. M. Butler to J. M. Cattell, 12 November 1914, James McKeen Cattell Papers, Columbia University; Joseph Dorfman, "The Department of Economics," in *A History of the Faculty of Political Science, Columbia University,* ed. Ralph Gordon Hoxie (New York, 1955), p. 188; Frederick S. Breed, "A Guide for College Teaching," *School and Society* 24 (17 July 1926): 82–87. On the recognition that teaching and research could be separated, see chapter 6.

54. *Annual Report of the President of Harvard University, 1924–25,* p. 19; *President's Report* (University of Chicago, 1929–30), p. 5. Administrators at Yale, Johns Hopkins, and Michigan also approved of adding training in teaching techniques to their existing graduate programs. Wilbur Cross, *Reports to the President of Yale University, 1929–30,* pp. 65–67; President Goodnow, *Annual Report of the President* (Johns Hopkins University, 1929–30), p. 6; Alfred H. Lloyd, *President's Report, University of Michigan* (1925–26), p. 114. Charles Lipman, dean of the Graduate Division at University of California, went a little further than his colleagues and suggested that the university try to take the lead in offsetting specialization within graduate studies. *President's Report* (University of California, 1926–28), p. 79.

55. E. Birnbaum, "Graduate Study in English Literature," *English Journal* (college ed.) 17 (1928): 33–43; O. J. Campbell, "The Value of the Ph.D. to Teachers of English," *English Journal* 15 (1926): 190–202; J. V. Denny, "Preparation of College Teachers of English," *English Journal* 7 (1918): 322–26; W. B. Gates, "In Defense of the Ph.D. in English," *English Journal* (college ed.) 18 (1929): 482–87; George S. Wycoff, "On the Revision of Ph.D. Requirements in English," *English Journal* (college ed.) 17 (1928): 213–20; Irving Babbitt, *Literature and the American College* (Boston, 1908), p. 149; Oliver Farrar Emerson, "The American Scholar and the Modern Languages," *Proceedings of the Modern Language Association* 24 (1909): lxxix.

56. Charles P. Parker, "Letter to the Faculty" (14 June 1910), and "Rules for the Choice of Electives" (n.d.), Lowell Papers.

57. Roswell Angier (dean of freshmen), in *Report of the President of Yale University, 1920–21,* pp. 254–55; J. A. Bursley, *President's Report, University of Michigan*

(1926–27), p. 149; *President's Report, University of Michigan* (1927–28), p. 159; Edward H. Kraus and Lloyd S. Woodburne, "The Administration and Curriculum," in *University of Michigan,* p. 433.

58. Jordan quoted in Orrin Leslie Elliott, *Stanford University: The First Twenty-five Years* (Stanford, 1937), p. 449..

59. Adam Leroy Jones, "Personnel Technique and Freshmen Guidance," in *The Effective College,* pp. 96–97; Marks, *Which Way Parnassus,* p. 124; *President's Report, University of Michigan* (1927–28), p. 159. See also Henry J. Doermann, *The Orientation of College Freshmen* (Baltimore, 1926), pp. 82–83. For criticism of faculty advisers, see Trow, "Dangers of the Doctorate," p. 36.

60. "Present Problems of Instruction in the University of Chicago," *University of Chicago Magazine* 3 (1910): 58–86; C. S. Boucher, *President's Report* (University of Chicago, 1925–26), pp. 23–24; Frederick Woodward, *President's Report* (University of Chicago, 1927–28), pp. xviii–xix. For an elaboration of the inadequacies of faculty advisers, see Ernest H. Wilkins, "The Orientation of the College Student," in *Problems of College Education,* pp. 253–54. Stanford had similar problems with departmental advisers and had to supplement them with special advisers. See Elliot, *Stanford University,* pp. 440–41. For an idealized discussion of the role of the dean, see Keppel, *The Undergraduate and His College,* chap. 11; for a critical discussion, see Little, *The Awakening College,* pp. 51–67. Both Keppel and Little believed that deans should have personal, sympathetic relations with students. Little, however, felt that few did because they were usually older faculty members. Little recommended that a committee of younger men serve as a replacement for the single dean.

61. *Annual Report of the President of Harvard University, 1929–30,* p. 12; *Report of the President of Yale University, 1919–20* p. 9; Jones, "Personnel Techniques," in *The Effective College,* p. 91. See also Doermann, *The Orientation of College Freshmen,* chap. 7; Edwards, Artman, and Fisher, *Undergraduates,* pp. 346–47.

62. Jones, "Personnel Techniques," in *The Effective College,* pp. 98–101; *President's Report* (University of Chicago, 1924–25), p. 21; *President's Report, University of Michigan* (1925–26), p. 89; *President's Report* (University of California, 1928–30), p. 225; *Reports to the President of Yale University, 1928–29,* p. 17. See also Doermann, *The Orientation of College Freshmen,* chap. 9; Wilkins, "The Orientation of the College Student," pp. 250–53.

63. Paula Fass, *The Damned and the Beautiful: American Youth in the Twenties* (New York, 1977), p. 173 and passim. Angell, *The Campus,* pp. 1–9. University officials recognized the potential moral value of extracurricular activities before the 1910s, but focused more attention on them as other, more traditional sources of moral training became obsolete. For early examples of interest in "indirect" forms of moral training, see "Statement of Entrance Requirements and Other Matters Preliminary to the Organization of the Work of Instruction for the First Year of the University," Leland Stanford Junior University Circular of Information 3 (Menlo Park, Calif., 1891); *President's Annual Report* (Columbia University, 1899), p. 106; Arthur T. Hadley, "Inaugural Address," in *Inauguration of Arthur*

Twining Hadley, LL.D. as President of Yale University, October 18, 1899 (New Haven, 1899), pp. 39–42;, *Annual Report of the President* (Johns Hopkins University, 1883), p. 5.

64. *President's Report, University of Michigan* (1920–21), p. 146.

65. *Annual Report of the President of Harvard University, 1918–19*, pp. 13–14..

66. Frederick Rudolph, *The American College and University: A History* (New York, 1962), chap. 7; Helen Horowitz Lefkowitz, *Campus Life: Undergraduate Culture from the End of the Eighteenth Century to the Present* (New York, 1987); Leslie, *Gentlemen and Community*, chap. 5; Elmer Harrison Wilds, *Extra-Curricular Activities* (New York, 1926).

67. Ronald Smith, *Sports and Freedom: The Rise of Big-Time College Athletics* (New York, 1988), chap. 9.

68. Ibid., chaps. 6–10.

69. Ibid., chap. 14. Educators who wrote books assessing higher education discussed extracurricular activities in depth. See, for example, Marks, *Which Way Parnassus;* Little, *The Awakening College;* Keppel, *The Undergraduate and His College;* Wilkins, *The Changing College;* Angell, *The Campus.*

70. Angell, *The Campus,* pp. 98–124; Edwards Artman, and Fisher, *Undergraduates,* p. 149; Howard J. Savage et al., *American College Athletics* (New York, 1929); Alfred E. Stearns, "What Is College For? The Place of Athletics," *Education* 35 (1914–15): 307–9; Wilkins, *The Changing College,* pp. 114–30; Keppel, *The Undergraduate and His College,* pp. 163–66; Little, *The Awakening College,* pp. 208–16; Marks, *Which Way Parnassus,* pp. 202–5; James Rowland Angell, "The Collegiate Sports Complex" (1934), in *American Education: Addresses and Articles* (New Haven, 1937), pp. 250–58.

71. A. A. Stagg quoted in Edwards, Artman, and Fisher, *Undergraduates,* p. 142. On Stagg, see also Amos Alonzo Stagg and Wesley Stout, *Touchdown!* (New York, 1927); Hugh J. Dawson, "Veblen's Social Satire and Amos Alonzo Stagg: Football and the American Way of Life," *Prospects* 14 (1989): 273–89. Edwards and his coauthors reviewed general attitudes toward athletics. They quoted at length a "psychologist in a men's college" who challenged the prevailing view that athletics had moral benefits, but the authors clearly treated his opinions as strange and unrepresentative. R. C. Angell acknowledged that athletics had moral benefits but thought that the damage they did was greater. He described his views as unusually critical and "iconoclastic." Angell, *The Campus,* p. 112. Even highly critical reports on athletics, such as the 1929 Carnegie Foundation report and the report of Committee G of the AAUP, acknowledged that sports had moral benefits. See Savage, *American College Athletics;* and Wilkins, *The Changing College,* p. 118.

72. Edwards, Artman, and Fisher, *Undergraduates,* pp. 143, 146; Savage, *American College Athletics,* pp. 294–95; Stearns, "What Is College For," pp. 305, 310.

73. Stearns, "What Is College For," pp. 310–11; Wilkins, *The Changing College,* pp. 126–29; Keppel, *The Undergraduate and His College,* pp. 157–80; Savage, *American College Athletics,* p. xxi; James Rowland Angell, "National Intercollegiate Athletic Association Address, 1930," in *American Education,* p. 248.

74. Little, *The Awakening College,* pp. 78, 88–89; Angell, *The Campus,* pp. 67–78;

Marks, *Which Way Parnassus,* pp. 156–92, 228; Fass, *The Damned,* pp. 187–88. University officials assumed that extracurricular activities distracted students from academic work. But early studies indicated that the most active students also did well in academic work. Plans to control the number of activities students could participate in were strongly motivated by a desire to restructure student social networks. See F. S. Chapin, "The Significance of Extra-Curricular Activities," in *Problems of College Education,* pp. 351–57..

75. Laurence Veysey, *The Emergence of the American University* (Chicago, 1965), pp. 67, 92–93. Although student housing was not a high priority among university reformers, they did build dormitories if benefactors wanted to donate money for them. New universities, such as Stanford and University of Chicago, assumed that they needed some student housing. Coeducational universities generally had more dormitory space for women than for men, because educators assumed that women students required more oversight than men.

76. Butler, "Introduction," in *College Teaching,* p. xv.

77. *Annual Report of the President of Harvard University, 1928–29,* p. 12; *Annual Report of the President of Stanford University, 1920–21,* pp. 34–35. See also *President's Report* (University of California, 1921–22), p. 18; and *President's Report* (University of Chicago, 1926–27), pp. 3–4.

78. Robert C. Angell, "A Tentative Plan for the Promotion of Satisfactory Living Conditions and Social Contacts among Students at the University of Michigan," in *President's Report, University of Michigan* (1925–26), p. 126.

79. Kerr D. Macmillan, "The Effective College Home," in *The Effective College,* pp. 17–21; Angell, "A Tentative Plan," pp. 126–35.

80. On the Harvard House plan, see Yeomans, *Abbot Lawrence Lowell,* chap. 15; Levine, *The American College,* pp. 106–7; Marcia G. Synnot, *The Half-Opened Door: Discrimination and Admissions at Harvard, Yale, and Princeton, 1900–1970* (Westport, Conn., 1979), pp. 111–24. On the Yale College plan, see J. R. Angell, "The College Plan," in *American Education,* pp. 259–82; George Wilson Pierson, *Yale: College and University, 1871–1937,* 2 vols., 2:chaps. 10 and 11. For examples of presidential appeals for funds for dormitories: *President's Report* (University of Chicago, 1926–27), pp. 3–4; *President's Report, University of Michigan* (1920–21), pp. 147–50; *President's Report* (University of California, 1921–22), p. 18; *Annual Report of the President of Stanford University, 1923–24,* p. 1.

81. Levine, *The American College,* chap. 7; Synnott, *The Half-Opened Door,* pp. 13–25; Harold Wechsler, *The Qualified Student: A History of Selective College Admission in America* (New York, 1977), chap. 7; Roger Geiger, *To Advance Knowledge: The Growth of American Research Universities, 1900–1940* (New York, 1986), pp. 129–39.

82. Little, *The Awakening College,* p. 25.

83. "Report of the Harvard Student Council Committee on Education," p. 23; Wilkins, *The Changing College,* pp. 76–77.

84. *Annual Report of the President of Stanford University, 1924–25,* pp. 11–17. On new admissions procedures, see Edwards, Artman, and Fisher, *Undergraduates,* pp. 356–57; J. B. Johnston, "The Selection of the College Student," in *Problems of*

College Education, pp. 239–46. On character tests, see Percival M. Symonds, "The Present Status of Character Measurement," *Journal of Educational Psychology* 15 (1924): 484–98.

85. For an example of the distinction between inculcating and developing existing moral characteristics, see Savage, *American College Athletics,* pp. 294–95..

86. Synnott, *The Half-Opened Door;* Thomas Bender, *New York Intellect: A History of Intellectual Life in New York City, from 1750 to the Beginnings of Our Own Time* (New York, 1987), pp. 288–92.

87. Reading Synnott's account of the origins of selective admissions at Harvard, it is easy to conclude that it was simply politically acceptable cover for discrimination against Jews. It may have been so for President Lowell, but others viewed selective admissions primarily as a means to social and moral improvement, and not necessarily as a means to reduce the number of Jewish students. For example, C. C. Little, former secretary to the Harvard Corporation and later president of University of Michigan, was firmly opposed to discrimination against Jewish students at Harvard, but was a strong advocate of selective admissions. See Synnott, *The Half-Opened Door,* p. 73; and Little, *The Awakening College,* pp. 13–29.

88. For an example of the equation of morality with morale, see Angell, *The Campus,* pp. 204–26.

Conclusion

1. Warren Sussman, "Personality and the Making of Twentieth-Century Culture," in *Culture as History: The Transformation of American Society in the Twentieth Century* (New York, 1984), pp. 271–85.

2. Advocates of emotivist theories of ethics did not necessarily deny that ethics were also cognitively true. Guy W. Stroh, *American Ethical Thought* (Chicago, 1979), chap. 7; Laurence Smith, *Behaviorism and Logical Positivism: A Reassessment of the Alliance* (Stanford, 1986).

INDEX